D0701708

NESTED IDENTITIES

Nationalism, Territory, and Scale

Edited by
GUNTRAM H. HERB
and
DAVID H. KAPLAN

ROWMAN & LITTLEFIELD PUBLISHERS, INC.
Lanham • Boulder • New York • Oxford

ROWMAN & LITTLEFIELD PUBLISHERS, INC.

Published in the United States of America
by Rowman & Littlefield Publishers, Inc.
4720 Boston Way, Lanham, Maryland 20706

12 Hid's Copse Road
Cumnor Hill, Oxford OX2 9JJ, England

British Library Cataloguing in Publication Information Available

Library of Congress Cataloging-in-Publication Data

Nested identities : nationalism, territory, and scale / edited by
    Guntram H. Herb and David H. Kaplan.
        p.   cm.
    Includes bibliographical references and index.
    ISBN 0-8476-8466-0 (cloth : alk. paper). — ISBN 0-8476-8467-9
(pbk. : alk. paper)
    1. Nationalism.   2. Geopolitics.   I. Herb, Guntram Henrik, 1959– .
II. Kaplan, David H., 1960– .
JC311.N45   1999
320.54'09'045—dc21   98-28143
                                                                    CIP

Printed in the United States of America

⊗ ™ The paper used in this publication meets the minimum requirements of
American National Standard for Information Sciences—Permanence of Paper
for Printed Library Materials, ANSI Z39.48–1984.

To Patricia, Henrik, and Natalie
To Veronica and Elliot

Contents

vii

Part IV. Micro-Scale

Illustrations

Figures

Tables

Introduction: A Question of Identity

David H. Kaplan and Guntram H. Herb

Identities are not fixed or immutable but are accumulated over the course of a lifetime; they are a part of the process of creating psychological stability (Bloom 1990). Territorially based identities are just some of the myriad identities possessed by people. Yet, such geographic affiliations can be among the most salient and provoke the greatest degree of ambivalence and conflict. It is possible for a geographic identity to be devoid of much additional meaning. Of the multitude of territories that surround us, many are little more than artificial jurisdictional divisions, such as census tracts or water districts. But even the most seemingly arbitrary geographic units have the capacity to accumulate additional meanings, particularly if they encompass something vital (Sack 1986). This is enhanced by the fact that territories enable us to exert control from within and to restrict access from without. For example, a water district can become essential if the supply of water becomes scarce. Suddenly its limits will constitute the boundaries between haves and have-nots. An identity begins to develop. Markers, which are often composed of the characteristics or elements contained within the territory, are crucial in this process. Gerald Suttles (1972: 28) mentions how residents of an inner-city ghetto distinguish themselves based on the color of their building, with opposition between red and white buildings.

But what is the precise role of territory in the process of identity formation? Does the territory simply "spatialize" already existing social and cultural phenomena, putting on the ground any classifications that exist but not adding any additional significance? Anssi Paasi (1996: 52) argues that for a given territory to become an important aspect of identity, it requires a "complex group of other elements" that

1

interact with the territory. The nature of interaction is key. The territory actively transforms the elements contained within it, adding an additional layer of meaning and so "achieving a specific identity (the identity of the region), which cannot be reduced merely to the regional consciousness (regional identity) living in it" (Paasi 1996: 33–35). Thus, territory becomes a vital constituent of the definition and identification of the group living within it. This is especially true when examining what has emerged as the most potent of all geographically based identifications, that of national identity.

The Role of Territory

In recent history, national identity has succeeded in placing itself at the apex, "overriding claims of lesser communities" and of larger allegiances (Emerson 1960). Ernest Renan's classic definition of nationhood (1996, speech delivered in 1882)—"a spiritual principle" constituted from the legacies of the past and the present desire of all its members to live and work together—does not rule out geographical attributes. In fact, territory is a basic requirement in organizing other attributes that form a specific identity (Greenfeld 1992). As a result, the preservation of the territory that is occupied and sometimes controlled by the nation is the goal of the nationalist mission—arguably even more than the preservation of the people. However, the relationship between national identity and national territory has not loomed large in past treatments of the subject. When they mention it at all, many scholars have taken the view that the territory and its name functions as a kind of "shorthand for a network of ideas concerning nations" (Breuilly 1994: 8). It adds definition to what would otherwise be an ambiguous mix of characteristics based on language, religion, heritage, habits, and other criteria. Anthony Smith (1991), for example, considers territory to be an important but external function of national identity that helps to position the shared culture and the social bonds among members. Territory is certainly important in this scheme but more as a derivative rather than as a primary attribute.

The contributions in this volume are premised on the belief that such a perspective is insufficient. Territory is so inextricably linked to national identity that it cannot be separated out. Neither the identity, or consciousness, shared by members of a nation nor the physical territory of the nation itself can be viewed in isolation. What complicates such a holistic investigation is that territories of national identity have to be viewed in the context of the existing territories of political power: the world political map of states. Nationalist movements politicize space and create geographically bounded homelands within which national groups claim sovereignty. This means that nations aspire to have their own states because only states hold sovereign power. The ideal of the nation-state—an entity in which the territory of the nation and the territory of the state are congruous—still reigns as the primary goal of the modern world. However, national identities and homelands are ill-defined and challenged by the territoriality of existing states.

Nation and State Identities

The spatial identity of a national group is composed of land deemed essential to its security and vitality (Kaplan 1994). This may consist of many parts: the actual space inhabited by members of a group, the particular terrain that helps define the group, the locational context vis à vis other powers, the historic legacy of a specific area, or specific natural features with economic or military-strategic importance. In contrast to nations, states have clearly demarcated territories. Yet, states also need an identity to ensure that their populations remain loyal to them, even if this identity has no salience other than its connection to governmental control.

In addition to the lack of correspondence between the territorial regions of "state" and "nation," both identities are relatively recent historical phenomena. The modern "state" is maybe 500 years old, and the modern "nation" is even younger than that (Smith 1983: 27). They did not emerge spontaneously throughout the globe but have undergone a long and uneven process of diffusion. Moreover, although the two entities are connected to one another, state and nation have rarely coevolved. In some countries, the state emerged long before a nation was constructed that took hold of its territory (a process still taking place in many situations), and in others, the sense of nationhood came first (with several national identities as yet unfulfilled by the existing state structures). As a result of the unevenness in their historical evolution a state territory may contain several groups who define themselves as separate from the majority nation, or a nation may extend far beyond the boundaries of the existing state.

The United States best exemplifies the problematic relationship between state and nation identities and their territories. Composed of several ethnic groups, there is no clear ethnic bond to provide cohesion as in the case of pre-World War II Germans who used this as a rationale to unite all ethnically German lands in a campaign of aggressive expansionism. The main unifying element of the population of the United States is birth within the borders of the state. This raises the question of whether a bond based on a territorial institution is equal to a bond based on the legacy of an ethnic community. In both cases the territory is an integral aspect of identity, but scholars disagree whether they should both be considered nations. The true complexity of the issue is revealed by the fact that such territorial identities occur at a variety of scales.

The Importance of Scale

This volume also adds to the existing literature on nationalism by adding a further element—that of scale. Although any discussion of national identity hinges on the level of the state, which assumes central importance given its exclusive claim to power, we are expressly interested in how national identity is negotiated within a hierarchy of geographical scales. These can extend above the state, such as an identity that encompasses a group of countries or a continental region, and below the state, such as a collection of localities and regions within countries. These spatial identities are roughly nested within one another, but each may have some claim on individual loyalties. Although quiescent at a particular point in time, both smaller and larger affiliations may flare up under any number of circumstances and thus threaten the status quo of the world political map. Taken for granted nations encompass smaller communities that can compete at some level for loyalty. They are also embedded within larger supranational (or superstate) identities. These scales must be negotiated but, as the dismantling of Yugoslavia and the creation of a united Europe bear out, this is rarely easy.

Regional conflicts occurring throughout the world further expose the importance of scale: They represent overlaps in spatial identities. This pertains especially to people whose spatial identity is unfulfilled by the existing state structure. The inability of minority national groups to attain some degree of sovereignty over a particular territory provokes frustration and may generate conflict. The degree of correspondence between the separate spatial identities of national groups within a plural state illuminates each group's conception of its own national identity and helps to determine the tenor of intergroup relations. Thus, a smaller-scale identity cannot be understood outside of the context of larger identities that cover its territory in its entirety or divide it. Similarly, a large-scale identity is more than the sum of its constituent parts and is also defined by its relationship with other overarching identities.

Organization of Book

This book is unique because it is the first volume to explicitly examine how national identity relates to territory and how it coexists and competes with other identities at different geographic scales. To structure such a complex investigation, we outlined three major scale divisions: a macro- (or superstate) scale, a meso- (or state) scale, and a micro- (or substate) scale. We are aware of the arbitrariness of such a classification and do not perceive either of its elements to be definable on its own. In addition, such a taxonomy is contextual, as Gary Elbow's discussion in Chapter 4 reveals. In our thinking, the meso-scale is by far the most contentious, given the great variety in the size of states. Yet placing the most dominant political entity in the center of two extremes—a macro-scale that supersedes the existing group of supposedly equal state actors and a micro-scale that segments the individual states—offers a sensible way to deal with issues of identity in different geographic contexts.

Because these scales are not only fluid but also interconnected or nested, we asked our contributors to address a set of questions to elucidate the negotiation of identity in the nexus of territory, power, and scale.

- Questions on territorial aspects dealt with the role of territory in a nation's perception of itself; the extent to which territorial aspects of national identity might bolster, compete with, or supersede more ethnic aspects of identity; and whether an aspatial national identity is a possibility.
- Power issues were raised in questions, such as how can identities be operationalized in jurisdictional terms, such as citizenship, voting, and minority rights? How has territory been used by a group with a shared identity to exert power, for example in trying to make an area more ethnically homogeneous or in trying to acquire additional territory? Are there differences between a regional identity, such as a minority within a state, and a national identity?
- Finally, there were specific queries on the negotiation of scale. Can a group coexist within a larger society and still retain its integrity? The term *nation* connotes some degree of primacy. But is it possible to have two primary identities? Is it possible to develop an overarching identity that encompasses several national identities? How might one identity compete with identities at lower or higher scales?

Thus, each case study in this volume shares a similar orientation, and because this necessarily entailed the examination of two and sometimes three separate levels, there is continuity between the three major scale divisions of the book. For example, Chapter 5 on Russian identity deals with the macro-scale issue of a multinational empire as well as with the Russian "nation-state" and links the macro- to the meso-scale. Chapter 9 on Sri Lanka cannot avoid the challenge of the substate Tamil identity and provides a connection with the micro-scale. Further coherence of the volume is provided by the editors' chapters, which clarify terminological confusion, lay a conceptual groundwork, and offer a larger context.

References

Bloom, William. *Personal Identity, National Identity, and International Relations.* Cambridge: Cambridge University Press, 1990.

Breuilly, John. *Nationalism and the State.* 2d ed. Chicago: University of Chicago Press, 1994.

Emerson, Rupert. *From Empire to Nation: The Rise to Self-Assertion of Asian and African Peoples.* Cambridge, Mass.: Harvard University Press, 1960.

Greenfeld, Liah. *Nationalism: Five Roads to Modernity.* Cambridge, Mass.: Harvard University Press, 1992.

Kaplan, David H. "Two Nations in Search of a State: Canada's Ambivalent Spatial Identities." *Annals of the Association of American Geographers* 84 (1994): 585–606.

Paasi, Anssi. *Territories, Boundaries, and Consciousness: The Changing Geographies of the Finnish-Russian Border.* Chichester, U.K.: John Wiley and Sons, 1996.

Renan, Ernest. "What Is a Nation?" In Geoff Eley and Ronald Suny, eds., *Becoming National: A Reader.* Oxford: Oxford University Press, 1996, 42–55.

Sack, Robert D. *Human Territoriality: Its Theory and History.* Cambridge: Cambridge University Press, 1986.

Smith, Anthony. *Theories of Nationalism.* 2d ed. New York: Holmes and Meier, 1983.

———. *National Identity.* Reno: University of Nevada Press, 1991.

Suttles, Gerald. *The Social Construction of Communities.* Chicago: University of Chicago Press, 1972.

Part I

Conceptual Issues

Discussions of national identity often threaten to descend into a terminological and conceptual morass. The most common error, of course, is the interchangeable usage of *nation* and *state*. But there are other terms that create problems too, even for specialists in the field. Moreover, the study of nationalism benefits from a chorus of voices from many different disciplines that at times descends into disharmony. The number of issues involved and the overwhelming variety of contexts make it especially difficult to arrive at a scholarly consensus. The emphasis on territory and scale in this volume may help to sharpen the focus somewhat, but much of the complexity remains.

Guntram Herb looks at the relationship between nations and states and discusses some of the dominant perspectives that have sought to make sense of national identity and nationalism. He then analyzes the role territory plays: how identity is inextricably tied to the land, how territory animates the nations' sense of self, how the "nation" is contained within an area, and how nations seek to control and modify their territory.

Dave Kaplan investigates how national identity fits within a continuum of geographic scales. He examines how the scale of national identity relates to the scale of state identity and why the two identities, though separate, are dependent on one another. He then notes asymmetries in spatial identities and how these generate forms like substate nationalisms, borderlands, and diasporas. Finally, he speculates on challenges to the dominance of national identity, at scales that are larger and smaller, and where territory may be less significant than it is today.

1

National Identity and Territory

Guntram H. Herb

With *globalization* and *shrinking world* as catchwords of the day, the sovereign state increasingly looks to some authors like a ghost from the past (Ohmae 1995; Guéhenno 1995). Yet, despite attempts to create structures such as the European Union, the Association of Caribbean States, or NAFTA, which challenge the power of states, there is little evidence for this assertion. States continue to dominate world politics and remain the sole entities to hold absolute or sovereign power (Murphy 1994). Moreover, their number has proliferated rather than declined. There were only around fifty states at the end of World War II, whereas today we have more than 190. As evidenced by separatist movements in Chiapas and Quebec, for example, there is potential for even further increases. Because only states guarantee freedom from outside interference, groups yearning to preserve their unique identity tend to inevitably demand independent statehood. Thus, the nation-state is still the primary goal in contemporary politics.

Globalization has intensified contact among the world's population and even contributed to the emergence of feeble macro-regional identities that encompass several states, such as the European Union or the Caribbean (see Chapters 3 and 4), but it has not succeeded in creating a global identity (Marden 1997). Instead, global social mobilization has enhanced the awareness of differences among groups of peoples and spurred new national identities. So, although the forces of globalization have reduced some of the divisive effects of boundaries between states, they have also encouraged new divisions among national groups within states. As a result, the territoriality of political power as expressed in the patchwork of colors on the world political map, is discordant with the territoriality of national identity.

Bounded space or territory is the crucial element in the tension between power and identity. Political power—particularly in the form of a sovereign state—is almost exclusively defined and exercised territorially. National identity is similarly dependent on territory because only territory provides tangible evidence of the nation's existence and its historical roots, and a nation needs a clearly demarcated national territory to demand its own state. But why are there such territorial tensions between power and identity, and how can we negotiate them? This chapter seeks to answer these questions in several steps. First, it will investigate how the exercise of political power in the modern state has evolved to reveal the increasing importance of territoriality, popular sovereignty, and self-determination. Second, it will examine theoretical perspectives on the formation of national identities to help to clarify and define that most ambiguous of concepts, the nation. Third, the chapter looks at the way territory defines the content and extent of national identity and exposes the ill-defined nature of national territory. Fourth, it will map out the process by which nations seek to maximize their territorial control. Finally, it will attempt to assess the future configuration of national identity in the modern state system.

Political Power and the Modern State

The origins of states can be traced back thousands of years and are customarily linked to warfare, the production of food surpluses, or the need to organize irrigation schemes. However, these early states were fundamentally different from the current system of states founded on the idea of territorial sovereignty. Absolute or exclusive control over a clearly defined territory only came to dominate politics around the fifteenth century. Before, political power was predicated on the personal allegiance between subjects and rulers rather than the bounds of a specific territory. Laws were based on customs and tradition, not on territorial codes. In addition, universalist concepts of power, such as the divine authority of the pope, challenged the power of individual rulers in their domains (M. Anderson 1996: 17–19).

The shift from a social to a territorial definition of power, or what Jean Gottmann (1973) has called the shift from cosmopolitanism to isolationism, was spurred by the accumulation of wealth associated with mercantilism, advancements in military technology, overseas discoveries and colonization, and the decline in the power of the church in the Reformation (Murphy 1994: 210). Increasing wealth in Europe meant larger and more complex economies, which required more control and administration (Häkli 1994: 43–45). This led to the emergence of a bureaucratic state apparatus and ultimately an economic world system based on independent states. In addition, technological progress enabled rulers to exert effective control over their territories either directly, such as through improved weaponry, or indirectly, such as through more accurate censuses and mapping.

Overseas discoveries also revealed the advantages of using a territorial definition of power, because it allowed for exclusive and unambiguous claims to new possessions without the need to know what these exactly entailed. This is exemplified by the division of Spanish and Portuguese colonial spheres along a line of longitude in the Treaty of Tordesillas in 1494 (Sack 1986: 131–132). The vestiges of a universalist conception of power in this legal arrangement—the arbiter for that line was the Pope—were finally abandoned in the Treaty of Westphalia of 1648. The treaty ended the thirty-year religious struggles of the Reformation period that undermined the power of the Catholic Church and codified the inviolable or sovereign territorial power of individual rulers. Although the Treaty of Westphalia is often cited as the legal document that marks the beginning of the modern state system, the true legal origin of the concept of territorially sovereign states can be found in earlier writings by scholars such as Hugo Grotius and Francisco de Vitoria (Murphy 1994: 210).

Although territorial sovereignty came to be accepted as the foundation of international law, it was not associated with a particular form of government before the French and American Revolutions popularized the notion of self-determination. Derived from the contractarian political philosophies of Locke, Montesquieu, and Rousseau, self-determination argued that political power should rest in the people of a given territory (M. Anderson 1996: 19, 37–38). The people, who were believed to share a common interest and bond, came to be identified by the term *nation,* and as a result the entire political institution by the term *nation-state.* The state apparatus used its repertoire of control and administration to ensure that the cohesion of the population and its identification with the state was maintained. For example, the enforcement of a uniform language and education and the creation of an iconography to erase existing local differences (Häkli 1994: 48–54). It is during this time period that encompassed the French and American Revolutions that most scholars of nationalism place the origins of nations and the ideology of nationalism (Smith 1983: 27).

In France and the United States—the first cases in which self-determination was applied—there was little difficulty conceiving of the entire population within their territories as a unified group with a common identity, because neither of them contained significant opposition groups. When the concept was applied to other areas, especially Central and Eastern Europe, problems arose. In these areas, identity developed along ethnic lines, independent of the territorial container of existing states. Thus, two different types of identities came into existence: a civic identity (also identified as a "political" or "civic nation"), which was focused on and mostly congruous with the territory of the state, and an ethnic nation, which stressed the commonality of language and culture and sought to unite all members in a contiguous territory. Although the role of territory and state power in these two types of identities were fundamentally different, the distinction between civic identity and nation became conflated because the concept of self-determination identified both of them as "nations" or "peoples."

Self-determination—the idea that all "nations" or "peoples" have the right to control their own affairs in a sovereign state—was popularized and applied in the territorial settlements that ended World War I, which attempted to create several new nation-states such as Czechoslovakia and Yugoslavia. It received further recognition by being explicitly mentioned in the charter of the United Nations: "To develop friendly relations among nations based on respect for the principle of equal rights and self-determination of peoples" (Charter of the United Nations, Article 1.2.; http://www.undcp.org/charter.html). Yet, as the wording in the UN charter shows, there is great potential for terminological confusion and ambiguity. Not only does the charter use the term *nation* to refer to the political entity of the state, but it does not offer a definition for the term *people*. Thus, *people* could signify the population within an existing state territory, that is, a civic identity, or an ethnic group with its own identity within a state, that is, an ethnic nation.

Because the UN was established to ensure the territorial integrity of the existing system of states, it is not surprising that it only has recognized the first type of identity; *people* is interpreted as the entire population within a state (Knight 1988: 119–122). For example, in the period of decolonization that followed World War II, national self-determination was granted to the people as a whole in existing colonial territories, such as the population of Nigeria, but not to ethnic minorities within these states, such as the Ibo of Eastern Nigeria. This means that self-determination was only acceptable in the case of colonization by an external power and not when a majority dominated and oppressed minorities inside an existing state territory (Knight 1988; Nietschmann 1994). Yet, as Rex Honey indicates in Chapter 8 of this volume, even if the Ibo's claims to Biafra had been recognized, the charge of internal colonization could still have been levied: Minority groups in Eastern Nigeria opposed the creation of Biafra, because they feared domination by the Ibo.

The ill-fated history of states that were established as "nation-states," such as Yugoslavia and Czechoslovakia, as well as secessionist movements in other states, reveals the difficulty of combining territorial sovereignty with national self-determination. In the modern state, territory defines the extent of political power. Its boundaries are considered sacrosanct and inviolable, and attempts to breach them even justify war, as witnessed by the coalition response to the Iraqi invasion of Kuwait. Despite numerous infringements on this territorial sovereignty, such as environmental pollution and the spread of the global economy, the idea of territorial sovereignty still dominates international relations (Murphy 1994). National self-determination attempts to transfer this territorial sovereignty onto the territory of the nation by creating a nation-state. There are two problems in this process. First, the concept of the nation is ambiguous and lacks a generally accepted theory or definition. Second, although it is recognized that a nation occupies a territory, its role is complex, and it often resists precise delimitation.

The Concept of National Identity

In light of the overwhelming number of publications on national identity, it is surprising to still find a great deal of confusion regarding terminology and the origins and nature of nations. As a result of the blurred distinction between civic identities and ethnic nations, it is a common practice to use *nation* and *state* as synonyms, despite the significant differences between them: For example, international relations really refers to interstate relations, and the United Nations represents the states of the world, not national groups. Similarly, *nationalism* is used to describe the ideology that seeks to make a population identify with the institution of the state, even though *patriotism* would be a more appropriate term (Connor 1977, 1978; Kecmanovic 1996).

In addition to terminology, there is confusion about the origins and nature of national identity and nationalism because a variety of perspectives have been applied to its study. As a necessarily subjective and incomplete selection of the most influential contemporary theorists shows, experts from several fields have grappled with the origin and definition of nationalism: Benedict Anderson (1991) is an anthropologist and political scientist, Ernest Gellner (1983, 1994), a philosopher, Anthony Smith (1983, 1986, 1992), a sociologist, John Breuilly (1994) and Eric Hobsbawm (1992) are historians, and Walker Connor (1994) and Elie Kedourie (1993), political scientists. If one expands the focus to authors who have made recent theoretical contributions to different aspects of nationalism, the fields of cultural studies, gender studies, literary theory, and geography have to be added.[1]

Among the plethora of perspectives, two main theoretical strands can be identified, the primordialist, or essentialist, view and the constructivist, or instrumentalist, view (cf. Eley and Suny 1996; Conversi 1997; Smith 1983). The former argues that nations are organically grown entities and that the world is inevitably and fatally divided into nations. It believes that there are national spirits or essences and that nations are collective answers to the call of the blood. Johann Gottlieb Fichte (1922, originally published 1808) and Hans Kohn (1944) are traditional representatives of this view, but more recently these ideas have been given new impetus by proponents of Fourth-World theory. For example, the geographer Bernard Nietschmann (1994) claims that there are 5,000–8,000 nations in the world. He considers them the only true or organic group identities and crucial for the survival of the planet because these nations have evolved through a harmonious relationship with the local environment.

The second main strand, the constructivist, or instrumentalist, view, argues that nations are artificial creations, founded on a myth. They are, in Benedict Anderson's (1991) words, "imagined communities." Yet, because nationalist movements have appeared in different time periods and different contexts, it has proven difficult to develop a universal explanation of how and why nations are constructed. Four versions of the instrumentalist, or constructivist, view have sought to offer insight. They define a nation as 1) the product of structural change; 2) the project of elites; 3) a discourse of domination; and 4) a bounded community of exclusion and opposition.

Authors who explain nations as products of structural change argue that modernization, industrialization, and advanced capitalism dissolved ancient, isolated communities into societies that were stratified by class. This shift from *Gemeinschaft* to *Gesellschaft* created a need for solidarity with and membership in the larger social structure. Literacy-based abstract culture filled this void and replaced the tradition-based communal bonds. Thus, nationalism is regarded as a sociological necessity of modern society. For example, Ernest Gellner's work (1983) shows how states arranged and financed "national" education systems as functional responses to new needs of the modern state, Tom Nairn (1981) analyzes the effects of the uneven diffusion of industrialization, Karl Deutsch (1966) stresses the role of social communication in establishing and enforcing a cohesive national identity, and B. Anderson (1991) reveals how national communities emerged as a consequence of print capitalism.

Confronted with the problem that modernization could not explain why some nations already appeared in late agrarian societies or why some ethnic communities did not turn nationalist, some scholars focused their attention on the role of elites. Miroslav Hroch (1985) documents that the construction of nations involved groups of actors that progressed in size from a small elite to a larger network of patriots and finally resulted in popular mobilization. John Breuilly (1994) examines the connection of elites with the state apparatus, and E. J. Hobsbawm (1992) focuses on the role of schoolteachers in disseminating the national idea. Anthony Smith (1986) emphasizes that historians were instrumental in creating and justifying the mythical past of the nation but believes that they could build on existing premodern entities, which he terms *ethnies*. His stress on such organic precursors of the nation establishes a link to the other major theoretical strand and reminds us that the dichotomy of primordialist and instrumentalist views should only be taken as a heuristic device.

Positing that nationalism constitutes a hegemonic political ideology, scholars such as Partha Chatterjee (1986), Kumari Jayawardena (1986), Peter Jackson and Jan Penrose (1993), Anne McClintock (1993), Virginia Sapiro (1993), and Sarah Radcliffe and Sallie Westwood (1996) have investigated how nationalism is connected to imperialism, racism, and gender roles. They have exposed the construction of the nation as part and parcel of larger processes of domination and thus as a construction of the Other. Nationalism is linked to the domination of the lesser-developed world by the West because it reflects the superiority-inferiority dichotomy on which colonialism is predicated. The exclusive nature of the national community also lays the foundation for the oppression of racial minorities in the postcolonial world. At the same time, the struggle against colonialism was a formative power in the establishment of Third World nationalism because the colonial oppressors served as a unifying foe image. Feminist movements were instrumental in these independence movements, but women were not emancipated because such a change was deemed a threat to the nascent national unity. This transfer of the individual domination by men in households to a collective domination of women is a general feature of national discourse that values women mainly for their role in the reproduction of the nation.[2]

Elaborating on the idea that nations are communities that are defined in juxtaposition to other groups, some authors have focused on the importance of their boundaries. Thus, nations are considered bounded communities of exclusion and opposition. For example, Daniele Conversi (1997) posits that the tendency of nations to stress antagonisms against other groups is dependent on the strength of their internal cultural content. Nations with few ethnic markers or core values, of which a shared language is the most common element, are more prone to resort to violence. This "oppositional dynamics" of nationalism, as he calls it, shows that the activities of Basque terrorists are connected to the fragmented nature of Basque nationalism (see Chapter 10).

Prasenjit Duara (1996), who rejects the idea that nations are a radically novel form of consciousness, suggests that nations are formed when a "master narrative of descent" (p. 168) privileges certain identity-forming principles and thus hardens the existing communal boundaries; the group closes itself off. He cautions that this should not be understood as an evolutionary process that leads to a stronger and stronger national consciousness, but that this boundary creation is always in flux, an argument that allows him to conceive of premodern national identities as well as identifications with multiple communities.

Despite the variety of explanatory models for nations, three commonalities emerge that help us define them. First, a nation evokes a stronger loyalty from its members than other communities. This sense of belonging can be interpreted as having evolved over time, that is, as an organic phenomenon, or as an artificial construction. Membership is collectively self-defined, and the cohesive power derives from an "usthem" distinction that stresses superiority over other groups. As a social activity, such a collective identity is not static but influenced by discursive processes. Second, a nation shares an idyllic and often primordial past. This long history fleshes out the identity of the nation, reveals it as a community of fate, and gives it genetic legitimacy. It can be based on events that have actually taken place or on myths that were purposely constructed. Third, a nation has a goal or destiny: It actively seeks to enforce and preserve the unique character of its community. This makes the nation a politicized entity. It yearns to be independent, which inevitably leads to the demand for its own state. It is only in a sovereign state that a nation can determine its own affairs without interference from other groups. The fact that some nations, such as the Catalans, seem to be content with a large degree of autonomy within an existing state does not contradict this. At a pragmatic level, this might simply be the most expedient solution. However, as soon as the political realities threaten crucial aspects of the nation, the demand for an independent state will resurface.[3]

The politicized nature of the nation points to a key difference between a nation and an ethnicity. Only a nation is considered worthy of the ultimate sacrifice—to give one's life for its continued existence. However, because the continued existence of a nation is only fully ensured in its own state, one element acquires prime importance: territory. For, as we have seen, the state's power is predicated on territory. The territorial focus does not just apply to nations that have acquired their own state. Territory is equally important for nations who have settled for autonomous control or who are still striving to get a state because autonomous control can only be exercised over a specific territory, and to make demands for a state tangible, a nation has to identify the specific territory it seeks to control. Yet, the relationship between territory and the nation is only implied or hinted at in the majority of the existing theoretical literature (Paasi 1997). Even the concept of nations as bounded communities neglects territory, because the boundaries it examines are social, not geographical. Geographers have incorporated theoretical aspects of national territory into their works, but a comprehensive geographical theory of nationalism is still missing.

National Territory and National Boundaries

Identities of state and nation are tied to territory and space; they are what David Kaplan (1994) has termed *spatial identities* (see also Knight 1982, 1994; Paasi 1996). Territory is vital to national feeling, and nationalists have long used images of place to link people to the land. In one respect, territory clarifies national identity by sharpening more ambiguous cultural and ethnic markers. Over time, as a group occupies and narrates a particular territory, a transformation occurs. Instead of the group defining the territory, the territory comes to define the group (Burghardt 1973; Knight 1982; Williams and Smith 1983; Lutz 1985; Sack 1986). This interaction between the nation and its space is expressed in Häkli's concept of "discursive landscape" (see Chapter 6).

There is something about the territory itself—composed of the actual space inhabited by members of a group, the particular terrain that helps define the group, the locational context vis-à-vis other powers, the historic legacy of a specific area, and the boundaries surrounding the national territory—that adds an essential component to national identity. Paasi (1996) terms this *spatial socialization*. As the territory becomes reified, individual members of the nation become socialized within the territorial unit that exists. The space itself helps to weld together fragmented individual and group experiences into a common nation story. The territory creates a collective consciousness by reinventing itself as a homeland.

Thus, nations cannot be conceived without a specific territory or homeland. Territory situates the nation, giving it roots and boundaries. In other words, territory expresses internal cohesion and external differentiation (J. Anderson 1986: 118). Given this dual function, the way territory defines national identity can be addressed from two angles: from the inside, that is, how the national community is linked to the land, and from the outside, that is, how the national community is delimited in relation to other groups.

An inward look reveals that territory makes the unique character of the nation tangible. All national anthems make reference to the special qualities of their natural environment to underline their unique character (Lowenthal 1994: 17). The Welsh nationalist party, Plaid Cymru, considered the mountains such an important expression of Welsh identity that it used a stylized rendering of three mountain peaks as its symbol (Gruffudd 1995: 223). In Denmark, the Jutland Heath fulfilled a similar ideological function (Olwig 1984). Even the changing skies and cloud formations can be a distinguishing expression of national identity (Gruffudd 1991: 19). However, since nations often share the same physical landscape with their neighbors, the claim to uniqueness needs to be given added support by incorporating cultural elements. Specific architectural styles, settlement structures, and land use and folklore practices are singled out as evidence of the superior culture of the nation and celebrated in national narratives, such as films and paintings.

The rural landscape, which expresses continuity, holds special significance in national discourse because it links the nation to the land as well as to the shared past. This is most forcefully expressed in the image of the peasant living in harmony with the land. The peasant welds the nation to its idyllic or primordial past and hearkens back to a time when life was pure and community meant a "morally valued way of life," not just a geographic setting (Agnew 1987: 232). These idyllic origins of the nation are presented as a bulwark against the disruptive forces of modernity, as a source of inner strength. Such links to the land are not just a feature of the blood and soil ideology of *völkisch* nationalism, which was a precursor of national socialism, or of Romantic nationalism in general. French nationalism celebrated the diversity of traditional ways of life and their intimate connection to the environment (Lowenthal 1994: 19), and the emerging nationalist movements of the Fourth World are heralded for the same natural harmony (Nietschmann 1994). The intimate relationship between unspoiled nature and by extension an unspoiled national community can also be seen in the shared agenda of environmental groups and extreme nationalist organizations. To its surprise, the Green Party in Germany found itself a magnet for Neo-Nazis in the early years of its existence.[4]

Territory not only represents the harmonious origins, the primordial past of the nation, but also embodies the collective memory of its evolution. The struggle against outsiders who seek to destroy the nation transforms the territory into holy ground. The soil is soaked with the blood of national heroes, the mountains are sacred, the rivers carry the national soul (Williams and Smith 1983: 509). Much like the places and icons of religious worship, the reified landscape becomes the altar of the nation and invokes supreme loyalty. For example, in Switzerland, a rather plain looking meadow in Rütli holds special significance because it is believed to be the place where the original three cantons took a solemn oath that marks the birth of the Swiss nation. At the beginning of World War II, the Swiss Army gathered all officers on the very same meadow to renew the pledge to defend the homeland.[5] However, although such bonds to the territory are crucial for the undivided loyalty of the national community, the continued existence of the nation can only be ensured via a clearly bounded territory. Virtually all laws are defined territorially, and full protection from outside interference can only be achieved in a territorially sovereign state.

At first glance establishing the territorial limits of a nation appears to be a straightforward process. Nations are commonly perceived as occupying distinct areas (e.g. Guéhenno 1995: 4–5), and history is replete with attempts to give nations sovereignty over them. The best example is the creation of states on the basis of national self-determination in the aftermath of World War I. Yet, it poses great difficulties to find an indicator that adequately defines the spatiality of the nation. Three main categories of indicators have been employed: social, historical, and geographical.

Social indicators employ attributes that are distinctive for the individual members of national communities. The most common is language use (i.e., the "mother" tongue), data that is readily available in censuses. However, as the role of Swedish in early Finnish nationalism demonstrates, language cannot be considered a true expression of national consciousness (see Chapter 6, and Hobsbawm 1992: 11–12). Social indicators that are based on surveys that directly measure national preferences, such as plebiscites, are also no panacea. Nations have distinct core areas but the peripheries are ill-defined. In these margins, the density declines and nations intermix with neighboring groups.

The lack of awareness about the ill-defined national periphery can be traced to the most commonly used method to depict the distribution of social data, such as language use: areal shading. In these types of depictions, areal units, such as administrative districts, are colored in the hue of the majority national group. The result is the familiar "ethnographic" map that appears to facilitate the delimitation of national territories along district boundaries but that completely obfuscates the presence of minorities (Herb 1997: 15–18, 178). Representing such data in the form of a dot map, which is closer to reality because it reflects the actual distribution of voters, reveals that it is difficult to draw a clear dividing line because of the intermixing in border regions (Herb 1997: chapter 3). Interestingly enough, it is precisely in these intermixed areas or in even more distant diaspora settlements that the most extreme nationalists can be found. There, the confrontation with other nations—which are portrayed as hostile and less cultured in nationalist discourse to create a feeling of superiority—is most intense. A case in point is the Nazi leadership whose members often had grown up or spent time in areas outside the national core (Wistricht 1984).

Historical occupancy is equally problematic. In many cases, national groups have partially or even completely abandoned their historic birthplaces. Other nations filled the vacant space, and the spatial disjuncture between historical roots and the current geography of nations is the source of much conflict. Many national groups, such as Jews and Palestinians, Germans and Poles, or Serbs and Albanians, have overlapping historical claims to certain regions because they occupied them during different periods. Neither of the opposing groups is willing to fully recognize the other's rights, and a compromise seems unlikely given the exclusive nature of national identity.

For example, Serbs claim the Kosovo as the cradle of their nation because it was the core of the Serbian territory in the Middle Ages. Yet, today the region is more than 90 percent Albanian. Abandoning the region to the majority of the current inhabitants would mean abandoning the "sacred lands" of Serbian national history, whereas Serb sovereignty over the region curtails the rights of the current inhabitants. The corridor along the Vistula River that was granted to Poland in the Treaty of Versailles was contested by Germans and Poles in the interwar period because both national groups could document dominant occupancy for separate time periods, especially because of large-scale in- and out-migration during the *Völkerwanderung* (large-scale migration of peoples in Central Europe at the end of the fourth century). Combined with the intermixed interwar distribution of their members and additional changes in population distributions during and after World War II, it is difficult to conceive precisely where the German national territory ends and the Polish one begins.

Geographical indicators scan the physical landscape for evidence that supports a nation's claim to a specific territory. Examples include features that are associated with a particular nation (e.g., settlement types and place names), boundaries that have strategic importance (e.g., mountain crests), and resources crucial for a self-reliant economy (e.g., minerals, agricultural land, or sea access). Given their spatial and more permanent character, these indicators seem to offer a solution.

However, their application raises other problems. For example, German geographers in the 1920s suggested that the national boundary between Germany, Poland, and Czechoslovakia should be determined by mapping the imprint of German and Slavic culture on the landscape (Penck 1925; Volz 1926). Although house forms, land use, or place names would have been distinctive enough to make such a definition fairly easy, it would have been biased by the century-long political administration of the area by Germans who were therefore more effective in modifying the landscape.

The strategic importance of specific boundaries, though often used in nationalist rhetoric, not only changes with technological development, but generally one nation's security means another's threat. Rights to resources are equally difficult to establish. The Poles argued during negotiations preceding the Versailles Treaty that Baltic Sea frontage was part of its identity as a seafaring nation and a necessity for its survival. After such access was granted in the form of a corridor along the Vistula River that separated East Prussia from the main German national territory, Germans posited that it was a deathblow to their nation because it destroyed the cohesion of their economy (Werner 1932; Ziegfeld and Kries 1933).

Nation Building and Territorial Control

As the previous discussion indicated, a national territory is neither uniformly significant nor unequivocally definable. In view of the clearly demarcated territory of a state, whose power nations strive to acquire, this is problematic. To overcome this predicament, nations seek to maximize their territorial control. They try to establish a consensus over their territorial boundaries and to increase internal cohesion by diminishing regional variations. This can be achieved by altering the territory and its representations. Such a process of territorial nation building, which Paasi (1997) has termed more generally "the institutionalization of territories," is not linear or universal but a contested discourse that needs to be negotiated between different factions within the nation as well as vis-à-vis other nations.

The situation is further complicated by the fact that this territorial identity construction takes place in the context of the existing mosaic of sovereign states whose precise territorial boundaries cut across national territories. Thus, some nations are able to use a state structure they dominate as a vehicle to maximize control over their national territory, whereas others need to carry out their nation-building activities against such powerful opposition. In addition, states are involved in identity formation: They strive to create a civic identity and to make their population identify with their territorially based institution. In a sense, states try to emulate the loyalty inspired by nations. The distinction between this state identity building and nation building becomes blurred in the case of states with a multitude of ethnic groups, as the case of Nigeria shows (see Chapter 8). It is the blurred distinction in these types of cases that contributes to the confusion of the terms *nation* and *state*.

Nationalist modifications of territory can be targeted to specific places, along pathways, or over entire regions. Monuments, settlements, and other places are "concentrated nodes" and "circuits of memory" of national identity (Johnson 1997: 361). They focus national ceremonies and rituals and make them tangible. Nationalist places can serve as bridgeheads for expansion into areas where control is challenged by other national groups, such as the Jewish settlements in the West Bank, or they can act as centripetal forces and direct attention to the center, such as the Rütli meadow pledge in Switzerland (see also the discussion of nationalist places in Transylvania in Chapter 12). John Agnew's (1987) theory of place reveals their multidimensionality: The significance of these places for national territorial control is defined by their physical characteristics (locale), the meaning that is ascribed to them in the national narrative (sense of place), and their position in the larger territorial setting of the nation (location).

For example, the decision to make Berlin the capital of unified Germany did not just offer a more cosmopolitan environment and a hybrid of East- and West-German cities (locale), more central position in Europe, an eastern gateway for an expanding European Union, and a strategic place to control the East-German *Länder* (location), but it embodied historical roots for the German nation that went back further than the division after 1945 (sense of place). Yet, this desire for historical continuity also opened up the Pandora's box of German national identity because Berlin symbolizes Prussian militarism and the center of National Socialism. The official decision to move the capital from Bonn to Berlin was made in June 1991, but there is still debate whether it was the right one (Rössler 1994).

Symbolic and material control over national territory can also be channeled along specific paths. Placing markers of national culture along the perimeters of a region make national boundaries appear real, even if there is little other evidence of the presence of the nation. Mahatma Gandhi's salt march in 1934 was an effective challenge to the British tax authority as well as a means to unify a diverse region in the national liberation struggle. The construction of the *Autobahn* system in Germany not only made remote areas more accessible and thus more integrated with the remainder of German national territory, it also brought Germans together in a large national project and symbolized the industriousness and modernity of the German nation (*Amtlicher Führer* . . . 1936: 142, 146–147; Rollins 1995). Welsh nationalists proposed to physically unite their nation through a north-south route starting in 1917. The argument was that the current transport system with its east-west orientation favored penetration by the English. However, although Plaid Cymru saw economic as well as symbolic benefits similar to the German case, other nationalists cautioned that the road would allow invasion of foreign elements and lead to the destruction of the organic unity that had so far been protected by geographic isolation (Gruffudd 1995: 232–236).

Even entire regions can be modified with success for greater nationalist control. Although specific places and pathways are usually involved in this process, such as the construction of dams as a basis for large-scale irrigated colonization schemes (see Chapter 9), the landscape of regions can be transformed in toto without any clear concentrations of national power. When heritage trusts and environmental associations single out regions for conservation or reclamation, it is not just an attempt to preserve biodiversity but also a nationalist project to ensure continuity of a landscape that is deemed representative of the national spirit (Lowenthal 1994; Olwig 1984). National dominance is enforced effectively by stamping it on the landscape of an entire region, as exemplified by the mandatory French language signs in Quebec. Surveying is an act of national hegemony and the straight lines that are reproduced on the landscape through roads, agricultural fields, and fences are successful in erasing opposing claims from a region (Edney 1997: chaps. 1, 10). Planning and zoning are equally tainted and seemingly harmless development projects can be exposed as carefully designed nation-building strategies that serve the interest of one nation at the expense of another.[6]

Taken to its extreme, national modifications of territory entail a nationalist cleansing of the landscape. After expelling or killing members of other nations, all visible traces of their previous occupancy are erased from the land. For example during the civil war in Bosnia, Serbs dynamited mosques and Muslim villages not simply to prevent Muslims from returning but to have a tabula rasa for the creation of an indisputably Serb national region. The Muslims and Croats quickly emulated the practice: The "reality" of the new landscape was powerful evidence for the rightfulness of territorial claims (see also Bell-Fialkoff 1993).

Direct interaction with the landscape for purposes of nation building are complemented and reinforced by representations of national territory in writing, painting, music, and mapping. As numerous studies attest, these discursive practices are crucial in establishing a strong attachment to the national territory.[7] However, except when nations occupy islands, the national identity that these artistic endeavors generate has fuzzy boundaries. For example, the reference to rivers and straits in the first verse of the German anthem identifies national parameters in all four cardinal directions, but still leaves considerable areas undefined.

Only maps are able to communicate a precise image of the limits of a nation and foster a territorial consensus (Herb 1997: 7). Their perception as accurate and truthful representations of reality makes them powerful tools of persuasion (Harley 1989; Pickles 1992). Thus, the presence of national groups that pose a challenge can be silenced easily and convincingly by simply omitting them from the map. For example, in Weimar Germany, numerous maps disseminated in schoolbooks, atlases, and posters clearly indicated a purely German area in Czechoslovakia, called Sudetenland, and portrayed Bohemia and Moravia as German cultural territory. This made the annexation of the Sudetenland and the establishment of a German protectorate over the area by Hitler in 1938 appear justified (Herb 1997).

Conclusion

At first glance, it appears that the territorial tensions between power and identity are irreconcilable. Political power is premised on precisely delimited territories whereas nations as social formations are by necessity ill-defined, even though they derive much of their cohesive strength from their interaction with territory, that is, their *territorial narrative*. To be sure, nations strive to lessen these tensions and actively delineate a specific national territory so as to give their exclusive community a visible expression and provide the foundation for a state. But does this mean that the territories of nations and states might someday be in agreement?

If increasing power means greater effectiveness in control, nations that are able to dominate a state with a dictatorial form of government or military law should be best at creating uniform and clearly delimited national territories. Yet, challenges to the majority nationalism are the most virulent and most vocal under these regimes. For example, Palestinian identity only began to show signs of a national identity when Palestinians were faced with British policies that discriminated against them, and this national identity further crystallized with the establishment of a Jewish state and the military occupation of the West Bank and Gaza (Mayer 1994). Thus, the maximization of territorial control by one nation will be opposed by other nations as they become more aware of their limited place in the dominant national identity. The central characteristic of national identity, the "us-them" distinction is heightened and with it the resolve of the group that is oppressed. And because acts of resistance, such as terrorism, are predicated on the ability to influence public opinion, the global spread of mass communication might alter the balance in favor of weaker nations (Adams 1996). The Palestinian national movement became a recognizable force after news of the terrorist attack in Munich was beamed around the world as part of the TV coverage of the 1972 Olympics. Without the ability of the Chiapas guerrillas to spread their message via the Internet and other electronic media, the Mexican government might have been able to silence the revolt, just as it had in the past.

This leaves two possible scenarios for the future: The state system could be characterized by states that create a homogeneous identity by force—Nietschmann's (1994) ultimate nightmare—or by smaller units in which the "cultural container" of the state corresponds closest to the distribution of ethnic groups (Taylor 1994: 159). Neither one would herald a peaceful equilibrium. The Janus-faced attitude of nationalism toward an idyllic past and modernization reveals that national identity is a contested discourse. As a result, if a clear threat to the national group dissipates, the internal cohesion that is predicated on the us-them distinction will give way to internal rifts. And new disputes, based on any number of possible attributes, will emerge.

Notes

1. See for example Williams and Smith (1983), J. Anderson (1986), Walby (1992), Jackson and Penrose (1993), Häkli (1994), Kaplan (1994), Radcliffe and Westwood (1996), and Paasi (1997) as well as some of the authors in Johnston, Knight, and Kofman (1988) and in Bhabha (1990).

2. See also the chapter "Nationalism and Masculinity" in Enloe (1990) and the edited volume by Mayer (forthcoming) on the intersection of nation, gender, and sexuality.

3. Oren Yiftachel argues that the Catalans should not be considered a true nation but a collective identity that occupies an intermediary position between an ethnic group and a nation, because they do not openly express the desire to have a separate state (see Chapter 11).

4. The frontier thesis of Frederick Jackson Turner (1935) employs such imagery for American identity: The early pioneers represent the idyllic "national"

past, and their mastering of the wild frontier environment establishes their unique and superior "national" character. However, the identification of the United States as a true nation is problematic given its short existence and its multiethnic character.

5. Recent historical scholarship established that there was no pledge in 1291, but the myth is still commonly accepted (see Kamm 1994).

6. See the debate on Israel's "Judaization" policy in *Political Geography*, vol. 10, no. 3, 1991.

7. See for example Albert Boime (1993), Stephen Daniels (1993), John Lucas (1990), Homi Bhabha (1990), Carl Dahlhaus (1980), and Herb (1997). The role of mapping is also discussed in Chapter 6, that of music in Chapter 7.

References

Adams, Paul C. "Protest and the Scale Politics of Telecommunications." *Political Geography* 15 (1996): 419–441.

Agnew, John. *Place and Politics: The Geographic Mediation of State and Society.* Boston: Allen and Unwin, 1987.

Amtlicher Führer durch die Ausstellung Deutschland, Berlin 1936, 18. Juli bis 16. August. Berlin: Gemeinnützige Berliner Ausstellungs-, Messe- und Fremden-verkehrs-G.m.b.H., 1936.

Anderson, Benedict. *Imagined Communities: Reflections on the Origins and Spread of Nationalism.* London: Verso, 1991.

Anderson, James. "Nationalism and Geography." In James Anderson, ed., *The Rise of the Modern State.* Atlantic Highlands, N.J.: Humanities Press International, 1986, 115–142.

———. "Nationalist Ideology and Territory." In R. J. Johnston, David B. Knight, and Eleonore Kofman, eds., *Nationalism, Self-Determination, and Political Geography.* London, New York: Croom Helm, 1988, 18–39.

Anderson, Malcolm. *Frontiers: Territory and State Formation in the Modern World.* Oxford: Blackwell, 1996.

Bell-Fialkoff, Andrew. "A Brief History of Ethnic Cleansing." *Foreign Affairs* (Summer, 1993): 110–121.

Bhabha, Homi K., ed. *Nation and Narration.* London, New York: Routledge, 1990.

Boime, Albert. *The Art of the Macchia and the Risorgimento: Representing Culture and Nationalism in Nineteenth Century Italy.* Chicago: University of Chicago Press, 1993.

Breuilly, John. *Nationalism and the State.* 2d ed. Chicago: University of Chicago Press, 1994.

Burghardt, A. "The Bases of Territorial Claims." *The Geographical Review* 63 (1973): 225–245.

Chatterjee, Partha. *Nationalist Thought and the Colonial World: A Derivative Discourse.* Minneapolis: University of Minnesota Press, 1986.

Connor, Walker. "Nation-Building or Nation-Destroying?" *World Politics* 24 (1977): 319–355.

———. "A Nation Is a Nation, Is a State, Is an Ethnic Group, Is a . . ." *Ethnic and Racial Studies* 1 (1978): 377–400.

———. *Ethnonationalism: The Quest for Understanding.* Princeton, N.J.: Princeton University Press, 1994.

Conversi, Daniele. "Reassessing Current Theories of Nationalism: Nationalism as Boundary Maintenance and Creation." In John Agnew, ed. *Political Geography. A Reader.* New York: John Wiley and Sons, 1997, 325–336.

Dahlhaus, Carl. *Between Romanticism and Modernism: Four Studies in the Music of the Later Nineteenth Century.* Berkeley, Los Angeles: University of California Press, 1980.

Daniels, Stephen. *Fields of Vision: Landscape Imagery and National Identity in England and the United States.* Princeton, N.J.: Princeton University Press, 1993.

Deutsch, Karl. *Nationalism and Social Communication: An Inquiry into the Foundations of Nationality.* Cambridge, Mass., London: MIT Press, 1966.

Duara, Prasenjit. "Historicizing National Identity, or Who Imagines What and When." In Geoff Eley and Ronald Grigor Suny, eds., *Becoming National: A Reader.* Oxford: Oxford University Press, 1996, 151–177.

Edney, Matthew H. *Mapping an Empire: The Geographic Construction of British India, 1765–1843.* Chicago: University of Chicago Press, 1997.

Eley, Geoff, and Ronald Grigor Suny. "Introduction: From the Moment of Social History to the Work of Cultural Representation." In Geoff Eley and Ronald Grigor Suny, eds., *Becoming National: A Reader.* Oxford: Oxford University Press, 1996, 3–37.

Enloe, Cynthia. *Bananas, Beaches, and Bases: Making Feminist Sense of International Politics.* Berkeley, Los Angeles: University of California Press, 1990.

Fichte, Johann Gottlieb. *Addresses to the German Nation.* Chicago, London: The Open Court Publishing Company, 1922 [1808].

Gellner, Ernest. *Nations and Nationalism.* Ithaca, N.Y.: Cornell University Press, 1983.

———. *Encounters with Nationalism.* Cambridge, Mass., Oxford: Blackwell, 1994.

Gottmann, Jean. *The Significance of Territory.* Charlottesville: University Press of Virginia, 1973.

Gruffudd, Pyrs. "Reach for the Sky: The Air and English Cultural Nationalism." *Landscape Research* 16 (2) (1991): 19–24.

———. "Remaking Wales: Nation-Building and the Geographical Imagination, 1925–50." *Political Geography* 14 (1995): 219–239.

Guéhenno, Jean-Marie. *The End of the Nation-State.* Minneapolis, London: University of Minnesota Press, 1995.

Häkli, Jouni. "Territoriality and the Rise of the Modern State." *Fennia* 172 (1994): 1–82.

Harley, J. B. "Deconstructing the Map." *Cartographica* 26 (2) (1989): 1–20.

Herb, Guntram Henrik. *Under the Map of Germany: Nationalism and Propaganda 1918–1945.* London, New York: Routledge, 1997.

Hobsbawm, E. J. *Nations and Nationalism Since 1780: Programme, Myth, Reality.* 2d ed. Cambridge: Cambridge University Press, 1992.

Hroch, Miroslav. *Social Preconditions of National Revival in Europe: A Comparative Analysis of the Social Composition of Patriotic Groups among the Smaller European Nations.* Cambridge: Cambridge University Press, 1985.

Jackson, Peter, and Jan Penrose. "Introduction: Placing 'Race' and Nation." In Peter Jackson and Jan Penrose, eds., *Constructions of Race, Place, and Nation.* Minneapolis: University of Minnesota Press, 1993, 1–23.

Jayawardena, Kumari. *Feminism and Nationalism in the Third World.* London: Zen Books, 1986.

Johnson, Nuala. "Cast in Stone: Monuments, Geography, and Nationalism." In John Agnew, ed., *Political Geography: A Reader.* New York: John Wiley and Sons, 1997, 347–364.

Johnston, R. J., David B. Knight and Eleanore Kofman. *Nationalism, Self-Determination, and Political Geography.* London, New York: Croom Helm, 1988.

Kamm, Henry. "The Swiss Debunk William Tell and All That." *New York Times,* March 30, 1994, A4.

Kaplan, David H. "Two Nations in Search of a State: Canada's Ambivalent Spatial Identities." *Annals of the Association of American Geographers* 84 (1994): 585–606.

Kecmanovic, Dusan. *The Mass Psychology of Ethnonationalism.* New York: Plenum Press, 1996.

Kedourie, Eli. *Nationalism.* 4th ed. Cambridge, Mass., and Oxford: Blackwell, 1993.

Knight, David B. "Identity and Territory: Geographical Perspectives on Nationalism and Regionalism." *Annals of the Association of American Geographers* 72 (1982): 514–531.

———. "Self-Determination for Indigenous Peoples: The Context for Change." In R. J. Johnston, David B. Knight, and Eleanore Kofman, eds., *Nationalism, Self-Determination, and Political Geography.* London, New York: Croom Helm, 1988, 117–134.

———. "People Together, Yet Apart: Rethinking Territory, Sovereignty, and Identities." In George Demko and William Wood, eds., *Reordering the World.* Boulder: Westview Press, 1994, 71–86.

Kohn, Hans. *The Idea of Nationalism: A Study in Its Origins and Background.* New York: MacMillan, 1944.

Lowenthal, David. "European and English Landscapes as National Symbols." In David Hooson, ed., *Geography and National Identity.* Cambridge, Mass., Oxford: Blackwell, 1994, 15–38.

Lucas, John. *England and Englishness: Ideas of Nationhood in English Poetry 1688–1900.* Iowa City: University of Iowa Press, 1990.

Lutz, J. "From Primordialism to Nationalism." In E. Tiryakian and R. Rogowski, eds., *New Nationalisms of the Developed West.* Boston: Allen and Unwin, 1985, 203–253.

Marden, Peter. "Geographies of Dissent: Globalization, Identity, and the Nation." *Political Geography* 16 (1997): 37–64.

Mayer, Tamar. "Heightened Palestinian Nationalism: Military Occupation, Repression, Difference, and Gender." In Tamar Mayer, ed., *Women and the Israeli Occupation. The Politics of Change.* London and New York: Routledge, 1994, 62–87.

Mayer, Tamar, ed. *Nationalism, Gender, and Sexuality.* London and New York: Routledge, forthcoming.

McClintock, Anne. "Family Feuds: Gender, Nationalism, and the Family." *Feminist Review* 44 (Summer) (1993): 61–80.

Murphy, Alexander B. "International Law and the Sovereign State: Challenges to the Status Quo." In George J. Demko and William B. Wood, eds., *Reordering the World: Geopolitical Perspectives on the 21st Century.* Boulder: Westview Press, 1994, 209–224.

Nairn, Tom. *The Break-Up of Britain: Crisis and Neo-Nationalism.* 2d ed. London: Verso, 1981.

Nietschmann, Bernard. "The Fourth World: Nations Versus States." In George J. Demko and William B. Wood, eds., *Reordering the World: Geopolitical Perspectives on the 21st Century.* Boulder: Westview Press, 1994, 225–242.

Ohmae, Kenichi. *The End of the Nation State: The Rise of Regional Economies.* New York: Free Press, 1995.

Olwig, Kenneth. *Nature's Ideological Landscape: A Literary and Geographical Perspective on Its Development and Preservation on Denmark's Jutland Heath.* London: George Allen and Unwin, 1984.

Paasi, Anssi. *Territories, Boundaries, and Consciousness: The Changing Geographies of the Finnish-Russian Border.* Chichester, U.K.: John Wiley and Sons, 1996.

———. "Geographical Perspectives on Finnish National Identity." *GeoJournal* 43 (1997): 41–50.

Penck, Albrecht. "Deutscher Volks- und Kulturboden." In Karl C. von Loesch and A. H. Ziegfeld, eds., *Volk unter Völkern, Bücher des Deutschtums 1.* Breslau: F. Hirt, 1925, 62–73.

Pickles, John. "Texts, Hermeneutics, and Propaganda Maps." In Trevor J. Barnes and James S. Duncan, eds., *Writing Worlds: Discourse, Text, and Metaphor in the Representation of Landscape.* London: Routledge, 1992, 193–230.

Radcliffe, Sarah, and Sallie Westwood. *Remaking the Nation: Place, Identity, and Politics in Latin America.* London, New York: Routledge, 1996.

Rollins, William. "Whose Landscape? Technology, Fascism, and Environmentalism on the National Socialist Autobahn." *Annals of the Association of American Geographers* 85 (1995): 494–520.

Rössler, Mechthild. "Berlin or Bonn? National Identity and the Question of the German Capital." In David Hooson, ed., *Geography and National Identity.* Cambridge, Mass., Oxford: Blackwell, 1994, 92–103.

Sack, Robert D. *Human Territoriality: Its Theory and History.* Cambridge: Cambridge University Press, 1986.

Sapiro, Virginia. "Engendering Cultural Differences." In Crawford Young, ed., *The Rising Tide of Cultural Pluralism: The Nation-State at Bay?* Madison: University of Wisconsin Press, 1993, 36–54.

Smith, Anthony D. *Theories of Nationalism.* 2d ed. New York: Holmes and Meier, 1983.

————. *The Ethnic Origins of Nations.* Oxford: Basil Blackwell, 1986.

Smith, Anthony D., ed. *Ethnicity and Nationalism.* (International Studies in Sociology and Social Anthropology, vol. 60). Leiden: E. J. Brill, 1992.

Taylor, Peter J. "The State as Container: Territoriality in the Modern World-System." *Progress in Human Geography* 18 (1994): 151–162.

Turner, Frederick Jackson. *The Frontier in American History.* New York: Henry Holt, 1935.

Volz, Wilhelm, ed. *Der ostdeutsche Volksboden: Aufsätze zu Fragen des Ostens.* Breslau: F. Hirt, 1926.

Walby, Silvia. "Women and Nation." In Anthony D. Smith, ed., *Ethnicity and Nationalism.* (International Studies in Sociology and Social Anthropology, vol. 60). Leiden: E. J. Brill, 1992, 81–100.

Werner, Karl. *Weichselkorridor und Ostoberschlesien: Der weltwirtschaftliche Zusammenhang beider Probleme.* Zur Wirtschaftsgeographie des deutschen Ostens, vol. 2, ed. Walter Geisler. Breslau: M. and H. Marcus, 1932.

Williams, Colin, and Anthony D. Smith. "The National Construction of Social Space." *Progress in Human Geography* 7 (1983): 502–518.

Wistricht, Robert. *Who Is Who in Nazi Germany.* New York: Bonanza Books, 1984.

Ziegfeld, Arnold Hillen, and Wilhelm von Kries. "Das Korridorproblem—als Wirklichkeit." In Friedrich Heiss and A. H. Ziegfeld, eds., *Deutschland und der Korridor.* Berlin: Volk und Reich, 1933.

2

Territorial Identities and Geographic Scale

David H. Kaplan

National identity first, is bound up with the territory that helps define it; second, is not an enduring constant but a set of cultural attributes bundled with articulated political objectives; third, exists as an identity distinct from the state; and fourth, is situated within a hierarchy of geographically based identities that coexist and sometimes compete with it.

Our identities are arranged in zones of increasing geographic extent. Tribal groups, with little knowledge of the outside world, draw a circle around their immediate clan, and then a larger circle that includes other clans with whom they are related or otherwise aligned, and then perhaps an additional zone composed of the familiar, followed by the largest zone of all, which encompasses all that is unfamiliar and strange—the world as they know it. The Chinese sense of a "Middle Kingdom" follows a similar logic, from the Lan (or Chinese people), to the near neighbors and tributary kingdoms, to the barbarians that surround the known and familiar (Fitzgerald 1964).

Classification according to scale is a critical aspect of human ordering and is particularly important in helping to organize human identities. We are all part of the "global community," and we are all unique individuals. Between these two extremes lie several intermediary scales of identity, and, in our modern world, national identity has emerged as the single most significant of these; it is an identity both global and pervasive (Smith 1991).

This might appear as a fairly straightforward proposition. It is not. National identities are situated among a cascade of geographically based identities. Although in many cases national identities are conceived as "ethnic," ethnic affiliations range from the clan to the civilization. In this day and age, national identities embody the political goal of comprising a state. But both substate and superstate units proliferate and can spawn their own identities. The nation-state was once seen as the preferred unit of efficient economic production and exchange. But all parts of the world are now integrated into a global assembly line, and a standardized commercial culture diffuses to all the world's people. Will the nation-state have any relevance to this new global order?

To understand national identity, it is crucial to comprehend its place within the overall scheme of identities, especially its relationship to the identity of states. There is nothing "natural" about its preeminent position. It is a fairly recent phenomenon and continues to be challenged by alternative means of ordering. In this chapter, I will focus specifically on the scale aspects of national identity and attempt to engage a series of issues. These begin with the privileged status of national identity. I will explore how the primacy of national identity is a legacy of the states' claim to sovereignty. This follows through to the issue of how the spatial identities of nations differ, in nature and scale, from the spatial identities of states. Because identities are unevenly nested and viewed separately by various peoples, it is useful to consider the conflicts generated by the incongruence of national and state identities or between national identities at separate geographical scales. Finally, I will discuss whether the privileged position of national identity might be challenged and if it might be possible to consider alternative identities that exist beyond or below the scale of the nation.

The Privileged Status of National Identity

Most scholars of nationalism seem to agree that national identity has a claim to preeminence. Anthony Smith (1991) writes that we live in a world of exclusive nations, and Rupert Emerson (1960: 95–96) points to the overwhelming dominance of national allegiance as compared with all other forms of identity. "The nation is today the largest community which, when the chips are down, effectively commands men's loyalty, overriding the claims both of lesser communities within it and those which cut across it or potentially unfold within a still greater society."

The concept of nation has undergone a tremendous metamorphosis over the past millennium, from designating a group of foreigners, to a community of elite, to a category that distinguishes unique sovereign peoples (Greenfeld 1992). Some go so far as to argue that the creation of nations has come about because of the creation of states (Hobsbawm 1990), with Wallerstein (1991: 141) stating that "in most cases, it was the establishment of a state that was the single strongest force in creating a people." Others maintain that "nations" existed prior to the era of nationalism and the nation-state ideal (Smith 1996, Armstrong 1982), with Nietschmann (1994: 232) boldly asserting that "thousands of nations and associated peoples and cultures were already distributed over the earth's space before states were invented." Whatever the precise timing, categories of state and nation are inextricably linked. The modern state has challenged the primacy of national identity, although it has enabled national identity to assume its present characteristics and dominance.

This is partly a result of the international legitimacy of a world organized around states. Since the Peace of Westphalia in 1648, which sanctioned the sovereignty of independent state territories, the idea of a world made up of interlocking, discrete, sovereign state units gained widespread acceptance (Murphy 1996, Taylor 1996). There was nothing inevitable about the states' categorical claim on sovereignty; it progressed as a result of particular material conditions, strategic behavior, and a change in social mentality (Ruggie 1993). As a consequence, the state evolved to command a privileged international recognition not accorded to "stateless" entities. From the outside, "nation" has come to be conflated with the state; the national voice is considered analogous to the existing government to the point where a world association of state governments is termed the United *Nations*. This reality compels modern "stateless" nations to accommodate themselves to a state-centric order and to gain recognition as states in the making.

The global community has come to see a world of nation-states as the best guarantor of political stability and to this end has promoted the process of "nation-building." The state already has enormous advantages. Ideally, it enjoys a monopoly of power within its borders and is endowed with the singular ability—through education, media, propaganda, and "infrastructural power" (Bloom 1990, Paasi 1996)—to inculcate a sense of collective identity among its residents. This has achieved uniformity within state borders, but only up to a point and within some countries. Identity-building is quite difficult to consummate in many of the newly independent countries, which are less favored with the tools of national integration although they must contend with greater internal diversity. For these countries, national and state identity often come into sharp conflict. In Chapter 8, Rex Honey examines how a sense of Nigerian identity has still not been fully developed and must contend with a variety of identities at more localized scales. And although Estonia and Finland are far more uniform, they too must reconcile the dominant statehood with the existence of significant minority populations (see Chapters 6 and 7).

The political goals of nationalism make state sovereignty essential. Self-described nations are either in charge of their political destiny or share in the goals of eventual self-determination. Ernest Gellner argues that (1983: 4) "nationalism emerges only in milieux in which the existence of the state is already very much taken for granted." Much of the allegiance enjoined by the nation is a legacy of a world made up of states. If national identity commands the primary loyalty of individuals, it is because the state has become the preferred political container. And national identity in turn has been the means of legitimizing the authority of states. As Smith (1991: 144) writes, "such order as may be found in the community of states is premised on the norm of the nation as the sole unit of political loyalty and action."

Asymmetrical Identities of States and Nations

State and nation are symbiotically linked. Even though the two identities are not congruent, national identity sustains state identity. The political functions of the state and the cultural functions of a nation make up an integral dualism (see discussion in Tiryakian 1997). The state needs the nation for legitimacy, and the nation needs the state to fulfill its aspirations. They are also in competition. Except in rare cases, the geography of nations and the geography of states do not coincide (see Chapter 1). The tension between the identities associated with state and nation is echoed by Friedrich Meinecke's distinction between the cultural nation and the political nation (Smith 1991).

The modern state would prefer that primary loyalties be conferred on it, but for this it needs to offer the legitimation of national identity. Dusan Kecmanovic (1996) distinguishes between patriotism (loyalty to the state) and nationalism (loyalty to the nation). When the two allegiances conflict, loyalty to nation usually wins out (Connor 1983). The "patriotism" one feels for the state is generally weaker than the "nationalism" felt for the nation.

Gaps between state and nation result from their separate characteristics, their different scales of operation, and their distinct spatial identities. Nations in control of the state apparatus (and with little awareness of other nations challenging the status quo) can often perceive the two identities as one and the same, but these nations enjoy the luxury of control. Those nations without political control see it differently. For them, stark contrasts between state and nation often result in individuals giving their primary loyalty to an entity apart from the state. The spatial identities of state and nation differ sharply (see Kaplan 1994). State identity involves membership in a polity. It is concerned primarily with consolidating administrative authority—what Jouni Häkli (1994: 41) terms *system integration*. Therefore, its spatial identity will entail such things as the jurisdictional aspects of the state, the maintenance of internal order, the symbols of government as they exist on the ground, and vigorous demarcation and control of the border. Moreover, the spatial identities of states are much cleaner. The territories served by states interlock, they are discrete. There are some border disputes, but these are more an exception than the rule. It is a spatial arrangement based on absolute sovereignty within each spatial unit (Taylor 1996).

Although the color map of the political world displays a neat and ordered pattern of interlocking units (with only a few lines of discord), it is not surprising that the real world of national identities is one of blotches, blends, and blurs. National identity implies affiliation with a cultural group, even if the cultural affiliation may appear from the outside to be artificial. The national spatial identity will go deeper than the state spatial identity. It will include a primordial attachment to the land (Grosby 1995), it will incorporate a "discursive landscape" (see Häkli, Chapter 6), and it will be suffused with the culture of the people, from aspects of the historical past to the present day reflections of language and religion (Knight 1994)—what Smith (1996) describes as "territorialized memory."

This identity manifests itself in spatial forms that are distinct from the spatial identity associated with the state (Taylor 1996). The legacy of a state-dominant system has compelled the homogenization of language and norms. Discrete, uniform national spaces have come to coordinate imperfectly with the state system (Häkli 1994, Anderson 1983). But national spaces are not necessarily discrete. They are often gradational, moving from zones of greatest intensity to the margins, where they coexist with other national identities (Rokkan and Urwin 1983). They can be interlaced within other national identities, and they almost always overlap with other national identities.

The uneven coordination of national and state spatial identities, or between two national spatial identities, creates certain asymmetries. The resulting forms include substate nationalisms, borderlands, and diasporas. Although they may carry different political implications, all asymmetries call into question the affiliations of some or all of the individuals living within the disputed area, and usually, the identity of the surrounding territories.

Substate Nationalisms

The disjuncture in the spatial identities between those nations who have achieved sovereignty and those nations that have been bypassed sometimes foments separatist movements. Such movements have emerged both in states where newly won independence runs up against ancient tribal antagonisms and in states that have been united for some time (Connor 1972). Actually, "separatism" is only the most extreme of several goals that may be pursued by members of the by-passed nation (Mikesell and Murphy 1991), but it helps to illustrate the stakes involved.

The conflict arises because of a discordance between two national identities at separate spatial scales. The dominant group's national spatial identity coincides roughly with the entire state territory, including those areas occupied by minority populations (Williams and Smith 1983, Kaplan 1994). It is often part of a conscious process of consolidating internal differences into a single cultural entity: nation-building. The aggrieved group's identity is maintained through a number of channels less privileged than that offered to the dominant group, but still enough to provide a rallying point. So-called micro-scale identities are often small nations that must coexist or challenge the larger state structure (Knight 1994). The contributions to this text by Pauliina Raento and Chelvadurai Manogaran could be viewed as describing the articulation of a national identity at a level below the conventional size of a "nation-state" (see Chapters 9 and 10). In this case, the region the national identity inhabits takes on additional significance. It becomes *institutionalized* to use Paasi's (1996) terminology. The goal is often to further this institutionalization, to carve out greater regional autonomy as a means of preserving the substate identity. And although the dominant nation may accede to some of these demands, very often, the demands threaten to infringe upon the dominant nation's own sense of national identity.

This has been the case in a number of locations. I earlier wrote about the asymmetry in the spatial identities of many English Canadians—focused on the whole of the Canadian state—and many French Canadians, whose identity was increasingly bound within the province of Quebec (Kaplan 1994). J. Penrose (1990) cites a similar process at work in the Netherlands, where the state-encompassing Dutch identity, itself of relatively recent vintage, conflicts with a smaller-scale Frisian identity. Both cases spark a conflict in identities but with differing outcomes. In Quebec, identification and even primary loyalty is increasingly centered on the province; many Quebecois will insist that they are not Canadian. The Dutch have been able to finesse these more worrisome aspects of Frisian consciousness; most Frisians still base their loyalty on the Dutch nation.

Borderlands

Borderlands represent another type of asymmetry that results from an incongruence between cultural and political boundaries. As political boundaries shift, perhaps because of warfare or political concessions, the new state territory includes land occupied by culturally distinct populations. As a result, borderlands "tend historically to be zones of cultural overlap and political instability where the national identity and loyalties of the people often become blurred" (Augelli 1980: 19; see also the introduction to Rumley and Minghi 1991).

Within a borderland, there are often at least three separate spatial identities involved at distinct geographical scales. There is the identity based on the state controlling the area, there is the identity based on the nation within which the occupants most identify, and there is a third borderland identity that is generated from the occupance and symbolism of the borderland itself (see Paasi 1996). This third identity can become more important as time passes between the adjustment of the political boundaries; the "blur" becomes more concrete. In Chapter 11, Oren Yiftachel discusses the case of Israeli Arabs, molded by their Palestinian nationalism and their location within the Jewish state but with an emerging sense of a separate ethno-regional identity. This identity can involve tremendous ambivalence, as has been the case with the Alsatians who positioned themselves as variously French, German, and somehow apart from either (Gaines 1994).

In many cases, the identity of a borderland region is further complicated by its distance from the state center. In addition to being at the political boundary, these regions are often peripheries. As such, they feel isolated from the central region (Rokkan and Urwin 1983: 3). Center institutions are necessarily weaker here; it follows that other cultural influences can take root. These may be influences across the political boundary from neighboring states. They may also be influences indigenous to the borderland itself, allowing a stateless nation greater leeway in developing its own identity.

Borderland identities at odds with the center provoke anxiety insofar as they may form the genesis of an irredentist or a separatist movement. As a consequence, borderlands often spur state efforts to secure its borders culturally and ideologically. Paasi (1996: 176) mentions that Finland in the 1920s and 1930s sought to populate its Finnish-Russian boundary with "reliable, patriotic" Finns. The Dominican Republic used force to expel Haitians from the borderlands, reeducate the re-

maining population, and render the human landscape more suitably
Dominican (Augelli 1980). In Chapter 12, George White's discussion of
Transylvania bears out the nationalizing efforts of the Romanian state,
as it seeks to eradicate Hungarian influences.

Diasporas

A third area of asymmetry pertains to the geography of diaspora
nations. The premier examples of this phenomenon are the Jews, but
diasporas also describe Chinese within Southeast Asia and along the
Pacific Rim, Indians throughout the world, and many other groups
(see Sheffer 1986a). In fact the numbers of such groups have been increasing with increased labor migration. In an introduction to a volume on diasporas, Sheffer (1986b) describes the diaspora as a group
that leaves their homeland, either voluntarily or through forced expulsion, that becomes a minority population in another country controlled
by others and that preserves a strong identification as a distinct ethnicity and continues to maintain transnational contacts. For most diasporas, the homeland is vital, even though relations between the diaspora
and the homeland are sometimes uncertain and the homeland itself is
artificially constructed (Sheffer 1986b, Connor 1986). Robin Cohen
(1996) adds that, in the diaspora, many communities share a strong
political commitment to their homeland and a desire to return. Although as Anne Knowles shows in Chapter 13, this bond does not
necessarily develop.
    Diaspora communities gives rise to spatial identities that are mani-
fested at two geographic scales. They can be described as "transnational" in that they are dispersed across several countries. At the same
time, many diasporas are extremely national. Their identity is bound
up with their homeland, and inasmuch as they share a cultural and
political loyalty to this homeland (see Esman 1986), diasporas are an
extension of a specific nation. The diaspora community often suffers a
sense of ambivalence that develops because its members live also
within a particular host country and often must remain circumspect
about any external loyalties and identities (Tölölyan 1996). But, although those in the diaspora may be cautious about voicing their sentiments, divided loyalties becomes a key issue for diaspora communities
and an issue for individuals within the host country who see the diaspora as a threat. According to Cohen (1996: 517), the general ascen-
dance of diasporas may be a part of a larger challenge to nation-states,
where diasporas become one of a number of nonterritorial "communities not of place but of interest." Such transnational communities may

be less likely to pledge allegiance to their host society but to focus their attention on building up their individual enclaves.

Diasporas can be vital to the overall maintenance of nationhood. Without a country to call their own, diasporic Jews maintained their traditions within the diaspora. Today, diaspora communities can still refresh and sometimes even generate the sense of nationhood. According to T. Eriksen (1993), the sense of Mauritian nationhood is strongest in the European diaspora; the experience of being outside the country helps to minimize the ethnic cleavages that divide Mauritians at home. The nationalism of Nevisians is "deterritorialized" in the diaspora, according to Karen Olwig (1993), where the contacts between Nevisians outside the island are more important than any national project within the island.

Challenges to National Identity

The primacy of national loyalty is relatively new. It has emerged at this historical period and has come about in a world of nations that have achieved self-determination or aspire to this status. The character and salience of national identity is likely to change some time in the future. As Eric Hobsbawm (1990: 11) puts it, "we cannot assume that for most people national identification—when it exists—excludes or is always or ever superior to, the remainder of the set of identifications which constitute the social being." Alternative forms of geographical identity have been preeminent in the past (Ruggie 1993). Other forms exist now. In the present era, there have been appeals to identification based on social class, on ideology, on levels of economic development, on religion. Still other forms are emerging. Can these political entities attract loyalties that are considered to be the exclusive preserve of the nation? Rather than a singular focus on the scale of nations, is it possible to conceive of a multiplicity of sites within which identity might be manifested?

Imperial Legacy

Scales of identity stretching beyond the boundaries of the modern state have long been significant. Macro-scale entities existed long before the rise of nationalism, and it is these entities that trace much of human civilization. Empires, in which the political sovereignty of several peoples is controlled from a central government, were the historically dominant form of political organization. And although they did not generate the mass horizontal allegiance of nationalism, many empires did foster a sense of a larger identity that transcended smaller-scale clan, ethnic, or religious ties. For instance, the Roman Empire became more of a political community over time, leading to where residents felt themselves part of a common civilization and offered their willing allegiance (Doyle 1986). Similarly, zeal for the Islamic religion helped the Ottoman Empire "transcend the limits of tribal social organization" (Doyle 1986: 107). And as Nicholas Lynn and Valentin Bogorov point out in Chapter 5, as recently as 1989, most Russians identified more strongly with the multinational Soviet Union than with a more narrowly defined ethnicity. These identities would not be considered national. They were too broad and they comprise a wide panoply of ethnicities. However, they were the most salient sources of identification at the time. Rome's decline coincided with the breakdown of political integration; a sense of being part of a common enterprise (Doyle 1986).

Samuel Huntington (1996) argues that these macro-scale identities are still with us. Civilizations, he claims, are the "broadest cultural entity," surpassing that of nations. Identities based on religion or a more vaguely considered "civilization" set the parameters of understanding. The best articulated example may be in countries that compose the "Arab world." Pan-Arabness is promoted within several individual Arab states, and seven of sixteen constitutions expressly pledge support for the goal of eventual Arab unity (Connor 1986). For people within a civilization, according to Huntington, there can be true trust and friendship. For peoples across civilizational divides, at best there can only be wary cooperation and at worst a distrust that aggravates local skirmishes into much broader wars.

Many of these civilizations are legacies of former empires but, unlike nations, they do not necessarily aspire to political unity or uniform sovereignty. Most civilizations contain many sovereign states and self-defined nations. According to Louis Snyder (1984), even through there may be an impulse to extend political control over a single "pan"-nationalism (similar to Huntington's civilizations), these attempts are unsuccessful. Susanne Rudolph (1997: 12) likens transnational religions to transparent overlays that do not replace states (and by extension, nations) but that diminish "their effect, function, and finality."

Compartmentalization

Many of the functions now concentrated in the state were once delegated to other political, spiritual, and private agencies (Mann 1993). Separate needs are still served by separate entities, whether it is the need to clean up the environment or to rid the Holy Land of infidels.

These entities may lay claim to separate identities. Is it possible to conceive of an identity that is "multi-perspectival"?

Rudolph's (1997) metaphor of overlays is a good way of conceiving the variegated world of the new millennium. It evokes a somewhat functionalist view in which, instead of the nation-state monopolizing all decisions, alternative entities fulfill certain demands (DiMuccio and Rosenau 1992, Held 1996, Murphy 1996). These include territorial alternatives like macro-scale entities, semi-sovereign units, and multilayered organizations in which the scale of control would fit the problems at hand (Taylor 1996). In addition to the transnational religious communities mentioned by Rudolph (1997), there are also "communities" based on political principles (human rights, eradication of poverty), economic interests, environmental issues, and issues of race, gender, and religion. The expansion of these international nongovernmental organizations (NGOs) has been nothing short of phenomenal (Drake 1994). Now they are usually able to conduct conferences in parallel with the official meetings held between representatives of states (Marden 1997). Moreover, there has also been a marked expansion in multistate groupings (Drake 1994).

However, it is possible to conceive of situations where micro-sale identities emerge that are not necessarily "nations" per se, but that coexist with a larger national identity. Snyder (1982) argues that many of what he calls "mini-nationalisms" are desirous of a sort of semi-sovereignty that falls short of complete self-determination. Likewise, Marvin Mikesell and Alexander Murphy (1991) catalogue a range of demands among minority groups, from separation to autonomy to independence. Because group aspirations form along a continuum (albeit one that can rapidly change) there is no reason to believe that there exists a point of equilibrium where smaller-scale identity fits into a larger nation.

A few examples bear this out. Using Singapore as a model, C. S. Foon (1986) maintains that it is possible for individuals to retain a loyalty to an ethnic group and a nation because the two scales of identity serve separate functions; they are complementary. Eriksen's discussion of Mauritius describes a government that encourages smaller-scale ethnic loyalties, while constructing a vision for Mauritius as a mosaic. Switzerland, too, appears to have created a successful blend between small-scale cantonal loyalty and a larger sense of Swiss nationalism (Bendix 1992). Successful negotiations are indeed possible where each loyalty is strictly demarcated.

As another example of compartmentalization, one could look toward the "region-state." Kenichi Ohmae (1993) maintains that the world has subdivided itself into "natural economic zones": Hong Kong and adjacent China, Northern Italy, San Diego and Tijuana. These do not necessarily respect political boundaries, although they don't threaten them either. They are also smaller than most nations—with between 5 and 20 million people—enough to achieve efficiency while still encouraging local control. Ohmae's discussion implies that the functional economic integration within these regions spurs the establishment of a kind of identity based on material success. It is an argument reminiscent of Joel Garreau's (1981) *Nine Nations of North America* that (with the exception of Quebec) credited the establishment of strong regional identities to differences in available resources and economic production.

In the modern world, the compartmentalization of identities may be necessary to tackle a range of problems and issues as they occur at different scales. In Chapters 3 and 4, Murphy and Elbow discuss the compartmentalized identities associated with the European Union and the Caribbean. But does the emergence of these new forms represent a shift in primary loyalty away from the nation? Smith (1992) argues that such a thing as a European identity, for instance, would be essentially "memoryless," with few unifiers that tie together a nation. Although such multistate identities would probably infringe on aspects of state sovereignty, it is unclear whether allegiance to the nation (which must be kept separate from the power of the state) would be compromised. In most cases, differential identities may work until the point where the demands made by each identity come into conflict.

Bifocal Identities and Nonterritoriality

The emergence of a new global economy raises the specter that the old bases of territorial affiliation will be shattered. Economic interactions that were once largely contained within the boundaries of states now take place over vast spaces. The effects on economics are profound, but so may be the effects on culture and on the realms of mutual understanding. Benjamin Barber (1992) describes this as "McWorld," in which a market imperative requires a common language and behavior and an information imperative requires individuals to share common technical skills and information. Flows of information and resources are accompanied by a more global labor market and the further mobility of individuals to take advantage of opportunities at several sites.

What is the impact on identities? There may be a bidirectional shift both " 'outward' towards supranational or transnational entities" and " 'inward' toward subnational bodies, groups and institutions" (DiMuccio and Rosenau 1992: 60). Zdravko Mlinar (1992) maintains that postindustrial society has expanded interdependence beyond state boundaries. At the same time, individuals are less likely to have their life-paths determined by their territory of origin; their identity as individuals becomes more significant than their position within a national group. Individuals are less beholden to traditional structures and are guided instead by their ability to accomplish certain goals with enhanced skills. Existing entities (like states and nations) that stand in their way are cast aside in favor of smaller- or larger-scale entities.

These shifts carry implications for the significance of territory in general and for national identity in particular. Mlinar (1992) sees an increase in nonterritorial actors and a diminution in territorially based identities. Taylor (1996) proposes a set of nonterritorial alternatives based on flows of people, networks of cities, and increasing dual citizenship. As people move across national boundaries, they may be less willing to exchange one absolute identity for another, choosing instead to acquire multiple citizenships and multiple identities (Taylor 1996). And as people identify with a cosmopolitan culture, they may shed their old territorial loyalties altogether (Marden 1997). The collapse of territorial loyalties will undoubtedly damage the integrity of the nation-state system, based as it is on territoriality. New structures will eventually diminish the current hegemony of national loyalty (Teune 1992). Henry Teune sees macro-scale loyalties now developing in Europe and in the rest of the world.

Identities existing at a macro-scale are clearly connected to identities at a micro-scale. The creation of broad "economic" allegiances, say within a multistate economic federation, may make it more possible for groups to indulge their smaller-scale aspirations. Some might argue, for instance, that the regional integration of Europe has made the aspirations of Wales and Catalonia more feasible (Williams 1985). At an even smaller geographic scale, micro-scale identities—"a new localism"—have the capacity to unite neighborhoods throughout the world, threading them into a transnational network (Teune 1992). According to Benjamin Barber (1992), a world economy will not be able to meet all identificational requirements but will allow the expression of smaller-scale ethnic bonds, creating a bifocal identity that bypasses the nation-state altogether. But Barber's vision is far darker than the others. He forecasts the "Lebanonization of the World," in which existing national identities implode, to be replaced by very narrowly drawn ethnic identities. "They are cultures, not countries; parts, not wholes; sects, not religions" (Barber 1992: 59). Although sharing the cultural attributes of the nation, the implication is that the new entities would not concur in the national goal toward political maturity but would instead operate as a kind of mobilized militia movement.

These ideas are open to a great deal of disagreement. Despite the rapid changes in global economy, culture, and technology, this is still a world of state sovereignty and national loyalty. Michael Mann (1993) asserts that although some functions of the nation-state have been reduced by the new capitalist order, these have been replaced by enhancement of other functions. Peter Marden (1997) suggests that the main effect now may be in weakening the idea rather than the reality of state sovereignty. As to a loosening of the bounds to territorial structures, Steven Grosby (1995) insists that territoriality played a role in collective self-consciousness long before the creation of the modern world. Murphy (1996: 109) admits that, although territorial forms other than the present system of nation-states are conceivable, "there is little to suggest that the powerful ideological bonds that link identity, politics, and territory will be loosened."

Conclusion

In this chapter, I have sought to situate national identity within the array of geographically based identities. Nations and national identity cannot be taken for granted. Although national identity may have roots in a distant past or in commonalities of language and faith, it is something that is formed and negotiated within the structure of the world as it exists today. It is an intermediary identity between the familial scale and the global scale. It is an identity that insists that individuals personalize their relations with a group of strangers; if necessary, to lay down their lives for them in the face of "external" threats. It is protean enough to construct itself from other sources of identity and other points of grievance. What was formerly a region may through mutational alchemy become a new nation, or different ethnic groups within a state may forge a single national sensibility.

The scale of modern national identity owes much to the scale of the modern system of sovereign states. If we are to believe some estimates, there are literally thousands of nations of all sizes scattered throughout a world of 190 or so states (Nietschmann 1994). But nations have been forced to pattern themselves into a geographical template created by states. Gellner (1983: 139) likens the geography of nations before the emergence of the modern state system to a painting by Kokoschka, "the riot of diverse points of color is such that no clear pattern can be discerned in any detail." The geography of nations today resembles Modigliani, "very little shading; neat flat surfaces are clearly separated from each other, it is generally plain where one begins and another ends" (Gellner 1983: 140). Clearly the modern geography and scale of nations has been transformed, and modern national identity is constrained by these forms.

At the same time, and with some deviation from Gellner's vision, the spatial identities of states and nations continue to diverge in character and form. The "nation-building" project is far from complete. Differences in the spatial identities of states and nations and among different nations have created a world of asymmetries, of ambiguities and blurs. Often, the national identity in control of a state runs up against other "stateless" national identities, with territories of their own. The potential secession of these substate nationalisms threatens more than the state but assaults the integrity of the dominant national identity. Overlaps of national and state identities occur also at borderland regions, where there is often an imperfect mesh of political and cultural boundaries. The allegiance of borderland peoples is pulled in several directions—toward the larger state, the larger nation, and into their own smaller-scale affiliation. Diasporas represent yet another source of ambiguity. Diaspora nations are transnational, occupying several different states over a wide but dispersed field. At the same time as they are rooted in a much smaller homeland, they are also enmeshed within other states, in the midst of other national identities. Such a situation, although a reality, is often seen to be incompatible with the "Modigliani" vision of nationalism. Diasporas—as with borderlands and substate nationalisms—imperil the system of discrete, state-encompassing national identities. They threaten in part because they simultaneously occupy several points along the gamut of scale-based spatial identities, from the macro-scale of transnational identities to the meso-scale of the homeland to the micro-scale of each individual diaspora settlement.

What of the challenges to national identity? Whether the dominance of national identity is in decline has been subject to some debate, with a range of possible alternatives being broached. First, there is the question if other geographical identities will assume the salience of national identity. Historically, people have identified with a range of geographical entities at various spatial scales. Empires, for instance, made no claims on national uniformity but fostered a sense of a larger community. Civilizations may perform these same functions today and create the basic cleavages dividing humanity. Smaller units—city-states, manors, tribes—have also become the cynosure of identity; similar groupings are possible in the future. Others see the possibility that a new world economy and civic culture will foster bifocal identities, directed outward to the set of global exchanges and flows and inward toward the individual's choice of affiliation. Although people will continue to be nominally territorial, the influence of territory on human identities will be diminished. The contrasts across national boundaries will melt, and the differences among individuals within a territory will magnify. As Mlinar (1992: 22) describes it, "the whole world will be found in each locality and at the same time each locality, region, nation, will be found all over the world."

The conception of a world where territory no longer exerts an enormous influence on identity seems far-fetched, but there is nothing hard and fast about the endurance of national identity. The ideal of the nation-state has today concentrated many vital aspects of identity into a single container. Its preeminence is of recent vintage and will likely be replaced. There is no reason why future touchstones of identity might not become increasingly manifold, so that our monogamous relationship to nation will splinter into a more polygamous affair, with identities sited among a multiplicity of geographical scales.

References

Anderson, Benedict. *Imagined Communities: Reflections on the Origin and Spread of Nationalism.* London: Verso, 1983.

Armstrong, John. *Nations before Nationalism.* Chapel Hill: University of North Carolina Press, 1982.

Augelli, John. "Nationalization of Dominican Borderlands." *The Geographical Review* 70 (1980): 19–35.

Barber, Benjamin. "Jihad vs. McWorld." *The Atlantic* 269 (3) (1992): 53–65.

Bendix, R. "National Sentiment in the Enactment and Discourse of Swiss Political Ritual." *American Ethnologist* 19 (1992): 769–790.

Bloom, William. *Personal Identity, National Identity, and International Relations.* Cambridge: Cambridge University Press, 1990.

Cohen, Robin. "Diasporas and the Nation-State: From Victims to Challengers." *International Affairs* 72 (1996): 507–520.

Connor, Walker. "Nation-Building or Nation-Destroying?" *World Politics* 24 (1972): 319–355.

———. "Beyond Reason: The Nature of the Ethnonational Bond." *Ethnic and Racial Studies* 16 (1983): 373–389.

———. "The Impact of Homelands upon Diasporas." In Gabriel Sheffer, ed., *Modern Diasporas in International Politics.* New York: St. Martin's Press, 1986, 16–46.

DiMuccio, R. B. A., and James Rosenau. "Turbulence of Sovereignty in World Politics: Explaining the Relocation of Legitimacy in the 1990s and Beyond." In Zdravko Mlinar, ed., *Globalization and Territorial Identities.* Aldershot, U.K.: Avebury, 1992, 60–76.

Doyle, Michael. *Empires.* Ithaca, N.Y.: Cornell University Press, 1986.

Drake, Christine. "The United Nations and NGOs: Future Roles." In George

Demko and William Wood, eds., *Reordering the World*. Boulder: Westview Press, 1994, 243–268.

Emerson, Rupert. *From Empire to Nation: The Rise to Self-Assertion of Asian and African Peoples*. Cambridge, Mass.: Harvard University Press, 1960.

Eriksen, T. "A Future-Oriented, Non-Ethnic Nationalism? Mauritius as an Exemplary Case." *Ethnos* 58 (1993): 197–221.

Esman, Milton. "Diasporas and International Relations." In Gabriel Sheffer, ed., *Modern Diasporas in International Politics*. New York: St. Martin's Press, 1986, 333–349.

Fitzgerald, C. P. *The Chinese View of Their Place in the World*. London: Oxford University Press, 1964.

Foon, C. S. "On the Incompatibility of Ethnic and National Loyalties: Reframing the Issue." *Canadian Review of Studies in Nationalism* 13 (1986): 1–11.

Gaines, Jena. "The Politics of National Identity in Alsace." *Canadian Review of Studies in Nationalism* 21 (1994): 99–109.

Garreau, Joel. *The Nine Nations of North America*. New York: Avon Books, 1981.

Gellner, Ernest. *Nations and Nationalism*. Ithaca, N.Y.: Cornell University Press, 1983.

Greenfeld, Liah. *Nationalism: Five Roads to Modernity*. Cambridge, Mass.: Harvard University Press, 1992.

Grosby, Steven. "Territoriality: The Transcendental Primordial Feature of Modern Societies." *Nations and Nationalism* 1 (1995): 143–162.

Häkli, Jouni. "Territoriality and the Rise of the Modern State." *Fennia* 172 (1994): 1–82.

Held, David. "The Decline of the Nation State." In Geoff Eley and Ronald Suny, eds., *Becoming National: A Reader*. New York: Oxford University Press, 1996, 407–416.

Hobsbawm, Eric. *Nations and Nationalism since 1780: Programme, Myth, Reality*. Cambridge: Cambridge University Press, 1990.

Huntington, Samuel. *The Clash of Civilizations and the Remaking of World Order*. New York: Simon and Schuster, 1996.

Kaplan, David H. "Two Nations in Search of a State: Canada's Ambivalent Spatial Identities." *Annals of the Association of American Geographers* 84 (1994): 585–606.

Kecmanovic, Dusan. *The Mass Psychology of Ethnonationalism*. New York: Plenum Press, 1996.

Knight, David B. "People Together, Yet Apart: Rethinking Territory, Sovereignty, and Identities." In George Demko and William Wood, eds., *Reordering the World*. Boulder: Westview Press, 1994, 71–86.

Mann, Michael. "Nation-States in Europe and Other Continents: Diversifying, Developing, Not Dying." *Daedalus* 122 (3) (1993): 115–140.

Marden, Peter. "Geographies of Dissent: Globalization, Identity, and the Nation." *Political Geography* 16 (1997): 37–64.

Mikesell, Marvin, and Alexander Murphy. "A Framework for Comparative Study of Minority-Group Aspirations." *Annals of the Association of American Geographers* 81 (1991): 581–604.

Mlinar, Zdravko. "Individuation and Globalization: The Transformation of Territorial Social Organization." In Zdravko Mlinar, ed., *Globalization and Territorial Identities*. Aldershot, U.K.: Avebury, 1992, 15–34.

Murphy, Alexander. "The Sovereign State System as Political-Territorial Ideal: Historical and Contemporary Considerations." In Thomas Biersteker and Cynthia Weber, eds., *State Sovereignty as Social Construct*. Cambridge: Cambridge University Press, 1996, 81–120.

Nietschmann, Bernard. "The Fourth World: Nations Versus States." In George Demko and William Wood, eds., *Reordering the World*. Boulder: Westview Press, 1994, 225–242.

Ohmae, Kenichi. "The Rise of the Region State." *Foreign Affairs* 72 (2) (1993): 78–87.

Olwig, Karen F. "Defining the National in the Transnational: Cultural Identity in the Afro-Caribbean Diaspora." *Ethnos* 88 (1993): 361–376.

Paasi, Anssi. *Territories, Boundaries, and Consciousness: The Changing Geographies of the Finnish-Russian Border*. Chichester, U.K.: John Wiley and Sons, 1996.

Penrose, J. "Frisian Nationalism: A Response to Cultural and Political Hegemony." *Environment and Planning D: Society and Space* 8 (1990): 427–448.

Rokkan, Stein, and Derek Urwin. *Economy, Territory, Identity: Politics of West European Peripheries*. London, Sage Publications, 1983.

Rudolph, Susanne H. "Introduction: Religions, States, and Transnational Civil Society." In Susanne Rudolph and James Piscatori, eds., *Transnational Religion and Fading States*. Boulder: Westview Press, 1997, 1–24.

Ruggie, John. "Territoriality and Beyond: Problematizing Modernity in International Relations." *International Organization* 47 (1993): 139–174.

Rumley, Dennis, and Julian Minghi, eds. *The Geography of Border Landscapes*. London: Routledge, 1991.

Sheffer, Gabriel. *Modern Diasporas in International Politics*. New York: St. Martin's Press, 1986a.

———. "A New Field of Study: Modern Diasporas in International Politics." In Gabriel Sheffer, ed., *Modern Diasporas in International Politics*. New York: St. Martin's Press, 1986b, 1–15.

Smith, Anthony. *National Identity*. Reno: University of Nevada Press, 1991.

———. "National Identity and the Idea of European Unity." *International Affairs* 68 (1992): 55–76.

———. "Culture, Community, and Territory: The Politics of Ethnicity and Nationalism." *International Affairs* 72 (1996): 445–458.

Snyder, Louis. *Global Mini-Nationalisms: Autonomy or Independence*. Westport, Conn.: Greenwood Press, 1982.

———. *Macro-Nationalisms: A History of the Pan-Movements*. Westport, Conn.: Greenwood Press, 1984.

Taylor, Peter J. "Territorial Absolutism and Its Evasions." *Geography Research Forum* 16 (1996): 1–12.

Teune, Henry. "Multiple Group Loyalties and the Security of Political Communities." In Zdravko Mlinar, ed., *Globalization and Territorial Identities*. Aldershot, U.K.: Avebury, 1992, 105–114.

Tiryakian, Edward. "The Wild Cards of Modernity." *Daedalus* 126 (1997): 147–181.

Tölölyan, Khachig. "The Nation-State and Its Others: In Lieu of a Preface." In Geoff Eley and Ronald Suny, eds., *Becoming National: A Reader.* New York: Oxford University Press, 1996, 426–431.

Wallerstein, Immanuel. *Geopolitics and Geoculture: Essays on the Changing World System.* Cambridge: Cambridge University Press, 1991.

Williams, Colin. "Conceived in Bondage—Called unto Liberty: Reflections on Nationalism." *Progress in Human Geography* 9 (1985): 331–355.

Williams, Colin, and Anthony Smith. "The National Construction of Social Space." *Progress in Human Geography* 7 (1983): 502–518.

Part II

Macro-Scale

We begin our series of case studies with an examination of identities that focus on scales above that of the state. As with each of the other scales of geographically based identity, *macro*-scale is a relative term and can be defined only in opposition to other levels. However, it clearly has relevance as a result of the attempted integration of several states into larger economic regions, the continued legacy of imperial identities and the negotiation that must take place within successor states, and the forces of a new world order that may attenuate national ties.

The chapter by Alexander Murphy investigates European identity by paying particular attention to its reconceptualization via regional levels. He shows that the customary opposition of European versus state identities does not cover the complexity of the situation. Furthermore, his analysis exposes European identity as a dynamic process that should not be couched in terms of primary allegiance to one entity. Indeed, developments in Europe may herald a more compartmentalized layering of identities to fulfill certain demands.

Gary Elbow explicitly examines issues of scale and identity within the Caribbean region. He asks whether the Caribbean—long fractured by colonialism, language, and the sea itself—may be in the process of creating a true macro-identity. Part of the difficulty lies in the fact that different regional identities exist, each with separate visions of the "Caribbean's" spatial extent. Yet, Elbow argues that a Caribbean identity has long existed in some form and is being strengthened further through the establishment of regional organizations and a sense of distinctiveness from both North and South America.

Nick Lynn and Valentin Bogorov survey the challenges to Russian identity in the wake of the collapse of the Soviet Union. They argue that Russian nationalism has long been ambiguous and that it now is unable to fashion a strong cohesive identity. Complicating this task is the negotiation that must take place between the Russian identity and the Russian/Soviet imperial identity, as well as the fact of Russia as a multinational entity of its own.

3

Rethinking the Concept of European Identity

Alexander B. Murphy

Those who dreamed of a united Europe after World War II looked for ways to promote a strong sense of European identity in a region long racked by internecine conflict. Thoughts of a European identity would have been deemed absurd just ten years earlier, when Europe was on the verge of its second devastating conflict of the century. But the political, social, and economic upheavals associated with World War II fundamentally altered the European order. It became possible—even necessary—to think of Europe in different ways; the founding of the European Coal and Steel Community, and eventually the European Economic Community (EEC), were the results of those thoughts (see Williams 1987). A new era seemed to be at hand. By the time that barriers to trade within the EEC began to fall in the 1960s, it became fashionable to talk of an emergent United States of Europe. Such an entity was seen not just as a formal economic entity; it was posited as a potential focus of identity for its inhabitants.

Much has happened since then to undermine the grand designs of those who boldly predicted that Europeans were on the threshold of creating a meaningful superstate at the western edge of the Eurasian land mass. The oil shock of the early 1970s ushered in a period of "Eurosclerosis," the expanding regulatory reach of the European integration project fostered resentments, and the collapse of the post-World War II political order—the fall of the Iron Curtain, the reunification of Germany, and the war in the Balkans—irrevocably altered the geopolitical and social circumstances that had originally given rise to the project of European unity. It is thus not surprising that the mid-1990s is a time of growing public mistrust of European Union (EU) institutions and great skepticism about the Maastricht Treaty's goal of creating "an ever closer union among the peoples of Europe" (Baun 1996). It is also not surprising that many regard the very notion of a European identity as increasingly problematic.

The contemporary debate over the nature and meaning of European identity goes to the heart of many of the critical issues facing Europe today (see, e.g., Deflem and Pampel 1996; Delanty 1995; Hodgson 1993). Complicating the debate are the assumptions that are made about the very nature of identity itself. These assumptions are the product of political-territorial developments over the past several hundred years that have cast the state in the role of creator and symbol of international society (Murphy 1996; Taylor 1994). In the process, the concepts of nation and state have become conflated, and national (i.e., state) identities have come to be treated as if they were the only significant objects of analysis in studies of international relations (see generally Connor 1994). One manifestation of this state of affairs is the tendency for studies of European identity to see it as something that is necessarily equated with, or in opposition to, state identity (Ruggie 1993). European identity is assumed both to be incompatible with state identity and to involve a primary commitment by a European people to "Europe" as a discrete political-territorial entity operating in a world of "nation-states."

From the perspective of those who see identity largely in these terms, it is difficult to argue that European identity is particularly strong. By most measures national and local loyalties remain entrenched, and support for the further concentration of power in the centralized decision-making bodies of the EU appears to be waning (see, e.g., Jenkins and Sofos 1996). Yet if one takes a different view of European identity—a view less wedded to the ideas about territory and identity that developed along with the modern state system—the concept is not so easily dismissed. As this chapter shows, a growing number of Europeans are thinking of Europe as a meaningful social-territorial construct, albeit not as a superstate. This development both reflects and shapes a variety of social, economic, and political changes that are not reducible to individual states and that are in some cases undermining traditional state domains of authority. These changes are evident in the declining significance of international boundaries within the EU, in the growing willingness of substate groups to challenge existing political structures and arrangements, and in the efforts of former East European countries to redefine themselves in European terms (Haller and Richter 1994).

This chapter examines both the possibilities and the limitations of European identity. Its goal is not simply to review developments that point in one direction or the other, however. Instead, the chapter seeks

Chris Leatham

to show that an expanded concept of identity is needed to capture the complexities of the European situation at the close of the twentieth century. The developments documented in the chapter lead to the conclusion that a broadened concept of identity is important not only for understanding the present but also for imagining the future of Europe both as a functional region and as a socially significant perceptual construct.

European Versus National Identity

Measuring senses of identity is a notoriously difficult task. There is no simple measure of identity, because identity is often contextually

▶━━━◀

TIMELINE OF PERTINENT EVENTS LEADING TO THE CURRENT STATE OF THE EU

May 1945	End of World War II in Europe.
June 1945	The United Nations is founded.
June 1947	Marshall Plan (European Recovery Program) is launched.
April 1948	Organization for European Economic Cooperation (OEEC) is established.
May 1949	Council of Europe is formed.
April 1951	Treaty of Paris is signed, which establishes the European Coal and Steel Community (ECSC).
March 1957	Treaties of Rome are signed, which establish Euratom and the European Economic Community (EEC). Members of EEC are France, Netherlands, Belgium, Luxembourg, Germany, and Italy.
February 1958	Benelux Economic Union is founded.
July 1958	Common Agricultural Policy is proposed.
December 1960	OEEC is reorganized into the Organization for Economic Cooperation and Development (OECD).
August 1961	Denmark, Ireland, and the U.K. apply for EEC membership. (De Gaulle vetoes U.K. application twice: in 1963 and 1967.)
April 1962	Norway applies for EEC membership.
April 1965	Merger Treaty is signed, which consolidates the institutions created by the Treaty of Paris and Treaties of Rome.
July 1968	EEC customs union is finalized, and the Common Agricultural Policy is enacted.
January 1972	EEC membership negotiations concluded with U.K., Denmark, Ireland, and Norway.
September 1972	National referendum in Norway goes against its membership in EEC.
January 1973	U.K., Denmark, and Ireland join the EEC.
January 1974	Creation of the European Social Fund.

January 1975	Creation of the European Regional Development Fund.
June 1975	Greece applies for EEC membership.
March 1977	Portugal applies for EEC membership.
July 1977	Spain applies for EEC membership.
March 1979	European Monetary System is established.
June 1979	First direct elections of the European Parliament.
January 1981	Greece joins EEC.
January 1986	Spain and Portugal join the EEC.
February 1986	Single European Act signed in Luxembourg removing most of the remaining physical, fiscal, and technical barriers to the formation of a European common market. EEC is now referred to as simply EC.
June 1987	Turkey applies for EC membership.
July 1989	Austria, Finland, Sweden, and Norway apply for EC membership.
December 1989	Turkey's membership application is rejected.
July 1990	Malta and Cyprus apply for EC membership.
October 1990	German reunification brings the former East Germany into the EC.
February 1992	Treaty on European Union (Maastricht Treaty) is signed, which expands process of European integration and creates a timetable for European Monetary Union (EMU). The European Community (EC) is now referred to as the European Union (EU).
June 1992	Danish voters reject Maastricht Treaty.
May 1993	Danish voters approve Maastricht Treaty after certain compromises are inserted into the treaty.
January 1995	Austria, Sweden, and Finland join the EU after respective national referendums favor membership. National referendum in Norway rejects EU membership.
October 1997	Treaty of Amsterdam is signed, which aims, among other things, to equalize tax structures among members of the EU in preparation for upcoming monetary union.

Sources: Harrison, D. M. *The Organisation of Europe: Developing a Continental Market Order.* London: Routledge, 1995.
McCormick, J. *The European Union: Politics and Policies.* Boulder: Westview Press, 1996.

EUROPEAN UNION—FACTS AND FIGURES

Member States	Pop. 1997 (millions)	Area (sq. mi.)
Austria	8.1	31,940
Belgium	10.2	11,790
Denmark	5.3	16,380
Finland	5.1	117,600
France	58.6	212,390
Germany	82.0	134,850
Greece	10.5	49,770
Ireland	3.6	26,600
Italy	57.4	113,540
Luxembourg	0.4	1,000
Netherlands	15.6	13,100
Portugal	9.9	35,500
Spain	39.3	192,830
Sweden	8.9	158,930
United Kingdom	59.1	93,280
EU Totals	374.0	1,209,500

Source: 1997 *World Population Data Sheet,* Population Reference Bureau, Washington, D.C.

▶————————————————————————◀

defined. One might be an Oregonian in one context, an American in another, a woman in another, and a geographer in another. Despite these complexities, formal studies of identity—at least in the international arena—tend to equate identity with the map of so-called nation-states. As John Agnew (1987) argues, over the past several decades mainstream work in the social sciences has been heavily influenced by the nationalization thesis, an idea premised on the notion that the forces of modernization have swept away primordial attachments to community and place, replacing them with state-defined national identities. For those adopting this approach, national identities are treated as if they were manifest at a single scale—that of the state—and as if state-based identities were the only significant components of the international scene.

From the perspective of the nationalization thesis, the problematic of European identity is conceptualized in a narrow way. The central question is whether state-based national identities are being replaced by allegiance to a larger unit called Europe. To put it another way, European identity is seen both in terms of, and in opposition to, state identity. If European identity is coming into being, then it is assumed that Europeans are increasingly thinking of Europe as a superstate that can take its place alongside other states, big and small, in the international state system.

Conceptualized in these terms, it is difficult to argue that European identity is well developed. As a recent article in *The Economist* (1995: 46) puts it, "almost four decades after the treaty of Rome, there are few signs of a European identity emerging to replace old national loyalties." Instead, resistance is growing in many quarters to the concentration of powers in what is often seen as an unrepresentative EU bureaucracy in Brussels. Moreover, xenophobia is on the rise in certain parts of Europe, and the state tends to be the spatial scale at which issues of "us" versus "them" are most commonly posited. Thus, it has been very difficult to develop supranational policies on the immigration of non-EU nationals except in those cases where such policies are consistent with national policies (Leitner 1997).

Confirming the weakness of European identity in these terms is a recent opinion poll conducted under the auspices of the EU (Figure 3.1). The results show that in most EU member states, less than 10 percent of those surveyed think of themselves as "European only" and that those who consider themselves "European first" followed by a national (i.e., state) loyalty rarely account for more than another 10 to 12 percent of the population. When these figures are considered alongside recent evidence of the continued vitality of national identities (Ashford and Timms 1992), there is no sound basis for concluding that Europe is likely to become a primary focus of state-like identity in the foreseeable future.

Expanding the Concept of European Identity

It does not follow from the foregoing that Europe is a meaningless construct to which no feelings of identity are attached. Instead, there is much to suggest that Europe has significant meaning. A glance at the books for sale in the "European Studies" section of any bookshop will reveal a host of new titles in which the term *Europe* appears prominently. These books are not just about the emergence of the European Community (now EU); many are exploring the very nature of the "idea of Europe" (see, e.g., *The History of the Idea of Europe*, Wilson and van der Dussen 1993, or the *The Making of Europe* series that has resulted from the collaboration of five publishers in Germany, the United Kingdom, Spain, Italy, and France). At the same time, the organization of life and work in contemporary Europe increasingly brings peoples of different nationalities together in ways that promote transnational

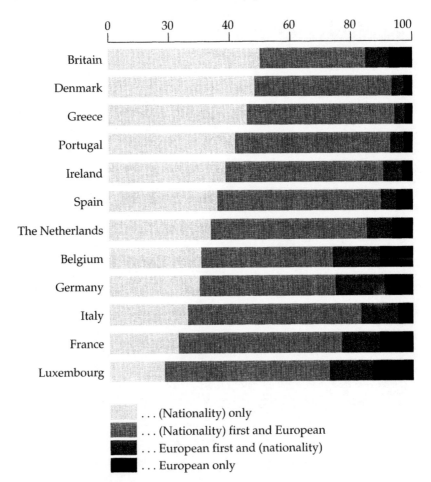

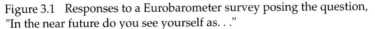
... (Nationality) only
... (Nationality) first and European
... European first and (nationality)
... European only

Figure 3.1 Responses to a Eurobarometer survey posing the question, "In the near future do you see yourself as. . ."

Source: The Economist 1995:46.

thinking. Developments such as the issuance of EU passports and the adoption of regulations that permit EU citizens to exercise defined citizenship rights throughout the union are encouraging people to think about Europe as a significant political-territorial entity (see, e.g., Séché 1988). And the very fact that Europe is treated as a cultural-cum-political construct in a variety of contexts—ranging from international trade associations to area studies programs—helps to fuel the idea that Europe has some meaning.

The significance of European identity in this expanded sense is evident in the same survey that shows the continued preeminence of state identities (see Figure 3.1). The survey shows that well over 50 percent of the population in most EU member states have some level of identification with Europe, and those figures would likely be even higher if parts of former Eastern Europe had been included (see, e.g., Dobroczynski 1989). Such figures reflect the fact that "Europe" is an ideological-cum-territorial construct that is deeply embedded in contemporary cultural, social, economic, and political discourses and that Europe is, as a result, an object to which feelings of identity can be, and often are, attached.

The nature of European identity in this broader sense is not easy to characterize. It differs from place to place and it is constantly changing. If there is one generalization that can be made, however, it is that European identity coexists with other identities—state, regional, ethnic, and local—in a way that is not strictly hierarchical. The idea of Europe is thus not analogous to the idea of the state; instead, Europe is one of several cultural-territorial constructs to which meaning is attached. The meanings imparted to Europe affect the ways that other cultural-territorial constructs are conceptualized and understood, but those other understandings are not derivative of "Europe" in the way that various smaller-scale identities are often seen as being derivative of national identities.

To gain some insights into what this expanded notion of European identity means, it is instructive to look at some of the ways in which the existence of Europe as a focus of identity shapes the evolution of European society. Such an inquiry could occupy the time and efforts of a multitude of scholars for years, but an examination of two developments that are being profoundly affected by the crystallization of Europe as a focus of identity provides a sense of the nature and scope of the matter. The two developments considered here are the changing activities and roles of substate regions in western Europe (primarily within the EU) and the culture and politics of geopolitical realignment in eastern Europe.

Regional Change

As in many parts of the globe, the boundaries between European states are becoming more permeable. What is different about Europe—at least EU Europe—is that the process is far more advanced than in other parts of the world. Throughout a considerable part of the EU, people can move between states without restrictions or formalities, and there is an unprecedented level of economic and cultural interaction occurring across state boundaries (see generally Wallace 1990). Many of these developments can be attributed to the institutional character of the EU. Over time, agreements have been reached facilitating a wide range of transnational activities. Many of these agreements are the products of initiatives and compromises that can be traced back to state institutions, ideas, and practices (Moravcsik 1993). As such, it is difficult to know what role a sense of European identity might have played in their original creation.

The growth of transnational interaction is not an ideologically neutral phenomenon, however. As the interests of peoples living in different places became knit together in new ways, the functional and perceptual geography of Europe inevitably changed. This change has taken a variety of directions, but one of its clearest manifestations is in people's mental maps of Europe. Those maps are no longer composed predominantly of the states of Europe; they include both regions that transcend state boundaries (Delamaide 1994) and smaller-scale regions—some of which are the focus of ethnonational movements (Dunford and Kafkalas 1992). Extrastate and substate regions have always had some significance for Europeans, of course, but by almost any measure their visibility has increased in recent decades. As a result, extrastate and substate regions are now routinely seen as important players in Europe. They are the subject of a rapidly expanding literature (see, e.g., Rhodes 1995; Harvie 1994; LaBasse 1991), and some even argue that the political activism of substate regional authorities is altering basic understandings of who and where the key players are in EU political affairs (Smart 1996).

It is almost impossible to comprehend the changing nature of regional understandings in Europe without reference to European identity, broadly defined. This is because Europe is an inescapable frame of reference that both reflects and shapes regional change. The existence of Europe as a meaningful cultural-territorial entity has been a catalyst to a wide array of regional initiatives, which in turn have reinforced the idea that Europe is much more than a collection of state interests.

The interdependent relationship between regionalism and European identity is evident in the overt political activities and discourse of regional authorities, in the growing number of transboundary cooperation schemes forged between regional governments in different European states and in the new spatial frameworks that are being used to address social and environmental issues in contemporary Europe. Turning to the first of these, regional activism has been one of the most notable features of the European political scene over the past two decades. This is certainly true in the EU policy arena. In 1985, representatives of regional governments in Europe banded together to form the Assembly of European Regions (AER) to lobby for regional representation in an integrated Europe (Cappelin 1993). By the early 1990s, the AER had established a secretariat in Strasbourg where the European Parliament meets and more than 150 European regions had joined. Not content simply to promote interregional interaction and to lobby the European Parliament, many substate European regions also established missions to the EU in Brussels (Cole and Cole 1993: 295). By articulating regional interests in ways that bypass the state, these missions are becoming increasingly important voices in European affairs. The activities associated with the missions bear witness to the changing role of Europe's regions in a world in which "Europe" has taken on greater economic, political, and cultural significance.

The growth in regional lobbying is a response in part to the promulgation of EU initiatives that disburse funds to state governments to promote the development of individual regions (e.g., programs concerned with the distribution of EU Structural Funds). Yet such initiatives cannot be seen purely in pragmatic political terms. Many of the lobbyists are bypassing the state and going directly to Brussels because they see in the EU a viable alternative to the state as a focus for the organization of cultural, social, and political life. Indeed, many are quite explicit in their efforts to "clamber out of the constraints of their association with poorer regions" in the states in which they are situated and instead adopt a more European posture (e.g., representatives of Lombardy in northern Italy; see Judt 1996: 8). They are pursuing strategies that are influenced by economic concerns, of course, but the larger regional-cum-territorial context within which they are framed is "Europe." Moreover, the pursuit of such strategies fosters structures and arrangements that lend credence to the idea that Europe does indeed matter.

A particularly vivid example of the importance of a European identity for substate regionalism comes from the many cases where regionalism is tied to a sense of ethnic difference. The recent activities of Welsh nationalists, for example, cannot be understood outside of a context in which Europe has some meaning (Jones 1992). Indeed, Welsh nationalists have used the EU as a basic framework for advancing their cause. They have established institutions that focus on the role of Wales in Europe, and they have argued that Wales should have a status somewhere between that of a constituent unit of the United Kingdom and that of a sovereign state. As Dafydd Elis Thomas, former leader of the Welsh nationalist political party Plaid Cymru, put it, "one day Wales may be able to be a region within a unified Europe without having to apply for UN membership" (Thomas 1992). Such an idea would be unthinkable if Europe were not seen as at least one of a number of units to which feelings of identity could be attached.

The issue of regional assertiveness is only one way in which regional change is being shaped by a certain kind of identification with Europe. Over the past decade some of the most interesting and important regional developments have grown out of efforts to forge linkages between regions in different EU member states (Murphy 1993; Cappelin and Batey 1993). As a result, meaningful transnational regions are developing directly across international boundaries and new social spaces are emerging as geographically dispersed regions enter into cooperation agreements (e.g., the Four Motors Agreement linking Rhône-Alps in France, Catalonia in Spain, Baden-Würtenberg in Germany, and Lombardy in Italy). These developments are tied to a confidence that Europe—or at least the EU—provides a meaningful umbrella within which new economic, social, and cultural relations can be established.

Several recent EU initiatives help to reinforce this confidence. In July 1990 the Commission of the European Community established a funded program called INTERREG to support cross-border cooperation schemes (Commission of the European Communities 1990a). The program was structured in a way that effectively bypasses the states; only regional representatives can apply for program funds, and those funds are disbursed directly to the regions. The program has been so successful that it has been renewed; it is now helping to foster a growing number of administrative and economic cooperation schemes across borders throughout the EU. Another program, adopted under the name "Exchange of Experience and Regional Network Scheme," has helped promote local-level cooperation initiatives by geographically disparate regions in different states (Commission of the European Communities 1990b). The program derives from an initiative of the European Parliament, the only major European Union institution with significant substate regional representation. It provides funds to encourage the exchange of ideas and information concerning local administration, transportation, research and technology, problems of environmental degradation, and tourism among substate regions and cities in different countries. Programs such as these are helping to bring into being a new functional and perceptual structure to Europe—one that both reflects a sense that Europe has some meaning and that makes it difficult to see Europe simply as a collection of discrete states.

Beyond the realm of regional activism, the significance of Europe as a meaningful conceptual construct is evidenced in the growing tendency for policymakers to frame issues and problems in innovative spatial terms. During the 1990s, scholars and policymakers have increasingly framed problems in ways that are not derivative of the map of European states; instead, starting with Europe as a larger-scale political-territorial construct, they have asked how issues might be addressed in ways that are compatible with their underlying geography. Such an approach was proposed in the "Thompson Report" in the 1980s, but as Allan Williams (1991: 130) notes, its recommendations were "politically unacceptable" at the time. The appearance of "Europe 2000" in the early 1990s, however, signaled a potential change in perspective (Commission of the European Communities 1991). The report identified a variety of different planning regions in Europe, most of which were not based on state boundaries. Instead, the regions grouped together areas sharing similar socioeconomic characteristics. The report identified a "capitals center" region in northwest continental Europe—encompassing parts of the United Kingdom, the Netherlands, Belgium, Luxembourg, Germany, and France—where regional inequalities are primarily associated with the decline of former centers of heavy industry. Similarly, it identified a "central Mediterranean" region—encompassing parts of Portugal, Spain, France, and Italy—where large numbers of relatively poor, agriculturally dependent communities can be found.

"Europe 2000" was based on a different conceptualization of space and place from that which had dominated in previous European Commission policy studies. It implicitly treated Europe as a large-scale framework within which common problems could be addressed in a coordinated and comprehensive manner. Such an approach is becoming increasingly common. In the environmental policy arena, for example, the European Environmental Agency is compiling a standardized geographic information system on the environment of the EU that is specifically designed so that data can be mapped and analyzed without reference to state boundaries (Moss and Wyatt 1994). Similarly, this approach has fostered interest in the possibility of bringing into being new politically and economically significant spaces of interaction and cooperation around bodies of water such as the Baltic Sea and the North Sea (see, e.g., Lundqvist and Persson 1993; Hunderi-Ely 1995).

In various ways, then, European identity is integrally woven into the evolving social and economic geography of late-twentieth-century Europe. This is not happening because people are seeing themselves as European above and beyond all else. Rather, it is happening because Europe has come to mean something more than a collection of states. Such a view of Europe is not just affecting regional developments in western Europe, however; it is also part of the unfolding political and social scene farther east.

European Identity and the Realignment of Eastern Europe

The fall of the Iron Curtain fundamentally altered Europe's geopolitics. In one sense it greatly complicated the ways in which people think about Europe. During the decades after World War II, most West Europeans had come to see Europe in ways that excluded the East (Judt 1992). Moreover, Communist Eastern Europe, with its Soviet overseer, was an important "other" against which notions of West European identity could be juxtaposed. The collapse of the post-World War II geopolitical order not only challenged the ideological underpinnings of West European concepts of Europe; it introduced enormous complexities into the effort to create a more unified Europe. Germany became distracted by reunification and the rebuilding of relationships with its eastern neighbors, the major powers of the European Community took different positions on political developments unfolding in the east, and widespread disagreements emerged over the role that former East European countries should play in the European unity project.

Against this backdrop, it would appear that geopolitical change in Eastern Europe has worked against European identity in the narrow sense. It has slowed, if not derailed, efforts to create a more powerful, functionally integrated EU, and it has raised questions about the boundaries and purpose of the EU that formerly could be easily ignored (see generally Reynolds 1992). If one adopts an expanded view of European identity, however, the verdict is not nearly as clear. Most obviously, the geopolitical upheavals of recent years are behind the aforementioned search for the meaning of Europe (see generally Johnson 1996). In the process, these upheavals have raised the visibility of Europe as an ideological construct. The consequences of this visibility are ambiguous in some parts of Europe, but that ambiguity declines as one moves east. In the hearts and minds of many citizens of the former Soviet Union's European bloc, the idea of "Europe" represents a future that is both different from the past and offers opportunity and promise.

The importance of Europe as an ideological construct for Eastern Europeans is rooted in a post-World War II history in which Europe represented an alternative to the post-Yalta reality. The significance of this point became evident after the Czechoslovak uprising of 1968, when "Back to Europe" became a popular slogan among those hoping to tie that country's fortunes to the West (Johnson 1996: 257). Since 1989, the idea of Europe has assumed even greater significance, particularly in those countries with strong historical connections to the West (i.e., Poland, the Czech Republic, Slovakia, Hungary, and Slovenia). As Thomas Simmons (1993: 239) argues, the driving force behind reform in the East-Central European countries has been the "deep and broad domestic political consensus for joining (or rejoining) Europe." Simmons goes on to note that "this hunger and thirst to become European, or become European 'again,' is strong, and it helps stabilize turbulent processes, because it provides a centrist core of belief and a program that resists the encroachment of the radicalisms proliferating at the margins of East European politics" (Simmons 1993: 234). If Simmons is correct—and there is much to suggest that he is—European identity is not merely a curious feature of the contemporary east European scene; it is fundamentally shaping the future of the region. It is pushing Eastern Europe toward liberal democratic models of governance and toward free market economics. It is also impelling the countries of Eastern Europe to seek membership in the EU.

Viewed from one perspective, the push for EU membership by Eastern European states is curious. Having so recently exited from a system in which the political autonomy of individual states was seriously compromised, why would the leaders of their successor governments be so eager to turn around and participate in an arrangement that requires the surrender of some degree of sovereignty to an outside power? The answer may lie partly in economics; EU membership would bring some clear fiscal advantages to Eastern European states. Yet economics alone cannot explain why Czechoslovakia's Vaclav Havel characterized the signing of an Association Agreement with the EU as "possibly the single most important event" in the country's postwar history (quoted in Wagner-Findeisen 1993: 261). The agreement was seen in these terms because of what it represented culturally and politically as well as economically. The agreement itself is specific on this front; it deals not only with economics and trade relations but also with political and cultural cooperation.

Most of the states in former Eastern Europe, along with the Baltic states, have signed association agreements with the EU (see Figure 3.2); some of these agreements have been formally ratified by the EU, and some are awaiting ratification. The agreements are tangible manifestations of a push toward EU membership in the eastern part of Europe that began in the immediate aftermath of the collapse of Communist regimes in the region (Kramer 1993). As early as 1989, the new leadership in Poland, Czechoslovakia, and Hungary began highlighting the advantages of EU membership. Consequently, these three states were the first to conclude association agreements with the EU in 1991. Most other east European states followed suit, albeit at a somewhat slower pace.

The efforts to which the political leadership has gone to prepare countries for membership in the EU provide a good indication of the

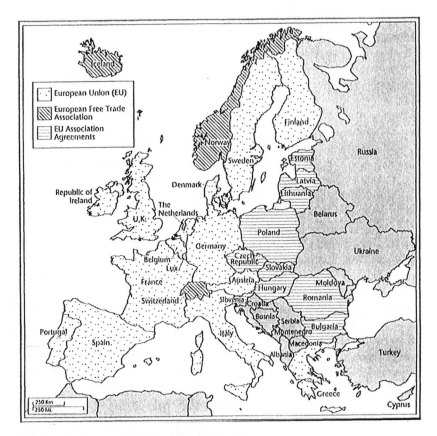

Figure 3.2   Suprastate affiliations in Europe

emphasis that has been placed on "joining Europe." The Hungarians
established a European Affairs Scrutiny Committee in 1992 to ensure
that new legislation was compatible with EU norms. The Poles and the
Czechs made compatibility with EU legal norms a requirement for any
new bill passed by their respective national legislatures. And after declaring its independence, Slovakia did the same (*The Economist* 1994).
How quickly the EU will accept expansion of membership is not at all
clear. Adding new Eastern European members would tax the EU budget to the extreme, and many in Western Europe are not eager to face
the challenges of integrating areas with new languages, complex cultural histories, and deep-seated economic problems. Nonetheless, the
case for EU membership that is being pushed in former Eastern Europe
cannot be ignored for long, precisely because it is being framed in
terms that go to the very heart of the European integration project.

Those terms emphasize the significance of Europe as a cultural-historical construct, not just as an economic zone. Viewed as such, they necessarily place the question of European identity at the center of debates over the future of Europe.

Implications and Conclusion

The modern state system is premised on the idea that the surface of the earth should be divided up into discrete national territories that are the foci of citizen identity (Mikesell 1983). That idea is currently being challenged by developments ranging from the growing independence of international capital to the rise of substate nationalism. Yet the inertia of the idea continues to shape the way we see the world. Nowhere is this more apparent than in traditional analyses of the EU, which posit European integration simply as a movement to create a large-scale state in Europe. But by casting integration in these terms, we implicitly treat the transfer of power from states to the central institutions of the EU as the critical determinant of success in the integration project. Those developments that push the EU closer to a state-like governmental and economic structure are interpreted as signs that integration is proceeding well, whereas those that challenge the concentration of power at the EU level are seen in opposite terms.

What lies behind this perspective on the integration process is the assumption that the EU is, or should be, engaged in "state building." The critical question for the EU is thus assumed to be whether the member states are willing to surrender increasing sovereignty to Brussels. Without denying that there is much to be learned from a consideration of this question, an emphasis on the allocation of power between state governments and EU institutions is an exercise in "top-down" thinking that focuses attention on governmental institutions as opposed to underlying social, political, and cultural processes. It also presents European integration fundamentally as a movement aimed at merging the interests of several states into one superstate rather than as a potential challenge to the concept of the state itself. At a time when the citizens of Europe appear to be rejecting the further concentration of powers in a centralized bureaucracy, such an approach seems increasingly anachronistic.

If we are to move beyond traditional interpretations of the integration process, the EU—and indeed Europe—needs to be seen in different terms. The peoples of Europe are currently facing issues ranging from environmental degradation to ethnic conflict to a grand geopolitical reordering in the aftermath of the fall of the Iron Curtain. None of these issues is neatly framed within the existing map of European states, and none of them can be adequately confronted solely at the European scale. It follows that analyses focusing largely on the interplay of power, meaning, and identity at the state and European scales miss the domain where Europe's best hopes arguably lie—a domain in which Europe is a framework within which social and political institutions are organized to accommodate and encourage new geographies of decision making and cooperation at a variety of scales. The EU of the late 1990s is a long way from realizing this ideal; indeed, for all the deference paid to "subsidiarity" in the Maastricht Treaty, the treaty assumes that there are only two levels of decision making: the EU and the state. Yet the idea that integration could give rise to a "Europe of the Regions" has always been part of the movement for European unity (Bray and Morgan 1985). The regions encompassed by this expression are usually understood to be simply administrative subdivisions of states, but there is no reason why a more imaginative approach to regionalism could not be adopted.

To the extent that Europe can remain a meaningful focus of identity, the possibility for more imaginative approaches to the spatial ordering of political and administrative life is enhanced. It becomes possible to see the state as one of many geographical arenas within which issues could be cast and to formulate affirmative obligations in the social and environmental realms in terms of territories defined along socioeconomic and ecological lines. These idealist notions are far from reality, but the tentative steps being taken to reshape the European political-territorial order are opening up small but important cracks in the foundation of the European state system and its attendant ideologies. These cracks are not the product of national identity writ large. Rather, they are being driven by new identity constellations that hold within them both the challenge and the promise of a new European order.

Acknowledgments

Research for this chapter was supported by the U.S. National Science Foundation under grant no. SBR-9157667. The author is grateful to Joanna Kepka for research assistance, to Sarah Shafer for comments on an earlier draft, and to Nancy Leeper for preparing the figures.

References

Agnew, J. A. *Place and Politics: The Geographical Mediation of State and Society.* Boston: Allen and Unwin, 1987.

Ashford, S., and N. Timms. *What Europe Thinks: A Study of Western European Values.* Aldershot, U.K.: Dartmouth Publishing Company, 1992.

Baun, M. J. *An Imperfect Union: The Maastricht Treaty and the New Politics of European Integration.* Boulder: Westview Press, 1996.

Bray, C., and R. Morgan. *The European Community and Central-Local Government Relations: A Review.* London: Economic and Social Research Council, 1985.

Cappelin, R. "Interregional Cooperation in Europe." In R. Cappelin and P. W. J. Batey, eds., *Regional Networks, Border Regions and European Integration.* London: Pion Limited, 1993, 1–20.

Cappelin, R., and P. W. J. Batey, eds. *Regional Networks, Border Regions and European Integration.* London: Pion Limited, 1993.

Cole, J., and F. Cole. *The Geography of the European Community.* London and New York: Routledge, 1993.

Commission of the European Communities. *INTERREG: Breaking through Borders.* Brussels: Commission of the European Community, Directorate General for Regional Policy, 1990a.

———. *Les interventions communautaires en matière de coopération interrégionale.* Brussels: Commission of the European Community, Directorate General for Regional Policy, 1990b.

———. *Europe 2000: Outlook for the Development of the Community's Territory.* Luxembourg: Office for Official Publications of the European Communities, 1991.

Connor, W. *Ethnonationalism: The Quest for Understanding.* Princeton, N.J.: Princeton University Press, 1994.

Deflem, J., and F. C. Pampel. "The Myth of Postnational Identity: Popular Support for European Unification." *Social Forces* 75 (1) (1996): 119–143.

Delamaide, D. *The New Superregions of Europe.* New York: Dutton, 1994.

Delanty, G. "The Limits and Possibilities of European Identity: A Critique of Cultural Essentialism." *Philosophy and Social Criticism* 21 (1995): 15–36.

Dobroczynski, M. "European Rapprochement." *Polish Perspectives* 32 (2) (1989): 19–26.

Dunford, M., and G. Kafkalas, eds. *Cities and Regions in the New Europe: The Global-Local Interplay and Spatial Development Strategies.* London: Belhaven, 1992.

The Economist. "Eastern Europe and the EU: Laying Down the Law." 333 (7893) (1994): 46–47.

———. "More-or-Less European Union." 336 (7929) (1995): 46.

Haller, M., and R. Richter. *Toward a European Nation? Political Trends in Europe— East and West, Center and Periphery.* Armonk, N.Y., and London: M. E. Sharpe, 1994.

Harvie, C. *The Rise of Regional Europe.* London and New York: Routledge, 1994.

Hodgson, G. "Grand Illusion: The Failure of European Consciousness." *World Policy Journal* 10 (1993): 13–24.

Hunderi-Ely, A. The Rise of Baltic Regionalism in a Rapidly Changing Europe. Unpublished master's thesis, Department of Geography, University of Oregon, 1995.

Jenkins, B., and S. Sofos, eds. *Nation and Identity in Contemporary Europe.* London and New York: Routledge, 1996.

Johnson, L. R. *Central Europe: Enemies, Neighbors, Friends.* Oxford and New York: Oxford University Press, 1996.

Jones, R. M. "Beyond Identity? The Reconstruction of the Welsh." *Journal of British Studies* 31 (4) (1992): 330–358.

Judt, T. "Ex Oriente Lux? Post-Celebratory Speculations on the 'Lessons' of '89." In C. Crouch and D. Marquand, eds., *Towards Greater Europe? A Continent without an Iron Curtain.* Oxford: Blackwell, 1992, 91–104.

―――. "Europe: The Grand Illusion." *The New York Review of Books* 43 (12) (July 11, 1996): 6–9.

Kramer, H. "The European Community's Response to the 'New Eastern Europe.'" *Journal of Common Market Studies* 31 (2) (1993): 213–244.

LaBasse, J. *L'Europe des régions.* Saint-Amand-Montrond, France: Flammarion, 1991.

Leitner, H. "Reconfiguring the Spatiality of Power: The Construction of a Supranational Migration Framework for the European Union." *Political Geography* 16 (2) (1997): 123–143.

Lundqvist, L., and L. O. Persson, eds. *Visions and Strategies in European Integration: A North European Perspective.* Berlin: Springer-Verlag, 1993.

Mikesell, M. W. "The Myth of the Nation State." *Journal of Geography* 82 (6) (1983): 257–260.

Moravcsik, A. "Preferences and Power in the European Community: A Liberal Intergovernmentalist Approach." *Journal of Common Market Studies* 31 (4) (1993): 473–525.

Moss, C., and B. K. Wyatt. "The CORINE Biotopes Project: A Database for Conservation of Nature and Wildlife in the European Community." *Applied Geography* 14 (1994): 327–349.

Murphy, A. B. "Emerging Regional Linkages within the European Community: Challenging the Dominance of the State." *Tijdscrift voor Economische en Sociale Geografie* 84 (3) (1993): 103–118.

―――. "The Sovereign State System as Political-Territorial Idea: Historical and Contemporary Considerations." In T. J. Biersteker and C. Weber, eds., *State Sovereignty as Social Construct.* Cambridge: Cambridge University Press, 1996, 81–120.

Reynolds, D. "Thawing History: Europe in the 1990s and Pre-Cold War Patterns." In C. Crouch and D. Marquand, eds., *Towards Greater Europe? A Continent without an Iron Curtain.* Oxford: Blackwell, 1992, 9–33.

Rhodes, M., ed. *The Regions and the New Europe: Patterns in Core and Periphery Development.* Manchester and New York: Manchester University Press, 1995.

Ruggie, J. B. "Territoriality and Beyond: Problematizing Modernity in International Relations." *International Organization* 47 (1) (1993): 139–174.

Séché, J. C. *A Guide to Working in a Europe Without Frontiers.* Luxembourg: Office for Official Publications of the European Communities, 1988.

Simmons, T. W. Jr. "Post-Communist Europe in Historical Perspective." In T. W. Simmons Jr., ed., *Eastern Europe in the Postwar World.* New York: St. Martin's Press, 1993, 226–264.

Smart, V. "Mighty Regions Unnerve Brussels." *The European,* August 15–21, 1996, 9.

Taylor, P. J. "The State as Container: Territoriality in the Modern State-System." *Political Geography* 18 (2) (1994): 151–162.

Thomas, D. E. "Together and Apart." *New Statesman and Society* 5 (199) (1992): 20.

Wagner-Findeisen, A. "From Association to Accession: An Evaluation of Poland's Aspirations to Full Membership in the European Community, 1989–1992." In M. B. Biskupski and J. S. Pula, eds., *Poland and Europe: Historical Dimensions.* New York: Columbia University Press, 1993, 243–281.

Wallace, W., ed. *The Dynamics of European Integration.* London and New York: Pinter Publishers for the Royal Institute of International Affairs, 1990.

Williams, A. M. *The Western European Economy: A Geography of Post-War Development.* Totowa, N.J.: Barnes and Noble Books, 1987.

———. *The European Community: The Contradictions of Integration.* Oxford: Blackwell, 1991.

Wilson, K., and J. van der Dussen, eds. *The History of the Idea of Europe.* London and New York: Routledge, 1993.

4

Scale and Regional Identity
in the Caribbean

Gary S. Elbow

This essay examines the development of regional identity in the Caribbean. A relatively large and fragmented region, the Caribbean provides an interesting example of the transition from micro- to macro-scale identity in a multistate setting. The Caribbean has long been noted as an example of physical, political, and cultural fragmentation, combined with strong association of individuals with their island of origin, all of which has inhibited the development of a strong macro-scale identity. This essay argues the role of fragmentation and diversity in the Caribbean may be overstressed; that there is more unity within the region than is generally recognized, and that recent events, both outside the region and within it, have caused Caribbean people and their governments to develop a more firm macro-scale identity as members of a broadly defined Caribbean community that is united by a number of shared cultural and historical elements and long-term goals of mutual interest.

In this essay, scale is interpreted within a cultural-historical context that extends beyond area alone to encompass broader concepts of identity (see also the Introduction to this volume). Micro-scale refers to units that have a common culture and history that impart a strong sense of identification to a small area. Micro-scale areas in the Caribbean are small islands within the Lesser Antilles or subregions of larger islands and mainland states such as, for example, the Cibao or Vega Real areas of the Dominican Republic, Cuba's Vuelta Abajo, or the Ulúa River valley of Honduras. Meso-scale areas also include groupings of small political units, generally with a shared colonial heritage, such as the Lesser Antilles, the British Caribbean, or the Hispanic

Caribbean, whereas larger agglomerations such as the West Indies, Central America, or the Caribbean (as defined in this paper) are macro-scale regions. In this construction, it is possible that certain micro-scale areas might be larger than some meso-scale regions and that a region defined as meso-scale could be larger than one classified as macro-scale.

Defining the Caribbean

The term *Caribbean* is widely used, but there is disagreement on what it means. The name is applied to areas as small as the Commonwealth Caribbean, a meso-scale region that includes only the islands affiliated with the British Commonwealth of Nations, whereas at the macro-scale, the "greater Caribbean area" has been said to extend from Virginia or Maryland in the United States to the central coast of Brazil (Hulme 1986, Taylor 1993). The United States-sponsored Caribbean Basin Initiative combined the insular Caribbean with the mainland states of Central America in its formulation of the region.

Gary Elbow (1997) defines the Caribbean in terms of three subregions (Figure 4.1). These regions occupy increasingly greater scales, with decreasing levels of Caribbean identity. The island arc of the Antilles, from Cuba to Trinidad, makes up the Caribbean core, a macro-scale region. This is the area included in nearly all delimitations of the Caribbean. The Caribbean fringe brings in the non-Hispanic mainland territories of Belize, Guyana, Suriname, and French Guiana, along with The Bahamas and Turks and Caicos Islands, which are Atlantic in location, but adjacent to Antillean islands. With the exception of Belize, these territories are not Caribbean in location, but they share important historical and cultural elements with the core. The Caribbean periphery is made up of Spanish-speaking mainland states that have a Caribbean coast and, in some cases, claim Caribbean island possessions. The affinities of the periphery with the core and fringe are largely defined by location; that is, peripheral states border the Caribbean Sea, but they lack the Caribbean centrality of the core and the strong cultural/ historical connections of the fringe territories. The situation of Panama—located astride the Central American Isthmus but not one of the five Central American Republics; formerly a province of Colombia but not a part of South America; and with a long Caribbean coast yet seldom included among the Caribbean states—is an extreme example of the level of incertitude that may exist with regard to regional placement of Caribbean peripheral territories.

The island Caribbean and its non-Hispanic mainland outliers do not

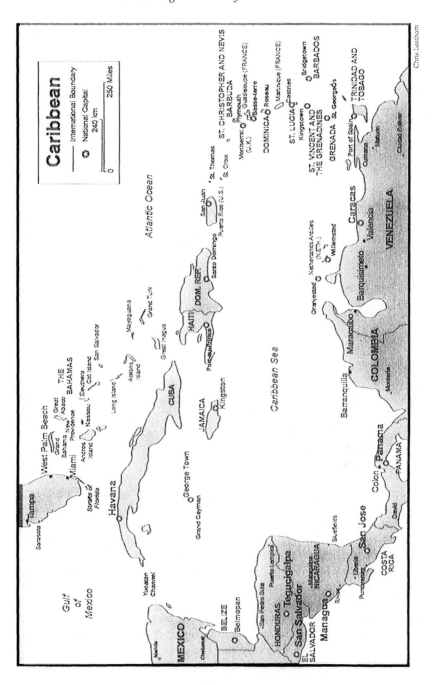

Caribbean

International Boundary
National Capital
240 km
250 Miles

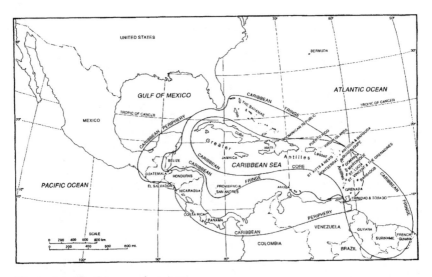

Figure 4.1   Caribbean subregions

Source: Reproduced from the *Journal of Geography* 1997, by permission of the National
Council for Geographic Education.

fit conveniently into either Anglo America or Latin America. Lowenthal (1972: 3) captures this aspect of the Caribbean as well when he
writes, "Alike is not being Iberian, the West Indies are not North
American either, nor indeed do they fit any ordinary regional pattern.
Not so much undeveloped as overdeveloped, exotic without being traditional, they are part of the Third World yet ardent emulators of the
West. Even from a statistical purview they lie outside, or are marginal
to, standard national categories."

Most of the region is made up of islands, as opposed to the adjacent
mainland states. In addition, the non-Hispanic Caribbean was shaped
by British, Dutch, and French colonial influences; and many of the islands, along with the mainland fringe states, still retain political ties to
one of those metropolitan powers or the United States. This distinction
is carried over into the international affiliations of different groups of
countries; for example, the English-speaking Caribbean countries
(along with Suriname) belong to CARICOM, the Caribbean Community and Common Market, and to the African-Caribbean-Pacific Group
(Lomé Agreements), whereas the Spanish-speaking mainland countries are members of the Latin American Integration Association and
subregional Latin American trade blocs such as the Central American
Common Market, the Andean Group, or the Group of Three (Figure
4.2).

AREA, POPULATION, AND ETHNIC GROUPS OF CARIBBEAN TERRITORIES

State/Territory	Area (km2)[a]	Population[b]	Ethnic Groups[c]
Spanish Caribbean	159,590	19,040,215	1, 9
Cuba	110,860	10,951,334	1, 4, 9
Dominican Rep.	48,730	8,088,881	1, 4
Spanish Mainland	4,524,324	186,671,134	7, 4, 2, 1, 3
Colombia	1,138,910	36,813,161	7, 4, 1, 2
Costa Rica	51,100	3,463,083	4, 7, 1
El Salvador	21,040	5,828,987	7, 2, 4
Guatemala	108,890	11,277,614	7, 2, 4, 1
Honduras	112,090	5,605,193	7, 2, 1, 4, 3
Mexico	1,972,550	95,772,462	7, 2, 4
Nicaragua	129,494	4,272,352	7, 4, 1, 2, 3
Panama	78,200	2,655,094	7, 1, 4, 2, 9
Venezuela	912,050	21,983,188	7, 4, 1, 2
British Caribbean	272,260	6,023,990	1, 4, 5, 2, 9, 8, 3
Anguilla[d]	91	10,424	1
Antigua and Barbuda	440	65,647	1, 4, 8
The Bahamas	13,940	259,367	1, 4
Barbados	430	257,030	1, 4, 5
Belize	22,960	219,296	7, 1, 2, 3, 4
Bermuda[d]	50	62,099	1, 4
British Virgin Islands[d]	150	13,195	1, 4, 9, 5
Cayman Islands[d]	260	34,646	1, 4
Dominica	750	82,926	1, 2, 3
Grenada	340	94,961	1
Guyana	214,970	712,091	5, 1, 2, 4, 9
Jamaica	10,990	2,595,275	1, 5, 4, 9
Montserrat[d]	100	12,771	1, 4
St. Kitts and Nevis	269	41,369	1, 4
St. Lucia	620	157,862	1, 5, 4
St. Vincent	340	118,344	1, 4, 5, 2, 3
Trinidad and Tobago	5,130	1,272,385	1, 5, 4, 9
Turks and Caicos[d]	430	14,302	1
French Caribbean	93,880	1,051,986	1, 4, 5, 2, 8, 9
French Guiana[d]	91,000	151,187	1, 4, 5, 9, 2
Guadaloupe[d]	1,780	407,768	1, 4, 9, 8
Martinique[d]	1,100	399,151	1, 4, 5, 8, 9

Netherlands Antilles	1,153	276,762	1, 2, 4, 5, 6
Aruba[d]	193	67,794	4, 5
Neth. Antilles[d]	960	208,968	1, 2, 4, 5, 6
U.S. Caribbean territory	9,456	3,916,143	1, 4
Puerto Rico[d]	9,104	3,819,023	1, 4
U.S. Virgin Islands[d]	352	97,120	1, 4
Independent States			
Haiti	27,750	6,731,539	1
Suriname	163,270	436,418	5, 1, 6, 3, 2, 9, 4

[a]Total area, including lakes, bays, etc.
[b]Population estimated as of July 1996.
[c]1 = Creole/Afro-Hispanic, 2 = Indian, 3 = Afro-Indian mix, Garifuna in Belize, Bush Negro in Suriname, 4 = Euro-American, 5 = East Indian, 6 = Indonesian, 7 = mestizo, 8 = Arab, 9 = Chinese
[d]Dependent Territory

Source: Adopted from 1996 *CIA World Factbook.* Central Intelligence Agency, Washington, D.C., 1996 (on line, http://www.ocdi.gov/cia/publications/nsolo/wfb-all.htm).

TWENTIETH-CENTURY CONFLICTS

Dominican Republic/Haiti. In 1937 Dominican troops massacred an estimated 30,000 Haitians who were living illegally along the Dominican side of the international border. Reflects deep-seated hostility between the predominantly African-origin Haitian population and the mulatto Dominicans.

Cuban revolution of 1958. Rebel forces led by Fidel Castro overthrew the government of Fulgencio Batista and led to Cuban affiliation with the Communist bloc and isolation from Caribbean neighbors. U.S. policy since 1959 has attempted to establish and maintain an economic blockade of Cuba and limit its economic and social interactions with Western, capitalist-oriented states of the Caribbean.

The Guatemalan civil war lasted from 1964 until 1996. At least 100,000 civilians were killed in this conflict, many of whom were Maya Indians.

El Salvador, civil war between 1980–1992. As many as 100,000 civilians and armed forces on both sides were killed.

Nicaraguan civil war, 1978–1979. An estimated 50,000 people were killed, with persistent unrest, followed by sporadic fighting between representatives of right and left. Miskito and Sumo Indians living along the Caribbean coast were also involved in this conflict fighting against the Sandinista-led government.

Colombia has had several bloody internal conflicts, including the War of 1,000 Days (1899–1902) and La Violencia (1948–ca. 1964). Currently the country is beset with violence as the government battles drug cartels and guerrilla organizations.

Venezuela has border claims with Colombia and Guyana. The dispute with Colombia involves jurisdiction over off-shore Caribbean waters and potential off-shore oil deposits. Venezuela has challenged a 1899 arbitration that awarded territory between the Essiquibo River and the mouth of the Orinoco to the United Kingdom. The territory is now part of Guyana.

Guyana has seen periodic political conflict between Afro-Guyanese and Guyanese of East Indian extraction as the two groups struggle for control of the country's political system.

Mexico, which was politically stable and largely free of ethnic and political conflict, has witnessed the rise of the Zapatista rebellion among Maya Indians in the southeastern state of Chiapas beginning in 1994, and political assassinations and additional civil unrest have occurred since the early 1990s.

HISTORICAL HIGHLIGHTS

The Caribbean is often characterized as fragmented and divided. The region was first colonized by Spain in the sixteenth century, and French, Dutch, and English occupation dates from the early seventeenth century. The seventeenth and eighteenth centuries were times of considerable conflict and turmoil, when many islands changed hands several times before settling into their final colonial affiliations. Caribbean economic and social history is dominated by the plantation system and replacement of native Indians by Africans in much of the region. After the end of slavery in the 1830s, the Guianas, Trinidad, and some smaller areas received thousands of indentured laborers from India and Indonesia, which added to Caribbean ethnic diversity. In the twentieth century the United States has emerged as the central power in the region, replacing European political colonialism with economic dominance and occasional military action to assert its influence.

The region has been characterized by failed attempts at political integration, including the United Provinces of Central America (1823–1836), Gran Colombia (1821–1830), and the Federation of West Indian

States (1958–1961). Beginning about 1960, emphasis shifted to economic integration, with the formation of the Latin American Free Trade Association (1960), the Central American Common Market (1961), and the Caribbean Free Trade Association (1968). The Reagan administration created the Caribbean Basin Initiative in 1983, bringing together Central America with the island Caribbean to develop trade. These efforts met with minor success but paved the way for more recent efforts such as the Caribbean Community and Common Market (CARICOM), the Group of 3, and the recently formed Association of Caribbean States. These efforts reflect a growing sense of regionwide Caribbean identity.

▶◀

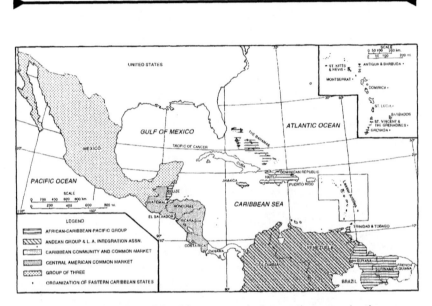

Figure 4.2 Membership of Caribbean states in integration organizations

A further indication of the ambivalent vision of this region is its North American placement in the United Nations and other statistical compendia, even though it is most frequently included as part of Latin America in regional surveys of history and geography.[1] For these reasons, one could argue that a part of the region's identity is derived negatively—the Caribbean does not fit conveniently into either of the generally recognized hemispheric cultural macro-scale regions, therefore it has acquired a separate identity.

The degree to which individual islands and mainland territories share common characteristics and mutual interests that lead to development of regional identity varies with scale. Micro- and meso-scale areas generally share language and colonial heritage and have stronger common identity than do macro-scale areas. For example, the seven small, English-speaking members of the Organization of Eastern Caribbean States form a more coherent regional grouping than the entire Lesser Antilles, which includes French- and Dutch-affiliated islands, or the entire Antillean island group, which takes in relatively large Spanish- and French-speaking countries along with U.S.-affiliated Puerto Rico and the Virgin Islands. The same may be said for Central America vis-à-vis the Caribbean Basin or other macro-scale configurations within the region.

The subregional distinctions described above also reveal that being located on the Caribbean Sea and identifying as Caribbean are different things. Mexico and Central America have Caribbean Sea locations, but they do not self-identify strongly as Caribbean states, and they are not so identified by others. On the other hand, Guyana and Suriname, which do not have a Caribbean location but share elements of common colonial history with British and Dutch Caribbean islands, tend to self-identify as Caribbean and are frequently included in groupings of Caribbean states. More to the point, Guyana has been an active participant in CARICOM since its formation, and Suriname recently joined the group, although these countries are not members of South American or Latin American trade groupings, despite their South American continental location (Figure 4.2). The discrepancy between Caribbean location and Caribbean identity suggests that a country's historic relationship with a specific colonial power (i.e., England, Spain, France, or Holland) and the kinds of institutions that were developed from that relationship are more important factors in the development of a "Caribbean" regional identity than is a Caribbean Sea location.

Caribbean Diversity

Fragmented, heterogeneous, insular, distinctive, and diverse are among the descriptive terms applied to the Caribbean (Boswell and Conway 1992, Knight 1990, Lowenthal 1972, Sandner 1985, Watts 1987, West and Augelli 1987). Few observers would argue against the appropriateness of these descriptors for a place as obviously diverse as the Caribbean. The region encompasses hundreds of islands and adjacent mainland extensions strewn around a sea that covers an area one-third the size of the United States. These islands range in area from the relative giant, Cuba, which is comparable in size to the state of Tennessee, to tiny uninhabited specks of land that appear only on the most detailed maps. Culturally, one finds in the Caribbean speakers of Dutch, English, French, Hindi, Javanese, and Spanish, along with locally developed languages such as Haitian Creole, Papiamento, and Surinamese (Sranan Tongo) and, on the mainland, numerous native-American languages that survived the European conquest. The countries that make up the extended Caribbean (i.e., core, periphery, and fringe) range from some of the smallest independent states in the world to countries with large and varied national territory; and populations are equally diverse, ranging from just over 40,000 for St. Kitts and Nevis to Mexico with over 95 million. Political status is also highly varied. The region comprises twenty-five independent states, three French overseas provinces, six islands that form two "autonomous countries" of the Kingdom of the Netherlands, six dependencies of the United Kingdom, one off-shore territory of the United States, the Commonwealth of Puerto Rico, and several Caribbean island territories of Spanish-speaking mainland states. Economies are heavily influenced by the metropolitan powers, especially the United States, but they also include socialist Cuba, along with important international players such as Mexico, Colombia, and Venezuela.

A history of colonization by competing European powers, followed by efforts on the part of the United States to establish hegemony in the area, also helps to explain Caribbean diversity. For a period of five centuries one or another outside power has attempted to assert control over all or some part of the region. The Spaniards began the process in the 1490s with their conquest of Hispaniola. English, Dutch, and French interests challenged the Spaniards in the seventeenth century, colonizing the Lesser Antilles and establishing a foothold on Hispaniola (Saint Domingue) and in Jamaica. Late in the same century these powers extended their colonizing efforts onto the South American mainland in what today are Guyana, Suriname, and French Guiana. Several Caribbean colonies changed hands a number of times during the seventeenth and eighteenth centuries as a result of European or local conflicts. During the twentieth century the United States has been the dominant outside actor in the region, playing an important role in shaping political and economic trends and establishing its own Caribbean colonial outposts.

The linguistic, political, and economic differences previously referred to are the result of this long history of colonial enterprise. Many of the smaller islands and one relatively large one (Puerto Rico) are associated with a metropolitan power or have dependent status, and most of the former British colonies are members of the British Commonwealth of Nations and retain close ties with the United Kingdom.

Only in the case of the former Spanish colonies have the economic and political ties with the mother country largely been severed. Elsewhere, economic, political, and cultural relations with former colonial rulers tend to focus the attention of the Caribbean territories toward the large power and inhibit interaction with Caribbean neighbors. Nevertheless, one can discern two major subgroups that have emerged from the colonial experience: the British Caribbean and the Spanish-speaking states. Both of these Caribbean subgroups developed relationships that led to the formal agreements for economic and political cooperation noted earlier, and they generally have been reluctant to enter into agreements that would reach across the subgroup boundaries.

Another factor that may contribute to an image of Caribbean disunity has to do with the orientation of many scholarly works on the region, which emphasize divisive rather than integrative elements. Jean Grugel (1995: 2), referring to the traditional separation of Central America from the insular Caribbean, supports this notion when he comments that it is common for writers on the Caribbean to stress in their work the cultural, political, and physical diversity of the region.

On the other hand, Elbow (1997: 16) notes that by placing an emphasis on unifying elements such as the Caribbean's shared history of plantation monoculture and slavery, the relative facility of movement among islands, interisland migration patterns, and shared themes in Caribbean culture, one is able to frame a picture that reveals the potential for cooperation and unity. Some of the stress on lack of unity may be stimulated by Western beliefs that the linguistic and political differences found in the Caribbean preclude collective action and militate against the formation of a common regional image or vision.

Yet, many countries outside of the Caribbean region have great cultural differences within their borders. India, Indonesia, and several African countries come to mind in this regard. Perhaps even more relevant is the recent formation of the European Union, a federation of fifteen independent states that have agreed to cooperate with each other at the expense of a portion of their sovereignty in behalf of the common good. These countries share far greater cultural differences than the Caribbean and emerged only fifty years ago from the second of two bloody and disastrous wars. The development of a strong regional identity among Western European countries, combined with their great progress toward regional cooperation, suggests that there is nothing inherent in the Caribbean situation that would preclude formation of a common macro-scale identity for that area, as well.

Compounding the difficulty in evaluating the relative importance of unifying and divisive forces in the region is the poorly developed state concept of many Caribbean countries (Knight 1990: 307–308). Most of the islands have been independent for a relatively short time: The exceptions are Haiti (1804), the Dominican Republic (1844), and Cuba (1902). The recently independent English- and Dutch-speaking territories retain ties to their former colonial rulers and lack strong identification as independent states; however, territorial identification may be quite intense. At the other end of the scale is Cuba, which had a protracted struggle to establish independence, first from Spain, then from U.S. political and economic domination. The Castro revolution, followed by challenges to the United States and the assumption of a leadership role in the Third World, give Cuba what is likely the strongest nation-state image in the region. The other Spanish-speaking states have also developed relatively strong national images, a product of longer independent histories and larger size, fewer ties to their former colonial ruler, Spain, and generally larger and more independent economies.

The differences between the recently independent Antillean states and the Spanish-speaking island and mainland states are manifested visually in the presence of nationalistic symbols in the latter, and their relative absence in the former. One would not have to spend very much time in Cuba to learn about José Martí, the martyr of Cuban independence, or in the Dominican Republic to find reference to the country's role as the first Spanish colony in the Americas. Even Haiti, which has a checkered political history, can look with pride on the accomplishments of Toussaint L'Ouverture and Jean Jacques Dessalines, heroes of the war for independence. But one looks in vain for monuments to similar figures on the other islands, which, of course, were awarded independence, rather than having to fight for it. Instead, one tends to encounter prominent remnants of the colonial past such as Nelson's Dockyard in Antigua or crumbling plantation houses or sugar windmill towers on St. Kitts and Nevis, or a French fort on Martinique. The relatively weak development of a sense of identity among the new, small Caribbean states might leave the way open for the emergence of an overarching macro-scale regional identity.

Another element that must be considered in evaluating the development of regional identity in the Caribbean is the existence of widely recognized subgroupings within the larger Caribbean. There seems to be little doubt that a survey of citizens of Guatemala, El Salvador, Honduras, Nicaragua, or Costa Rica would reveal that they identify far more readily with Central America than they do with the Caribbean. Likewise, the strongest regional identification of Mexican Yucatecans is surely with the Yucatan Peninsula, rather than with a (to them) distant Caribbean archipelago. Within the Caribbean, the identification of the Antillean core as the most "Caribbean" part of the larger region has already been noted. This distinctive meso-scale character interferes with the development of a strong macro-scale identity for the greater Caribbean, especially for areas on the Caribbean periphery.

Elements of Macro-Scale Identity

What factors contribute to a sense of Caribbean identity? The ambivalent position of the Caribbean with respect to Anglo and Latin America has already been noted. The difficulty, especially for the British Caribbean territories, of identifying with the Spanish-speaking states of Latin America intensifies their sense of belonging to a distinctive region within the hemisphere. Even for the Spanish-speaking islands, their relatively late independence compared with the continental states, physical isolation from the mainland, and Afro-Spanish heritage identifies them as different from most of continental Latin America. The mainland states, themselves, are characterized by intense cultural differences between their Caribbean coastal areas and the traditional Hispanic-oriented highland cores. Perhaps the best example of this is the Mosquito Coast of Nicaragua, which has very weak associations with the Hispanic majority of Nicaraguans, but one could point to many other examples of distinctive Caribbean-oriented populations living on the north and east coast of Central America (Jones 1970). John Augelli (1963) recognizes this distinction when he identifies the Rimland-Mainland dichotomy in Middle America.

The Caribbean Sea is an important common element in the region. Burghardt (1973: 236) has observed that water tends to separate territories, whereas land unites them, and speculated that the way we draw maps might be a cause for this perception. Perhaps this is why the Caribbean Sea is visualized as a divisive factor—but the sea also unites. The Caribbean has served as a route of interisland migration and trade since pre-Columbian times. After the European conquest, ships crossing the Caribbean carried at one time or another: Aztec and Inca treasure, along with pirates who tried to steal it, sugar and the slaves needed for its production, bananas and the plantation workers who planted and harvested them, along with oil, bauxite, iron ore, and loads of bulk cargo and manufactured goods bound from one coast to the other by way of the Panama Canal. The strategic role of the Caribbean as a major shipping route for Venezuelan oil exports and United States oil imports from around the world and the importance of passages between islands as access ways to the Panama Canal contribute to the sea's integrative character.

But the Caribbean is more than just a transportation route, as important as that might be. There are vital cultural, economic, and political links across the sea as well. Jamaican and Barbadian migrants helped to build the Panama Canal and worked on the banana plantations of Costa Rica and other Central American countries. Garífuna people from the Caribbean islands of Saint Vincent and Dominica settled in Belize and Honduras. West Indians emigrated to the Lake Maracaibo oil fields of Venezuela and to work in the refineries of Aruba and Curaçao in the early part of the twentieth century. Haitians once migrated in considerable numbers to harvest Cuban sugarcane, as they still do in the Dominican Republic (Boswell and Conway 1992: 45, Richardson 1989: 222).

More recently, the governments of the region have come to see the Caribbean Sea as an asset shared by all, but one that requires collaborative effort to gain the greatest benefit from its resources, and for its preservation. Andrés Serbín (1994: 62) refers to this integrating aspect when he observes that the Caribbean states have adopted the sea "with its economic potential, collective interests (both social and political), and similarity of threats posed to the ecology and security of its members—as a common good." This collective approach to management of the Caribbean is echoed in the charter of the recently formed Association of Caribbean States, which recognizes in its constitution "the importance of the Caribbean Sea which constitutes the common patrimony of the peoples of the Caribbean, and recall[s] the role it has played in their history and the potential it has to operate as a unifying element in their development" (Organization of American States 1995). This same document also notes the importance of collective action to accomplish the goal of Caribbean environmental preservation.

Not surprisingly, some of the most articulate expressions of macro-scale Caribbean identity have come from the region's writers. Antonio Benítez Rojo (1992: 4), a Cuban novelist and literary scholar, refers to the Caribbean as a "meta-archipelago," where shared characteristics of the region are repeated in an infinite variety of forms at the micro-scale on different "islands" (which would also include some mainland areas). For Benítez Rojo, the syncretization of Amerind, European, African, and Asian elements into a Caribbean culture gives the area its unique macro-scale identity, which is neither North nor South, Anglo nor Latin American. In this construction, the characteristics of "Caribbeanness" are instantly apparent in all of their manifestations and would be recognized by natives of the region, whether they come from Spanish-speaking Roman Catholic-Santero Cuba, Creole-speaking Roman Catholic-Vodun Haiti, or English-speaking Hindu-Moslem-Protestant Trinidad. The distinctive combination of Caribbean characteristics is generally lacking among the Spanish-speaking population

of the mainland, except for Caribbean coastal Colombia and Venezuela.

The idea of repeated themes is echoed by Derek Walcott (1992: n.p.)
in his Nobel prize lecture. "All of the Antilles, every island, is an effort
of memory; every mind, every racial biography culminating in amnesia
and fog. Pieces of sunlight through the fog and sudden rainbows, *arcs-
en-ciel*. That is the effort, the labour of the Antillean imagination, rebuilding its gods from bamboo frames, phrase by phrase."

In the introduction to a comparative analysis of myth in the work of
three Caribbean novelists, each of whom wrote in a different language,
Barbara Webb (1992: 4) notes that all Caribbean writers confront cultural dislocation and fragmentation brought about by the European
conquest and colonization of America. If one accepts her assertion that
there are common themes in Caribbean literature and that these
themes reflect elements that contribute to the possibility of integration,
the conclusion must be that the seemingly divisive qualities of dislocation and fragmentation are transformed by means of their appearance
throughout the region into elements that contribute to a sense of regional unity.

The Colombian Nobel prize-winning writer, Gabriel García Márquez, was born and raised in Aracataca, a town in the Caribbean
coastal lowlands in his country. García Márquez stresses the contrasts
between his Caribbean place of origin, which is vibrant, colorful, and
cosmopolitan, with the highlands, which he characterizes as drab, re-
pressed, and inward-looking (Mendoza 1982: 54–56). As a Caribbean
native, there is little with which he can identify in the highlands. On
the other hand, García Márquez finds reminders of his heritage
throughout the Caribbean and beyond. Of a trip to Angola, the writer
remarked how the visit reinforced his consciousness of African elements in Caribbean culture (Mendoza 1982: 73). Among the Afro-Caribbean traits that attract García Márquez are the carnival tradition and
African influences in the region's music (Bell-Villada 1990: 21).

The common strains in Caribbean music that García Márquez identifies make up another unifying factor in the region. The rhythms of
mambo, salsa, rumba, reggae, and calypso are instantly recognized
around the world as Caribbean in origin. Formed by a blend of African
and European musical traditions, Caribbean music is a distinctive element of local culture that contributes importantly to regional identity.[2]

The Process of Regional Integration

The 1950s and 1960s saw the rise of two important movements in the
Caribbean that both reflected meso- and macro-scale identity and in-

fluenced it. One of these movements was the granting of independence to former British colonies, and the other was a push for political or economic integration in the region.[3]

These two movements merged with the creation of the Federation of the West Indies in 1958. The British West Indian colonies were generally small and poorly developed. With the Federation of the West Indies the British colonial office hoped to create a more economically and politically viable state than would have been possible if each of the ten Caribbean colonies had become separately independent.[4] However, despite lengthy preparations, the federation collapsed in 1962, only four years after its formation.

The breakup of the Federation of the West Indies has been attributed to great differences in size and economic strength. Two members of the federation, Jamaica and Trinidad and Tobago, had seven-eighths of the population and controlled three-quarters of the group's aggregate wealth (Erisman 1992: 60). These members, along with Barbados, which had a stronger economy than its Windward and Leeward Island neighbors, feared that they would be forced to subsidize the smaller members, so they went their own way. With respect to identity, Thomas Anderson (1984: 22) observes: "fundamental [to the failure of the federation] was a nearly overpowering sense of personal identification with individual islands." It seems clear that, at the micro-scale, local identity far outweighed whatever perceived benefits might be gained through political union at the meso- or macro-scale levels.

At the same time as the experiment with the Federation of the West Indies was progressing toward failure, work was also moving ahead on formation of the Central American Common Market (CACM) in 1961. Based on the European Common Market model, CACM had an ambitious agenda that went beyond promotion of free trade to include creation of a regional development bank, improvement of regional transportation networks, and formulation of regionwide economic and social policies. After a promising beginning, CACM nearly collapsed in the 1970s and 1980s as a result of a 1969 war between Honduras and El Salvador and the civil conflicts that erupted in Central America during the late 1970s and the 1980s. Recently, efforts have been made to rebuild CACM, but to date, it has largely failed to fulfill the hopes of its founders to integrate meso-scale areas at the macro-scale level.

The two integration efforts previously noted were both organized within Caribbean subregions that each have a common colonial heritage. As would be expected, efforts to promote integration between Spanish- and English-speaking Caribbean groups or individual countries have also been troubled.

Following their independence, Jamaica and Trinidad and Tobago petitioned for membership in the Organization of American States. Reluctance by the overwhelmingly Spanish-speaking organization (at the time the United States and Haiti were the only non-Hispanic members) to accept British Caribbean states stalled action on the requests for admission for five years in the case of Trinidad and Tobago and seven years (until 1969) in the case of Jamaica. According to Serbín (1990: 30), the British Caribbean states were equally reluctant to join the Latin American–dominated OAS, but did so because membership was required to obtain credit from the Inter-American Development Bank.

Following Che Guevara's spectacular failure to export revolution to Bolivia and other mainland countries in the late 1960s, Fidel Castro turned toward the British Caribbean. The Cuban initiative began with meetings between Fidel Castro and British Caribbean political leaders in the mid-1970s. Subsequently, Cuba developed ties with the Manley government in Jamaica as well as with Trinidad and Tobago, Guyana, and Grenada, which resulted in bilateral technical cooperation and cultural exchange agreements. An important aspect of Cuba's ability to develop relations with the English-speaking Caribbean was to project the image of an Afro-Latin state that shared with them important elements of culture and history. Cuba was responding to the rise of interest in the African origins of the majority of the Caribbean population and attempting to change the British Caribbean image of Cuba as a white-dominated Hispanic state, a process that was reinforced by assignment of Black Cuban ambassadors to CARICOM countries (Serbín 1990: 61).

Despite these efforts, several factors weakened the relationship between Cuba and the English-speaking Caribbean. One of these was Cuban militarization, which was revealed in 1980 when Cuban aircraft attacked a coast guard patrol in the Bahamas and in 1982, when Cuban advisors helped to build an airfield in Grenada that might have had potential for military use. The 1982 Falklands (Malvinas) War between Argentina and the United Kingdom revealed the deepness of the differences, when all of the English-speaking Caribbean states except Grenada sided with the United Kingdom and Cuba allied itself with Argentina.

U.S. concern with the expansion of Cuban influence in the Caribbean reached its climax with the 1983 invasion of Grenada, which was urged by certain members of the Organization of Eastern Caribbean States (Williams 1996). Economically, the United States responded to the Cuban effort with the Caribbean Basin Initiative, which was announced in 1982 and implemented in 1984. This program created incentives for private U.S. investment in the region, which included reduction of tariffs on most Caribbean exports. Significantly, the

Caribbean Basin Initiative did not affect sugar, traditionally the region's most important export, which faces increasingly stiff competition in the U.S. market (Conkling 1987: 8, Serbín 1990: 27).

For the purposes of this chapter, the most important aspect of the Caribbean Basin Initiative was that it covered both the insular Caribbean and Central America, thus creating a macro-scale framework through which the United States could deal with the entire area as a unit.[5] The Caribbean Basin Initiative, by most accounts, failed to promote economic growth in the region (Conkling 1987: 7, Grugel 1995: 188, Serbín 1990: 29). But the inclusion of the insular Caribbean with Central America by the United States for policy purposes did provide a mechanism whereby the English- and Spanish-speaking sectors of the greater Caribbean increased their interaction and facilitated the later move toward greater regionwide cooperation.

The notable and well-publicized failures to achieve political or economic integration outlined previously contrast with important movements toward greater regional cooperation in the Caribbean region (Table 4.1). Chief among these within the British Caribbean was formation of the Caribbean Free Trade Association (CARIFTA) in 1968 among the former Federation of the West Indies members and Guyana. In 1973, CARIFTA was renamed CARICOM (Caribbean Community and Common Market), and its scope expanded beyond trade to include integration in the areas of economy, health, education, communication, transportation, and foreign policy (Erisman 1995: 45). With respect to regional identity, the most important result of the creation of CARICOM was formulation of a coordinated foreign policy. This allowed the member states to have much greater influence outside of the region than would have been possible acting independently, and it also helped to promote a common identity, both internally and with respect to the international community (Erisman 1992: 69–70). CARICOM also provided for creation of the Caribbean Development Bank and the University of the West Indies with campuses in Jamaica, Trinidad, and Barbados and open to enrollment of students from all CARICOM states.

The British Caribbean states have been reluctant to admit outsiders to CARICOM. Suriname first applied for admission in the mid-1970s, shortly after it became independent. It finally became the first non-English-speaking full CARICOM member in 1995. The Dominican Republic applied for admission to the group in 1991 and was granted observer status. Reluctance to admit non-British-affiliated members is probably a reflection of continuing suspicion of Hispanic countries on the part of the CARICOM members. The Dominican Republic had also joined the African-Caribbean-Pacific group, along with Haiti, which

TABLE 4.1   Selected International Affiliations of Caribbean States

State	ACP Lomé 4	AG	AMAZ	CARICOM	CACM/CABEI	CDB	G-3	IADB	LAES	LAIA	OECS
Antigua and Barbuda (E)	*			*		*		*			*
The Bahamas (E)	*			*		*		*	*		
Barbados (E)	*			*		*		*	*		
Belize (E)	*			*		*		*	*		
Dominica (E)	*			*		*					*
Grenada (E)	*			*		*		*	*		*
Guyana (E)	*		*	*		*		*	*		
Jamaica (E)	*			*		*		*	*		
St. Kitts and Nevis (E)	*			*		*					*
St. Lucia (E)	*			*		*					*
St. Vincent and the Grenadines (E)	*			*		*					*
Trinidad and Tobago (E)	*			*		*		*	*		
Suriname (D)	*		*	*		*		*	*		
Haiti (F)	*					*		*	*		
Colombia (S)		*	*			*	*	*	*	*	
Costa Rica (S)					*			*	*		
Cuba (S)									*		
Dominican Republic (S)	*							*	*		
El Salvador (S)					*			*	*		
Guatemala (S)					*			*	*		
Honduras (S)					*			*	*		
Mexico (S)						*	*	*	*	*	
Nicaragua (S)					*			*	*		
Panama (S)								*	*		
Venezuela (S)		*	*			*	*	*	*	*	

Key to acronyms: ACP = African-Caribbean-Pacific countries (total of 70 members), AG = Andean Group (also includes Ecuador, Peru, and Bolivia; in 1997, Peru indicated its intent to withdraw from the Andean Group), CARICOM = Carribean Community and Common Market (with Montserrat; associate members are British Virgin Islands and Turks and Caicos Islands; observers are Anguilla, Bermuda, Cayman Islands, Dominican Republic, Haiti, Mexico, Netherlands Antilles, Puerto Rico, and Venezuela), CACM/CABEI = Central American Common Market/Central American Bank for Economic Integration, CDB = Carribean Development Bank (also includes the dependent territories of Anguilla, British Virgin Islands, Cayman Islands, Montserrat, Turks and Caicos Islands with Canada, France, Germany, Italy, and the United Kingdom as nonregional members), AMAZ = Amazon Cooperation Treaty (other members are Bolivia, Brazil, Ecuador, and Peru), IADB = Inter-American Development Bank (46 countries are members of IADB), LAES = Latin American Economic system (other members are Argentina, Bolivia, Brazil, Chile, Ecuador, Paraguay, Peru, and Uruguay), LAIA = Latin American Integration Association (other members are Argentina, Bolivia, Brazil, Chile, Ecuador, Paraguay, Peru, and Uruguay), OECS = Organization of Eastern Caribbean States (with Montserrat).

(D) = Dutch-speaking, (E) = English-speaking, (F) = French-speaking, (S) = Spanish-speaking
Source: *1996 World Factbook.* Washington, D.C.: Central Intelligence Agency, 1996.

gave both countries access to European markets, a benefit that was not available to Central and South American countries or Mexico, but which was seen as a competitive move by CARICOM members. Venezuela applied for membership in CARICOM in 1992 and signed a non-reciprocal free trade agreement that went into effect in 1993 (Serbín 1994: 67). Venezuela has since been granted observer status, as have Haiti, Mexico, the Netherlands Antilles, and Puerto Rico, along with several English-speaking British dependencies (Table 4.1). Costa Rica and Colombia also applied for membership but their applications had not been acted upon as of 1995. Cuba has expressed an interest in developing closer relations with CARICOM, and a joint commission was established in 1993 to investigate areas of possible cooperation (Erisman 1995: 51).

CARICOM and CACM are not the only groups in the region with an interest in integration. Mexico, Colombia, and Venezuela formed the Group of Three (G-3) in 1990 and agreed to reduce barriers to mutual trade. Venezuela and Colombia later signed a far-reaching bilateral trade agreement. Venezuela and Colombia are also members of the Andean Group, along with Ecuador, Peru, and Bolivia, and they, along with Guyana and Suriname, are among the eight signatories of the Amazon Cooperation Treaty. This is not a trade agreement, but it is noteworthy because it includes the Guianas along with Portuguese- and Spanish-speaking states, a distinction it shares with the Latin American Economic System (Table 4.1). Mexico joined with the United States and Canada to create NAFTA in 1994, an event that focused additional attention on economic integration throughout Latin America and the Caribbean.

The clearest expression of the changed climate for cooperation in the Caribbean is the formation of the Association of Caribbean States in 1994 (Table 4.2). The ACS has as its mission to promote trade within the region and with countries outside the bloc and to promote international cooperation in the areas of energy, marine resources, higher education, industrial and agricultural development, and transportation and communication, among others (Inter-American Development Bank 1994, Serbín 1994). Because the objectives of ACS are economic in nature, the political status of the member states is not affected.

The ACS is an extension of earlier integrationist movements in the region, but it is also a response to external events. The failure of the Caribbean Basin Initiative to produce the economic benefits that were expected disappointed many Caribbean national leaders. At the same time, the signing of the North American Free Trade Agreement and the formation of MERCOSUR (Argentina, Brazil, Chile, Paraguay, and Uruguay) in southern South America highlighted the danger of eco-

TABLE 4.2   The Association of Caribbean States

Members	Associate Members
Antigua and Barbuda	Anguilla
The Bahamas	Bermuda
Barbados	Cayman Islands
Belize	Turks and Caicos Islands
Colombia	British Virgin Islands
Costa Rica	U.S. Virgin Islands
Cuba	Montserrat
Dominica	Puerto Rico
Dominican Republic	French Republic
El Salvador	(Guadaloupe, Martinique, and
Grenada	French Guiana)
Guatemala	The Netherlands (Aruba and Guyana
Haiti	Netherlands Antilles)
Honduras	
Jamaica	
Mexico	
Nicaragua	
Panama	
Saint Kitts and Nevis	
Saint Lucia	
Saint Vincent and the Grenadines	
Suriname	
Trinidad and Tobago	
Venezuela	

nomic isolation for the Caribbean. These events acted as catalysts that accelerated a process that already was beginning to develop.

Association of Caribbean States membership includes every territory that might be considered Caribbean except for the two giants of the extended region, the United States and Brazil. In view of the relative lack of success of earlier integration efforts, the ACS would seem to be an unlikely candidate for survival. However, the creation of MERCO-SUR and NAFTA within the Western Hemisphere along with the recent formation of the European Union and the possible development of Asian trade blocs provide a strong incentive for cooperation. Likewise, the end of the Cold War reduces the likelihood that small states will receive significant economic aid from outside sources. Finally, the emergence of the United States as the world's "superpower" calls for a cooperative effort to counter its influence in the region. With respect to the latter point, Cuba presents a special problem. Most of the states in the region oppose U.S. efforts to isolate the Castro regime, but many may be unwilling to pay the cost of dealing with Cuba under its current government, especially in light of the recently passed Helms-Burton Bill.

The increased need to work together for mutual benefit may be sufficient incentive for the Caribbean states to make the concessions necessary to make the Association of Caribbean States work. If this is true, it will be a major contributor to Caribbean integration, and it will further the development of a sense of macro-scale regional identity among Caribbean territories. In the short run, this may be the most important contribution of the regional economic integration movement.

Conclusions

The Caribbean has long been identified as a fragmented, diverse, and poorly integrated region that gained at least a part of its identity more because it was not part of Anglo America or Latin America than for any generally recognized shared regional characteristics. However, over the past few decades a growing sense of Caribbean regional identity has emerged. This sense of Caribbean identity is strongest at the meso-scale, among countries that share common colonial experiences. That is, there is a stronger common identification among the former British colonies or Spanish colonies than there is across these different groups. Caribbean identity, especially among former British colonies, extends beyond the Antillean core to include fringe areas on the mainland and non-Caribbean islands that share elements of Caribbean colonial history and modern economy. Thus, the Guianas, Belize, and the Bahamas share the meso-scale regional identity, even though they are not Antillean in location. Among former Spanish colonies on the periphery, Venezuela and Colombia have well-established Caribbean interests, albeit with equally strong links to Mexico, the Andes, and the Amazon as well. On the other hand, certain countries with Caribbean Sea locations such as Mexico and the Central American republics, are weakly identified with the region. This suggests that Caribbean regional identity is more tied to historic patterns that trace their origin to past political and economic linkages than it is to purely locational factors.

Beginning in the 1950s, several attempts were made within the Caribbean region to develop economic and political integration, with mixed success. The most recent of these initiatives is the Association of Caribbean States, formed in 1994. This organization is dedicated to promoting macro-scale cooperation, including states with strong regional identity as well as those that historically have had only weak links to the Caribbean. The initiative to develop the Association of Caribbean States is in part a response to the perception that Caribbean states will benefit from increased trade among themselves and from being able to confront competition from the European Community, NAFTA, and other emerging trade blocs as a group rather than individually or as members of smaller blocs such as CARICOM, CACM, or G-3.

If these regionwide efforts to develop economic integration and increased trade are successful, they will reinforce the existing macroscale sense of identity among states that already see themselves as Caribbean, and it will probably strengthen the relatively weak Caribbean identity of Mexico and Central American republics. And although it seems unlikely that any form of regionwide political integration will emerge in the foreseeable future, it does appear as if the Caribbean, with its vibrant· and attractive lifestyle, will continue to develop its unique identity as a recognized culture region of the Americas.

Notes

1. Sometimes the Caribbean merits a separate designation in regional textbooks, as in recently published works by Clawson (1997) and Blouet and Blouet (1997), both of which bear the title *Latin America and the Caribbean.*
2. It is worthy of note that Cartagena, on the Caribbean cost of Colombia and about 150 km west of García Marquéz's birthplace, hosts an annual Caribbean music festival that attracts entertainers and an audience from throughout the region.
3. The move for economic integration extended beyond the Caribbean to include most Latin American states by way of the Latin American Free Trade Association (see Elbow 1997).
4. Founding members of the Federation of the West Indies were Jamaica, Trinidad and Tobago, Barbados, Antigua-Barbuda, Dominica, Grenada, St. Kitts-Nevis, Anguilla, St. Lucia, and St. Vincent.
5. Significantly, the largest Spanish-speaking mainland states, Mexico, Colombia, and Venezuela, were excluded from the CBI. Later these states, especially Venezuela, were active promoters of the Association of Caribbean States.

References

Anderson, Thomas D. *Geopolitics of the Caribbean: Ministates in a Wider World.* New York: Praeger, 1984.
Augelli, John P. "The Rimland-Mainland Concept of Culture Areas in Middle

America." *Annals of the Association of American Geographers* 52 (1963): 119–129.

Bell-Villada, Gene. *García Márquez: The Man and His Work.* Chapel Hill: University of North Carolina Press, 1990.

Benítez Rojo, Antonio. *The Repeating Island.* Durham, N.C., and London: Duke University Press, 1992.

Blouet, Brian W., and Olwyn M. Blouet, eds. *Latin America and the Caribbean: A Systematic and Regional Survey.* 3d. ed. New York: John Wiley and Sons, 1997.

Boswell, Thomas, and Dennis Conway. *The Caribbean Islands: Endless Geographical Diversity.* New Brunswick, N.J.: Rutgers University Press, 1992.

Burghardt, Andrew F. "The Bases of Territorial Claims." *Geographical Review* 63 (1973): 225–245.

Central Intelligence Agency. *1996 World Factbook.* Washington, D.C.: Central Intelligence Agency, 1996.

Clawson, David L. *Latin America and the Caribbean: Lands and Peoples.* Dubuque, Ia.: William C. Brown, 1997.

Conkling, Edgar C. "Caribbean Basin Initiative: A Regional Solution for America's Threatened Enterprise?" *Focus* 37 (1987): 2–9.

Elbow, Gary S. "Regional Cooperation in the Caribbean: The Association of Caribbean States." *Journal of Geography* 96 (1997): 29–38.

Erisman, H. Michael. *Pursuing Postdependency Politics: South-South Relations in the Caribbean.* Boulder and London: Lynne Rienner, 1992.

———. "Evolving Cuban-CARICOM Relations: A Comparative Cost/Benefit Analysis." *New West Indian Guide/Nieuwe West-Indische Gids* 69 (1995): 45–66.

Grugel, Jean. *Politics and Development in the Caribbean Basin: Central America and the Caribbean in the New World Order.* Bloomington and Indianapolis: Indiana University Press, 1995.

Hulme, Peter. *Colonial Encounters: Europe and the Native Caribbean, 1492–1797.* London and New York: Methuen, 1986.

Inter-American Development Bank. *The Latin American and Caribbean Integration Process in 1992/1993.* Buenos Aires: Inter-American Development Bank/ Institute for Latin American Integration, 1994.

Jones, David R. W. "The Caribbean Coast of Central America: A Case of Multiple Fragmentation." *The Professional Geographer* 22 (1970): 260–266.

Knight, Franklin. *The Caribbean: The Genesis of a Fragmented Nationalism.* Rev. ed. New York and London: Oxford, 1990.

Lowenthal, David. *West Indian Societies.* New York, London, and Ontario: Oxford, 1972.

Mendoza, Plinio A. *El Olor de la Guayaba: Conversaciones con Gabriel García Márquez.* Barcelona: Bruguera, 1982.

Organization of American States, General Secretariat. *Convention Establishing the Association of Caribbean States.* OAS Foreign Trade Information System, 1995. [http://www.sice.oas.org/gen_coop/acstoc.html].

Richardson, Bonham. "Caribbean Migrations, 1838–1985." In F. W. Knight and C. A. Palmer, eds., *The Modern Caribbean.* Chapel Hill: The University of North Carolina Press, 1989, 203–223.

Sandner, Gerhard. *Zentralamerika und der Ferne Karibische Westen: Konjunkturen, Krisen und Conflikte 1503–1984.* Stuttgart: Franz Steiner Verlag, 1985.

Serbín, Andrés. *Caribbean Geopolitics: Toward Security Through Peace?* Boulder and London: Lynne Rienner, 1990.

———. "Towards an Association of Caribbean States: Raising Some Awkward Questions." *Journal of Interamerican Studies and World Affairs* 36 (1994): 61–90.

Taylor, Peter J. *Political Geography: World-Economy, Nation-State and Locality.* 3d ed. Essex, U.K.: Longman, 1993.

Walcott, Derek. *The Antilles: Fragments of Epic Memory.* New York: Farrar, Straus and Giroux, 1992.

Watts, David. *The West Indies: Patterns of Development, Culture and Environmental Changes since 1492.* Cambridge: Cambridge University Press, 1987.

Webb, Barbara J. *Myth and History in Caribbean Fiction.* Amherst: University of Massachusetts Press, 1992.

West, Robert C., and John P. Augelli. *Middle America: Its Lands and Peoples.* 3d ed. Englewood Cliffs, N.J.: Prentice Hall, 1987.

Williams Gary. "The Tail that Wagged the Dog: The Organisation of Eastern Caribbean States' Role in the 1983 Intervention in Grenada." *European Review of Latin American and Caribbean Studies* 61 (1996): 95–115.

5

Reimagining the Russian Idea

Nicholas J. Lynn and Valentin Bogorov

The former Soviet republics have all faced great difficulties in building stable, peaceful, and democratic states. Domestic political competition has often been divisive and violent, couched in terms of personalities and events. The management of economic reform has led to deepening uneven development, widespread impoverishment and the intensification of internal social divisions. The fragility of the new states has been further highlighted by their immersion within the global economy (subject to the influence of powerful international financial institutions and multinational companies) and also by the scale of the environmental problems left over from the Soviet period.

Particular difficulties have been faced by the largest successor country, Russia, which stretches from the Baltic (Kaliningrad) to the Pacific and from the Arctic to Central Asia, and has more than one hundred different nationalities residing within its boundaries, some living in "sovereign" national homelands. At the same time, more than 20 million ethnic Russians are now living outside the territory of the Russian Federation, in the other newly independent states. In response to these difficulties, political and intellectual elites have called for the reconstruction of a distinct "Russian idea" that will pull the country together territorially, socially, culturally, and morally. After winning his second presidential election in July 1996, the Russian president Boris Yeltsin fueled the debates by appointing one of his presidential aides to investigate the problem of Russia's missing national state idea (see Chinyaeva 1997).

State ideas have had an important influence on geographical accounts of modern political systems. Functional approaches to political geography, for example, emphasize the fundamental importance of state ideas for binding states together. Every state is said to require a basic raison d'être that is strong enough to counteract the centrifugal pull of regional inequality and diversity (see Hartshorne 1950). The problem with this kind of approach, however, is that it emphasizes the importance of the territorial organization of the state without consider- ing the social context within which states exist. In particular, it assumes that the state simply operates by and for itself, rather than recognizing that state formation is a process of social conflict and competition be- tween groups (Johnston 1982).

More critical readings have highlighted the need to focus on the so- cial construction of national and state identities. Gertjan Dijkink (1996), for example, stresses the importance of identifying the "geopolitical visions" of national groups: ideas concerning the relation between their own and Other places, feelings of insecurity or disadvantage, and notions of a collective mission. Such geopolitical visions require the construction of a "them and us" distinction and an emotional attach- ment to a sense of place. They incorporate a whole range of spatial and territorial symbols and signs: natural borders, core areas, geopolitical codes, and so on.

It is the aim of this chapter to develop a critical reading of the re- imagining of the Russian idea that has taken place since 1991. This analysis identifies the significance of territory and scale in the construc- tion of several competing Russian geopolitical visions, and it highlights the way in which all of these ideas have struggled to gain a footing during a period of chaotic systemic transition and during an apparent ideological vacuum in Russian politics. Anthony Smith (1995) de- scribes nation building as a process akin to archaeology in the way that particular historical artifacts are pieced together in order to construct a specific national history. This chapter examines how age-old debates in Russia over both its territorial structure and its Eurasian geopolitical "destiny" have been revisited in the post-Soviet scene. In coming to terms with the state's new political and territorial boundaries, several macro-scale visions of the Russian idea have been constructed by a range of different groups.

The Russian Question

In his recent assessment of three hundred years of Russian history Aleksander Solzhenitsyn (1995) focuses on the problem of "the Rus- sian question," by which he means the debate over the use of the terms *russkiy* and *rossiiskiy*. Both of them are normally translated into English as *Russian*, however, more accurately, the former refers to Russian lan-

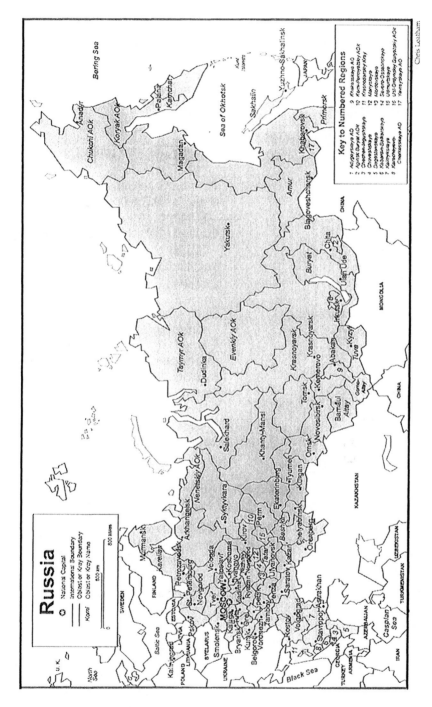

▶──◀

RUSSIA—THE RUSSIAN FEDERATION

Territory	17,075 (thousand square kilometers)
Population (1996)	148 million [27% rural and 73% urban]
Population growth rate (1995)	−5.7%
Ethno-demographic composition	Russians 81.5% (1989) and 82.9% (1994)
	Tatar 3.8% (1989) and 3.8% (1994)
	Ukrainian 3.0% (1989) and 2.3% (1994)
	Chuvash 1.2% (1989) and 1.2% (1994)
	Bashkir 0.9% (1989) and 0.9% (1994)
Administrative-territorial composition	21 republics (incl. Chechnya-Ichkeria)
	6 *krays*
	49 oblasts
	1 autonomous oblast
	10 autonomous *okrugs*
	2 "federal cities" (Moscow and St. Petersburg)
	1,868 *rayons*

THE ETHNO-DEMOGRAPHIC COMPOSITION
OF THE REPUBLICS

Republic	Total Population in 1989	Titular Share of Population in 1989	Titular Share of Population in 1994
Karelia	790,150	10.0	10.8
Komi	1,250,847	23.3	26.3
Mari-El	749,332	43.3	40.1
Chuvashia	1,338,023	67.8	68.8
Kalmykia (Khalmg Tangch)	322,579	45.4	52.6
Tatarstan	3,641,742	48.5	48.1
Adygeya	432,046	22.1	25.2

Dagestan	1,802,188	72.4	75.1
Kabardino-Balkaria	753,531	57.6	58.1
Karachay- Cherkessia	414,970	40.9	44.7
North Ossetia	632,428	53.0	59.3
Chechnya and Ingushetia	1,270,429	70.7	99.4
Bashkortostan	3,943,113	21.9	22.9
Udmurtia	160,566	30.9	31.3
Altay	190,831	31.0	30.6
Buryatia	1,038,252	24.0	28.6
Tyva	308,557	64.3	65.6
Khakassia	566,861	11.1	9.8
Sakha (Yakutia)	1,094,065	33.4	39.6
Mordovia	963,504	32.5	30.6

NOTE: Where more than one titular nationality is included in the republican name, the total of both nationalities (combined) is used. Titular nationality in Dagestan includes Avar, Dargin, Kumykh, Lezgin, and Lak.

REGIONAL CONFLICTS AND MOVEMENTS

Russia—The Russian Federation is the largest and the most populous of the post-Soviet states. It is also the most multinational in that, although ethnic Russians compose more than 80 percent of the total population, the last census recorded over 100 different nationalities resident in the Russian Federation.

Since the collapse of the USSR, Russia has been embarked on a "triple transition" as it attempts to dismantle the Soviet system of administrative command and establish new mechanisms for economic management, political control, and social provision. This has been a comprehensive process of systemic change, which politically, at least, has been characterized by uncertainty, volatility, and conflict.

The most serious conflicts have arisen in the North Caucasus, because of disputes over national and cultural rights as well as the control and ownership of land and resources. The most serious disputes have arisen between Ossetians and Ingush and between Abkhaz and Georgians. In the winter of 1994 the Russian army began an unsuccessful two-year bloody campaign in Chechnya-Ichkeria against "separatist rule." In the 1996 peace treaty Russia agreed to postpone any decision on Chechnya-Ichkeria's territorial status until the new millennium.

Elsewhere, Russia has continued to dispute ownership of the Kurile Islands/Northern Territories with Japan, islands the Red Army seized at the end of World War II. The Russian army has also acted in a "peace-keeping role" in several conflicts in other countries that belong to the Commonwealth of Independent States (Russia's self-declared "near abroad"), including Georgia, Moldova, and Azerbaijan.

More generally, Russia has recently tried to reestablish closer economic and political ties with several of the other post-Soviet states. In 1996 Russia signed a provisional treaty of union with Belarus as well as a quadripartite treaty with Belarus, Kazakhstan, and Kyrgyzystan over closer cooperation, especially in the economic sphere.

Sources: Goskomstat RSFSR. *Natsional'ny sostav naseleniya RSFSR* (Moscow), 1990. Goskomstat Rossii. *Raspredelenie naseleniya Rossii po vladeniyu yazykami* (Moscow), 1995. United Nations. *Human Development under Transition: Europe and CIS* (New York), 1997.

▶━━━━━━━━━━━━━━━━━━━━━━━━━━━━━━━━━━━━◀

guage and ethnicity and the latter to the Russian state and territorial Russia (*Rossiya*). Russkiy has a emotional and popular appeal, rossiiskiy has broader and more official connotations. For Solzhenitsyn such terminological distinctions epitomize the deep ambivalence that exists in modern Russian identities.

When labels are used to include persons in Russian homeland claims, moreover, the linguistic confusion increases. Rogers Brubaker (1996) recognizes five different identifiers: (1) *russkie,* which refers to a Russian ethno-cultural nationality; (2) *rossianie,* which interprets Russianness as an affiliation with the Russian state and territory; (3) *russkoizychnye,* which refers to Russian speakers and specifically those who use Russian as their primary language; (4) *sootchestvenniki,* meaning compatriots and which is often applied to people in the former USSR who consider themselves to have cultural ties with Russia; and (5) *grazhdane,* meaning citizen, which can also be used loosely to include all former Soviet citizens.

The complexity and ambiguity of this vocabulary demonstrates the way in which jurisdictional claims of Russianness overlap and compete in the popular consciousness. It illustrates the lack of an agreed-upon Russian idea and highlights the problems faced in constructing a new post-Soviet Russian identity. There is no agreement over who is a Russian or where the territorial limits of the Russian state should be (Beissinger 1995).

The historical reasons for the uncertainty of the Russian question are complex (see Shaw 1997). Unlike the empires of West European powers, the Russian empire expanded contiguously, which led to an ambiguous relationship between core and periphery. The process of imperial enlargement was evolutionary and gradual, many different ethnic groups were conquered and "assimilated," and it needed the conquest of Siberia to provide a non-European geographical Other for the westernization of the "European Russia" core (Bassin 1991). Moreover, imperial expansion was legitimized not only economically but also in terms of a religious mission to preserve and consolidate the center of orthodoxy. The religious project further confused the relationship between Russians and the czars' holy empire.

In a similar vein, although the USSR has often been called an empire in the West, that description requires a great deal of qualification. In particular, if the USSR was an empire, then who was it run by, and for whom? Certainly there was an ambiguous relationship between Russian and Soviet power. It may be possible to identify similarities between the Soviet Union and the Russian empire in terms of territorial extent, linguistic and cultural Russification, a tradition of absolutism and state sponsored colonization, but there were fundamental differences between the two, especially in the way they were structured territorially and administratively. Crucially, the Soviet Union gave some non-Russian groups the symbolic appearance of institutions of self-government through the establishment of a pseudo-federal system (see Kaiser 1994). The Soviet Union was structured in terms of a national-territorial principle with a hierarchy of different administrative-territorial units (see Figure 5.1), even though in reality republican autonomy was extremely limited; throughout the Soviet period the Communist Party headed a massive bureaucracy that centralized administrative and coercive power.

In national terms, the Russians had an ambiguous relationship with the Soviet state, therefore the Russian Soviet Federative Socialist Republic (RSFSR) lacked many of the symbolic national state institutions that other republics had. There was no specifically Russian Communist Party; for example, Russians belonged to the Communist Party of the Soviet Union (CPSU). There was no specifically Russian trade union organization or academy of sciences—as there were in the other Soviet republics—and these were the kinds of institutions that were important in codifying official notions of national identity in the USSR (see Suny 1993). Moreover, Geoffrey Hosking (1990) distinguishes between the assimilatory policies of the czarist and Soviet empires. In the USSR the dominant process was Sovietization rather than Russification, which involved subjecting all nationalities (including the Russians) to the centralized political control of the Communist Party and to the economic domination of the central planning apparatus.

Jonathan Steele (1994: 162) is one of several writers to have identified the imperial paradox that lay at the heart of the Soviet Union. "By the end of the 1980s, the Soviet Union, itself a continuation of the tsarist

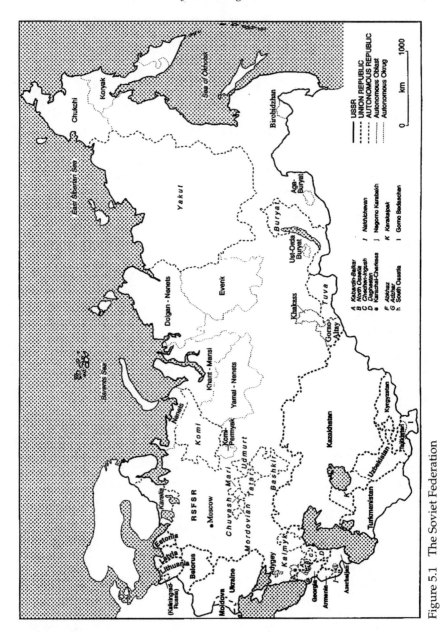

Figure 5.1 The Soviet Federation

empire, was the longest surviving European empire. But the Russians did not perceive it as that. They felt the Soviet Union was genuinely an international family. Because it was a continuous land mass with no customs posts or border controls, it felt like a single harmonious country. Russians saw no sign of the resentment and tension which non-Russians felt towards them."

The Russian polling center VTSIOM conducted a study of national identities in all of the constituent republics of the USSR in 1989, which provides an interesting insight into Russian national consciousness in the late Soviet period (see Levada 1993). Characteristically, Russians in 1989 very strongly identified themselves with a sense of belonging to the Soviet Union as a whole, rather than to the RSFSR (their "own" Soviet republic). The great majority of the Russian respondents designated the USSR as a whole, rather than the RSFSR, as their "motherland" (*rodina*), and asked whether they considered themselves to be primarily citizens of the USSR as a whole or citizens of the RSFSR in particular, the Russian respondents overwhelmingly identified themselves with the USSR as a whole. This differed sharply with the attitudes of respondents in the other Soviet republics for whom their territorial homelands had come to frame self-determination claims.

This macro-scale identity has been hard for many Russians to shake off in the post-Soviet scene. One response has been to attempt to re-imagine Russian identity within a discourse that celebrates Russia's hegemonic position in the heartland of Eurasia. This particular geopolitical vision has been used to reaffirm Russian influence over the other newly independent states—the countries Russian politicians refer to as "their near abroad."

Russia and Eurasia: The Politics of Heartland

Some groups in the post-Soviet scene have tried to reframe the Russian idea in terms of an identity that is "supranational" in extent. In this way Russianness is interpreted in terms of relatively broad definitions of civilization, historic power, and spiritual heritage, rather than ethnocultural definitions of nationhood. Russians are said to lack any strong sense of internal ethnic solidarity although Russianness is intrinsically tied to notions of space (*prostranstvo*) and nature (see Dugin 1994). This kind of interpretation reveals a desire for reintegration between former Soviet republics, in order to reaffirm Russia's self-association with empire. The reestablishment of some kind of "super-state" is not so much driven by the search for colonies to exploit or even in terms of a boost to Russia's geopolitical status, although that would be welcomed, but for the preservation of what is interpreted to be the Russian imperial state identity.

However, a key problem for this kind of approach is the lack of any effective ideological basis for the reestablishment of a new "supranational" state. Whereas monarchy and religion were the ideological cornerstones of the czarist empire and Marxism-Leninism was the official ideology of the Soviet Union, it is unclear what could provide the foundation for a new Russian imperial identity. The solution for those groups that have sought to reframe the Russian idea in terms of empire is said to lie in reexploring the concept of Eurasianism.

Eurasianism is a philosophy that emerged in the work of a group of Russian émigrés in the 1920s, who maintained that the Eastern Slavs and their non-Slavic neighbors who inhabit the steppes belong to a distinct Eurasian cultural realm, which is fundamentally different from both Europe and Asia. Many of the Eurasianists were deeply influenced by the concepts of environmental determinism, which was popular at the time (Bassin 1991). They believed that the natural features of the Eurasian landmass, such as vast open expanses, the absence of physical boundaries, the continentality of climate, and so on, exercised crucial influence on the development of a Eurasian culture. Although not refuting altogether the benefits of Russia's historical ties with Europe, the Eurasianists believed that Russia's "historical destiny" remained in the East, especially in uniting the peoples of Eurasia under its control. Despite their early anti-Bolshevism, many of the Eurasianists ultimately came to support the Soviet Union as a vehicle for realizing their dreams of a Eurasian commonwealth headed by Russia.

In the post-Soviet scene a new Eurasianism has emerged, most clearly in some aspects of Russian foreign policy. This new philosophy emphasizes the importance of Asia for both Russia's internal political stability as well as for its economic development, given that the Asian Pacific region is one of the most dynamic in the world economy (Kerr 1995). The new Eurasianism is an attempt to come to terms with Russia's new territorial boundaries (those of the former RSFSR rather than the USSR) and in particular, the narrowing of Russia's "routes to the sea to the west and south" and perceptions of its "shift away from Europe" as it is now a "separated country" (Bykov 1992).

Despite the appeal of the new Eurasianism, the predominant cultural orientation of Russians (and especially intellectuals) remains toward Europe, and this is reflected in Russian foreign policy as well as in other areas. Most people in Russia remain deeply skeptical about the political and cultural (if not the economic) consequences of defining Russia as a Eurasian rather than a European power (Kerr 1995). One place where Eurasianism does seem to have had an important impact, however, is on the reformed Communist Party of the Russian Federation (CPRF) led by Gennady Zyuganov. The CPRF was the major winner in the 1995 parliamentary elections, electing the largest fraction (more than one-third) of deputies to the Duma (receiving 22 percent of the vote in terms of candidates on the party list) and Gennady Zyuganov himself was Boris Yeltsin's major contender in the 1996 presidential elections (receiving 40 percent of the vote in the second round against Boris Yeltsin's 53 percent). The CPRF presents itself as the successor to the CPSU and capitalizes on widespread feelings of Soviet nostalgia among the vast strata of the Russian population that has been disoriented and impoverished by shock reform.

The CPRF under Zyuganov has detached itself from much of the ideological basis of Marxism-Leninism. Rather than talk about "scientific communism," Zyuganov (1995) talks about "scientific geopolitics." The major conflicts in the modern world are no longer said to be driven by class divisions but relate to fundamental competition between civilizations. Zyuganov characterizes the idea of Russia as "A special type of civilization, heir and successor to the millennium-old traditions of Kievan Rus, Muscovy, the Russian Empire and the USSR. From a geopolitical viewpoint Russia is the core and the major pillar of the Eurasian continental bloc, the interests of which run counter to the hegemonic tendencies of the 'sea power' of the United States and the Atlantic 'geopolitical space'. In national terms, Russia is a complex ethnic community based on the national core of Russians, Ukrainians and Belarussians" (Zyuganov 1995: 20).

Zyuganov thus makes reference to the sea power that is an essential ingredient of Halford Mackinder's (1919) heartland theory of geopolitics. This is some testimony to the continued prevalence of Mackinder's work, which remains probably the best known geographical model in the world, but it also reveals how the new Eurasianist discourse is couched within a familiar context of "geopolitical realities": pivot areas, world islands, and so on (see Hauner 1990). It also highlights what Gertjan Dijkink (1996) has called Russia's Eurasian imperative. That is, the opinion in Russia that in order to maintain its Great Power status it must occupy an autonomous intermediate position between Europe and Asia. Russia's place within the heartland of Eurasia is seen to provide it with a unique opportunity to reconstruct Russian identity by synthesizing both European and Asian traits.

Competing Geopolitical Visions in Russia

As well as Eurasianism, other models have been proposed for coming to terms with Russia's imperial past and its position vis-à-vis both Asia

and Europe. Competition between these different visions was especially evident in 1992 and 1993, a period characterized by intense political conflict. In particular, the political situation became polarized
around two key disputes: (1) arguments over the kind of state system
that should be constructed (especially questions relating to the establishment of a presidential or a parliamentary system and problems resulting from continued fragmentation and disintegration); and (2) conflicts between the center, the regions, and the republics over political
and economic authority in the Russian Federation (especially during
the drafting of the 1992 Federation Treaty and the 1993 constitution).
In both of these areas of conflict, it is possible to identify the relative
influence of competing models of the Russian idea.

Restructuring the State

Russia has faced specific difficulties in state restructuring because of
problems inherited from the USSR. In particular, a legacy of intense
"stateness" (the complex and contradictory relationship between state
and nation determined in the Soviet Union) has led to the privileging
of liberalization and independence over democratization in the post-
Communist scene (Linz and Stepan 1996). These difficulties also reflect
the influence of new statist movements in Russian politics. A number
of powerful political actors, including (at various moments) the former
Russian vice president Alexander Rutskoi, the speaker of the Supreme
Soviet Ruslan Khasbulatov, and the Russian prime minister Viktor
Chernomyrdin, have supported the establishment of strong central authority and demanded an assertive foreign policy with respect to both
the other former Soviet republics and the West.

Richard Sakwa (1996) identifies two influential statist movements
(*gosudarstvenniki*) in Russia. First, there are the national patriots who
stress the importance of reconstructing Russia's Great Power status (a
group loosely dubbed *derzhavniki*). Although they have much in common with Eurasianists, they focus particularly on rebuilding Russia's
military potential (mainly through revitalizing the military defense
complex). Moreover, their image of Eurasia is predicated on the belief
that Europe is morally inferior, rather than equal or even superior, to
Russia (Neumann 1996). The *derzhavniki* believe Russia should inherit
the international standing and the military superpower status of the
USSR, and the idea of Russia is equated with the global influence of
the Soviet empire. These groups largely comprise former Communists
and the former economic managerial elite, although they make up a
diffuse range of centrist and populist movements.

A second group of statists are Russian romantic-nationalists (conservatives who mainly emphasize the importance of building an ethnic Russian nation-state). Historically, they see imperialism as having "diluted" and "over-burdened" Russia's national base, and they blame Russia's continued demise on the West and certain groups (mainly Jews) within Russia. In particular, they focus on the effects of shock reform, which is seen as an attempt by the West at turning Russia into a dependent resource colony. Typified by the rhetoric of the leader of the "Liberal Democratic Party" (LDP) Vladimir Zhirinovsky, Russian nationalism has been characterized by xenophobia and racism. Zhirinovsky (most clearly in his 1993 autobiography) has constructed a distinctive geopolitical vision, which imagines Russia's future within "the South" (rather than "the East") and in direct opposition to the United States (the center of "the North"). However, Zhirinovsky's vision is as much about laying political claim to as many rival nationalist movements as possible, as about developing a single cohesive philosophy.

The LDP gained significant electoral support in the 1993 and 1995 Duma elections (in 1993 they won 23 percent of the vote in terms of candidates on the party lists and in 1995 they won 11 percent), and Zhirinovsky himself came in third in the first round of the 1996 presidential election (although with only 6 percent of the vote). The LDP has fared particularly well in the regions that have been hit hardest by the central government's reforms, like the Far East where in 1993 it gained the largest share of the vote in every administrative district. However, Russian romantic-nationalism has generally failed to gain a real foothold in the Russian political scene. Its role has been to reflect disenchantment with the economic problems caused by reform and also the rejection of the idea of democracy as it has been constructed in Russia since 1991.

Opposed to the nationalism of the *gosudarstvenniki*, some liberal and democratic politicians have proposed an Atlanticist model of the Russian idea. Atlanticism implies both a commitment to closer relations with the West and a desire for greater integration into the world economy. As such, it marks a break from Russian claims for distinctiveness, arguing instead that Russia should develop "in the Western tradition" (Sakwa 1996). In his early period in the foreign ministry, Andrei Kozyrev tried to adopt an Atlanticist line. The developed countries of the West were seen as Russia's "natural allies," and Russia was said to be a "returning European civilization." Rather than aspiring to superpower status, Russia needed to become comfortable with its postimperial identity as a "normal great power" (Kozyrev, quoted in Neumann 1996: 181–182). However, the influence of the Atlanticist model on foreign policy was brief and limited (see Malcolm 1994). Typically, Kozyrev was forced to resign as foreign minister in 1996, as policy became increasingly conservative. Although Mikhail Gorbachev and even Boris Yeltsin had talked of Russia's place within a "common European home," the new policy position became increasingly "restorationist": "Russia," it was said, "needed to get its own home in order first" (Borko 1993).

Refederalizing Russia

One important consequence of the influence of Eurasianism and statism in reconstructing Russian identity is a heightened vigilance against centrifugal forces both between the countries of the Commonwealth of Independent States (most of the former Soviet republics) as well as within the Russian Federation itself. The former has largely been achieved through the establishment of a Russian "Monroe Doctrine" (see Galeotti 1995). However, the fight against internal separatism within Russia is seen by many groups to be made more difficult because of the ethno-federal hierarchy inherited from the RSFSR.

Soviet federalism was based on a national-territorial principle that recognized some national groups' territorially based claims to political recognition. Although in reality this principle was little more than rhetoric, a conception of national statehood was made the foundation of the federal system in the Soviet Union. The Russian Federation (the former RSFSR) has inherited this national-territorial principle, which continues to impose institutional limits on the process of establishing new center-periphery relations. Issues surrounding how to deal with this legacy have been central to the reimagining of the Russian state idea since 1991 (see G. Smith 1996).

According to the 1992 Federation Treaty and the 1993 constitution, Russia comprises eighty-nine different administrative units (see Figure 5.2). There are twenty-one republics made up of the former autonomous republics and all of the former autonomous oblasts of the RSFSR (except the "Jewish" autonomous oblast in Siberia). There are also eleven autonomous "formations" in the Russian Federation (the Jewish autonomous oblast and the ten smaller nationality districts [okrugs] of the RSFSR) that signed a separate Federation Treaty in March 1992 to that of the republics. These autonomous formations are administered as distinctive parts of the remaining fifty-seven regions of the Russian Federation—the "regular" Russian oblasts and krays (provinces), which include the two city "regions" of Moscow and St. Petersburg. The oblasts and krays also signed a separate federation treaty in March 1992, thereby reinforcing the differences among the levels of the federal hierarchy of the Russian Federation (see Il'inskiy et al. 1992).

The present structure of the Russian Federation is not simply an in-

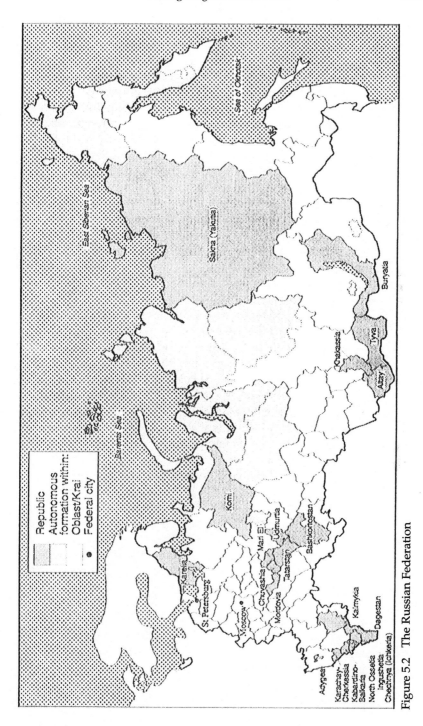

Figure 5.2 The Russian Federation

herited institutional form, it is also the result of a process of negotiation and debate among Moscow, the republics, and the regions (see Solnick 1995). The central argument has been over the basic principle that should underpin the organization of federation in Russia, and in particular two competing federal models have been proposed.

The first of these models envisages a strictly spatial division of power, which can be achieved by either a fundamental reorganization of the administrative-territorial composition of Russia into a smaller number of larger regions, or an equalization of the constitutional rights of the existing eighty-nine units. One of the best-known plans for reorganizing the Russian Federation into territorial units was Oleg Rumyantsev's 1990 proposal for establishing twenty regions (*zemli*) on the lines of the Länders of the Federal Republic of Germany (*Izvestiya* September 2, 1990). (Oleg Rumyantsev was the secretary of the Constitutional Commission of the Supreme Soviet of the Russian Federation, and his ideas had a wide influence.)

Early constitutional drafts were strongly influenced by liberal writers (like the former dissident Andrei Sakharov) and by ideas about federal evolution in the West. In particular, many proponents of a territorial principle looked to the United States as a model of successful federalism. The redrawing of the Russian idea was framed in terms of international experience, and Russia, like the United States, was said to need a constitution that guaranteed basic individual rights and freedom (Rumyantsev 1995). Many writers also adopted an economic approach to refederalization, according to which restructuring provides a number of advantages for the whole country: the advantages that result from a larger market and from the removal of tariffs and barriers to trade (see Zlotnik 1993).

In national terms, this approach seeks to establish a principle of "democratic cocitizenship" as the political basis for federation in Russia: That state building should involve a gradual depoliticization of interethnic relations and the promotion of a plural and "multileveled" civic identity (Tishkov 1995; see also Abdulatipov 1992). By embracing the concept of territorial reorganization it can also support the reconstruction of a macro-scale vision of the Russian idea, including reintegration among the newly independent countries of Russia, Belarus, and Ukraine.

The second model of Russian federalism proposes maintaining and even reinforcing the asymmetry of the national-territorial principle inherited from the RSFSR. According to this perspective national territoriality actually helps to preserve stability by granting non-Russian populations the right to some kind of statehood within the federation. Proponents of this view, which include most of the republican leaders, argue that the "titular" nationalities of the republics (and also the okrugs) have a right to their "own" national territory and that you cannot simply try to ignore the structures that have been in place for the last seventy years.

Rafael Khakimov (an adviser to President Mintimer Shaymiev of the Republic of Tatarstan), for example, vigorously opposed the moves that were made during the drafting of the 1993 constitution toward equalization—in his words, "towards limiting the republics' sovereignty" (*Nezavisimaya gazeta* June 24, 1993). Khakimov's approach stands in direct opposition to the center's proposals for restructuring state power in Russia. "It is not the federal government that should determine the powers of the members, on the contrary, the members should decide what kind of government should be formed and what kinds of functions and powers it should be given" (*Nezavisimaya gazeta*, June 24, 1993).

In this way Russia is seen as a smaller territorial version of the USSR, with a large number of minority national groups fighting against "assimilation" by the dominant ethnic Russians. This approach is far less comfortable with the idea of a macro-scale Russian idea, arguing instead that Russia needs to come to terms with its new boundaries and its new ethno-demographic composition. Rather than reintegration, either within the Russian Federation or among the countries of the CIS, proponents of the second model would like to see greater devolution and more regional self-government.

At the heart of the problem of reconstructing a Russian idea, therefore, lies a fundamental debate over the territorial administrative structure of the federal state. The Russian Federation has inherited a distinctive internal territorial arrangement, composed of a variety of different types of units that have different levels of political authority at a range of scales. The foundation for this structure is a national-territorial principle first established by Lenin and the Bolsheviks in the 1920s. However in the post-Soviet scene, this principle has had the effect of legitimizing non-Russian (republican) voices that are strongly opposed to both the idea of constructing an ethnically based Russian nation state and the idea of recreating any kind of new Russian empire.

Conclusion: Nation Building and State Formation During Systemic Transition

Sytemic transition may appear to provide the conditions (rising inequality, social exclusion, alienation and lawlessness, etc.) within which extreme nationalist movements could potentially mobilize large sections of the population. However at the moment in Russia, imperial-ist, Eurasianist, and nationalist movements are actually quite small in number. Moreover they are politically diffuse, comprising a whole range of small and largely ineffective marginalized organizations (see *Transition: A Special Edition on Extremism in Russia* June 23, 1995; and Laqeur 1993). Only the "Liberal Democratic Party" and the CPRF really have an effective infrastructure established across the Russian Federation. But in both these cases their leaders have surprised West-ern observers by their preparedness to be pragmatic and cooperative with the central authorities in government.

The general lack of popular support for these types of organizations reflects the fact that ordinary Russians have to a large extent lost any belief they may once have had in grand ideology and utopianism. Any awareness of common national goals or unifying political programs has become extremely faded. In fact opinion poll research has shown that there are hardly any positive ideas capable of mobilizing a large proportion of the Russian population (Miller et al. 1995). Most observ-ers have referred to this state of affairs as an "ideological vacuum" in Russia's post-Soviet society.

According to Peter Rutland (1997) the political situation in Russia has been restructured in terms of access to power (pragmatism) rather than ideology. The political game consists of espousing whatever is the political flavor of the month in order to maneuver oneself closer to the center of power. Although ideological conflict no longer provides the fault line for Russian politics, events are increasingly polarized around individual personalities and particular themes.

It is within this context of social upheaval, political uncertainty, and ideological vacuum that any attempt at reimagining the Russian idea must be seen. In searching for concepts capable of mobilizing the mass of the population, political and intellectual elites have been largely in-effectual in terms of their reexploration of past debates on Eurasianism and new ideas on territorial restructuring. Boris Yeltsin may regret the absence of any unifying national mission in Russia, but most people at the present time seem to believe that the reinvention of a Russian idea should take place in a gradual, evolutionary, and above all peaceful manner. In analytical terms, the process of reimagining demonstrates the extent to which territory and scale provide the bases for a number of competing and distinct geopolitical visions of Russia at the end of the twentieth century.

References

Abdulatipov, R. G. "Federativnyy Dogovor. Dokumenty." *Kommentariy*. Mos-cow: Izdanie Verkhovnogo Soveta Rossiyskoy Federatsii, 1992.

Bassin, M. "Russia between Europe and Asia: The Ideological Construction of Geographical Space." *Slavic Review* 50 (1991): 1–17.

Beissinger, M. "The Persisting Ambiguity of Empire." *Post-Soviet Affairs* 11 (1995): 149–184.

Borko, Yu. "O Nekotorykh Aspektakh Izucheniya Protsessiv Zapadnoevropeyskoy Integratsii." *Mirovaya ekonomika I mezhdurnarodnye otnosheniya* 32 (1993): 35–50.

Brubaker, R. *Nationalism Reframed: Nationhood and the National Question in the New Europe.* Cambridge: Cambridge University Press, 1996.

Bykov, A. "Rossiya, SNG, Evraziya: Geopoliticheskie Aspekty Vneshneekonomicheskikh Svyazei." *Vneshnyaya Torgovlya* 11 (1992): 3–10.

Chinyaeva, E. "The Search for the 'Russian Idea.' " *Transitions* 4 (1997): 40–46.

Dijkink, G. *National Identity and Geopolitical Visions: Maps of Pride and Pain.* London: Routledge, 1996.

Dugin, A. *Konservativnaya Revolutsia.* Moscow: AKIRN, 1994.

Galeotti, M. *The Age of Anxiety: Security and Politics in Soviet and Post-Soviet Russia.* London: Longman, 1995.

Hartshorne, R. "The Functional Approach in Political Geography." *Annals of the Association of American Geographers* 40 (1950): 95–130.

Hauner, M. *What Is Asia to Us? Russia's Asian Heartland Yesterday and Today.* London: Routledge, 1990.

Hosking, G. *A History of the Soviet Union.* Rev. ed. London: Fontana, 1990.

Il'inskiy, I. P., B. S. Krylova, and N. A. Mikhaleva. "Novoe Federativnoe Ustroystvo Rossii." *Gosudarstvo i pravo* 11 (1992): 29–37.

Johnston, R. J. *Geography and the State: An Essay in Political Geography.* London: MacMillan, 1982.

Kaiser, R. *The Geography of Nationalism in Russia and the USSR.* Princeton, N.J.: Princeton University Press, 1994.

Kerr, D. "The New Eurasianism: The Rise of Geopolitics in Russia's Foreign Policy." *Europe-Asia Studies* 47 (1995): 977–988.

Laqeur, W. *Black Hundred: The Rise of the Extreme Right in Russia.* New York: Harper Perennial, 1993.

Levada, Yu A., ed. *Sovetskii Prostoi Chelovek: Opyt Sotsial'nogo Portreta na Rubezhe 90-kh Moscow.* Moscow: VTSIOM, 1993.

Linz, J., and A. Stepan. *Problems of Democratic Transition and Consolidation.* Baltimore, Md.: Johns Hopkins University Press, 1996.

Mackinder, H. *Democratic Ideals and Reality.* London: Constable, 1919.

Malcolm, N., ed. *Russia and Europe: An End to Confrontation?* London: Royal Institute of International Affairs, 1994.

Miller, A., V. Hesli, and W. Reissinger. "Comparing Citizen and Elite Belief Systems in Post-Soviet Russia and Ukraine." *Public Opinion Quarterly* 59 (1995): 1–40.

Neumann, I. *Russia and the Idea of Europe.* London: Routledge, 1996.

Rumyantsev, O. G. "The Present and Future of Russian Constitutional Order." *The Harriman Review* 8 (1995): 21–35.

Rutland, P. "Russia's Broken 'Wheel of Ideologies.' " *Transitions* 4 (1997): 47–55.

Sakwa, R. *Russian Politics and Society*. 2d ed. London: Routledge, 1996.

Shaw, D. "Geopolitics, History, and Russian National Identity." In M. Bradshaw, ed., *Geography and Transition in the Post-Soviet Republics*. London: Wiley, 1997, 31–42.

Smith, A. D. "Gastronomy or Geology?—The Role of Nationalism in the Reconstruction of Nations." *Nations and Nationalism* 1 (1995): 3–24.

Smith, G. E. "Russia, Ethno-Regionalism and the Politics of Federation." *Ethnic and Racial Studies* 19 (1996): 391–410.

Solnick, S. "Federal Bargaining in Russia." *East European Constitutional Review* Fall (1995): 52–58.

Solzhenitsyn, A. *The Russian Question at the End of the Twentieth Century*. London: Harvill, 1995.

Steele, J. *Eternal Russia: Yeltsin, Gorbachev and the Mirage of Democracy*. London: Faber and Faber, 1994.

Suny, R. G. *The Revenge of the Past: Nationalism, Revolution and the Collapse of the Soviet Union*. Stanford: Stanford University Press, 1993.

Tishkov, V. "Rossiya: Ot Mezhetnicheskikh Konfliktov k Vzaimoponimaniyu." *Etnopolis* 8 (1995): 36–51.

Zhirinovsky, V. W. (1993). *Posledniy Brosok na Yug*. Moscow: LDP.

Zlotnik, M. "Vliyanie Regional'nykh Faktorov na Razvitie Rossiyskoy Federatsii." In The Heritage Foundation, ed., *Federalizm, Regionanlizm i Konstitutsionnaya Reforma v Rossii*. Washington, D.C.: The Heritage Foundation, 1993.

Zyuganov, G. A. *Rossia i Sovremennyi Mir*. Moscow: Obozrevatel, 1995.

Part III

Meso-Scale

The term *meso-scale* is problematic, because it spans a wide range of intermediate identities between the micro and the macro. Despite this, we feel that meso-scale has real relevance in two senses. First, as a scale that in some way balances off identities at higher and lower levels, and second, as a scale that approximates the geographic extent of the state and the scale at which dominant national identities may or may not develop. It is this second sense with which we categorized the chapters in this section.

Jouni Häkli's chapter analyzes Finnish national identity from the vantage point of what he terms *discursive landscapes*, which represent the material and abstract signification of a region as national territory. He explores this meso-scale identity by comparison with the smaller Swedish-speaking and Sami minorities that have contested the creation of the Finnish national image.

Tim Unwin traces the origins of Estonian national identity to an intimate relationship with nature and a rural way of life that emerged in the nineteenth century. For most of its history, the Estonian nation was dominated by others but managed to preserve its unique identity. Unwin shows that the nation still faces challenges since it became independent in early 1990. Its current identity is a contested discourse between those embracing this traditional origin and those who emphasize a more modern, urban, and commercial orientation.

Rex Honey's chapter examines the problems of nationalism in the postcolonial era, particularly among those states that have been formed from boundaries imposed by European powers. The question is whether Nigeria—a land of hundreds of ethnic groups and dozens of languages—can really be considered a nation or simply an assemblage of very different nations. And is that national identity powerful enough to stand up against the deeply sedimented local identities that color each of Nigeria's regions?

Chelvadurai Manogaran introduces the problems inherent in a situation when the spatial identities of two nations come into conflict within a single state. Sri Lanka hosts two major nations. The dominant Sinhalese nation has framed its identity in terms of the entire Sri Lankan state. The minority Tamil have a national claim to the northeastern portion of the island. The two territorial visions are asymmetrical and incompatible, leading to an intractable conflict that has flared into a brutal civil war.

6

Cultures of Demarcation: Territory and National Identity in Finland

Jouni Häkli

This chapter explores the significance of geographical scale in the negotiation of spatial identities and especially attempts to understand the processes of nation building in Finland, which stands out as an exceptional case among the several "successor states" born out of the European geopolitical turmoil in the nineteenth and twentieth centuries. I pay particular attention to the role of territory both as a political reality and as an image or symbol in the shaping of the Finnish identity and also discuss the different scales and sources of ethnic identity within the Finnish territory. By looking at two historically very different minority groups and their relationships to the Finnish majority culture, I wish to show that territorial identities should be studied as multilayered and complex phenomena, embedded in their particular historical contexts and material circumstances.

The contextual character of majority-minority relations is evident in the differences in how territoriality and the geographical scale are appropriated in ethnic groups' self-definition as well as in the different paths along which the attitudes of minority groups develop toward the majority with which they reside territorially. For instance, a territorial emphasis in the group's self-definition may turn into a positive and inclusive identification—a "peaceful coexistence"—with the majority identity. On the other hand, cultural demarcations may come to express longstanding contradictions and ambiguity in the relationships between ethnic minority and majority (Kaplan 1994). In Finland the Swedish-speaking Finns exemplify the former case, whereas the Sámi minority has a history of more difficult relationships with the Finnish majority.

In highlighting the role of territory in nation building I wish to put forward the concept of "discursive landscape," which points at the several ways in which geography is involved in the evolution of national identities. As has become abundantly clear from the research on cultural landscapes, "landscape" is a socially constructed relation of the natural and cultural environment. It is a way of seeing, experiencing, and interpreting things and events irreducible to their objective qualities. Nevertheless, "landscape" also has a more substantive nature because perception and interpretation, which make up a landscape, always take place in some material and cultural context. Landscape is not only looked at but also lived in.

There are different kinds of social and personal identities that may give shape to, and be formed by, cultural landscape. National identity is a particular case in that it is often formed in connection with political aspirations. Hence the term *nation building*. It is possible to address the particular relation between national identity and cultural landscape by focusing on the structured aspects of landscape, that is, by looking at the ways in which things and events are systematically drawn to signify nationality, and nationhood. The fact that there are certain textual or text-like materials through which this can be done—the result of reading and writing national space—justifies the term *discursive* in connection with the landscape. National landscape is not only read from nature and culture, it is also written therein.

I argue that the concept of discursive landscape has the potential to make us better understand the intertwined nature of national identity and territory. However, it is a dubiously vague and abstract notion unless contextualized within particular social activities and processes of nation building, for example, those that took place in Finland over the nineteenth and twentieth centuries. Thus, the "discursive landscape of Finland" reflects the historically and geographically specific social activities and processes of nation building that have given rise to things and events firmly interpreted in terms of Finnishness, within the Finnish territory. It is a relatively fixed system of nationalizing signification with both virtual and concrete existence over space. The idea is well captured by A. Paasi (1992), who points out that a nation-state's territory can be thought of as a container that the nation-building processes gradually fill with national consciousness.

The focus here is not on the Finnish discursive landscape as a whole, which would entail the analysis of the entire network of ideas, symbols, and practices associated with Finnishness, and thus constitutive of the Finnish identity. Instead, my emphasis is on the particular role of territory in this landscape—that is, representations of the Finnish

Chris Leatham

territory and the concrete territorial settings that have given shape to the majority national and minority ethnic identities in Finland.

The chapter begins by exploring the larger European context of the Finnish national identity. Finland is analyzed as one of the "second generation" nation-states established after World War I. When compared with other successor states, Finland stands out as a state that had a relatively "stable" territorial shape and unified state apparatus long before it formally gained independence. This territorially stable foundation and the emerging discursive landscape is further scrutinized by looking at the development of the majority-minority relations in Finland, with a particular focus on two cases that reflect different cultures and histories of demarcation within the territoriality hegemonic Finnish identity.

Although pointing to the hegemonic position of the Finnish national culture in present-day Finland and acknowledging some form and degree of unity in the Finnish identity, the concept of discursive landscape does not denote a closed, clearly defined and instrumentally applicable device of social control. The specific knowledges, images, and symbols giving shape to national identity cannot be fully reduced to the direct motivations and aspirations of the elites who produced them. Rather, it should be noted that all collective identities are subject to historical transformation, and because they arise from different social bases, they consist of various contestable and contradictory elements. Thus, although on some level national identity is something that unites the whole population, there are cleavages in it too, because the identity is differently appropriated and reproduced and sometimes contested by different groups (Johnston 1995). It is this type of cleavage in Finland that this chapter attempts to illuminate.

Finnish Nation Building in European Context

World War I brought about the complete collapse of three empires— Russia, Austria-Hungary, and the Ottoman Empire. The dismembering of these great multinational empires made possible the consolidation of national minorities and resulted in the "new nations" of Albania, Bulgaria, Czechoslovakia, Estonia, Finland, Latvia, Lithuania, Poland, Hungary, Romania, and Yugoslavia (Alapuro 1988: 7). As products of the second wave of the creation of distinct national states in Europe, the successor states were latecomers in the international political stage dominated by the already well-established, large European national states (Engman 1989: 102).

Understandably, the state-making processes in the successor states

▶ ◀

CURRENT COUNTRY/REGION DATA
(all statistics are from the end of 1996)

Finland

Total population	5,132,320
Total area (excluding seas)	338,145 km²
Swedish-speaking population	294,233 (5.7% of the total population)
Land area of the municipalities with Swedish-speaking majority	11,681 km² (3.5% of the total area)
Sámi population	6,500 (0.1% of the total population), of whom 1,712 are Sámi speakers
The area designated as "Sámi homeland area"	32,000 km² (9.5% of the total area)

POPULATION BY RELIGIOUS AFFILIATION

Lutheran National Church	4,396,823 (85.7%)
The Greek Orthodox Church in Finland	54,019 (1.0%)
Other religious communities	54,551 (1.1%)
Persons not members of any religious community	626,927 (12.2%)

Source: Official Statistics of Finland, 1997.

PERTINENT CONFLICTS

- No violent ethnic or language-based conflicts
- Civil war waged from January to May 1918, over 24,000 killed in battles and aftermath
- The Russo-Finnish War, also called the Winter War, waged by the USSR against Finland from November 30, 1939, to March 13, 1940; over 23,000 killed in action
- The Finno-Russian War, also called the Continuation War, June 26, 1941–April 25, 1945; over 60,000 killed in action

Jouni Häkli

HISTORICAL BACKGROUND

Finnish polity was formed in 1809 when Finland, thus far a collection of provinces under Swedish rule, became the Grand Duchy of Russia. Over the nineteenth century there was an increasing desire among the mostly Swedish-speaking educated elites to create a sense of common national identity among the Finns, who were linguistically a distinct group in the Russian empire.

In 1917 Finland gained independence and the Finnish identity assumed a hegemonic position in the country. The reaction among the Swedish-speaking elites was to strive for a cultural and political vitality for the linguistic minority. This was largely achieved by means of legislation that granted the Swedish-speaking population a degree of cultural autonomy in the form of educational and cultural institutions designated particularly for Swedish speakers. Consequently, the early twentieth-century concerns about forming a territorially distinct Swedish-speaking political community have moderated into a deterritorialized struggle against voluntary assimilation.

The relationships between Finns and the Sámi people have a long history marked by the colonization of the north by Finns as well as different cultures and sources of living. Despite attempts at times to assimilate the Sámi people into the Finnish majority culture, the group has been able to maintain many of its ethnic characteristics, including the Sámi language and lifestyle. Recent governmental actions have brought Sámi people increasing recognition as an ethnic minority, more cultural autonomy, and even political power in matters related to the Sámi people.

▶─────────────────────────────◀

differed from those of the early substantial states like Germany, France, England, Spain, or Sweden. This makes it interesting to compare the role of territory in early state making with that in the less-studied successor states, Finland in particular. Research on early state-making and nation-building processes has shown that an emerging congruence took place between established political and administrative control over a state territory on one hand, and the building of national homogeneity on the other (Gellner 1983, Giddens 1985, Häkli 1994a). The large national states thus emerged by winning out and producing territoriality, whereas the political and territorial structures of the latecomer states were heavily influenced, and sometimes fully imposed, by an earlier metropolitan power or several states in some cases.

Finland is no exception here. The state's legal and administrative systems were inherited from the period of the Swedish rule, whereas the territorial shape and the state governmental structures were formed during Finland's autonomy as a Russian Grand Duchy. Formerly a collection of "the eastern provinces" of Sweden, Finland became a unified polity as a result of Sweden's defeat against Russia in the Napoleonic Wars. In 1809 Czar Alexander I assumed the title Grand Duke of Finland (Jutikkala 1962).

However, the Finnish case differs from the rest of the successor states in one interesting respect. None of the other states gained independence on a territory with such an evident historical continuity from the imperial period. Sometimes the new state territory was actually an agglomeration of regions that had belonged to different earlier states. This was the case with Poland, Czechoslovakia, Yugoslavia, and to a certain extent Romania, which all had been divided among various earlier states and empires and thus inherited regionally varying political and legal traditions (Alapuro 1988: 7, Engman 1989: 108). In other cases new states emerged with a territory that had not existed in an established form prior to their gaining independence (Albania, Bulgaria, Hungary, Estonia, Latvia, and Lithuania).

However, when Finland became the autonomous Grand Duchy of Russia, and the province of Viborg was attached to its territory three years later, Finnish nation building assumed a territorial framework that would remain virtually intact until 1940. This territorial continuity was accompanied by a political and administrative one, as the Finns were also allowed to retain their old Swedish constitution. By the end of the nineteenth century the Grand Duchy of Finland had its own parliament, government, administration, law and courts, postal services, army (until 1904), and currency. To be sure, the Russian governor-general represented the supreme executive power in the country, but this could not considerably hinder the state-making efforts in Finland (Engman 1989, Jussila 1992). All in all, it can safely be asserted that the formative years of national identity in Finland took place in a stable geographical setting.

Research on the history of territoriality has shown how the early national states rose both as fields of action and fields of knowledge, that is, they were the territorial outcome of not only warmaking organizations but also of placemaking endeavors where the knowledge and communication of territory were essential (e.g., Revel 1991, Häkli 1994a). The close interconnections between warmaking, military reconnaissance, and the popularization of the state's mapped image clearly indicate that the consolidation of territoriality was as much a concrete process of tightening the governmental control over the state's domain as it was a matter of the conceptual production of space (Harley 1988, 1989, Ruggie 1993).

However, the role of territoriality in the late nation-building processes, especially in Finland, was different from that of the "old continuous nations" of Europe. Because Finland had already assumed its territorial shape during metropolitan rule, it was more the imagined and social unity of the territory that had to emerge, rather than the territory as the state's domain, which, in fact, had already been established by the inherited state apparatus. This is why in Finland the territory produced in and through the nation-building process was more a symbolic unit (and community) than a result of political and military attempts to demarcate and control space. The task that the elites aspiring for national self-determination faced was the production of "Finland" both as a field of knowledge tied to governmental activities and as a symbolic landscape in the popular realm. The term *discursive landscape* highlights the fact that these two spheres needed to be brought together to form and support the self-understanding of a coherent ethnic nation.

Of course it was only possible to produce the discursive landscape of Finland with reference to the territorially defined Finnish space. But as mentioned before, this territory, although belonging to the Russian empire, had already been established as a distinct unit both geographically and politically. The task remaining to the nationalists was to build a sense of "Finnishness" into the governmental activities, the particular lands, and the identity of the population. In short, in the case of Finland territoriality may have figured more importantly in the politico-administrative discourses of the government and the social memory of the population, than in the practices of the production of Finland's territorial domain.

Territory and the Discursive Landscape of Finland

The discursive landscape of Finland emerged along with a broad range of cultural and political activities, events, and projects producing the symbolic fabric that linked the self-understanding of a people with a particular territory, concrete places, everyday practices, and imagination. The geographical dimension of national identity represents the webs and nets of "Finnishness," consisting of, among other things, the images of space and lands designated as Finnish and experienced usually, albeit not necessarily, within the Finnish territory.

Here the shaping of the discursive landscape of Finland is treated periodically, so that different phases and degrees of national consciousness may be distinguished. The discussion focuses particularly on how the Finnish territory was brought into the emerging discursive landscape in different historical, cultural, and political contexts: the preautonomy period (before 1809), the age of autonomy (from 1809 to 1917), and the age of independence (since 1917). Of these, the first two periods are interesting as far as the rise of national consciousness is concerned, whereas the last period will be approached from the point of view of majority-minority relations in Finland.

The different periods show different degrees to which territory, its images, and discourses have been vital constituents of the Finnish identity. This is especially clear with the preautonomy period, which witnessed little or no nationalist sentiments centered on the Finnish nation. Finland was the name of a geographical area, not a concept referring to a sovereign political unit (Jussila 1992). Furthermore, because the Finnish language and culture were not yet regarded as criteria of distinct nationality, there was little to be popularized within the vague territorial framework of Finland. Toward the end of the period peripheral nationalisms occurred, but there was not any concerted effort to build Finnish identity in the popular symbolic realm (Engman 1995).

Thus, it makes little sense to discuss the discursive landscape of Finland before the age of autonomy. There simply was not enough political will or consciousness of a distinct nationality to give rise to the processes of nation building. Of course, compared with other successor states, the Finnish case is not exceptional. Most of the nationalist fervor in these states, and in Europe overall, emerged first in the course of the nineteenth century, after the Napoleonic Wars and the Congress of Vienna in 1815 (Hobsbawm 1983, Hutchinson and Smith 1994).

When Sweden had to cede Finland to Russia in 1809, the conditions for Finnish nation building changed dramatically because now for the first time Finland was defined unambiguously as a territorial and political unit. I would argue that in consequence, territory assumed a vital place in the emerging self-concept of Finnish elites. A factor that also greatly contributed to this was the particular socioeconomic structure of the Finnish society. No strong, politically independent landed aristocracy existed, and the peasants formed a broad and disperse, but nonetheless central, group in the possession of land. Therefore, the elite status was reproducible practically only through the professional system and high offices provided by the state apparatus (Alapuro and Stenius 1987: 12). Simply put, the upper classes were both attached to and dependent on the newly born state's continuing autonomy.

The territorial state provided a relatively stable and undisputed ground for several groups of Finnish elites interested mostly in securing the autonomy of the state apparatus on which their own position so clearly depended. The state-dependent aristocracy was not a local extension of the Russian metropolitan power like, for instance, the German nobility in Estonia and Latvia (Kionka 1992, G. Smith 1992, Engman 1995). The elites were mostly Swedish-speaking or bilingual (Swedish- and Finnish-speaking), usually not of Russian origin, and seldom loyal to the Russian empire as a whole. Although separated from the subject population of Finns by language and status, the aristocracy came to define itself as Finnish, not Russian or Swedish. Of course, the elite was loyal to the emperor as it was expected to be. But this loyalty was based on the elite's own interests, and indeed, so well did the Finnish aristocracy perform that when it came to "public temper" and calmness, Czar Nicholas I regarded the Grand Duchy of Finland as an exemplary case among the empire's foreign territories (Jutikkala 1962: 197–200).

In the shelter of these mutually good relations between the metropolitan power and the local Finnish elite, patriotic sentiments grew stronger in Finland. Although this was detected in St. Petersburg, it was quite well tolerated, thanks to the Finns' unwavering loyalty to the throne (Jutikkala 1962). Interesting in the rise of nationalism in Finland is the fact that, in contrast to most other successor states, where nationalism took shape as the masses' struggle _against_ its elite oppressors and the repressive state apparatus, in the Finnish case nationalism was broadly supported by the state-minded aristocracy (e.g., G. Smith 1992: 56). This may explain why in Finland the nationalistic movement consolidated with relative ease, encountering only few contradictions. Nationalism was the project of those in power (Hroch 1985, Alapuro and Stenius 1987).

Overall, the discursive landscape of Finland began to emerge during the first half of the nineteenth century. The most active group was made up of intellectuals, among whom there grew an urge to promote the use of the Finnish language in official as well as cultural activities (Wilson 1976, Vuorela 1977). This was in accord with the ideals of the early nineteenth-century romantic nationalism, which had made language one of the most significant markers of a distinct national culture (see, for example Hobsbawm 1990: 102).

With the asserted importance of vernacular language and folk culture, the Finnish territory began to gain both explicit visibility and implicit weight in the imagination of the Finnish nation. On one hand, through books and articles published since roughly 1835, a growing reading public became aware of the particularity of the land they inhabited. Among the most significant contributions to the Finnish discursive landscape was _Kalevala_, an epic collection of rural folk poetry masterfully compiled and partly created by physician Elias Lönnrot while practicing medicine in the eastern frontier region. This book soon became an admired work all over Europe, and was evidence of a vital culture expressing a definite "national history" (Wilson 1976, 1985). Importantly, it established Karelia, the eastern frontier region (Figure 6.1), as an authentic core of historical Finnishness, thus providing the emergent discursive landscape with a distinct regional base (Sihvo 1996).

Another important work was Zacharis Topelius's *Maamme kirja* (*The Book of Our Land*), which describes Finland and its landscape in an idealistic, stereotypical, and easily accessible way. Published in 1875, it quickly became popular reading and a standard bookshelf item both in schools and at home (Lehtonen 1983, Paasi 1992). In territorial terms

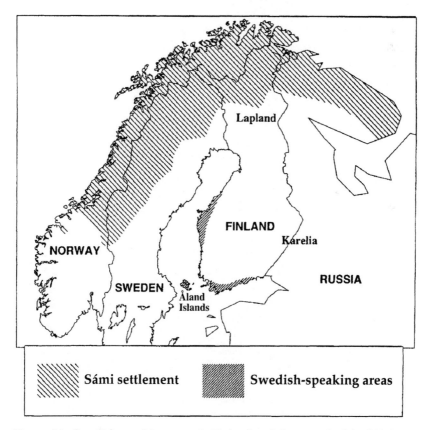

Figure 6.1 Swedish-speaking areas in Finland and the spread of the Sámi settlement in Northern Scandinavia

the book is significant not only in that it described a land and a landscape with which the ordinary people could identify, but also in that it popularized a poetic representation of the Finnish territory as a person. The "Maiden of Finland," portrayed against the landscape "of the thousand lakes," soon became the symbol of Finnish nature and nation and an image of the Finnish territory as a human figure (Titta 1982: 22, Reitala 1983: 59).

On the other hand, because it was only through extensive "field trips" that the protagonists of Finnish folklore were able to collect their materials, the discourses of Finnish cultural originality also took an implicit territorial tone. In addition to the fact that symbols and discourses of Finnish lands and nationhood were disseminated over the Finnish territory via newspapers, books, and school education, all ethnographic knowledge implicitly reflected and recognized the territorial extensions of Finland (see, for example, Vuorela 1977, R. Räsänen 1989, Pentikäinen 1995). The fact that folklore was collected and recorded from both sides of the Russian border only strengthened the territorial consciousness among nationalistic intellectuals. After independence this consciousness took shape in ideas of a "Greater Finland" covering large areas of the Russian side of the eastern border (Paasi 1990, 1996).

The different ethnographic endeavors and the rise of ethnology as a science can also be understood as an expression of the discursive development I have elsewhere termed *the invention of region* (Häkli 1994b, 1998). By the nineteenth century in many fields of social activity and knowledge regions came to be conceived of as unified wholes, consisting of social, cultural (linguistic), economic, or political relations. Thus, within attempts to make visible the European national cultures, there also was present an implicit geographical, or rather territorial, conception of the principles of organization of the social world.

This was the case with Finnish folklore studies, too. Toward the end of the period of autonomy, extensive "mappings" of the ways of Finns had been recorded and preserved in museums and archives (Vuorela 1977). Thus, the territory established during early political autonomy came to be tightly knit into the discursive landscape of Finland (for the significance of museums, see Anderson 1991: 163–185). This process had two dimensions that can only be distinguished analytically. On the one hand, representations of Finnish culture, nature, and nation made increasingly visible the lands that made up the Finnish territory and also provided symbolic infrastructures for the various discourses of Finnishness within which the Finnish identity was being constructed. On the other hand, these symbolisms and discourses, produced mostly by the educated elites, were disseminated over the Finnish territory via newspapers, books, and primary education as well as via material items such as monuments, museums, and public buildings. The resulting discursive landscape of Finland emerged as a "fixed picture of the Finnish cultural 'semiosphere', its symbols and boundaries" (cf. Paasi 1992: 94).

From Language Strife to Collective Identity

The rising Finnish vernacular culture gradually changed the position of the Swedish-speaking Finns. This is evident when looking at the language situation in the nineteenth-century Grand Duchy of Finland. As mentioned previously, the aristocracy was mostly Swedish-speaking so that with few exceptions the distinguishing boundary between social classes ran along linguistic lines (Lönnqvist 1981, Engman 1995). Furthermore, the language of secondary and higher education was exclusively Swedish, until the establishment of the first school with Finnish as the language of instruction in 1858. Also the official language was Swedish, both at the central bureaucracy and in the minutes kept of the local self-governing agencies' meetings. Even much of the literary work promoting the Finnish nationalist cause was in Swedish because of its strong position among the learned elite.

Thus, one of the most urgent nationalist goals was to replace Swedish as the language of the educated class and to introduce Finnish into official as well as cultural use. No particular attention was paid at this point to the position of the small Swedish-speaking rustic population, settled mostly along the coastal areas of the Finnish territory (Jutikkala 1962: 201). Despite the hegemony of the Swedish language, a Finnish-speaking elite grew surprisingly rapidly—an educated class capable of integrating ideologically and practically the Finnish-speaking masses with the state. By the end of the nineteenth century many Swedish-speaking families had adopted the Finnish language, and some even changed their family names from Swedish to Finnish (Jutikkala 1962: 206, Alapuro and Stenius 1987: 14–18).

However, a reaction to the victorious advance of the Finnish language from some members of the Swedish-speaking side of the educated elite gave rise to a movement that sought to compete with Finnish nationalism. It was suggested that the Swedish language and culture were a vital part of the Swedish heritage in Finland and should not be dismissed in favor of the "rustic" Finnish culture. Furthermore, it was held that the Swedish-speaking elite and common people living mostly along the western and southern coasts of Finland formed a sep-

arate nation, which should not be betrayed by forsaking the Swedish
language (Lönnqvist 1995, Engman 1995).

A few hostile bursts of opinion notwithstanding, Swedish-speaking
nationalism did not cause too much disturbance in the steady nation-
building process that gradually established the hegemony of Finnish
culture and language in Finland. There were two reasons for this. On
one hand, the language question never surpassed in importance the
goal of forming an independent nation-state, accepted both by the
Swedish and the Finnish-speaking elite (Engman 1989). Thus, the dispute was on the means and forms of the process rather than on its
ultimate aims. On the other hand, the Swedish-speaking elite experienced no linguistic difficulties in school any more than in public life.
The Swedish movement, therefore, was more concerned with language
as a practical instrument of social activity than as a mystic source of
culture, and for the most part they were content to secure the position
of the Swedish language in a bilingual Finland (Jutikkala 1962: 210).
These practical goals also set the tone for much of the Swedish-speaking politics in independent Finland.

By the nineteenth and twentieth centuries the foundation of Finnish
identity was already well established. It had been negotiated in a
"counter-cultural" spirit first inspired by romantic nationalism but
from 1890 onward, as a response to direct policies of Russification (Jutikkala 1962, R. Räsänen 1989). The two peculiarities that distinguish
Finnish nation building from that of the other successor states, the
"ready made" territorial frame together with the state-dependent
upper classes, had an important effect on Finnish identity. First, in
their attempts to make the ordinary masses, especially the peasants,
loyal to the state, the Swedish-speaking or bilingual upper classes were
encouraged to adopt the language and culture of the Finnish-speaking
(quantitative) majority. A passage from Topelius's *Maamme kirja* illustrates this willingness to identify with a common nation and destiny.
"This is my fatherland. Whether I call it 'Suomenmaa' in Finnish, or
'Finland' in Swedish makes no difference, it is always the same country. All its sons and daughters belong to the same nation, no matter
what language they speak" (Topelius 1945; my translation).

Second, because of the central role of peasants in the national romantic historiography, the ideals and cultural elements of the Finnish identity could most unambiguously be found in the agrarian "free peasant
life." This was reflected in the discursive landscape of Finland, which
up until the 1960s was largely constructed around the symbols of rural
lands and lifestyles (M. Räsänen 1989). Finnishness was held to be rooted
in the rustic folk culture embedded in a distinctive natural landscape,
which from early on was brought into the discourses of national iden-

tity through ethnographic activities. In addition to several distinguished ethnologists and learned societies, student nations at the University of Helsinki voluntarily participated in the "recording and preservation of the Finnish peasant culture" (Vuorela 1977). The "nationally coded" items of folk culture were then distributed across the country by means of temporary displays, permanent national and local museums, and printed works like Topelius's *Maamme kirja* (Smeds 1987, Korhonen 1989). Agrarian motives and the landscapes of wilderness were also dominant in Finnish poetry, music, painting, and literature, which by the end of the nineteenth century had eagerly adopted the great national mission (Tiitta 1982).

Yet another important medium in Finnish nation building was the breakthrough of mass organization after 1870. Leaders of the Finnish nationalist movement had founded *Kansanvalistusseura* (the Society of Popular Education) and made it into a house organ for the movement's ideals and organizatinal activities. Thus, the Finnish movement gained an organization whose network of representatives extended into all areas of the country (Liikanen 1995). Soon after, a temperance movement followed with even more effective means of encouraging local organization (Sulkunen and Alapuro 1987). Mass movements were instrumental in the building of the Finnish identity and cultural hegemony both in that they popularized and disseminated political consciousness of Finland, and in that they introduced modern principles of public life to cities and countryside alike (Alapuro and Stenius 1987). This rapidly gave rise to a modern political field in Finland, which already by 1918 had come to experience two dramatic events: a declaration of independence from Russia and a civil war.

The bloody civil war was a traumatic experience for the Finnish society at large. It was only after World War II that the wounds would really start to heal and the legacy of hatred separating the "whites" and the "reds" would grow into a unified political culture. However, on the perhaps less-conscious level of territorial identity, national unity had survived the dramatic changes and turns of Finnish political life. Numerous important social (and socializing) practices continued to produce the image of Finland as a unified whole. After all, it was largely in and through school education and mass mobilization that Finns had become aware of their distinct history, culture, and nationality. This discursive landscape had consistently been built on the idea of a larger territorial unity rising above, but not suppressing, regional identities. Also the meaning of linguistic, social, and ethnic differences was continually downplayed (Paasi 1992, Liikanen 1995). Thus, from the point of view of the increasingly hegemonic Finnish identity, the

Swedish-speakers and "Lapps" were just as important "elements" in Finnishness as were the Finns themselves.

It is therefore possible to argue that the political cleavages and instabilities in the young republic were not mirrored in the territorially stable discursive landscape of Finland as such. Rather it was the new, culturally and politically less-secure position in which the Swedish-speaking Finns found themselves after independence that brought about a desire for a "smaller-scale" political territorialization.

Lines of Demarcation: The Swedish-Speaking Finns

With independence, the formative years of the Finnish discursive landscape were over. I therefore approach the third period, the age of independence, first from the point of view of the Swedish-speaking Finns and then the Sámi people, and focus on their different responses to changing minority position. This is not to say that the Finnish identity and its reflections in the national discursive landscape had somehow reached a stage of finality in 1917. Quite the contrary, the postindependence time has been characterized as a continuous "search for national identity" (e.g., M. Räsänen 1989). For instance, the dramatic changes in the Finnish territory after World War II necessarily affected the Finnish self-image, because the mythic lands of Karelia, which only recently had figured in aspirations toward "Greater Finland," had to be ceded to the Soviet Union (Kärkkäinen 1987). During the Cold War era that followed, Finland was imagined as part of the Scandinavian family of nations, largely for official neutrality policy reasons. More recently the Baltic Sea region and the European Union have again become foci of larger-scale identity building.

There is no doubt that rapid urbanization, globalization, and cultural changes have shifted the emphases in the expressions of Finnish identity. However, it is equally possible to argue that the discursive foundation created and canonized by the nineteenth and twentieth centuries has continued to guide the "search" for identity as one of its fundamental layers (Tiitta 1982, Reitala 1983). It is here that the comfortable and secure images of the Finnish nature, lands, tradition, and territory have been cherished and preserved, although not without internal cleavages.

Mobilization based on ethnic identity had begun among the Swedish-speaking people during the latter part of the nineteenth century as new questions and problems emerged. The group became increasingly politicized through participation in various mass organizations and the Swedish People's Party (Lönnqvist 1981, Stenius 1987). This was largely a response to the strengthening position of Finnish as an official language, on the one hand, and to the increasing migration of Finnish-speaking people to the predominantly Swedish-speaking coastal areas, on the other hand. The balance between the political importance of these two areas of "confrontation" with the hegemonic Finnish culture has changed over the twentieth century (Lönnqvist 1981).

The Swedish-speaking "cultures of demarcation" can be described in terms of the change in emphasis in the group's identity and political goals from territorial to ethno-linguistic. In the beginning of the twentieth century most of the Swedish-speaking people lived on the southern and western coasts of Finland and in the Åland Islands (Figure 6.1). As many as 80 to 100 percent of the people living in these regions spoke Swedish (Klövekorn 1960). This concentration of the "Swedish nation" was the foundation upon which, beginning in the 1910s, claims were made of territorially based Swedish-speaking self-government, even autonomy.

The "Swedish regional policy" *(bygdesvenskhet)* emphasized the Swedish settlement areas and their culture in sustaining the lines of demarcation against the Finns (Engman 1995). Among the first concrete signs of a territorialized Swedish policy was the adoption of the term *Swedish-Finland* as the name of the Swedish settlement region (Lönnqvist 1995). This was soon followed by plans for self-government, which aimed at comprehensive regional self-government, either for the Swedish-speaking provinces separately, or for a union of provinces under one governor. Further demands included cultural autonomy in church and education and a separate military unit (Engman 1995).

These plans were never realized, however, partly because the Swedish opinion remained divided on the issue and partly because a limited Swedish cultural autonomy was already being prepared through institutional arrangements and legislation. For example, a Swedish diocese was established including all Swedish congregations in the country, and a separate Swedish department was instituted in the government's Board of Education. Furthermore, the demands of linguistic and cultural equality were realized in the 1919 constitution, which decreed that both Finnish and Swedish were the national languages of the republic and that the needs of both language groups were to be satisfied on the same basis. In addition, the 1922 language law secured the rights of citizens to use their mother tongue in their business with authorities (Lönnqvist 1991).

Thus, favorable institutional arrangements and legislation should perhaps be regarded as a success of the "Swedish cultural policy" *(kultursvenskhet)* rather than the territorial faction of the Swedish movement. Whatever the case, the achievements of the Swedish nationalists were hardly considered a great victory within the movement. A measure of the advantageous political position of the Swedish-speakers was their lack of interest in the treaties on protection of minorities drawn up at the Paris Peace Conference after World War I. They were considered inadequate and in all ways unsuitable for the situation of the Swedish-speaking population in Finland (Engman 1989, 1995).

Territorial strategy was more successful in the case of the Åland Islands, which had strong historical and cultural ties to Sweden and a population that spoke Swedish with the exception of small groups of Finnish immigrant workers. At the end of 1917 the so-called Åland Movement arose requesting association with Sweden. This was said to embody an ancient wish for "reunion with the motherland," but it has been suggested that the real reasons were fear of Russian anarchy, a strong Finnish nationalism, and the uncertain political future of an independent Finland (Engman 1995).

In contrast to mainland Swedish regional policy, which remained an internal question, the Åland Movement became an international issue because of its goal to be united with Sweden. In 1921 the League of Nations stated that Åland should go to Finland and recommended that Finland and Sweden together should seek to guarantee the position of Swedish-speaking Finns as well as a neutral status for the islands (Lönnqvist 1981). However, the Finnish government had already, under international pressure, granted Åland autonomy by law in 1920, and two years later new guarantees were incorporated into a law on the islands' self-government (Engman 1995).

The solution didn't fully satisfy any of the parties involved. Having lost the battle for Åland the Swedes were disappointed, the Finns had made the decision for autonomy under pressure, and the Ålanders had not achieved their goal to be united with Sweden. The situation quickly stabilized, however, and none of the parties complained to the League of Nations (Engman 1995).

After the most vital interests of the Swedish-speaking group were protected and the Åland question was solved, the Swedes dismissed much of their territorial policy. Also the language question, which had occasionally turned into open political conflict, gradually became unimportant as the Swedish-speaking minority found its position secured (Lönnqvist 1995: 58). World War II and wartime unity further contributed to the stabilization of the language issue, so that after the war the Finns saw themselves as a nation that spoke two languages (Engman 1995). The Swedish-speaking minority has managed to establish or maintain a political party (the Swedish People's Party); primary and secondary schools; several institutions of higher education; newspapers; television and radio programming; a multitude of cultural organizations, institutions, and foundations; and, most importantly, a lively, although proportionally shrinking, Swedish-speaking community. In 1967 Swedish also became a compulsory language in the comprehensive school (Lönnqvist 1981).

Hence, it may be justified to say that the lines of demarcation by the Swedish-speaking minority have, over the course of this century, changed from territorial to cultural—that is, the Swedish regional policy has largely been rejected in favor of the more ethno-linguistically oriented Swedish cultural policy. At the same time the tone of Swedish nationalism has changed from being aggressive to more diplomatic, having achieved the goal of Swedish-speakers being equally represented in the centers of power and cultural life and the aim of supporting bilingualism (Engman 1995).

The Sámi Movement Emerges

If the development of the Swedish-speaking minority has progressed from a strong political "awakening" toward a more moderate cultural presence, for the Sámi minority almost the opposite is the case. Although there have been waves of political mobilization, caused by the consolidation of state power in the northern periphery, it was really World War II that gave rise to the Sámi ethnic revival in Finland (Aikio 1994). The differences in the groups' reactions to a rising Finnishness derive from their different histories as national minorities.

The Sámi have been living in Northern Scandinavia since before it was settled and colonized by Norwegians, Swedes, Finns, and Russians. Over their history the Sámi have faced problems and challenges similar to many other indigenous groups. Among the most critical issues have been the preservation of Sámi culture and language as well as its material foundation, the land title rights. The focus here is on the Sámi people living in northern Finland, where three groups can be distinguished on linguistic grounds: the North Sámi, the Inari Sámi, and the Skolts (East Sámi). Earlier the divisions also corresponded relatively well to differences in sources of livelihood (Aikio 1994). However, because the "Sámi question" has often concerned the three groups equally, in the following, I will use the collective term *the Finnish Sámi*.

The period from 1850 to World War II has been called the century of Sámi assimilation policies in Scandinavia (Aikio 1994, Salvesen 1995). Yet, few explicitly political responses arose from the Sámi minority in Finland. The first concrete step toward Sámi mobilization was taken as late as 1932, when *Lapin Sivistysseura* (Society for the Promotion of

Lapp Culture) was formed in Helsinki (Siuruainen 1976). A number of
Sámi participated but most of the members were non-Sámi. The society
was active primarily in publishing books and a newspaper in the Sámi
language as well as increasing awareness of (and among) the Sámi people. Some attention was also directed at concrete "social questions"
(Sillanpää 1994).

World War II was a crucial watershed in Sámi mobilization in Scandinavia, especially in Finland. The war marked the politicization of the
Sámi culture. It was a period during which the Sámi identity was first
given a discursive form and later territorialized when used for claiming rights to cultural autonomy and the land title (Asp 1993). The Sámi
mobilization was largely a response to hardships experienced during
and after the war. First, as the German army withdrew from Finland
through Lapland and Norway, many Finnish Sámi lost their homes
and were evacuated to more southerly regions of Finland until other
accommodation could be found. The reconstruction of the northern-
most Sámi areas took many years. Second, some 650 Skolt Sámi were
displaced from their native homeland in the Petsamo area when it was
ceded to the USSR in 1944. The Skolt Sámi were resettled by the Finnish government in the northeastern part of Inari (Sillanpää 1994).

Each of these events served to accentuate the Sámi situation in the
eyes of the Finnish authorities. The Sámi themselves first began to organize in 1945 when *Sámii Litto* (Sámi Union) was founded. However
the political weight of this organization never reached the level of its
Swedish and Norwegian counterparts. More successful in this respect
was the Sámi Delegation organized by the Finnish state as a committee
for advisory purposes. The delegation was juridically a state authority,
but it soon also became a permanent institution representing the Sámi
people; an elected body that the Sámi renamed the *Sámi Parliament*
(Jones 1982). The chosen term points to the committee's position as the
first truly national Sámi federation capable of setting its own agenda
and priorities. However, despite its popular designation as a parliament, the delegation was not able to make decisions in matters concerning the Sámi people; it could only make recommendations, or it
could respond to proposals by the Finnish state (Aikio 1994).

However, it was through the Sámi Parliament that the Sámi were
first able to voice their demands for recognition as a national minority
as well as for greater cultural autonomy and, perhaps most importantly, for the Sámi land title rights (Jones 1982, Sillanpää 1994, Pentikäinen 1995). The last of these demands has given the traditional Sámi
conception of territory a more consciously political tone, while also
allowing for nonterritorial solutions to be sought (Asp 1993). Because
Finnish legislation does not grant the Sámi a legal monopoly to their

traditional livelihood of reindeer herding, Sámi activists have wished to promote a form of cultural autonomy in which the rights to land and water are strongly emphasized (Pääkkönen 1995). In this way the practically unattainable goal of Sámi regional autonomy has been moderated while maintaining a political conception of the territorial rights of the Sámi people in Finland.

The most recent Sámi legislation has been aimed at further improving and protecting the Sámi cultural self-government. Effective from the beginning of 1996, the legislation changed the Sámi Delegation into the Sámi Assembly, which no longer is a state authority but a self-governmental body in the Sámi homeland with twenty-one representatives elected every four years (Hallituksen esitys 1994). In addition to advisory tasks, the assembly has some decision-making power, which, even in its limited form, is a step toward both more territorially based Sámi politics and the territorialization of the Sámi identity.

Also the definition of who are counted as ethnic Sámi, and thus have the right to vote in the Sámi elections, was broadened in the new legislation. Now in addition to Sámi-speakers and the people whose parents or grandparents were Sámi-speakers, the descendants of the practitioners of traditional Sámi sources of livelihood can register as Sámi (Hallituksen esitys 1994). This has caused severe disputes between the Sámi and the Finns living in Lapland, because the former are afraid of being outnumbered by the latter in the voting registers. In heated debates, terms like *racism* and *cultural genocide* have been wielded, even though the legislation was actually intended to do justice to those Sámi who lost their native language under the pressures of the Finnish state's assimilation policies. According to some estimates, tens of thousands of Finns could register as Sámi. Even though this would increase the Sámi's political weight, the identity of a small minority would be compromised. It is not surprising then that the Ministry of Justice recently promised to reestablish the definition of Sámi ethnicity on purely linguistic grounds (Tahkolahti 1997a, 1997b).

The Finnish Sámi minority has been able to compensate for its small size (about 6,400 persons in 1992) through participation in the Nordic Sámi Council, which is an inter-Nordic pan-Sámi organization, as well as by resorting to international human rights organizations (Aikio 1994). In this respect the Sámi minority has had to adopt policies that differ from the Swedish-speaking minority's largely internal channels of influence. This reflects tellingly the fact that within the discursive landscape of Finland these two minority groups occupy very unequal positions, the one being a relatively large group with a history of cultural and political affluence in Finland, the other being a small "Fourth

World" nation with a history of struggles against cultural assimilation and subjugation.

The difference between the Swedish-speaking and the Sámi minorities is also reflected in the ways in which their relationships to the Finnish-speaking majority have developed over the course of the twentieth century. It can roughly be asserted that the stronger group started with a more aggressive and territorialized emphasis and ended up with a relatively diplomatic "Swedish cultural policy." The Sámi movement, on the other hand, began largely as an attempt to make the group's culture more visible and only after that adopted more territorial emphasis in its policies.

Conclusion: Some Theoretical Considerations

Since the 1970s nationalism and national identities have attracted increasing attention among social theorists. Much of this revival of interest has been a reflection of the upsurge of ethnic protest in the United States and the emergence of peripheral nationalisms in Europe since the 1960s. When theoretically oriented, the research has sought to explain the origin as well as the revival of ethnic and nationalistic sentiments and thus deepen our historical understanding of these phenomena.

Along with an increased understanding of its history and associated social phenomena, nationalism has been portrayed by a number of variants and in many contexts. The sheer number of different nationalisms depicted in the proliferating literature has made it difficult to appreciate what they have in common and what it is about the late-modern world that has made national or ethnic identities such a powerful basis for political legitimation, contestation, and rivalry.

This is not to claim that attempts have not been made to extract the root causes of nationalism and thus reduce its empirical and explanatory diversity. Any broader review of the research on nationalism soon reveals a tendency to argue for causality in the emergence of the ideologies, languages, and politics of nationalism as coupled with the rise of national identities, democracy, and the principle of national self-determination (e.g., Deutsch 1966, Tilly 1975, Breuilly 1982, A. D. Smith 1991).

Social, economic, and political transformations in European societies, their historical and geographical contexts, the French and American Revolutions, mass education, and the development of the means of communication have all figured in attempts to explain why national phenomena gained such a powerful impetus both politically and in the realm of "civil society" during the eighteenth and the nineteenth centuries. However, each assertion of causality has also been contested when approached from a different point of view or with a different set of questions. In fact, often the phenomena that are portrayed in causal relationship seem both to presuppose one another and follow from each other, depending on the particular case or aspect under scrutiny.

In this chapter it is suggested that the focus on territory in relation to nationalism and national identity may in a useful way lead us to think about the "common ground" on which these phenomena—nationalism, nations, self-determination, and democracy—have flourished. Encompassing both symbolic formations of nationhood and the landscapes situated within the physical state territory, the term *discursive landscape* may be helpful in the theoretical reflection of this common ground.

Two deeply rooted imaginations have made nations perhaps the most pervasive discursive landscapes of the modern age: the rise of historical consciousness in the beginning of the nineteenth century and the invention of "region" as a field of knowledge tied to governmentality (Häkli 1994b, 1998). As pervasive models of world perception and knowledge production they have molded the overwhelming reality of twentieth-century international relations and territorial politics. They have also made claims to nationhood and ethnic cultural autonomy rational in themselves. The consciousness of "history" and "region" come together in the emergence of national discursive landscapes, giving them both legitimacy and territorial extension on different geographical scales.

Territories form the "geographical backdrop" against which both students of nationalism and nations themselves often view national landscapes of the modern world. Independent of whether nations overlap territorially with a particular state or whether there is a discrepancy between the state and nation, the territorial imagery is, thus, part and parcel of the historical negotiation of national identities. It may be possible to imagine a community in almost aspatial terms, as an extended family rooted in history (e.g., the Jewish identity), but it is always the territorial mosaic of the world map against which such images are cast.

Yet, despite the significance of territory in nation building, in much of the literature on nationalism territory has been viewed as a relatively fixed and immutable reality over a given period of time. Although justified with respect to some essential traits of state power, this conception has tended to lead scholars to underestimate the dynamic and active character of territory. In reality, territory is a multidimensional social construct continually reproduced in different social practices. Therefore, instead of "taking territory apart," it was here viewed as part and parcel of the cultural, social, and political practices involved in the rise of national consciousness and its political mobilization. In order to maintain in sight the constructed nature of modern territoriality, territory was here conceptualized as ideas and their discourses, as much as the physical and political realities of land, movement, and demarcation.

The territory of Finland was fundamental both to the growing spatial extension of national identity and to the imagination of nation as such. The process in and through which a region called "Finland" was invented—first by the educated elite and later by the masses—involved an extraction from the people's everyday practice of certain cultural traits, their association with the "Finland-object," and the elevation of the resulting object into the status of enduring, unified, historical entity—a political subject.

The discursive landscape thus produced gradually made the Finnish culture and language hegemonic in Finland. It also provoked reactions from the Swedish-speaking and Sámi minorities, the responses reflecting the groups' particular, and very different, histories. The historically dominant position and larger size of the Swedish-speaking population has tended to bias the Finnish minority policy so that, until very recently, the authorities saw only one minority in the country. The situation is being corrected now, for the benefit of the Sámi people. These omissions notwithstanding, the Finnish case is usually not considered a bad example of minority-majority relations (Tägil 1995). An especially encouraging fact is that in Finland inter-ethnic questions have been settled with relatively little conflict, and in any case, nonviolently.

References

Aikio, S. "The History of the Sámi." In S. Aikio, U. Aikio-Puoskari, and J. Helander, eds., *The Sámi Culture in Finland*. Helsinki: Lapin Sivistysseura, 1994.

Alapuro, R. *State and Revolution in Finland*. Berkeley: University of California Press, 1988.

Alapuro, R., and H. Stenius. "Kansanliikkeet Loivat Kansakunnan." (Mass Movements Created the Nation). In R. Alapuro et al., eds. *Kansa Liikkeessä (Nation on the Move)*. Helsinki: Kirjayhtymä, 1987, 7–52.

Anderson, B. *Imagined Communities*. Rev. ed. London: Verso, 1991.

Asp, E. "The Lapps as a Minority Group in Finland. In E. Asp, ed., *Ethnic Minorities*. University of Turku, Department of Sociology and Political Research, ser. A, no. 20, 1993, 30–48.

Breuilly, J. *Nationalism and the State*. Manchester: Manchester University Press, 1982.

Deutsch, K. *Nationalism and Social Communication.* 2d ed. Cambridge, Mass.: MIT Press, 1966.

Engman, M. "Finland as a Successor-State." In M. Engman and D. Kirby, eds., *Finland: People, Nation, State.* London: Hurst, 1989, 102–127.

———. "Finns and Swedes in Finland." In S. Tägil, ed., *Ethnicity and Nation Building in the Nordic World.* Carbondale and Edwardsville: Southern Illinois University Press, 1995, 179–217.

Gellner, E. *Nations and Nationalism.* Oxford: Blackwell, 1983.

Giddens, A. *The Nation State and Violence.* Cambridge: Polity Press, 1985.

Häkli, J. "Territoriality and the Rise of Modern State." *Fennia* 172 (1) (1994a): 1–82.

———. "Maakunta, Tieto, ja Valta." (Region, Knowledge and Power). *Acta Universitatis Tamperensis* ser. A, vol. 415. Tampere, 1994b.

———. "Discourse in the Production of Political Space. Decolonizing the Symbolism of Provinces in Finland." *Political Geography* 18 (3) (1998): 331–363.

Hallituksen esitys. HE 248 Hallituksen esitys Eduskunnalle saamelaisten kulttuuri-itsehallintoa koskevien säädösten ottamisesta Suomen Hallitusmuotoon ja muuhun lainsäädäntöön. (GP 248 government's proposal to the Parliament for statutes concerning the Sámi cultural self-government in the Finnish constitution and other legislation), 1994.

Harley, B. "Maps, Knowledge, and Power." In D. Cosgrove and S. Daniels, eds., *The Iconography of Landscape.* Cambridge: Cambridge University Press, 1988, 277–312.

———. "Deconstructing the Map." *Cartographica* 26 (2) (1989): 1–20.

Hobsbawm, E. "Introduction: Inventing Traditions." In E. Hobsbawm and T. Ranger, eds., *The Invention of Tradition.* Cambridge: Cambridge University Press, 1983, 13–14.

———. *Nations and Nationalism since 1780.* Cambridge: Cambridge University Press, 1990.

Hroch, M. *Social Preconditions of National Revival in Europe.* Cambridge: Cambridge University Press, 1985.

Hutchinson, John, and Anthony D. Smith, eds. *Nationalism.* Oxford, U.K.: Oxford University Press, 1994.

Johnston, N. "Cast in Stone: Monuments, Geography, and Nationalism." *Environment and Planning D: Society and Space* (13) (1995): 51–65.

Jones, M. "The Sámi of Lapland." Minority Rights Group, report 1982, 55. London.

Jussila, O. "Suomen Valtion Synty" (The Emergency of the Finnish State). In P. Haapala, ed., *Talous, Valta, ja Valtio (Economy, Power, and State).* Tampere: Vastapaino, 1992, 17–28.

Jutikkala, E. *A History of Finland.* New York: Praeger, 1962.

Kaplan, D. "Two Nations in Search of a State: Canada's Ambivalent Spatial Identities." *Annals of the Association of American Geographers* 84 (4) (1994): 585–606.

Kärkkäinen, L. "Suomen Valtakunnan Vanhat Rajat ja Itärajan Käynti 1934." (The Old Borders of Finland). *Maanmittaushallituksen Julkaisu* 59, 1987, Helsinki.

Kionka, R. "Estonians." In G. Smith, ed., *The Nationalities Question in the Soviet Union*. London: Longman, 1992, 40–53.

Klövekorn, M. "Die Sprachliche Struktur Finnlands 1880–1950." (The Linguistic Structure of Finland 1880–1950). *Bidrag Till Kännedon af Finlands Natur Och Folk* 105, 1960, Helsinki.

Korhonen, T. "Museoitu Suomi." (Finland in Museums). In T. Korhonen and M. Räsänen, eds., *Kansa Kuvastimessa: Etnisyys ja Identiteetti. (Nation in a Mirror: Ethnicity and Identity)*. Helsinki: Suomalaisen Kirjallisuuden Seura, 1989, 103–134.

Lehtonen. "Valtiovalta ja Oppikirjat." (The State and School Textbooks). *Helsingin yliopisto kasvatustieteen laitoksen julkaisuja* 9 (1983), Helsinki.

Liikanen, I. *Fennomania ja Kansa. (Fennomania and the People,* English Abstract). Helsinki: Suomalaisen Kirjallisuuden Seura, 1995.

Lönnqvist, B. *Suomenruotsalaiset. (Finland's Swedes)*. Jyväskylä: Gummerus, 1981.

———. "What Does It Mean to Be a Swedish-Speaking Finn?" *Life and Education in Finland*, no. 3, 1991, 25–27.

———. "Rhetorik im Dienste der Ethnischen Mobilisierung." (Rhetoric in the Service of Ethnic Mobilization). *Ethnologica Europaea* 25 (1995): 55–60.

Pääkkönen, E. "Saamelaisuus Sirkumpolaarisena Etnisyytenä. (Sámi as a Circumpolar Ethnicity). Sámi Instituhtta; Diedut 1. Guovdageaidnu, 1995.

Paasi, A. "The Rise and Fall of Finnish Geopolitics." *Political Geography Quarterly* 9 (1990): 53–65.

———. "The Construction of Socio-Spatial Consciousness. Geographical Perspectives on the History and Contexts of Finnish Nationalism." *Nordisk Samhällsgeografisk Tidskrift*, no. 15 (1992): 79–100.

———. *Territories, Boundaries, and Consciousness*. Chichester: John Wiley, 1996.

Pentikäinen, J. *Saamelaiset: Pohjoisen Kansan Mytologia. (The Sámi: Mythology of a Northern People)*. Helsinki: Suomalaisen Kirjallisuuden Seura, 1995.

Räsänen, M. "Kansankulttuuri Kansakunnan Identiteetin Rakennuspuuna." (Folk Culture in the Construction of National Identity). In T. Korhonen and M. Räsänen, eds. *Kansa Kuvastimessa: Etnisyya ja Identiteetti. (Nation in a Mirror: Ethnicity and Identity)*. Helsinki: Suomalaisen Kirjallisuuden Seura, 1989, 10–28.

Räsänen, R. "Kotiseutuaate ja Kotiseutuliike Suomalaiskansallisessa Prosessissa." (Home District Movement in Finnish Nationalism). In T. Korhonen and M. Räsänen, eds., *Kansa Kuvastimessa: Etnisyys ja Identiteetti. (Nation in a Mirror: Ethnicity and Identity)*. Helsinki: Suomalaisen Kirjallisuuden Seura, 1989, 144–161.

Reitala, A. *Suomo-Neito: Suomen Kuvallisen Henkilöitymisen Vaiheet. (The Maiden of Finland: On the Development of the Personified Images of Finland)*. Helsinki: Otava, 1983.

Revel, J. "Knowledge of the Territory." *Science in Context* 4 (1) (1991): 133–161.

Ruggie, J. G. "Territoriality and Beyond: Problematizing Modernity in International Relations." *International Organization* 47 (1) (1993): 139–174.

Salvesen, H. "Sámi Aednan: Four States—One Nation? Nordic Minority Policy and the History of the Sámi." In S. Tägil, ed., *Ethnicity and Nation Building in the Nordic World.* Carbondale and Edwardsville: Southern Illinois University Press, 1995, 106–144.

Sihvo, H. "Karelia: History, Ideals, Identity: Karelian History from the Finnish Viewpoint." In E. Varis and S. Porter, eds., *Karelia and St. Petersburg: From Lakeland Interior to European Metropolis.* Joensuu: Joensuu University Press, 1996, 11–26.

Sillanpää, L. "Political and Administrative Responses to Sámi Self-Determination." The Finnish Society of Sciences and Letters, 1994, 48. Helsinki.

Siuruainen, E. "The Population in the Sámi Area of Finnish Lapland." *Acta Universitatis Ouluensis,* ser. A, no. 40. Oulu, 1976.

Smeds, K. "Joukkotapahtumat ja Suomi-Identiteeti." (Mass Events and the Finnish Identity). In R. Alapuro et al., eds., *Kansa Liikkeessä (Nation on the Move).* Helsinki: Kirjayhtymä, 1987, 91–107.

Smith, A. D. *National Identity.* Reno: University of Nevada Press, 1991.

Smith, G. "Latvians." In G. Smith, ed., *The Nationalities Question in the Soviet Union.* London: Longman, 1992, 54–71.

Stenius, H. "Ruotsinkieliset Järjestäytymisperinteet." (Traditions of Mass Organization among the Swedish-Speakers). In R. Alapuro et al., eds., *Kansa Liikkeessä (Nation on the Move).* Helsinki: Kirjayhtymä, 1987, 173–175.

Sulkunen, I., and R. Alapuro. "Raittiusliike ja Työväen Järjestäytyminen." (Temperance Movement and the Workers Organization). In R. Alapuro et al., eds., *Kansa Liikkeessä (Nation on the Move).* Helsinki: Kirjayhtymä, 1987, 142–156.

Tägil, S. "Ethnic and National Minorities in the Nordic Nation-Building Process: Theoretical and Conceptual Premises." In S. Tägil, ed., *Ethnicity and Nation Building in the Nordic World.* Carbondale and Edwardsville: Southern Illinois University Press, 1995, 8–32.

Tahkolahti, J. "Uusi Saamelaismääritelmä Teki 'Kiinteistöstä Ihmisen.'" (The New Definition of Sámi Ethnicity Equates "Real-Estate with a Human Being"). *Helsingin Sanomat,* January 8, 1997a.

———. "Saamelaisuuden Määritelmä Palautetaan Kielipohjaiseksi." (The Linguistic Definition of Sámi Ethnicity Will Be Reestablished). *Helsingin Sanomat,* January 9, 1997.

Tiitta, A. "Suomalaisen Maiseman Hahmottuminen Kirjalisuudessa ja Kuvataiteessa." (Finnish Landscape in Literature and Art). *Terra* 94 (1) (1982): 13–26.

Tilly, C. "Western State-Making and Theories of Political Transformation." In C. Tilly, ed., *The Formation of National States in Western Europe.* Princeton, N.J.: Princeton University Press, 1975.

Topelius, Z. *Maamme kirja (The Book of Our Land).* 47th ed. Porvoo: Wsoy, 1945.

Vuorela, T. "Ethnology in Finland before 1920." The Finnish Society of Sciences and Letters; 14b. Helsinki, 1977.

Wilson, W. *Folklore and Nationalism in Modern Finland.* Bloomington: Indiana University Press, 1976.

———. *Kalevala ja kansallisuusaate. (Kalevala and Nationalism).* Helsinki: Työväen sivistyslitto, 1985.

7

Place, Territory, and National Identity in Estonia

Tim Unwin

This chapter explores the contrasting forces shaping Estonia's national identity following the republic's independence from the Soviet Union in 1991. It argues that there are always competing ideas and images of what constitutes a nation's identity and that currently in Estonia these can broadly be grouped around two central themes. On the one hand there are those who argue that Estonia's identity is essentially rural and that it is derived primarily from the country's national awakening in the nineteenth century. This imagery owes much to the creation of institutions and socioeconomic structures during Estonia's first period of independence between 1918 and 1939. In contrast to this, there are those who seek to forge a new identity for Estonia in the context of the republic's increasing linkages with Europe and its aspiration to join both the European Union and the North Atlantic Treaty Organization. Advocates of this approach seek to create an identity for Estonia that is modern, forward looking, and based essentially on the success of its urban commercial economy (Lauristin and Vihalemm 1997). The resultant tensions find their expression both within the political arena, as represented by contrasting patterns of support for the various political parties in different parts of the country, and also in the dramatic changes taking place within rural society and economic activity (for a broader discussion of rural change elsewhere in eastern Europe, see Conte and Giordano 1995).

After a discussion of the historical context and the currently contested nature of Estonian identity, the chapter addresses three of the book's key themes. First, it explores the importance of size in influencing the character and durability of national identity. Second, it examines the relationships between ethnic identity and national identity, both through an exploration of the ways in which ethnic groups can retain their identities within larger societies and also through an examination of how territorial identity can be used to suppress aspects of ethnic identity. Third, it investigates the role of the physical environment and interpretations of nature in shaping particular national identities.

Historical Context in Contemporary Practice

A central tenet of this chapter is that much of the debate over the creation of an Estonian national identity since the republic's latest independence in 1991 has been based around questions of Estonian identity in the past. Whereas "modern" forces seek to emphasize Estonia's new role in a free market and liberal democratic Europe, other voices reflect past Estonian interests in the land and in a particular kind of rural identity. To understand these debates, it is crucial to have some awareness of the emergence of Estonian national identity during the nineteenth century and the first half of the twentieth century.

Before the nineteenth century, the territory of Estonia and the majority of the people who lived there were subject to a range of different cultural influences, including Danish, German, Swedish, and Russian (Raun 1991, Taagepera 1993, Lieven 1994, Tarand 1996). Throughout this period, the meaning of being Estonian was largely forged from opposition to an alien ruling elite, and Estonian identity was largely a rural peasant identity. This has been stressed by J. Kahk (1994a: 10), who notes that, "For centuries the Baltic area was a battleground between East, West and North. Estonians were ruled over by the Knights of German Orders and by catholic bishops, by Polish, Danish and Swedish kings and Russian tsars. For over six hundred years, Estonian life as such was almost wholly the life of the countryside and village people. . . . (T)he Estonian countryside was in many respects a closed world." He goes on to emphasize that research on Estonian folklore indicates that the views of the peasantry underwent significant change over this period, as expressed in folksongs that indicate that "Earlier heroic themes and sentiments were pushed into the background and feelings of envy and vengeance became more prominent" (Kahk 1994a: 11). Significantly, Kahk not only highlights the importance of a rural peasant tradition but also that this identity was expressed in song.

It was in the nineteenth century that these various threads were first brought together to create a specific Estonian identity; indeed this period has widely been referred to as Estonia's cultural awakening (Raun

Estonia

International Boundary
⊙ National Capital
85 km
0   90 Miles

FINLAND

Gulf of Finland

Tallinn
Rakvere
Haapsalu   .Turi
Hiumaa   Lake
Baltic Sea   Mustvee Peipus   RUSSIA
Parnu
Saarema
Tartu
Gulf of
Riga
LATVIA   LATVIA

Chris Leatham

1991, Taagepera 1993, Abrahams and Kahk 1994, Kahk 1994b, c). Four factors were of particular importance in shaping the character of this national identity that emerged between 1860 and 1885. First, although the movement was led by an indigenous Estonian middle class, it was in essence a peasant movement; second, it was closely linked with land reform; third, it was considerably enhanced by the introduction of technological innovation in agriculture; and fourth, it was advanced by the use of Estonian language publications, both epic works such as the *Kalevipoeg* and also more prosaic texts such as agricultural periodicals.

Kahk (1994b) emphasizes that the crucial change that took place in this period was essentially a change in peasant attitudes toward property. The Peasant Laws of 1816 and 1819 had led to Latvian and Estonian peasants being declared free from serfdom, but this legislation nevertheless also stated that all land, including that which the peasants had traditionally farmed, belonged to the landlords. The conceptual worlds of the peasantry and the Baltic German nobility were vastly apart on this issue, and it proved difficult for the peasantry to adjust from their traditional conceptualization of feudal rent to the idea that what they saw as "their" land could actually be taken from them (Kahk 1994a). A powerful peasant protest movement thus emerged,

▶───◀

CURRENT COUNTRY DATA

Area:	45,227 km² (Tartu Peace Treaty of 1920 defined area as 47,549 km²), fifteen counties (*maakond*)
Population:	1,462,130 (as of January 1, 1997)
Population density:	32.6 inhabitants per km² (January 1, 1996, official estimate)
Mortality rate:	12.09 per thousand (January 1, 1996, official estimate)
Urban population:	69.4% (January 1, 1996, official estimate)
Ethnic groups:	Estonians 65%; Russians 28.2%; Ukrainians 2.6%; Belarussians 1.5%, Finns 0.9%; others 1.8% (January 1, 1996, official estimate)
Religions:	Lutheran, Orthodox, Baptist, Methodist
Languages:	Estonian is the official language. The other main languages spoken include Russian, Finnish, English, and German
GDP growth rate:	4.0% for 1996; 4.3% for 1995
Average monthly gross wage:	3,463 kroons (approx. US$250) for 3rd quarter of 1997
Unemployment rate:	10.7% (3rd quarter 1997)

Source: Derived from official figures published by the Bank of Estonia (http://www.ee.epbe/) and the Estonian Ministry of Foreign Affairs.

PERTINENT CONFLICTS

1914–1918	World War I
1918, 24 February	Proclamation of Independence for Republic of Estonia
1920, 2 February	Tartu Peace Treaty fixing boundary between Estonia and Russia
1939, 23 August	Molotov-Ribbentrop pact
1940, 17 June	Estonia invaded by Russian troops
1941, 6 June	6,400 Estonians deported
1941, July–August	Summer invasion by Germany
1944, July–October	Russians reinvaded

| 1949, March | Deportation of some 22,000 people by Soviet government |
| 1991 | Independence |

Source: Derived in part from Taagepera 1993, Lauristin and Vihalemm 1997

BRIEF HISTORICAL BACKGROUND

The nineteenth century saw the awakening of a specific Estonian national identity, following centuries of rule by Germans, Danes, Swedes, and Russians. The republic's first period of independence emerged in the wake of the dissolution of the Russian empire during the 1914–1918 war, with a proclamation of independence being declared on February 24, 1918. The boundaries between Russia and Estonia were eventually settled in the Treaty of Tartu in 1920. In the ensuing years of the 1920s and 1930s, Estonia emerged as a largely agricultural and rural state, with around three-quarters of its farms under 20 ha. The 1939–1945 war saw Estonia being invaded in turn by Russian, German, and then again Russian troops, leading eventually to its incorporation into the Soviet Union during the postwar period. The Soviet occupation led to substantial urban and industrial growth linked to considerable foreign immigration, although the agrarian economy continued to be based largely on dairy production. Increasing unrest during the 1980s associated with the broader fragmentation of the Soviet Union, but also in part linked with the rise of an environmental movement in Estonia, led to the republic's independence in 1991. Since then, Estonia has been eager to realign itself with Western, particularly Scandinavian, traditions of liberal democracy and a free market economy.

▶━━━━━━━━━━━━━━━━━━━━━━━━━━━━━━━━━━━━━━━◀

involving emotions and concepts much more complex than simply issues of rights to land. As Kahk (1994a: 20) notes, "from the German-Scandinavian conquest onwards, the antagonism between peasants and their lords was coloured by national feelings. Peasants hated their lords, exploited wars to attack their estates, and often declared that they wished to obey only the king or tsar. But when they spoke about historical rights to land, they did not presuppose the rights of individual peasants to concrete pieces of land, so much as the status and rights of Estonians more generally with regard to their country."

Kahk (1994a: 20) goes on to suggest that in these circumstances "The idea of 'historical rights' thus points to the ties of a nation with its land; all other nations are aliens, people who have come from far away and

therefore have less rights than the natives. It is also in this sense . . .
that the 'rights' of the Estonian nation were understood by the leaders
of the Estonian 'national awakening' in the middle of the 19th century." This is highly significant, because ideas about a particular relationship between people and the land were to find their practical expression in the creation of the landholding system created during the
republic's first period of independence in the 1920s and 1930s. This in
turn was to act as a central symbol of Estonia's emerging national identity in the 1980s as its people sought to overthrow what they perceived
as the Soviet yoke.

The Estonian national awakening in the 1860s, though, was not only
about land reform and the contested emergence of the peasants as
owners of their own land. It also involved the creation of an intelligentsia and the emergence of a distinctively Estonian "high culture." Any
summary of the processes involved in this awakening must be highly
selective, but in linking this national awakening with recent events in
the 1990s, it is pertinent to note the key elements identified as being
significant by those involved in the creation of the new post-Soviet
Estonian national identity. The Estonian Institute (1995a: 4–5), which
provides an official information service for the republic, has highlighted five main themes in Estonian nationalism, which are widely
accepted by Estonians as having been of central significance to the development of Estonia's national identity: the role of the Estonian language, the importance of education, the significance of local Estonian-
language newspapers and journals, the role of the national theater and
epic poetry, and the importance of song festivals and singing. By reas-
serting these core elements of Estonia's culture and identity during the
first years of the republic's new independence in the 1990s, the institute is thus seeking to provide an important element of continuity with
the past.

However, it is also salient to note that the imagery of the institute
provides a somewhat different gloss on past events to that provided
by historians such as Kahk (1994a, c), who continue to stress the importance of the links between the peasantry and the land in the emergence
of Estonia's independent identity. Another significant aspect of this
particular relationship between people and the land was the traditional
importance of magic ritual and Shamanism in the lives of many Estonians. Such rituals were also incorporated into the nineteenth-century
epic poems written about the ancient Finno-Ugric peoples, such as the
Kalevala, first published in 1835 by the Finnish scholar Elias Lönnrot,
and the *Kalevipoeg*, written by the Estonians Faehlmann and Kreutz-
wald and published in 1861 (Taagepera 1993, Lieven 1994: 119–121).
These folk epics, as well as having been important for the formulation

of specific Finnish and Estonian national identities in the nineteenth century, represent the survival among Finno-Ugric peoples of a relationship between people and nature that was fundamentally different from that which had emerged in Christian Romanized Europe.

In the late nineteenth century, following the death of Jakobson and the intense Russification program initiated by Czar Alexander III, the Estonian nationalist movement suffered a severe setback. However, in the turmoil of the 1914–1918 war and the disintegration of the Russian empire in 1917, a three-man Salvation Committee issued a proclamation of independence for the Republic of Estonia on February 24, 1918. German forces invaded the next day, and with the collapse of German power later in the year, Russian Red Army Units once again invaded in 1919. It was not until the Tartu Peace Treaty of February 2, 1920, that the national boundaries between Russia and Estonian were fixed and Russia agreed to recognize Estonia's independence in perpetuity.

In 1919 a constitutional assembly was elected, and one of the Parliament's first acts was to pass a radical land reform law on October 10, 1919. In 1918, 58 percent of the total area of Estonia was still in large landed estates, with the remaining 42 percent of the land being divided into some 51,640 small freehold farms, averaging only 34.1 hectares (Pullerits 1937, Kahk 1994a). The Land Reform Law subsequently led to the redistribution of over 2.3 million hectares of land and established an additional 83,514 new independent holdings. At last, the Estonian vision of small independent rural farm holdings, for which the peasantry had been campaigning ever since the passing of the Peasant Laws in 1816 and 1819, was fulfilled.

Despite the existence of an Estonian urban middle class with its own "high culture" and a more developed industrial base than many of its neighbors, Estonia remained fundamentally a rural country during the 1920s and 1930s (Pullerits 1928, 1937). By the end of the 1930s, just under three-quarters of all farms were less than 20 hectares, and a similar percentage of farms were run on a single-person ownership basis (Raud 1953, Aunap and Mander 1991; Van Arkadie and Karlsson 1992). This creation of an independent small-scale farming sector had crucial economic, social, and cultural implications for the identity of the Estonian Republic prior to the 1939–1945 war (White 1994).

Throughout the 1920s and early 1930s, Estonian politics were highly unstable (Lieven 1994), and with the global recession of the 1930s, the fears of the middle class, concerned both about their economic future and the political implications of the Communist regime on their eastern border, led to the emergence of various right-wing groups. In particular, the League of Veterans of the War of Independence gained a strong following, with an ideology that "was strongly nationalist, anti-communist, anti-parliamentary, anti-semitic, and opposed to ethnic minorities in general" (Lieven 1994: 69). In municipal elections in January 1934, the league won absolute majorities in Estonia's three main cities. Anxious over the implications of this and supported by the Socialists, Prime Minister Konstantin Päts declared martial law and arrested the league's leading members (Taagepera 1993). The following year, after growing opposition to his views, Päts banned all political parties and replaced them with his own Fatherland League. Subsequently, Estonian political life became ever more authoritarian. Although not as extreme as the fascist rhetoric of the League of Veterans, Päts was unwilling to return Estonia rapidly to a democracy and proved very reluctant to relinquish his own powers as president.

On the eve of the 1939–1945 war, Estonia was thus in the hands of a right-wing authoritarian ruler (for an excellent summary, see Kasekamp 1996). Around two-thirds of the population was classified as rural, and the vast majority of farms were still small scale and privately owned. For the majority of Estonians, this close link with their newly acquired land was central to their understanding of what it meant to be Estonian. However, this rural identity was soon to be challenged during the period of Soviet occupation, which lasted for almost half a century.

Under the secret protocols of the Molotov-Ribbentrop pact, Estonia was invaded by Soviet troops on June 17, 1940, leading to a period of terror, arrests, and deportations. During the summer of 1941 the Germans then reinvaded Estonia, and given the mass deportations that had preceded the German attack, most of the Estonian population initially welcomed them. However, following the repressions of the Nazis, resistance against the invading German forces in its turn grew, until the Soviet army once again invaded Estonia in September 1944. There followed a further period of mass deportation and genocide, so that by 1945 it is estimated that the population of Estonia was only three-quarters of what it had been in 1939 (Lieven 1994). The period of warfare and Estonian guerrilla resistance to the Soviet forces has been detailed at length elsewhere (Taagepera 1993, Lieven 1994, Kahk 1994d), and it is not the intention to summarize the history of Soviet occupation here at any length. However, it is salient to emphasize the violence and oppression that characterized the early years of Soviet rule. Immediately on the annexation of Estonia, the Soviet authorities initiated a program of land reform leading to collectivization. However, this was resisted by large numbers of Estonian farmers, and so the Soviet government ordered the deportation of some 22,000 people in March 1949 (Kahk 1994d). This broke the back of Estonian resistance, and thereafter the process of collectivization continued apace so that by 1955 there were 908 collective farms and ninety-seven state farms in Estonia.

Although direct resistance to Soviet rule was extremely difficult and was stamped out with harsh retaliatory measures, indirect resistance was still possible. This was mainly reflected in the cultural sphere and largely resorted to images and practices derived from the period of cultural awakening in the nineteenth century. The Estonian Institute (1995b: 1) thus comments that "Despite the all-pervasive Communist ideology which tried to stamp out independent thinking and national identity, Estonians continued to resist, shifting to the preservation of cultural identity and family values. Traditional song festivals, organized every five years, offered an opportunity to express national unity." However, the maintenance of a specifically rural Estonian national identity during the period of Soviet occupation also rested on five other features (Unwin 1997): the continued importance of agriculture in the Estonian economy; the close links with the countryside retained by many urban Estonians; the urban bias in Soviet occupation, which meant that by 1989 although Estonian speakers accounted for only 49 percent of the urban population, they represented some 87.5 percent of the rural population of the country (Marksoo 1992); the location of armed resistance by the Forest Brothers *(Metsavennad)* specifically in rural and forested areas; and the environmental degradation resulting from the Soviet program of heavy industrialization and the extraction of vast areas of oil shale and phosphorite in the north and east of the country, which provided the basis for an increasingly vehement Estonian environmental movement during the 1980s (Taagepera 1993, Lieven 1994).

Above all, the images of Estonia that were sustained during the period of Soviet rule were essentially those looking back to what was seen as a rather idyllic rural past, where the majority of Estonian families each had their own farm (Figure 7.1). It was this identity that was continually reemphasized in the words of Estonian songs. Taagepera (1993: 207–208) thus poignantly recalls events after the achievement of Estonia's independence again in 1991 in the following words: "there was a day of exhilaration, the event called the Song of Freedom (September 8, 1991), a more modest repeat of the Song of Estonia exactly three years earlier that 250,000 attended. Now the crowd was around 100,000. In the intermittent rain showers we sang the unaccustomed words 'jää vabaks, Eesti pind!' (stay free, soil of Estonia), whereas for most of the last fifty years, it had been a hushed 'saa vabaks, Eesti pind!' (be free again, soil of Estonia)." Such rhetoric once again reinforces the significance of the links between a particular relationship with the land and Estonia's national identity.

Figure 7.1 Traditional image of Estonian national identity:
the windmills at Angla

Contested Images of Independent Identity

The crisis of the Soviet economy during the 1980s and the increasing failure of its system of legitimation provided the context in which Estonian claims for independence were able to find their realization. Much has been written about the emergence of the Baltic states as independent entities in the 1990s (Taagepera 1993, Lieven 1994, Smith 1994, Lauristin and Vihalemm 1997). Instead of seeking to summarize this material the purpose here is rather to emphasize three key features: the role of rural agendas in the independence movement, the contested nature of the postindependence rhetorics of identity, and the increasing impoverishment of rural areas in Estonia during the 1990s.

Rural agendas played a significant part in the complex arena of political opposition to Soviet rule that emerged during the latter part of the 1980s. Two themes in particular can be highlighted. First, in May 1987 a number of students and intellectuals protested successfully against plans to dramatically expand phosphorite mining in northeastern Estonia, arguing that this would have had damaging ecological impacts. Second, considerable pressure for the disintegration of the collective farming system emerged in the late 1980s, with the first private farm being declared as early as 1987 (Unwin 1994, 1996). By the beginning of 1988 some 200 private farms existed, and by the end of 1990, under growing pressure from the newly independent farmers, the Supreme Soviet of Estonia declared collectives illegal.

Thus, well before independence in 1991, fundamental changes were beginning to take place in rural areas. In October 1991, a land reform law was passed, establishing the basic principle that anyone who was a citizen of the republic on June 16, 1940, or who is an heir of such a person, had the right to demand return, substitution of compensation for land that was unlawfully alienated. Overnight, as Abrahams (1992; see also Abrahams and Kahk 1994) has emphasized, this therefore provided the context for subsequent rural change by setting the clock back to the 1930s and to a landholding structure that was likely to be incapable of providing the basis for a competitive agricultural sector in the context of Europe in the 1990s (Figure 7.2). However, such a system of landownership was perfectly consonant with the symbolic significance that small private farms had retained throughout the period of Soviet rule. In the late 1990s, with the benefit of hindsight, it is easy to criticize the policies introduced in the fervor of independence at the beginning of the decade, but at that time the Estonian Farmers' Central Union as well as foreign advisors, such as the Danish Agricultural Advisory Centre, were predicting that there would be some 40,000–60,000 private farms in Estonia by the year 2000 (Unwin 1994).

Figure 7.2   Recreating a rural national identity: a recently privatized farm near Tartu

Although such aspirations toward the reconstruction of a rural identity as it had existed in the 1930s were being advocated by many Estonians, others were eager to see Estonia move as rapidly as possible toward a modern, Western capitalist economy (Rausing 1996). The key words in their rhetoric were *democracy* and a *free market*, and it was this latter view of Estonia's future that was to convince the majority of the voters in the first postindependence elections. Three central principles have thus come to underpin Estonia's postindependence economic policies: a stable currency, a balanced budget, and liberal foreign trade. The net outcome has been that Estonia is widely seen as being one of the countries of eastern Europe and the former Soviet Union to have benefited most from the economic transformations that have taken place in the region (Lauristin and Vihalemm 1997). However, such policies have not been without their problems, and these have mainly been encountered in rural areas.

Tensions between those advocating different conceptualizations of Estonia's future identities have been clearly expressed in the voting patterns in elections since independence in 1991. The first elections to be held following the adoption of the new constitution took place in September 1992 and were contested by some thirty-two parties. They were won by the Fatherland Party *(Isamaa)* with twenty-nine seats, followed by the Secure Home Party *(Kindel Kodu)* with seventeen seats, and the Popular Party with fifteen seats. As Lieven (1994: 285) has noted, the Fatherland Party "had stood on a mixture of free-market economics, restitutionalism, and moderate nationalism, under the overall slogan 'cleaning house,' represented by an election poster depicting a man with a broom." This election therefore brought into power a government eager to align the Estonian economy closely with a free-market policy involving minimal government intervention.

Although such policies undoubtedly benefited the urban commercial sector, the refusal of the government to permit subsidies for agriculture was a point of considerable grievance to many of those in rural areas. Agricultural production collapsed (Unwin 1994, CCET 1996), and many more elderly and rural voters became increasingly dissatisfied with the style of government and approach adopted by the new generation of young politicians. This concern was expressed in the March 1995 elections, which were contested by thirty parties, divided into seven electoral unions and nine individual parties. Although the Reform Party-Liberals *(Reformierakond)*, campaigning on a policy of continued economic restructuring, gained the largest single number of seats (nineteen), the overall winners of the election were the Coalition Party and Rural Union *(Koonderakond ja Maarahava Ühendus* KMU) with forty-one seats. This coalition consisted of a range of different parties who had been opposed to the economic program introduced by the previous government and reflected pensioners' interests and the concerns of rural people and farmers as well as those of the Coalition Party.

The KMU's victory did initially lead to some change of direction in policy, although not to the extent that substantial numbers of rural people who voted for them would have liked. However, the collapse of the government in October 1995 once again threw the country into political turmoil. Discussions between the KMU and the Reform Party, intended to create a new coalition, led to the removal of various policies that would have directly benefited farmers. The agreement thus stated quite clearly that protective tariffs, subsidies, donations, and other direct support measures would not be used by the government in achieving its aims. This was nevertheless balanced by the inclusion of a statement to the effect that transfers would regularly be made into a budget for the development of rural life and that a new law would be adopted in 1996 specifically on the support of rural life. This, however, failed to materialize, and the overall thrust of the coalition agreement reflected the continued dominance of free market economic principles.

In the local elections held in the autumn of 1996 the Reform Party once again performed well, particularly in urban areas, and this provided them with a platform from which they tried to argue for greater influence in the government. During November, the Coalition Party then signed a cooperation agreement with the Centre Party, apparently without first having consulted the Reform Party. This resulted in the Reform Party leaving the coalition, with all six of its ministers submitting letters of resignation on November 22. Such political volatility reflects the continuing contested views of different groups within Estonia concerning the future path of economic change and thus the construction of the republic's national identity. It is not easy to generalize about these contested identities, but the electoral voting patterns and support for different parties clearly reflect a major divide between, on the one hand, urban commercial interests, and on the other, farmers and rural people. As the historical introduction to this chapter emphasized, this tension is one that reflects very deep-seated feelings of Estonian people concerning their past identity.

Size, Ethnicity, and Nature in the Construction of Estonian National Identity

Size and National Identity

With a population of some one and a half million and an area of less than 50,000 km^2, it is in many ways remarkable that Estonia should have been able to survive centuries of external rule and domination to emerge as a newly independent state in the 1990s (Ruutsoo 1997). Other small states undoubtedly exist in the world, but the majority of these are endowed with some distinct economic asset, such as plentiful oil reserves in the cases of Bahrain or Kuwait. Estonia has no such resource base, but its people have nevertheless retained a deep sense of their cultural identity.

In explaining the survival of Estonian identity, Taagepera (1993: 5–6) has stressed that "Estonia became the smallest continental language area in the world to break through to modern culture because a small quasi-insular area (1) had a language very different from that of most of its neighbors, (2) was geographically and politically isolated from its linguistic kinfolk, and (3) was strategically set so that its peculiarities could fix a major religious cultural border at that location and thus reinforce its distinct identity." These arguments, though, do not provide a complete interpretation of the survival of Estonia's identity, particularly during the twentieth century. Three other factors need to be considered as having played their part during the period of Soviet rule between 1940 and 1991.

First, it was highly significant that Estonia, along with Latvia and Lithuania, was able to retain a sense of separate identity as a distinct Soviet Socialist republic. This enabled some Estonians to gain positions of political power and influence during the Soviet era, through which a small number sought to maintain elements of Estonia's national identity. Lieven (1994: 93) has thus observed that "After the death of Stalin, many native Communist officials extended a measure of protection to cultural figures, and indeed justified their own collaboration in terms of preserving the nation's cultural heritage." The links between the intelligentsia and Communist officials are well exemplified in the following account by Lieven (1994: 93) of the tensions represented by the life of Ingrid Rüütel, the wife of the Communist Chairman of the Estonian SSR Supreme Council:

> As the process of "nativization" of the Baltic Communist Parties proceeded, leading Communists inevitably had close links with the intelligentsias, the majority of whom, even if they did not brave outright dissent, were nationalist in spirit and, above all, committed to preserving their national cultures. . . . As the daughter of Neeme Rüüs, Ideology Secretary of the Estonian Communist Party in 1940–41, who was executed by the Nazis, Ingrid Rüütel came from the very heart of the Communist establishment. Yet by profession she was an ethnographer, a branch of academia full, throughout the Soviet years, of crypto-nationalists.

A second factor that helped Estonians to sustain their identity through the Soviet period was their close proximity to Finland (Lauristin and Vihalemm 1997). The possibility that Estonians had of receiving Finnish radio and television programs meant that they could relatively easily maintain links with another Finno-Ugric speaking people. This not only allowed them to gain news unbiased by the Soviet censors, but more importantly it enabled them to retain a sense of linguistic distinctiveness that was not entirely isolated. A third significant factor in influencing the survival of Estonian identity during the Soviet period, though, was that being Estonian was itself a way of opposing Soviet rule. Throughout history, Estonians have forged their own identity in opposition to a sequence of alien rulers, and in this respect the Soviet occupation, however unwelcome, was therefore nothing new (Huntington 1993, Ruutsoo 1997).

More generally, these arguments suggest that small size by itself is not necessarily an overwhelming obstacle to the creation and maintenance of national identity. Another significant conclusion that can be drawn from the Estonian example, though, is that even with small nations, identity is something that can be highly contested. Although opposition to alien rule is highly important in uniting people around a single concept of identity, ideas of national identity become much more readily contested once such opposition is removed. This is clearly reflected in the arguments over the future meaning of Estonian identity that have risen to the fore since independence in 1991 (Ruutsoo 1997).

Ethnicity and Estonian National Identity

The relationship between ethnic identity and national identity is central to an understanding of what it means to be Estonian. Although the territory of Estonia has usually in the past been ruled by people from a range of different ethnic groups, Estonians have managed to retain their own independent identity. It was this identity that emerged as the dominant force in the republic's first period of independence in the 1920s and 1930s. Aware of their own oppression in previous centuries, Estonians are eager to emphasize that their Law on Cultural Autonomy of Ethnic Minorities promulgated in 1925 was the first of its kind anywhere in the world. This granted the right for ethnic minority groups of over 3,000 people to establish their own cultural self-government, including the rights "to organize, administrate and monitor public and private educational institutions in their native language" and "to attend to the respective ethnic minority's other cultural needs and administrate institutions and enterprises established for that purpose" (Estonian Institute 1994).

During Estonia's first period of independence, people of Estonian ethnic origin accounted for between 87 percent and 89 percent of the population. In 1934, ethnic Russians represented a further 8.2 percent, Germans, 1.5 percent, Swedes, 0.7 percent, Latvians, 0.4 percent, and Jews, 0.4 percent (Estonian Institute 1995c). However, following the Soviet conquest of Estonia, the percentage of Estonians in the population of the republic fell rapidly to 74.6 percent in 1959, 64.7 percent in 1979, and 61.5 percent in 1989 (Estonian Institute 1995c). Although people of Russian ethnic origin dominated the minorities, with 30.3 percent of the total population in 1989, the 1989 census recorded 121 different nationalities in Estonia. The very large number of non-Estonian immigrants exacerbated social and cultural tensions, and the enforced Russification policies of the Soviet era were widely disliked by Estonians. Nevertheless, it is highly significant that Estonians were able to retain a sense of their own ethnic identity throughout the period of Soviet rule. This was in part achieved by looking back to their "cultural awakening" in the nineteenth century and to the economic, social, and political structures that were created during the first period of independence in the 1920s and 1930s.

Following independence in 1991, the role of the ethnic minorities in the newly independent republic has been one that has aroused considerable discussion and debate (Jasinskaja 1996). Article 1 of the 1992 Constitution states that "Estonia is an independent and sovereign democratic republic wherein the supreme power of the state is held by the people." Herein, lies an unambiguous claim to democracy. However, the constitution also emphasizes that only those who were citizens of the interwar republic or their descendants have an automatic right to citizenship. For all other people, a period of residency, linguistic competence in Estonian, and an oath of loyalty were required (Smith 1996). This therefore excluded from citizenship most of the Russian speaking people who had entered the territory of Estonia between 1940 and 1991. In the light of these arrangements, Smith (1996) has suggested that Estonia should be considered an ethnic democracy in which the dominance of one ethnic group is institutionalized. Smooha and Hanf (1992: 32) see such ethnic democracies as a viable option for deeply divided and nondemocratic societies, and they suggest that "Since nationalism in Eastern Europe tends to be integral and exclusionary as opposed to Western nationalism which tends to be open, inclusive and coterminous with citizenship, there is a strong possibility for some of the democratizing states there to become ethnic democracies."

One of the central problems facing the newly elected Estonian government was how best to incorporate a substantial ethnic minority within the republic's territory, a problem not made any easier because this minority had once formed part of the politically dominant social group. Estonian governments since 1992 have therefore placed great emphasis on Article 9 of the new constitution, which states unequivocally that "The rights, liberties and duties of everyone and all persons, as listed in the Constitution, shall be equal for Estonian citizens as well as for citizens of foreign states and stateless persons who are present in Estonia." The main difficulty with this claim is that Article 57 states that "The right to vote shall belong to every Estonian citizen who has attained the age of eighteen." So, although there is a claim that basic human rights apply to all people within Estonia, a large number of Russian speaking people who have not chosen to take Estonian citizenship have been excluded from voting in national elections. This tension has been emphasized by Russian politicians in their dealings with Estonia, as well as by some Russian-speaking groups within Estonia. In October 1993, though, the Law on Cultural Autonomy for Ethnic Minorities in existence between 1925 and 1940 was restored, and this led to the registration of some sixty different new associations by October 1995 (Estonian Institute 1995c). Further international pressure led to the passing of a new Law on Citizenship in January 1995, which was designed to make it easier for Russian speakers to become Estonian citizens if they so wished. Despite these attempts to reduce external criticism, particularly in the context of Estonia's planned accession to the European Union, accusations of discrimination and human rights abuses continue to be quite common in the Russian-language press.

Estonia's emerging national identity has therefore been closely bound up with conceptions of ethnic identity. As yet the ethnic tensions outlined previously have not erupted into serious violence. Many Estonians are thus eager to emphasize their history of ethnic harmony. In this context, The Estonian Institute's (1995c: 4) conclusions on Estonia's ethnic policies make interesting reading.

> Estonians are willing to support the aspirations of other peoples, because they know well from their own historical experience what it means to live without freedom or recognition. Sociological studies commissioned by the Ethnic Minorities' Round Table in 1993 concluded that the Estonians' attitude towards non-Estonians is neither aggressive nor vengeful. Foreigners, who choose to stay permanently in the country are accepted, provided they learn the Estonian language and are loyal to the country. Although some non-citizens may find it difficult to get used to their changed status from that of a powerful representative of a colonial empire to being a member of an ethnic minority in a foreign country, attitudes will change in time. The Republic of Estonia will try to solve problems concerning citizenship, minority policies or human rights, peacefully, legally and in a humane manner.

Two key factors need to be taken into consideration in any long-term appraisal of the future of Estonia's ethnic identity. The first is that the Russian-speaking population living within Estonia over the last fifty years has had some advantages in terms of living standards compared with people living elsewhere in the former Soviet Union. This is still largely true today, although if unemployment rates among the non-Estonian population remain high, then this is likely to give rise to increasing ethnic tension. Second, the presence of Russia on Estonia's immediate eastern border remains a source of considerable uncertainty (Ruutsoo 1997). As long as there are Russian politicians eager to regain territory in the Baltics, the position of Russian minorities in countries such as Estonia is one that they will continue to exploit. This has been seen most recently in debates over the expansion of NATO, and despite Estonia's wishes to join at the earliest opportunity, it seems likely that Russian sensitivities over the accession of former Soviet republics to NATO will remain a stumbling block for some time to come.

Nature and National Identity

This chapter has stressed throughout that Estonian national identity has been closely linked to a particular interpretation of the meaning of the physical world. Unlike in much of western Europe, where "people" and "nature" are often seen as opposites, the traditional Finno-Ugric interpretation of this relationship, mediated by the role of Shamans, is very different. For Estonians, the meaning and significance of the forest is thus something very different from that experienced by most people in western Europe or North America. Rather than being something rather alien or "other," to be cut down and exploited (Schama 1995), Estonians thus see the forest as very much an element of their internal home environment. J. G. Frazer (1981), for example, notes the Estonian belief in the forest spirit Metsik, to whom prayers and sacrifices continued to be offered in return for protection of the cereal crop and cattle.

Throughout the period of Soviet rule, opposition to Russian domination was in part expressed through this particular Estonian relationship with the physical environment. Russians were thus frequently caricatured by Estonians as steppe people, unfamiliar with the forest and only interested in the exploitation of Estonia's physical resources, such as oil shale and phosphorite. During the 1980s, the emergence of the environmental movement was thus one way in which opposition to Moscow could be expressed. Furthermore, immediately following independence a range of academic publications on "man" and nature appeared, seeking to integrate this Estonian concern with the environment with broader international agendas associated with sustainable development. Typical of these were *Estonia: Man and Nature* (Kaare et al. 1992) and *Ida-Virumaa: Man, Economy, Nature* (Kaasik, 1995). The latter of these emphasizes even more so than for the rest of Estonia the significance of the Russian domination of the easternmost part of Estonia, Ida-Virumaa. The chapter by Hallik and Vseviov (1995: 10) captures the essence of this ethnic domination:

> Soviet authorities pushed the Estonian-Russian ethnic border deep into the area traditionally settled by Estonians. The capital Tallinn, Estonian coastal areas, the major transportation junctions as well as areas bordering on Russia became footholds of colonization. The urban and mining centres of Ida-Virumaa wee turned into areas with Russian majority. Today, non-Estonians make up over 80 per cent of the population of this area. The uniform ethno-territorial and ethno-cultural area of Ida-Verumaa has ceased to exist.

The significance of the link between a particular conception of nature and Estonian national identity has been expressed in a range of ways since independence, but two highly visible examples are in the images portrayed in tourist brochures and on the republic's banknotes. Although most Estonian tourism has been focused on the capital, Tallinn, increasing attempts are being made to encourage the development of rural tourism (Unwin 1996). Indeed, almost all Estonian tourist brochures place heavy emphasis on the country's rural beauty and the value of its unspoiled "nature." Typical of these is the tourist map and booklet produced by the Huma Publishing Company (1996: 3), which emphasizes the country's rural heritage in the following terms:

> The beauty of animate and inanimate nature with its wide variety, and the preservation of naturalness—this is the greatest treasure of Estonia. Land and sea, jagged coastline and more than a thousand islands, high banks and picturesque dunes, stone-covered areas side by side with patches of fertile soil, hills and primeval valleys, springs and a thousand lakes, karst areas and marshland, extensive territories covered with forest, flora extremely rich in species, habitats of waterfowl, landscapes long forgotten in many European countries.

A second example of such emphasis on Estonia's rural landscape heritage is to be found on the republic's banknotes. In its drive to create a modern free-market economy, Estonia was the first country in the former ruble zone to implement currency reform, pegging its new currency, the kroon, to the Deutschmark at a rate of 8:1 in June 1992. The images used on the banknotes are full of historical and cultural resonances, with many of them reflecting aspects of Estonia's rural environment. On one side, the notes have pictures of key figures in Estonia's cultural awakening, including, for example, Lydia Koidula (100 kroon), Anton-Hansen Tammsaare (25 kroon), and Jakob Hurt (10 kroon). On the other side, there are historical buildings, but also the largest oak tree in Estonia (10 kroon), the rural farm where Tammsaare was born (25 kroon), and waves crashing onto the rocks of the north Estonian coast (100 kroon). These banknotes wonderfully represent the tensions encountered in the creation of Estonia's independent identity. The new currency is forward looking, a key element in Estonia's drive to create a modern capitalist economy, and yet the banknotes look back to an idealized historical past, in which rural identities, close to nature, have deep symbolic and practical significance.

Contested Identities

This chapter has sought to explore the historical traces of Estonia's national identity and to examine their implications for the construction of the newly independent state. It has throughout emphasized two key arguments: that national identity is something that is highly contested; and that traditionally the meaning of being Estonian has been intimately tied to a rural way of life. Moreover, Estonian identity has generally been forged through opposition to alien dominating powers, most recently those of the former Soviet Union.

Estonia has emerged as an independent state in the 1990s at a time when economic and political forces are creating an ever-more integrated global political economy. In this context Estonian governments have been eager to apply for membership in the European Union as rapidly as possible. Estonia became a member of the Council of Europe on May 14, 1993, and signed a free trade agreement with the European Union on July 18, 1994, which became operational on January 1, 1995. Since then, Estonia has sought to move ever closer to an economic policy that will enable it to become a full member of the union. Such policies, though, are helping to shape a national identity very different from that which was advocated in the past. The dominant forces in Estonia's economy today are urban commercial interests, and the collapse of the agrarian economy is leading to a rapid transformation of Estonia's rural landscapes, with large areas going out of production (Unwin 1997).

These tensions have been expressed in the political arena in Estonia's recent history of elections: For some Estonians, the most important objective is to become a modern European state with a thriving market economy; for others, it is to retain a sense of continuity and meaning with the past. The challenge for future Estonian governments will be to prevent such tensions from irrevocably dividing the republic. So far, they seem to have been successful (Lauristin and Vihalemm 1997). Although Estonia's national identity was maintained throughout the period of Soviet rule, specifically because it was a way of expressing opposition to an alien power, it seems likely that in their desire to integrate Estonia fully into a "modern" Europe, those in positions of political power will let important aspects of Estonia's cultural heritage gradually fade away. Being European may become more important than being Estonian. Paradoxically, in such circumstances, national identity will have been preserved much more strongly under alien domination than under conditions of so-called democracy and political freedom.

Acknowledgments

I am grateful to funding from The British Academy and the Estonian Academy of Sciences, which has enabled this research to be undertaken. Many Estonians have contributed to my attempts to understand what it means to be Estonian, and in this context I am particularly appreciative of the help and advice I have received from Anton Laur, Reet Karukäpp, Jaan-Mati Punning, Anto Raukas, Tiina Peil, and Kristi Tarand.

References

Abrahams, R. "The Emergence of New Family Farmers: The Countryside in Transition." In D. Lane, ed., *Russia in Flux*. London: Arnold, 1992.

Abrahams, R., and J. Kahk. *Barons and Farmers: Continuity and Transformation in Rural Estonia (1816–1994)*. Göteborg: Department of History, University of Göteborg, 1994.

Aunap, R., and Ü. Mander. "Estonian Agriculture." In K. Sepp, ed., *European Workshop on Human Impact on Environment: North-east Estonia Excursion Routes*. Tallinn: Institute of Ecology and Marine Research, 1991, 73–80.

Buttimer, A. "Edgar Kant and Balto-Skandia: Heimatkunde and Regional Identity." In D. Hoosen, ed., *Geography and National Identity*. Oxford: Blackwell, 1994, 161–183.

CCET (Centre for Co-Operation with the Economies in Transition). *Review of Agricultural Policies: Estonia*. Paris: CCET-OECD, 1996.

Conte, E., and C. Giordano. "Sentiers de la ruralité perdue. Réflexions sur le post-socialisme." *Etudes Rurales*, 1995, 138–140, 11–34.

Estonian Institute. *The Cultural Autonomy of Ethnic Minorities in Estonia*. Tallinn: The Estonian Institute (Estonia in Facts), 1994.

————. *A Glance at Estonia's History: From Pre-History to the Second World War*. Tallinn: The Estonian Institute (Fact Sheet, September 1995a).

————. *The Restoration of Estonian Independence*. Tallinn: The Estonian Institute (Fact Sheet, January 1995b).

————. *Ethnic Issues in Estonia*. Tallinn: The Estonian Institute (Fact Sheet, October 1995c).

————. *Facts about Estonia*. Tallinn: Estonian Institute, 1996.

Frazer, J. G. *The Golden Bough: The Roots of Religion and Folklore*. New York: Avenel Books, 1981.

Hallik, K., and D. Vseviov. "Population and Its Formation." In T. Kaasik, ed., *Ida-Virumaa: Man, Economy, Nature. (A Survey of the Problems Facing Ida-Virumaa in the Context of Sustainable Development)*. Tallinn: Stockholm Environment Institute, and Commission on Sustainable Development of Ida-Virumaa, 1995.

Huma. *Estonia for Tourists*. Tallinn: Huma Publishing, 1996.

Huntington, S. P. "The Clash of Civilisations." *Foreign Affairs* 72(3) (1993): 22–49.

Jasinskaja, T. "Baltic Russians in 1989–1995: Adaptation to a New State System." *Anthropological Journal on European Cultures* 5(2) (1996): 97–110.

Kaare, T., H. Mardiste, L. Merikalju, and J.-M. Punning, eds. *Estonia: Man and Nature*. Tallinn: Academy of Sciences of Estonia, and Estonian Geographical Society, 1992.

Kaasik, T., ed. *Ida-Virumaa: Man, Economy, Nature. (A Survey of the Problems Facing Ida-Virumaa in the Context of Sustainable Development)*. Tallinn: Stockholm Environment Institute, and Commission on Sustainable Development of Ida-Virumaa, 1995.

Kahk, J. "Historical Roots." In R. Abrahams and J. Kahk, eds., *Barons and Farmers: Continuity and Transformation in Rural Estonia (1816–1994)*. Göteborg: Faculty of Arts Europaprogrammet, University of Göteborg, 1994a, 9–49.

————. "Uue Põllumajanduse Algus Eestis 1860–1880." *Eesti Teaduste Akadeemia Toimetised: humanitaar-j a Sotsiaalteadused* 43(2) (1994b): 105–123.

————. "About the Birth of Modern Life in an Estonian Village (An Attempt to Methodologically Study Problems of Periodization)." *Eesti Teaduste Akadeemia Toimetised* 43(3) (1994c): 336–345.

————. "The Years of Soviet Occupation." In R. Abrahams and J. Kahk, eds., *Barons and Farmers: Continuity and Transformation in Rural Estonia (1816–1994)*. Göteborg: Faculty of Arts Europaprogrammet, University of Göteborg, 1994d, 50–85.

Kant, E. *Problems of Environment and Population in Estonia*. Tartu: Publicationes Seminarii Universitaties Tartuensis Oeconomico-Geographici, 7, 1934.

————. "Estland und Baltoskandis. Bidrag till Östersjöländernas Geografi och Sociografi." *Svio-Estonia*, 1935, 80–103.

Kasekamp, A. "The Nature of Authoritarianism in Interwar Estonia." *International* 33(1) (1996): 57–65.

Lauristin, M., and P. Vihalemm, eds. *Return to the Western World: Cultural and Political Perspectives on the Estonian Post-Communist Transition.* Tartu: Tartu University Press, 1997.

Lieven, A. *The Baltic Revolution: Estonia, Latvia, Lithuania, and the Path to Independence.* 2d ed. New Haven, Conn., and London: Yale University Press, 1994.

Lugus, O., and G. A. Hachey Jr., eds. *Transforming the Estonian Economy.* Tallinn: International Center for Economic Growth, 1995.

Maide, H. "Transformation of Agriculture." In O. Lugus and G. A. Hachey Jr., eds., *Transforming the Estonian Economy.* Tallinn: International Center for Economic Growth, 1995, 169–186.

Marksoo, A. "Dynamics of Rural Population in Estonia in the 1980s." In *Estonia: Man and Nature.* Tallinn: Estonian Academy of Sciences and Estonian Geographical Society, 1992, 129–153.

Pullerits, A., ed. *Eesti Põllumajandus Statistiline Album.* Tallinn: Riigi Statistika Kesküroo, 1928.

———. *Estonia: Population, Culture, and Economic Life.* Tallinn: Tallinna Eesti Kirjastus-Ühisuse Trükikoda, 1937.

Raud, V. R. *Estonia: A Reference Book.* New York: The Nordic Press, 1953.

Raun, T. O. *Estonia and the Estonians.* 2d ed. Stanford, Calif.: Hoover, 1991.

Rausing, S. "Reforming Habitus: The Appropriation of Western-ness on a Former Collective Farm in NW Estonia." *Anthropological Journal on European Cultures* 5(2) (1996): 135–158.

Ruutsoo, R. "The Estonians: Identity of Small Nation in Past and Present." *Anthropological Journal of European Cultures* 7(1) (1997): 73–100.

Schama, S. *Landscape and Memory.* London: HarperCollins, 1995.

Smith, G. "When Nations Challenge and Nations Rule: Estonia and Latvia as Ethnic Democracies." *Coexistence* 33 (1996): 25–41.

Smith, G., ed. *The Baltic States: The National Self-Determination of Estonia, Latvia, and Lithuania.* Basingstoke: Macmillan, 1994.

Smooha, S., and T. Hanf. "The Diverse Modes of Conflict-Regulation in Deeply Divided Societies." In A. Smith, ed., *Ethnicity and Nationalism.* Leiden: E. J. Brill, 1992, 25–41.

Taagepera, R. *Estonia: Return to Independence.* Boulder: Westview Press, 1993.

Tarand, K. *I'd Like to Show You My Town.* Tallinn: ReMall, 1996.

Unwin, T. "Structural Change in Estonian Agriculture: From Command Economy to Privatisation." *Geography* 79 (1994): 246–261.

———. "Tourist Development in Estonia: Images, Sustainability, and Integrated Rural Development." *Tourism Management* 17(4) (1996): 265–276.

———. "Agricultural Restructuring and Integrated Rural Development in Estonia." *Journal of Rural Studies* 13(1) (1997): 93–112.

Van Arkadie, B., and M. Karlsson. *Economic Surveys of the Baltic States: The Reform Process in Estonia, Latvia, and Lithuania.* London: Pinter, 1992.

White, J. D. "Nationalism and Socialism in Historical Perspective." In G. Smith, ed., *The Baltic States: The National Self-Determination of Estonia, Latvia, and Lithuania.* Basingstoke: Macmillan, 1994, 13–40.

8

Nested Identities in Nigeria

Rex D. Honey

Nigeria is an African place created by Europeans. It is a powerful place; the "Giant of Africa" with some 90 million people. It is the world's sixth ranking oil exporting state and the leading military power of West Africa. Nigeria is also a place in chaos. Successive military governments have ruled for more than 70 percent of its independent history. Despite its oil riches, it has plummeted from the ranks of the emerging economic powers to join its West African neighbors among the world's poorest countries. The once vibrant night life of its cities has evaporated in an atmosphere of trepidation as people try to evade the dual dangers of military oppression and armed robbers. One consequence is that Nigeria is a place of multiple and ambivalent identities.

Nigeria is a fascinating example of the interplay between territory and identity. At one extreme is the national identity, shared to varying degrees by all Nigerians, some fully committed to being part of what they see as a global power, others bothered by the excesses of oppressive governments. At the other extreme are village and town identities, tied to traditional patterns of associational life, with many people taking their primary identity from their patrilocal places of origin. Other crucial identities in Nigeria are based on ethnic group, religion, and jurisdictional organization. Nigeria has over 300 ethnic groups, ranging in size from the Hausa with a population surpassing 30 million and the Yoruba with close to 20 million down to a number of groups with only hundreds of members. The myriad traditional African religions have in the last two centuries been buffeted by the onslaughts of both Islam and Christianity, with the competing proselytizing faiths now constituting the most significant cultural divide in the country.

Jurisdictionally, the country has moved from three regions at independence to thirty-six states in the late 1990s, with each successive round of state creation altering jurisdictional structure and identity. As will be seen, these factors influencing identity have been remarkably fluid over the last 200 years in the place that has become Nigeria. This chapter examines that fluidity, looking in turn at the political geography and identities of precolonial Nigeria, the transformation of territory and identity during the colonial period, and the continuing alterations of identity that have marked Nigeria since independence. Before the infamous European "scramble for Africa," there was no Nigeria (Gavin and Betley 1973). Identities were based on other things. Now those other things compete with the national identity in a variety of ways and with a range of commitments. Let us see how.

Territory and Identity in Precolonial Nigeria

Culturally, Nigeria is an incredibly complex place. The Nigerian sociologist Onigu Otite identifies 374 separate ethnic groups in the country (Otite 1990: 175). He does so on the basis of five criteria that are important to the issues of territoriality and identity. The first, in fact, is that each group has a "core-territoriality," a place to which members of a group can retreat in times of emergency and with which they identify, even though many, perhaps even a majority, have moved away. The second is cultural identity, including but not limited to language. The third is shared patterns of normative behavior, the fourth exclusive membership, and the fifth shared myths of kinship ideology (Otite 1990: 16–19). Together these criteria yield a lengthy list of identifiable ethnic groups, most quite small in terms of numbers. In precolonial times, they had their own histories, legends, social structures, political structures, and ways of providing sustenance; in many ways, they still do.

Even today an important part of the geography of Nigeria is the geography of ethnic groups. As Figure 8.1 shows, Hausa is now the dominant language of the north, Yoruba, of the southwest, and Igbo, the southeast. Several smaller groups dominate their own areas: for example, the Izon (often spelled "Ijaw") in the Niger Delta and the Kanuri near Lake Chad in the northeast. Ethnic identities, as defined by Otite, follow the same distribution. Ethnic identities, though, are not cast in stone. Who belongs to an ethnic group can change, as can how the ethnic group is known. People speaking the same language may not really identify with each other at one time but do so at another.

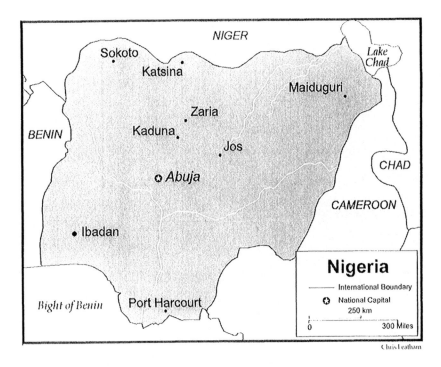

NIGER

Sokoto
Katsina

Lake Chad

Maiduguri

Zaria

BENIN

Kaduna

Jos

CHAD

⊙ *Abuja*

CAMEROON

• Ibadan

Nigeria

International Boundary
⊙ National Capital
250 km

Bight of Benin Port Harcourt

0 300 Miles

Chris Featham

Consider the identity of the Yorubas. *Yoruba*, pronounced as three two letter syllables with a long *o* and long *u*, is a Hausa word adopted by Europeans and only later by the Yorubas themselves (Isichei 1983: 1). Yorubas do speak—and for centuries have spoken—the same language, although with a range of dialects. They all trace their origin to a single progenitor, *Oduduwa*, in the city of Ile Ife. Politically, though, the Yorubas have never been unified. In the centuries just before the twentieth, various Yoruba political entities flowed and ebbed; some of them grew to imperial status whereas others remained small. The mid-nineteenth century was the time of "the Yoruba wars," with major Yoruba states fighting each other (Johnson 1921: 15–16). These wars led to one of the more picturesque forms of identity among the Yorubas, tribal markings. These are distinctive facial scars that allow the people of different communities to identify each other in times of emergency, especially in battle. The core identity of Yorubas was the locality with its kinship-related ties. We shall see how identities below the level of the Yoruba ethnic group remain important in the story of state creation in postcolonial Nigeria.

Though mutually distinctive, Nigerian cultures were not isolated from each other in precolonial times. Indeed, many of these cultures

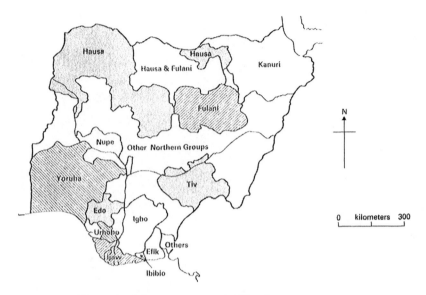

Figure 8.1   The major language groups in Nigeria

shared attributes. For example, only two Nigerian languages origi-
nated far from the borders of Nigeria: Shuwa, brought across the Sa-
hara from the northeast; and Fulani, brought from what is now Senegal
(Isichei 1983: 5). The interactions among the various cultures led to a
number of changes, including identities and locations. Among these
interactions were trade, warfare, and religion, sometimes all at the
same time. For example, Africans, including West Africans, traded
with each other long before they traded with Europeans. Flourishing
exchanges of such things as palm oil and kola nuts were central to
West African ways of doing things, from cooking practices to ceremonies. Sizable trading centers emerged in such places as Ibadan in the
west, Onitsha in the east, and Kano in the north. In each of these, as
well as other marketing centers, peoples of different ethnic groups
came together. Outsiders typically lived in "strangers quarters." These
strangers came to identify with each other as well as to provide the
major connections between the trading centers and these peoples'
places of origin.

The political structures of precolonial Nigerian cultures ranged from
the very egalitarian to the highly autocratic. Among some, as with the
Igbos in what became southeastern Nigeria, decentralization was the
norm (Isichei 1977: 1–7). The truism that "the Igbos have no king" was
a popular saying among the egalitarian Igbos in contrast with the more

CURRENT COUNTRY DATA (1998)

Population	Approximately 100 million
Area	356,700 square miles; 923,800 square kilometers
Major ethnic groups	30 million Hausa-Fulanis, mainly in the north; 20 million Yorubas, mainly in the southwest; and 17 million Igbos, mainly in the southeast
Major religions	50 percent Muslim, mainly in the north; 40 percent Christian, mainly in the south; 70 percent Traditional African Religions, throughout the country

PERTINENT CONFLICTS

The Nigerian Civil War lasted from May 1967 to January 1970, with a loss of life varyingly estimated at from one to two million, many of whom were civilians who died of starvation.

Sporadic armed conflicts among various groups led to scores or hundreds of deaths. Most common among these were purges of Christians in the north. Igbo-Edoma clashes, Izon-Itsereke clashes, and Tiv violence against various neighbors have all led to deaths this decade.

The Nigerian Civil War prevented the secession of the eastern region. In the spring of 1967, the Igbo leaders of the east declared the independence of the state of Biafra. Their action was precipitated by extensive violence against Igbos in the north, subsequent to a pair of military coups. The first coup, in January 1966, was largely led by Igbo officers. The second, in the summer of 1966, was basically a reassertion of power by Hausa-Fulani forces in the military.

Biafran leaders expected the western region also to secede, but this did not occur. Nigerian leaders succeeded in maintaining the allegiance of non-Igbo minorities in the east.

Hausa-Fulani military and political leaders have maintained a monopoly over state power in the decades since the civil war. Periodically violence flashes in the north, especially when Muslims object to Christian proselytization, as occurred in 1991. The other clashes usually involve land disputes.

centralized, monarchical polities of other cultures. Among these others were the Yorubas in what became southwestern Nigeria and the south of the Republic of Benin. They tended to have strongly hierarchical polities, including empires that waxed and waned (Adediran 1994: 175–178). The areas controlled by the various ethnic groups changed as their fortunes changed, particularly their military fortunes.

External forces also altered ethnic relations in precolonial Nigeria. Chief among them were the slave trade and penetration of monotheistic religion. The slave trade had a number of impacts. One was a keen competition to control trade routes, especially those up the various rivers. This trade altered the wealth and military power of various groups, and it pitted them against each other in their pursuit of slaves to trade.

Two major religious transformations altered the cultural landscape of what became Nigeria: Islam and Christianity. Beginning in 1804, the Fulani Jihad swept from Sokoto in what is now northwestern Nigeria, either spreading the faith of Islam to nonbelievers or "purifying" the faith by getting those who were nominal adherents back to orthodox practices (Adamu 1978: 23–27). Eventually most people of the north and some in the southwest adopted Islam. The jihad gave the Sokoto caliphate control over most of the area of what is now Nigeria as well as adjacent parts of what are now Niger and the Benin Republic. This had a profound influence on social reproduction. Koranic schools brought literacy, but it was a limited literacy, focused almost wholly in reading the Koran. It brought with it, too, a particular interpretation of gender relations, with fertile women in many communities segregated. It also changed the language of northern Nigeria. The jihad was led by a Fulani governing structure, but it enhanced the adoption of Hausa as a lingua franca for the Sahelian band across West Africa (Hunwick 1965: 269–277). Even today Hausa is the main language of many people across northern Nigeria but the lingua franca of all people in that region. The impact of the jihad on Nigerian identities was profound. For many people it refocused life from the locality to the caliphate. Further, it brought a tie to the larger Islamic world.

In the nineteenth century European contact with West Africa changed. The slave trade diminished, but other kinds of interaction expanded, particularly the penetration of capitalism and Christianity. Before the century was over this penetration had become full-fledged colonialism. The European penetration of West Africa was inward from the coast—in Nigeria meaning from the south. Those involved from the beginning were traders and missionaries. Most southern groups—and many in what became known as "the Middle Belt"— eventually adopted Christianity (Udo 1970: 6). The penetration of

Christianity continued during the colonial period with the British authorities virtually excluding missionaries from the predominantly Muslim north. Where the missionaries were allowed, they took (in addition to their faith) education, teaching their charges to read and inculcating them with western political and economic values. Hence the missionaries sowed the seeds that eventually would bring colonialism to an end. The division of the country between a Muslim north and a Christian south would long impact the country in very significant ways. Indeed, it is the major cultural divide in contemporary Nigeria.

The religious transformations clearly changed the lives of many people, redirecting their attention and aspirations in many cases. These changes were quickly followed by others as the domination by outsiders increased, culminating in the political and economic hegemony of British colonialism. This is not to say that African societies ceased being African. An example is the ways that many Nigerians practice their Islam or Christianity, incorporating aspects of traditional African religions, even when doing so violates the letter of the creed for those monotheistic religions. In other words, the deep-seated social structures changed but did not disappear. Significant social identities remained intact, albeit in somewhat altered form.

Colonial Transformation

These identities received further challenges during the colonial period, a time when nationalism and the preeminence of national states became the global norm (Tilly 1992: 161–183). Those who endured the dominance of colonialism faced decades of external control, along with a redefinition of who they were. European contact with the peoples of what became Nigeria began early with sustained Portuguese contact from the sixteenth century (Hodgkin 1975: 124–128). The Portuguese established a trading post at Lagos, named after a small port on Portugal's south coast. Eventually what became Nigeria had several ports active in the slave trade. Among them were Bonny, Brass, and Badagery as well as the larger ports of Calabar and Lagos. European contact increased during the years of the trans-Atlantic slave trade. British contact increased after Britain abolished the slave trade within its own empire and attempted to enforce the ban generally. Contact, of course, was great with coastal peoples, but trade up the Niger River and along the smaller rivers pushed a considerable distance inland.

By the time of the European scramble for Africa, Lagos was a British protectorate, and British commercial interests had regular contact up the Niger River and elsewhere in what became Nigeria. French traders,

coming down the Niger from what became the country of Niger, constituted the only significant European challengers, and their efforts
ceased after the Berlin Conference of 1884 and 1885. At that conference,
which had no African representation, the European imperial powers
carved Africa into spheres of influence, each country agreeing to leave
the sphere of other countries in return for "the right" to colonize its
own sphere. Hence other European states agreed to stay out of what
became Nigeria in return for British agreement to leave "their" areas
alone. Each of the imperial countries was then able to proceed to con-
quer a portion of Africa with no competition from the other imperial-
ists, concentrating their efforts on the under-armed indigenous peoples
rather than on each other (Gavin and Betley 1973: xv–xxvii).

By the early twentieth century Britain, through treaties and military
conquests, established its hegemony over all of Nigeria, first as a series
of four separate colonies. In 1914, against the press of World War I,
Britain began to administer Nigeria as a single entity with a hierarchical structure of territorial subdivisions. British efforts to redefine Nigerian societies—and Nigerian identities—were in full flower. Europeans, in Berlin and later in the British Foreign Office at Whitehall in
London, first determined the dimensions of Nigeria, then strove to re-
make their creation to their own benefit (Crowder 1968: 198–216).

The British Influence

To accomplish this task Britain sent Lord Lugard, who had been Britain's governor-general in India. He took with him to Nigeria the administrative system that had been successful for the British in India.
This was the system of indirect rule with most administrative tasks
executed by indigenous people rather than more expensive British personnel (Okafor 1981: 42–62). Indirect rule transformed political power
within Nigerian societies. The British preferred to work with local
leaders who had clear-cut powers and long tenure. Where the tradition
was rotating the leadership position, the British intervened by appointing a person who would serve at their pleasure. Where tradition called
for shared power rather than a traditional ruler, the British created a
new tradition, with a ruler of their liking. As a consequence, the Igbos
found themselves ruled by kings, even though this was contrary to
their traditions and wishes. Where a ruler failed to satisfy their interests, the British replaced him with one more acquiescent. The sad tale
of JaJa, who rose from being a slave to king only to be deposed by the
British, became a Nigerian legend—and a warning to even powerful
rulers to toe the British line (Isichei 1983: 229).

Indirect rule had significant impacts, including impacts on Nigerian identities. Indirect rule allowed the British to rule with a quite small staff of expatriates. This required a trained workforce of literate Nigerian administrators. Furthermore, it imposed a fairly uniform system of governance over peoples who before lived under highly varying systems. In the process, the imposition of indirect rule rearranged powers among many of the indigenous societies, strengthening the power of leaders relative to their subjects in many instances, as well as emphasizing the symbols of office, for example, "stools" for chiefs, mimicking Britain's throne, and an emphasis on titles, even where none had existed before. Indirect rule influenced Nigerian identities in several ways. One was to create a class of civil servants who saw themselves as Nigerians. They often worked far from their places of origin with transfer over large distances commonplace. Another is that it provided a common experience, something shared by those inside Nigeria but not shared by those across the borders in the neighboring French or German colonies. A third is that it provided for a hierarchical system of administration with at least nominal identification with the jurisdictional spaces of that hierarchy.

British rule also led to a Nigerian identity. Indeed, the British coined the colony's name. They created an administrative jurisdiction with all the territorial trappings of a jurisdiction, for example, boundaries and the consequent channeling of human movement. Rules from Whitehall and edicts from the governor-general provided Nigerian-wide rule, at least in some aspects of administration. In others British rule bifurcated Nigeria into north and south. The people of Nigeria thus came to have new levels of identity—regional identities and an incipient national identity, not in the usual sense of a nation as a culture but in the more modern sense of the peoples who lived under the same rule and the same place name, in this case, Nigeria (Okafor 1981: 177–179).

Lugard found that governing the north was fairly easy as long as he worked with the Sultan of Sokoto and the caliphate structure of leaders subservient to the Sultan. Hence he left the native court system fairly intact, and he prohibited Christian missionaries from moving into the Muslim north (Isichei 1983: 368). Clearly Lugard minimized conflict through these actions; just as clearly, he assured a lasting distinction between the two parts of the country.

Under British rule capitalism penetrated Nigeria, again more completely in the south. British investment developed ports, railways, industries, and plantations. Furthermore, the indigenous inhabitants were taxed to fund government projects. First the obligations could be met through labor, but as early as the 1920s they required payment in cash. The colonial power thus forced people into a commodified economy and away from their traditional subsistence. The rulers encour-

aged people to raise export crops as a way of gaining the cash necessary to pay their taxes. This led to significant increases in the
production of such crops as cocoa and coffee in place of the foodstuffs
that were previously grown.

The numerous societies of this new "place" Nigeria yielded part of
their influence over social reproduction to a new phenomenon, Western education. Outsiders, particularly missionaries with their very different religion and ways of doing things, controlled the content of formal education—and with it, a significant amount of social
reproduction. Those who gained literacy clearly gained advantages because they could work for and with the colonial rulers. Education
spread quickly in the south, particularly in the densely populated
southeast with its corresponding shortage of arable land (Udo 1970:
68–71). Traditional rulers in some cases kept their own sons from the
missionary schools until seeing that this strategy was creating an alternative source of power (Crowder 1968: 283–284).

Western education helped transform Nigerian societies in several
significant ways. One was further differentiating north and south
(Kukah 1993: 1–24). Indigenous responses to external influences had
already made the two quite different. Islam in the nineteenth century
came to dominate the north. Preimperial changes in the south were
more the product of trade with Europeans, including the slave trade.
The British enhanced the regional differentiation: They kept the missionaries and their schools out of the north at the request of caliphate
leaders. Because of this, southerners dominated the class of educated
workers, in the private as well as public sector. Education helped Igbos
to become particularly prominent, a fact that became important later
as ethnic groups struggled over influence (sometimes literally as in the
case of the attempted Biafran secession of 1967 to 1970). The pace of
transformation quickened in the south relative to the more traditional
north. This included interest in British political and economic ideas. By
creating a class of literate people, education empowered much of the
Nigerian population with ideas from other cultures as well as their
own. In many cases, education provided opportunities for significant
career advancement, and this altered the power structures in many
southern communities. Many Nigerians became much more receptive
to change than would have been the case without the expansion of
Western education. Some faces of change were, of course, more palat-
able than others.

Economic transformation within this new political entity of Nigeria
led to considerable migration, both rural-rural and rural-urban (Fadayomi 1988: 42). The migrants—usually young men, and in the cities
often educated young men—found themselves far from home and

without the traditional support of their extended families. Building on Nigerian traditions of associational life and encouraged by the colonial government, they tended to form social support organizations. These organizations, widely known as hometown associations, strengthened migrants' ties with their places of origin (Okafor and Honey 1998: 9). Typically, the young men would join with others from the same place. Gradually these organizations became common, especially among southern Nigerians. They had two places of emphasis: the place where the migrants lived while "abroad," that is, away from their hometown, and the hometown itself. For those abroad, the hometown association became a substitute extended family and a way of maintaining ties with the customs practiced back home. For the hometown these organizations became important sources of development assistance. In many cases the hometown association built the first schools, churches, community buildings, electrical distribution systems, and water systems in a small town or village. These organizations reinforced the significance of local identities in the face of competing identities at the regional and national levels.

Regional Attitudes toward Independence

Even before World War II, southern intellectual leaders were arguing for an end to colonial rule. Whether educated in Britain, as with Obafemi Awolowo, or the United States, as with Nnamdi Azikewe, Nigerian intellectuals argued for the recognition of political rights in Nigeria. Northern leaders, for a series of reasons, preferred a slower approach. They were happier with the status quo, which rendered them quite powerful. Furthermore, they feared that southerners would dominate an independent Nigeria, given that southerners were the ones prepared to take the administrative positions. Northerners also feared that political dominance would be added to the economic dominance southerners had achieved thanks both to their higher levels of education and the trade advantages of being closer to the coastal ports.

The British, in no hurry to leave anyway, found allies in the northerners. A decade of domestic self-government preceded full independence. In a break from their own tradition, the British structured a federal system for Nigeria with significant powers at the regional rather than federal level. The three regions, for example, controlled education and their own civil servants. This assured northern control over northern institutions of social reproduction. With regard to the kind of democracy adopted, though, the British followed their own parliamentary model rather than a presidential system with American-style checks and balances. This allowed significant concentration of power if one party or coalition could gain a stable majority in parliament. (To understand the point, consider how much more readily Margaret Thatcher was able to restructure British government with her parliamentary majority than Ronald Reagan was able to restructure U.S. government dealing with a Democratic Congress.)

The system of governance that would see Nigeria through into its first few years of independence had three regions. The northern region covered almost two-thirds of the national territory and included just over half the population. It was dominated by the Sokoto caliphate, with its Hausa-Fulani political base. The Niger River divided the rest of the country into a western region heavily dominated by Yorubas and an eastern region less heavily dominated by the Igbos. The distribution of seats gave the northern region a decided advantage—one that most southerners believe exaggerated northern population and therefore representation (Olusanya 1980: 78). Furthermore, the government of the northern region was able to determine the northern delegation to the Nigerian parliament, assuring the north not only control over social reproduction but also control over national issues. These political maneuverings influenced social identity but not so much the making of a Nigerian identity as the making of a regional one. For example, the Yorubas and Igbos formed ethnic unions, each with a regional rather than national political base, in order to mobilize political power. In addition, the emergence of political parties with strong ethnic ties worked to strengthen ethnic identities, particularly among the large ethnic groups (Joseph 1987: 129–150). Nevertheless, Yorubas and Igbos had greater affinity—and identity—with their localities than with the larger ethnic groups. This became readily apparent later when the regions were divided into states. Still, the formation of regions by the British government exacerbated the ethnic divisions of the country, not only by pitting the three largest ethnic groups against each other but also by making minorities out of other ethnic groups in each of the three regions (King 1988: 71–89).

The way the British manipulated the jurisdictional system gave the Hausa-Fulani and their leaders in the Sokoto caliphate an opportunity to overcome their disadvantages in education and economic clout so that they could control the emerging independent country. They succeeded in part because of the inability of the Yoruba and Igbo leaders, Awolowo and Azikewe, respectively, to meld a common strategy. This was the final British success in Nigeria at a divide-and-rule strategy.

The colonial experience left a very different Nigeria from what had been there before—in fact, before there had been a Nigeria at all. As the colonial period drew to a close in 1960, Nigerians had many competing identities. Among the important ones were a national identity, three regional identities, two major religious identities, hundreds based on ethnicity, and thousands based on place of origin. The new national identity, an identity that did not exist just two generations before, competed with remaining, though sometimes transformed, identities. The identities of this emerging Giant of Africa were nested at a range of scales as independence approached. The hope at independence was that the federal structure, with sovereignty shared by the regions and federal government, would work precisely because it had multiple identities. The regions would control such aspects of social reproduction as education, health, and the broadcast media. The federal government would control international affairs and related economic issues in a division that mirrored the different identities recognized by Nigerians. Within a few years the form of the state became less important than control over it.

Becoming Nigerian since Independence

States, empowered as they are, become significant conduits of social change. This has certainly been the case in Nigeria, as it has in the other postcolonial countries of Africa and elsewhere. As Edward Soja long ago pointed out, states use such symbols as flags and anthems to foster a sense of territorial identity and such tactics as tariffs and visas to enforce a sense of territorial exclusiveness (Soja 1971: 23–25). The Nigerian state has used the full continuum of state powers in its efforts to build a Nigerian identity. Exhortations range from anthems and television jingles to adoption of a national curriculum (Datta 1984: 15). Police action ranges from currency regulations to the imposition of national rather than regional or local police (Nwabueze 1993: 222–224). Participation ranges from governmental control over banking to governmental control over irrigation. Development ranges from control over waterways to control over oil.

Ah, yes, oil. Though by the standards of the industrialized countries the states of the developing world are weak, they are in general the most powerful institutions in their respective countries. Oil helps the Nigerian state to be exceedingly more powerful than most. Oil has overwhelmed the political forces that usually operate within a country (Dayomi and Alokan 1992: 361). Oil funds the Nigerian state in such a way that it essentially makes the state immune from the usual requirements of maintaining public support. Most of the country's income comes from oil revenue rather than taxes. Much of the revenue is used to support a military that prevents the people from challenging national leadership. The consequences are many. One is that the most important struggle in the country is over control of the government. Another is that the military is the only potent player in that struggle. A third is that much of the population is so disillusioned that it turns to other identities for pride and other entities for solace. Understanding these contested identities requires understanding the major events of the historical geography behind Nigeria's political geography. Let us proceed by examining the ethnic basis of Nigerian politics, the impacts of a major civil war, the dominance of the country by the military, and the way the government has used state creation to divide and rule.

The Ethnic Basis of Nigerian Politics

The colonial division of Nigeria into three regions, each dominated by a large ethnic group, saddled Nigeria with ethnic politics. As we have seen, the Hausa-Fulani with their caliphate structure rules the north, the Igbos rule the east, and the Yorubas, the west. Nnamdi Azikewe, one of the leaders of the independence movement, led a political party that included many Yoruba followers even though he was an Igbo. Indeed that party won the first regional election in 1952 as part of the transition to independence. Obafemi Awolowo, Azikewe's great rival, played the ethnic card, getting his fellow Yorubas to reject "Zik" and his party in the next election. Nigeria has never recovered. Hostilities between Yorubas and Igbos have time and again allowed northern leaders to put together ruling coalitions under northern leadership by playing off the Yoruba-Igbo feud. Minority groups have joined the political struggles in efforts to further their interests, too (Jibo 1993: 3–9). These struggles have focused peoples' attention on their ethnic and local roots rather than their shared status as Nigerians.

The excesses of ethnic politics have twice led the Nigerian military to wrest control of duly elected civilian governments, first in 1966, then again in 1983. Political squabbling degenerated to the point that most Nigerians cheered military intervention in 1966; many, though not as many, cheered again in 1983. After years of unbroken rule, though, the military has clearly out-lasted its welcome. Nigerians no longer see the military as an institution protecting the people or even as the lesser of evils (Olowu 1995: 26–29). Successive military regimes have assumed greater and greater powers, reaching status as the paramount institution in the country. Though Nigeria's government is still officially a "federal republic," its military nature means it cannot truly be federal because that would require shared sovereignty between two levels rather than a military chain of command.

The Nigerian Civil War

Two military coups actually occurred in Nigeria in 1966. The first was largely an Igbo affair, followed by a coup that struck directly at Igbo leadership in the military. In the ensuing months Igbos in the north endured a series of violent attacks, including considerable loss of life. Emboldened by the finding of abundant oil deposits in their portion of the Niger Delta, eastern leaders moved toward secession. War broke out at the end of May 1967, but it was quickly overshadowed by the Six Day War in the Middle East. Eastern leaders expected the western region likewise to secede, virtually guaranteeing success of the effort. This did not happen. The Nigerian government succeeded in gaining the support of non-Igbos in the east. An important consideration was the government's decision to divide the regions into twelve states. The new jurisdictional structure allowed eastern minority groups to be in states not dominated by Igbos. As the late Ken Saro-Wiwa explained in his memoir of the war, this strategy worked (Saro-Wiwa 1989: 127–142). After thirty months of fighting and as many as two million deaths, the secession attempt ended in failure.

The termination agreement was much more conciliatory than what had happened in the United States 100 years earlier. With oil production coming on line and a major rise in global oil prices, Nigeria appeared to be on a trajectory toward significant economic prosperity. The national question—whether there should be a single entity known as Nigeria—appeared to be solved once and for all. Sadly what has happened in the ensuing decade has not been so rosy.

The Nigerian Military

The Nigerian military's timing has been fortuitous—for the military. The men in uniform have benefited, in turn, from the Cold War, increases in the significance of oil as a political and economic weapon, and the laissez-faire aura of the post–Cold War era. Africa was the scene of many Cold War skirmishes with the First and Second Worlds funding, supplying, and training armies of allies, however nefarious those allies might have been. The credo clearly was that the enemy of my enemy is my friend. Britain, Nigeria's favored trading partner, and the United States, as leader of the Western alliance, supplied Nigeria's military rulers with whatever was necessary to keep them allied to the West. This, despite the partial demobilization that occurred after the Nigerian Civil War, allowed the military to become far and away the most powerful institution in the country. With the military dominated by a succession of northerners, this has meant that northern interests have monopolized power over the government.

Nigeria's emergence in the 1970s as a significant oil exporter gave the Nigerian military—and with it the northern elite—power unavailable to the military governments ruling other African countries. Governing by decree, the military leaders simply took the oil revenue as their own. When money was not a problem, the military bowed to international pressure and returned control of the state to civilian officials in 1979, only to promulgate another coup four years later. The military aborted a similar promised return to civil rule in 1993, then concocted a sham election in 1993 with the military ruler nominated by all five of the approved political parties. The oil money is no longer as abundant. A widely held view in Nigeria is that factions in the officer corps expect "their" shares of the oil wealth. Even if the current rulers would agree to go, their subordinate officers would expect their own turn rather than yield power to civilians. The oil money allows the military to rule without deference to civilian support; essentially the military has immunity from checks by the Nigerian people. It depends on them for neither money nor votes.

Tilly (1992: 16–20) argues that the national state became the global norm because of a conjunction of abilities—those of accumulating wealth and those enabling coercion, both externally and internally. Timing has given Nigeria's military both. The Nigerian military, armed with technologies undreamed of by tyrants in earlier ages, has a monopoly on the powers of coercion in Nigeria. With oil revenue, the military is effectively immune to the need for public support, and it will be as long as the world continues to buy Nigerian oil; indeed, as long as the United States continues to buy Nigerian oil, because the United States in recent years has bought more than half of what Nigeria has sold.

A glance at the identity of military rulers and their main aides shows that the rule of Nigeria has been an almost unbroken line of northerners. All Nigerian heads of state have either been al Haji (a Muslim who has made the pilgrimage to Mecca) or a general. Most have been both. With Nigeria's economic performance down and corruption and crime up, many residents of Nigeria are disgusted. They no longer feel pride in being Nigerian, or at least no longer feel unfettered pride. Rather, they are turning to other institutions for their protection—and their identity.

Social identity in Nigeria has traditionally been tied to one's ethnic group through a hierarchy of social and territorial levels. In some of the Nigerian societies—the Yoruba, for example—these hierarchies are mirrored by hierarchies of traditional rulers. Many, but certainly not all, Yorubas recognize the Alaafin of Oyo or the Ooni of Ife as the paramount king, or oba. Below them are the subordinate obas attached to other places. Monarchists would have one believe that part of the justification for these traditional and titled positions is that the occupants assure the protection of their subjects. Alas, the picture in Nigeria is not one to further arguments for monarchies. All too often in Nigeria traditional rulers have been co-opted by the military rulers. The top grades of traditional rulers are provided government funds. All too often this is enough to silence the obas, although exceptions occur. In 1995, the Oba of Benin, one of the more exalted traditional rulers in the country, reminded the military head of state that people in Nigeria were starving. This "affrontery" was chastised in the government-controlled press but widely lauded elsewhere. More typically, the traditional rulers act as sycophants for whoever is paying their bills. Opposition to the whole enterprise of traditional rulers may not be strong, but it is growing.

The institutions that have proven truly useful for the people in the face of the failures of both military and traditional governments are the hometown associations that provide support for people through most Nigerian societies. These associations bring together people of common origin when they are working or living away from their homes, and they bring many material improvements to the hometowns themselves (Honey and McNulty 1994: 67). The hometown associations rather than the traditional rulers are providing the positive social identity for Nigerian peoples today.

Religion remains an important aspect of social identity in Nigeria. Many Yorubas thought one of their own could be elected president if the candidate were Muslim—as well as rich, popular, and acceptable to the military. They were partly right. Their 1993 presidential candidate, Mashood Abiola, was Muslim, rich, and popular, and he was acceptable to the sitting military head of state. Other officers simply let it be known that only they were acceptable, so the election was annulled as the early returns foreshadowed an Abiola victory. A southern Muslim, Abiola was able to gain the votes of a majority of those who took part in the election, including in the north. Suffice it to say that religion is, simultaneously, a significant aspect of social identity and a divisive element in Nigerian life.

Divide and Rule through State Creation

As mentioned earlier, Nigeria had three regions in its federal structure at independence in 1960. Now it has thirty-six states, the last six added by the military government in 1996. The expansion has come in stages—four regions, then twelve, nineteen, twenty-one, thirty, and thirty-six states. With the sole exception of the First Republic's addition of the fourth region in 1963, all the additions have been military acts. We saw how the first, a transparent effort in 1967 to forestall the civil war, divided the regions so that the Igbos were no longer able to dominate other ethnic groups in the east. Successive military governments have used the creation of new states as a means of currying favor with smaller ethnic groups and regional subdivisions of the larger ones. The purpose has been to gain support by playing to the desires people have for their own clans or ethnic groups to gain control of a state and all the resources that will follow (Dayomi and Alokan 1992: 374). This does nothing to solve the country's problems, rather it is a circus that attracts the spotlight away from those problems. Consequently people continually petition sitting governments to create more states (and local government areas, too).

One consequence has been the creation of small states without the resources to provide their own budgets. They do not have to provide their own budgets because virtually all money comes from oil sales, but consequently these states have few genuine powers, rendering Nigeria a federation in name only. Furthermore, many of the new states make little sense as potential partners in a truly federal system with shared sovereignty and shared responsibilities. This is because they have few resources of their own and because they were defined by political opportunism rather than administrative viability. The central government is thus able to monopolize significant power at the same time that it deflects attention away from its malperformance. The social identity focus is on entities that are smaller and smaller. What had been the western region at the time of independence is now nine states, seven of them (all but the two that were hived off to form the midwestern region in 1964) almost entirely Yoruba except in the multiethnic urban areas. The concentration of attention—and identity—is at or below the state level rather than at the all-Yoruba ethnic level. Yorubas now squabble among themselves, thanks to this divisive action of state creation by a succession of Nigerian military governments. At a time when the military government is currying favor by recognizing more and more states (and local government areas), it succeeds in focusing people's attention on continually more local scales of identity.

The national government is able to use its divide-and-rule strategy because of what many Nigerian intellectuals bemoan as the tragedy of oil, a peculiar phenomenon in light of the economy and political power held by oil-exporting countries. Among the critics, of course, are many people from the oil-producing areas, among them Ken Saro-Wiwa, who was executed to silence his criticism of government policies despoiling riverine environments. Other critics, though, are not from the oil-producing areas. They include prominent international figures, such as Nobel laureate Wole Soyinka.

In a nutshell the argument goes this way. Oil has allowed Nigerian governments to rule without the support of the people. The lack of popular control has allowed these governments to ignore environmental safeguards and squander the oil without substantial benefit to the people at large. Rather than oil being the source of genuine Nigerian development, it is a means of Nigerian degradation. The corruption and rent-seeking behavior coming out of the oil economy have damaged the country rather than help it (Odekunle 1986: 1–7). Too many people are more interested in making a deal than in being productive. Nigeria, then, is not the positive place of hardworking, publicly minded people that it could and should be. Rather, it is a sycophant country run by thugs for their own aggrandizement (Joseph 1987: 184–189). This is not a country to be emulated or admired. Hence, it is not a level of identity that its people any longer find attractive.

Will Nigeria Survive?

A decade ago the survival of Nigeria was no more in doubt than the survival of the United States or the United Kingdom. No one asked "The National Question," that is, should Nigeria be one country or more? The disappointments of the three decades of independence, coupled with the collapse of such states as the Soviet Union and Yugoslavia, have brought this question back to the surface.

The American Civil War settled once and for all the unity of the United States. In the eyes of its citizens, the Nigerian Civil War seemed to have done the same. In the United States, though, the national rather than state identity became much more important for most people. The people of the area that tried to secede are arguably the most patriotic people in the country. Many factors have been involved in this transformation; the point for the moment is that in the United States the transformation has occurred.

In Nigeria, that transformation has not occurred. National identity is not the primary identity. Among the large ethnic groups of the south, even ethnic identity is not the primary one; local identity is. Hence, when the obvious examples of dissolution occur elsewhere, and when the government has so clearly failed to meet people's aspirations, "The National Question" returns. Consider the view of R. K. Udo, a renowned Nigerian geographer. In 1970, just after the Nigerian Civil War, he published his *Geographical Regions of Nigeria* through the University of California Press. He dedicated the book, "To those who died in the fight to keep Nigeria one" (Udo 1970: iv). Udo, from one of the minority groups in the east, opposed the secession of the eastern region. He had a vision of Nigeria as an African giant that would be productive and humane as it moved toward the twenty-first century. Reality has depressed him. He himself now questions whether Nigeria will survive—even whether it ought to survive if its leaders perform no better than they have been (Udo 1996). So many rulers have feasted on the national treasury rather than fostering genuine development, and so many people think raiding the treasury is an obligation to one's ethnic group, that people like Udo question whether the dream of a strong, competent, and compassionate Nigeria can be fulfilled. Even those who strove courageously to produce a viable Nigerian national identity are having a hard time maintaining that identity themselves.

Disappointment with the broken promises, bad management, and duplicity of governments have made many Nigerians very cynical. The author's personal contacts, most of them university people, spoke disparagingly of efforts to elect the officials for Nigeria's Third Republic. Elections of local officials began in 1990 and continued in stages to the election of the president in 1993. Many in 1990 voiced a view that the exercise was one in futility, expressing the opinion that their votes would not matter. As the events proceeded, many of these people became involved, even helping in electoral campaigns. Twin blows gave life to their cynicism in 1993. The first was the annulment of the presidential vote; the second was the military's removal of civilian officials elected to local and state offices through ballots in 1991 and 1992. A common attitude was that being fooled this time was bad enough, one would not be fooled again by participating in the next set of elections. Consequently turnouts at local government elections in 1997 and state government elections in 1998 were very low. Mistrust magnified; alienation grew. In the face of this cynicism, the commitment of Nigeria's citizens to its survival is in doubt.

Many forces pull the people of Nigeria together, so the country's obituary should not be written yet. Despite the disappointments, many of Nigeria's citizens retain their hope for their "Giant of Africa." Like Texans, they take pride in being big. They have hope for themselves, retaining a glimmer of optimism because of the view that the mass of the people are honorable and willing to work with others (Seidman and Anang 1991: 1–5). If Nigeria were to live up to its potential, being a Nigerian would be a very good thing, indeed, and many people hold on to this hope that Nigeria's potential will be realized. For many, the height of Nigerian achievement was claiming the Olympic gold medal in men's soccer in Atlanta in 1996.

Despite its abuses, the Nigerian state is itself a centripetal force. By devoting resources for communications, education, and development, the national government is able to bring attention to the idea of a Nigeria, calling on people to think of themselves as Nigerians. The leaders tend to interpret all criticisms of themselves as criticisms of Nigeria, and, as is the case in all countries, some people fall for it. Nigeria's resource base is also a centralizing force. Despite the waste, Nigeria still has a resource base more impressive than those of its neighbors. As long as the oil lasts, many of the peoples who constitute Nigeria will benefit from maintenance of the national identity—as long as they, or more accurately military officers from their ethnic groups, continue to control power.

Finally, some people will support the preservation of Nigeria because the alternative is too frightening. If the country were to disintegrate, what would follow? The prospect for bloodletting is too great for many people to contemplate as a serious option. Hence, Nigerian survival benefits from the lack of an obviously acceptable set of successor states. Eastern and probably northern minorities would resist dividing the country into three sovereign states matching the old regions, and any other option would face committed opposition, too, given the complexity of the ethnic and cultural map.

Still, the forces of disintegration are significant, at least as significant as those that were apparent in the Soviet Union or Yugoslavia two decades ago. These include the divisive social attachments that dominate people's lives, defined by ethnicity, religion, and locality. They also include the enormous mistrust of the Nigerian government and Nigerian institutions. These are the deep-seated identities that inhibit the development of a more broadly based national identity.

Conclusions

A century has given the peoples of Nigeria a national identity, but it is not a deep-seated identity, not an identity that transcends the fundamental identities that preceded colonial times. People first see themselves as citizens of Asaba or Osogbo (or whatever place is their ancestral home) rather than as Nigerians. Colonialism strengthened regional identities and the identities of the large ethnic groups. It also provided a common Nigerian experience, even if that experience did not supplant other identities and experiences. By controlling institutions of social reproduction, the Nigerian state has provided identities that compete with the traditional ones, but the disdain people have for that state has weakened the ability of those new identities to supplant those that were there before.

Furthermore, in the Nigerian case, politics has created and is creating places—at a series of scales from the national through the regional to the local—through a combination of external and internal decisions that redefine jurisdictional organization, creating new entities where they did not exist before and reshaping those entities as people struggle for control. In Nigeria the regional structure of government at the time of independence led to an emphasis on ethnic politics, a phenomenon that undercut the development of a national consciousness. The regions and subsequent states have become the organs of public administration, the significance of which has expanded under military rule. In Nigeria, what it means to be a member of a particular culture has changed as the rules of that culture have changed, sometimes with British rules, sometimes with rules from the central government of Nigeria. Nevertheless, the core identities have remained, altered in emphasis but still there. The balance between local and regional identities has varied as the different levels have varied in their ability to provide what people want and need.

Whether Nigeria, cobbled together by Europeans more than a century ago, will survive in an age of emergent nationalism and political decentralization is not clear. In terms of survival, the best thing that Nigeria has going for it is the fact that there is no obvious set of successor states. The Giant of Africa is troubled. Almost four decades after independence Nigeria's strength remains its potential rather than its performance. In terms of human and other resources, that potential remains, just as Nigerians still have a series of identities at a range of scales as they strive to determine for themselves who they really are and which level of identity is really important.

References

Adamu, Mahdi. *The Hausa Factor in West African History.* Zaria, Nigeria: Ahmada Bello University Press, 1978.

Adediran, Biodun. *The Frontier States of Western Yorubaland: 1600–1889.* Ibadan: French Institute for Research in Africa, 1994.

Crowder, Michael. *West Africa under Colonial Rule.* London: Hutchinson, 1968.

Datta, Ansu. *Education and Society: A Sociology of African Education.* London: Hutchinson, 1984.

Dayomi, Mathew A., and Olabode Alokan. "The Economic Context of Democratic Transition and Democracy in Africa: The Case of Nigeria." In B. Caron et al., eds., *Democratic Transition in Africa.* Ibadan: CREDU, Nigeria, 1992, 359–377.

Fadayomi, T. O. *Rural Development and Migration in Nigeria.* Ibadan: Nigerian Institute of Social and Economic Research, 1988.

Gavin, R. J., and J. A. Betley. *The Scramble for Africa.* Ibadan: Ibadan University Press, 1973.

Hodgkin, Thomas. *Nigerian Perspectives: An Historical Anthology*. Oxford: Oxford University Press, 1975.

Honey, Rex, and Michael L. McNulty. "Nigeria's Approach to Decentralized Development." In R. J. Bennett, ed., *Local Government and Market Decentralization*. Tokyo: United Nations University Press, 1994, 67–85.

Hunwick, J. O. "The Nineteenth Century Jihads." In J. F. A. Ajai and Ian Espie, eds., *A Thousand Years of West African History*. Ibadan: Ibadan University Press, 1965, 267–282.

Isichei, Elizabeth. *Igbo Worlds*. London: MacMillan, 1977.

———. *A History of Nigeria*. London: Longman, 1983.

Jibo, Mvendaga. *Tiv Politics since 1959*. Zaria: Ahmadu Bello University Press, 1993.

Johnson, Samuel. *The History of the Yorubas*. Lagos: C.S.S. Bookshops, 1921.

Joseph, Richard A. *Democracy and Prebendal Politics in Nigeria*. Ibadan: Spectrum Books, 1987.

King, Mae C. *Localism and Nation Building*. Ibadan: Spectrum Books, 1988.

Kukah, Matthew Hassan. *Religion, Politics, and Power in Northern Nigeria*. Ibadan: Spectrum Books, 1993.

Nwabueze, B. O. *Military Rule and Social Justice in Nigeria*. Ibadan: Spectrum Law Publishing, 1993.

Odekunle, 'Femi. *Nigeria: Corruption in Development*. Ibadan: Ibadan University Press, 1986.

Okafor, S. O. *Indirect Rule: The Development of Central Legislature in Nigeria*. Lagos: Nelson Africa, 1981.

Okafor, Stanley I., and Rex Honey. "The Nature of Hometown Voluntary Associations in Nigeria." In Rex Honey and Stanley I. Okafor, eds., *Hometown Associations: Indigenous Knowledge and Development in Nigeria*. London: Intermediate Technology Publications, 1998.

Olowu, Dele. "Transition to Democratic Governance in Africa." In Dele Olowu et al., eds., *Governance and Democratisation in Nigeria*. Ibadan: Spectrum Books, 1995, 15–31.

Olusanya, G. O. "Constitutional Developments." In Obaro Ikeme, ed., *Groundwork of Nigerian History*. Ibadan: Heinemann, 1980, 63–82.

Otite, Onigu. *Ethnic Pluralism and Ethnicities Nigeria*. Ibadan: Shoreson, 1990.

Saro-Wiwa, Ken. *On a Darkling Plain: An Account of the Nigerian Civil War*. Port Harcourt: Saros Publications, 1989.

Seidman, Ann, and Frederick Anang. *Twenty-First Century Africa*. Worcester: Clark University Press, 1991.

Soja, Edward. *The Political Organization of Space*. Washington, D.C.: The Association of American Geographers, 1971.

Tilly, Charles. *Coercion, Capital, and European States*. Cambridge, Mass.: Blackwell, 1992.

Udo, Reuben K. *Geographical Regions of Nigeria*. Berkeley: University of California Press, 1970.

———. Personal interview, January 10, 1996.

9

Space-Related Identity in Sri Lanka

Chelvadurai Manogaran

Ethnic identity has become a potent force, fomenting ethnonationalist movements and undermining the internal structure and territorial limits of many states. Ethnic minorities, in many parts of the world, are asserting their own geographical and their cultural identities and demanding the creation of new nation-states out of the existing multiethnic states. Many of the existing multiethnic states are considered nation-states, even though they are identified exclusively with dominant ethnic groups claiming to be the original settlers. In some of these multiethnic states, myths and legends were contrived to attribute the greatness of nations to specific ethnic groups (Mikesell 1983: 257–258). In the extreme, some ethnic majorities have been driven by their feeling of superiority over other groups to demand special status in their respective nations; this type of ethnonationalism can often lead to the ethnic cleansing, mass killings, and violations of human rights vis à vis ethnic minorities.

Ethnic minorities consider their traditional homelands as treasured possessions because these help to preserve their cultural and political identities in multiethnic states. Ethnic minorities, such as African-Americans in the United States, cannot even claim the status of distinct nationality, or the right to "build a separate national consensus," because they are widely dispersed throughout the state (Poulsen 1995: 14). Ethnic minorities aspire to have the right of self-determination for their traditional homelands, because they, after having inhabited these homelands for centuries, "have gradually come to identify with their environments, perceived as archetypal, endowed with love and celebrated in songs and poetry," and become convinced of their intrinsic value for the group's economic well-being (Hooson 1994: 1). Although the territorial dimension of nationalism continues to provoke conflicts between ethnic or cultural groups within states, few scholars, including geographers, have focused on the role of space-related identity in explaining the origin of intranational conflicts.

In Sri Lanka, conflicting claims between the Sinhalese majority and the Tamil minority over their respective space-related identities have contributed to one of the most bitterly fought civil wars of the second half of the twentieth century. The space-related identity of the majority Sinhalese has run up against the distinct cultural and spatial identity of Sri Lankan Tamils, intensifying the nationalist crisis now gripping the island and hindering any negotiated settlement between the two groups.

Sinahelese nationalism rests on three territorial assumptions. One, Sinhalese-Buddhists, as the original settlers, inhabited all parts of the island from ancient times, including those areas currently dominated by Sri Lankan Tamils. Second, Tamil-Hindus from south India established permanent settlements in the northern and eastern parts of the country as the invading armies of south Indian rulers drove the Sinhalese population from these areas to the southwest from the tenth century A.D. Third, Tamils are accused of having destroyed and plundered the once prosperous Rajarata Kingdom of rice fields, irrigation tanks, and Buddhist places of worship. Tamil nationalism is a mid–twentieth century phenomenon that rose in direct response to Sinhalese nationalism and that has sought recognition of their ancestral ties to a portion of Sri Lanka and various degrees of autonomy for Tamil majority provinces.

Sinhalese-Buddhist Identity

The beginnings of Sinhalese nationalism can be traced to the nineteenth century when, for the first time, Tamils from their traditional homeland in northern and eastern Sri Lanka and Tamils from south India, who were brought to the island by the British to work on the tea and rubber plantations in Sinhalese areas, came into direct contact with Sinhalese. Although both communities trace their ethnic heritage to India, each developed its own sense of group identity, differentiated from the other on the basis of ethnic origin, language, religion, cultural attributes, and ancestral territory. Sinhalese, the majority of whom are Buddhists, claim to be descendants of fair-skinned Aryan people of north India, distinct from the darker-skinned Hindu-Tamils of south India. The Sinhalese language is related to the Indo-European group of languages and uses a script that is very different from the Dravidian

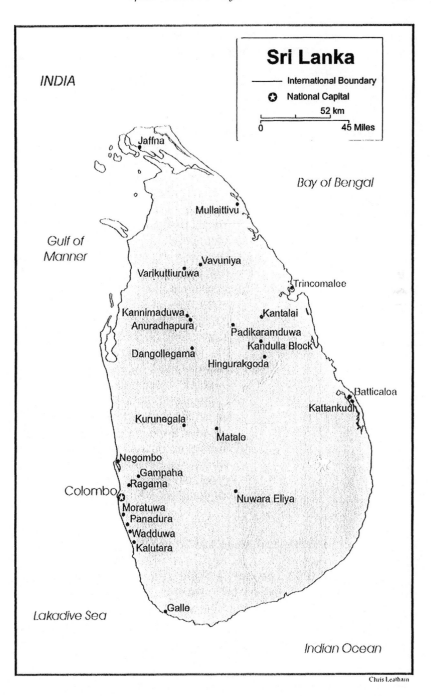

◄──►

CURRENT COUNTRY/REGION DATA

No official census has been conducted since the escalation of the civil war in the early 1980s.

Area of Sri Lanka	25,252 square miles
Population	Estimated to be 18,342,660 in July 1995 (*Source:* Sri Lanka Tourist Board, Central Bank of Sri Lanka, and the CIA's *The World Fact Book*).
Ethnic Divisions	Sinhalese 74%, Tamils 18% (7% include Tamils of Indian origin), Moors 7%, Vedda 1%
Religions	Buddhists 69%, Hindus 15%, Christians 8%, Islam 8%
Geographic Distribution of Ethnic Communities	According to the last official census of 1980, 73% of Sri Lankan Tamils, 2.51% of Sinhalese, 9.39% of Indian Tamils, and 34.94% of Moors live in the northern and eastern provinces. Approximately 97.5% of the Sinhalese population is concentrated in the rest of the island. 90% of the Indian Tamils live in the predominantly Sinhalese areas of the central hill country. Indian Tamils are descendants of indentured workers whom the British settled in the predominantly Sinhalese areas in the 1830s to work on tea plantations.

PERTINENT CONFLICTS (INCIDENTS)

Mob Violence of 1956. The Federal Party, in a show of disapproval over the tabling of the Sinhala Only bill in the legislature, led 300 of its members to stage a demonstration in the vicinity of parliament on June 5, 1956. This prompted a violent reaction by Sinhalese mobs, accompanied by more widespread anti-Tamil riots.

Mob Violence of 1958. The Federal Party called a convention in May 1958 to launch a mass disobedience campaign in Vavuniya in the northern province. This gathering was opposed by Sinhalese activists, and what began as the stoning of buses and trains, erupted in an anti-Tamil riot of a more violent nature resulting in the massacre of Tamils in many areas, especially in Colombo.

Mob Violence of 1977. The anti-Tamil riots of August 1977 were sparked when the Tamil United Liberation Front, formed by the amalgamation of Tamil parties, won the support of the Tamil people of the northeast on a mandate to establish a separate Tamil state called Eelam at the general elections of 1977.

Mob Violence of 1983. Riots began in July 1983 when a truckload of thirteen Sinhalese army personnel was ambushed by the Tamil Tigers in retaliation for the killing of 175 Tamils. This set the stage for the most violent confrontation between Tamil militants and government forces, which has continued into the late 1990s. It also led to an exodus of 100,000 Sri Lankan Tamils to south India and about 40,000 to various countries in Europe. By the beginning of 1990, almost 300,000 Tamils had taken refuge in various countries, including the United States and Australia.

Indian Intervention and the Indo-Sri Lanka Pact of 1987. The Indian peace-keeping force was deployed in Tamil areas to maintain peace and to carry out the terms of the Indo-Sri Lanka Accord, which was signed on July 29, 1987. The Tamil Tigers, which was not a party to the agreement, failed to abide by the terms of accord, and an unfortunate incident involving the arrest of seventeen Tigers, who were armed in violation of the accord, led to the confrontation between the Tigers and the Indian peace-keeping force. By the time the Indian peace-keeping force departed from Sri Lanka in 1991, 1,155 Indian soldiers had lost their lives and three times as many had been wounded. It is alleged that the Tamil Tigers were responsible for the death of Prime Minister Rajiv Gandhi.

The Capture of Jaffna Peninsula and the Escalation of the Civil War: 1995. In December 1995, government forces captured the capital of Jaffna, which the Sri Lankan Tamils consider the cradle of their civilization. Almost three-quarters of the 700,000 Tamils from the Jaffna Peninsula fled from the path of the advancing government forces toward the city of Jaffna. Only half the number has returned to their original villages, and the others continue to live in make-shift shelters in the mainland or in rented apartments and homes in Colombo and its vicinity.

HISTORICAL BACKGROUND

Sinhalese and Tamils evolved their own distinct identities by inhabiting different areas of the island, which were ruled as separate units beginning in the thirteenth century. The whole country was brought under a single administrative unit by the British in 1833. During the British period, disputes over Tamil representation in the legislature and in public services began to create a rift between the communities, and when the country became independent in 1948, the Sinhalese majority in the parliament introduced laws and regulations making it difficult for Tamils to use their own language to communicate with the government, to secure employment in the public service, and to gain admission to universities. Tamil areas were also neglected and rapidly colonized by Sinhalese peasants. Tamil youth, convinced that peaceful methods were ineffective in persuading the government to resolve the Tamil problem, formed militant movements, such as the Liberation Tigers of Tamil Eelam, and adopted violent methods to demand the creation of a separate Tamil state. The war between the Tamil Tigers and government forces has since resulted in the death of thousands of civilians and untold destruction to portions of Sri Lanka. None of the Tamil grievances have been resolved since the conflict started in 1956, and many of the peace initiatives have failed.

▶————————————————————————◀

language of the Tamils. Indeed, Sinhalese and Tamils have, through centuries of evolution, developed such distinct language and cultural traits that they were strangers to each other in the nineteenth century. They continue to be self-conscious of their respective identities.

When the British government began developing the Sinhalese-dominated Wet Zone during this period for commercial purposes, English-educated Sri Lankan Tamils took the opportunity to seek employment in these areas because they faced problems of overcrowding, landlessness, and acute unemployment in their northern, water-deficient provinces. Over the course of time, Tamils, by virtue of their proficiency in the English language, competed successfully with the Sinhalese and acquired a disproportionate share of jobs in government services and other professions. To Tamils, the opportunity to acquire an English education, a requirement for employment in public service, came with the arrival of Christian missionaries to the island. Unlike Sinhalese-Buddhists, the Hindu-Tamils invited Christian missionaries to establish schools and churches in the Tamil areas, especially in Jaffna Peninsula, the cultural heart of the Tamil homeland.

Sinhalese nationalists, Buddhist activists, and politicians revived the ancient fear of a Tamil threat to the survival of the Sinhala race, Sinhala language, Buddhist religion, and the Sinhala-Buddhist nation as Tamils moved into Sinhalese areas. They used semilegendary narratives, historical accounts, and religious tracts in the Pali Chronicles, *Mahavamsa* and *Culavamsa*, composed by the Buddhist clergy between the fourth and the sixth centuries A.D., to link Sinhalese people's unique ethnic, linguistic, religious, and cultural identity with the geographical entity of the state of Sri Lanka. According to the Pali Chronicles, Buddha himself asked Sakka, the king of Gods and the protector of Buddha's doctrine, to furnish protection to Vijaya and his 700 followers, who arrived from north India on the very day Buddha attained nirvana, about 500 B.C., in order to establish and preserve the Sinhalese-Buddhist nation of Sri Lanka (Geiger 1912: 51–61). Gananath Obeyesekere states that the "myths are an expression of the self-perceived historical role of the Sinhalese as a nation" and that the Buddhist clergy has convinced generations of Sinhalese that the very existence of Sri Lanka as a sovereign nation is under the constant threat of racial and cultural assimilation from Dravidian "racial and cultural assimilation from South India" (Obeyesekere 1979: 282, Matthews 1984: 192). Underlying intergroup prejudices also aroused communal self-consciousness among the members of each community, setting the stage for the rise of Sinhalese nationalism. Sinhala Buddhist activist Anagarika Dharmapala and others in the Buddhist Revivalist Movement gave a new lease on life to older forms of identity, thereby contributing to the rise of Sinhalese nationalism in the late nineteenth century (Jayawardena 1984: 57)

The Making of Sri Lankan Tamil Nationalism

Sri Lankan Tamil nationalism did not become a political force until the second half of the twentieth century, although Tamil politicians of the British colonial period were cognizant of the rising tide of anti-Tamil sentiment among the Sinhalese-educated, upper caste elite and Buddhist activists in the 1930s. The Sinhalese elite and politicians began linking the cultural identity of the Sinhalese-Buddhist people with the nation-state of Sri Lanka in order to seek special recognition for their race at the expense of the Tamils. They even accused the Tamils of conspiring with the British to monopolize most of the public service jobs and to obtain political leverage through communal representation in the legislative councils. It was not surprising, therefore, that the Sinhalese-dominated Parliament passed laws depriving the Indian Tamils of their voting rights and citizenship as soon as the country became independent of British rule in 1948.

Some Sri Lankan Tamil politicians continued to cooperate with the ruling United National Party, even after the passage of this anti-Indian Tamil legislation, but others, like, S. J. V. Chelvanayakam, formed the Federal Party in 1949. Chelvanayakam believed that Sinhalese leaders were determined to deprive the minorities of their rights. The Sri Lankan Tamil people, however, did not comprehend the extent to which the rising tide of Sinhalese nationalism would threaten the very survival of their ethnic identity, as well as the integrity of their traditional homeland. Whereas Chelvanayakam was determined to defend the rights of the Tamils, S. W. R. D. Bandaranaike, a prominent Sinhalese politician, quit the ruling United National Party and formed the Sri Lanka Freedom Party in order to champion the cause of the Sinhalese masses. He demanded the overhaul of the administrative, educational, and political structures, which he and other Sinhalese nationalists claimed bestowed undue privileges upon Sri Lankan Tamils. He formed an alliance with other Sinhalese parties opposed to the United National Party to form the Mahajana Eksath Perumuna, winning a landslide victory in the general elections of 1956. The newly elected government made Sinhala the only official language of the nation during the same year and pledged to settle large numbers of Sinhalese peasants in Tamil districts.

The Federal Party, which contested the general elections on a pledge to establish, through peaceful and parliamentary methods, a Tamil linguistic state within a federal union of Sri Lanka, received the overwhelming support of the Tamil people. The Federal Party made it known to the Sinhalese electorate that, to Tamils, the right of self-determination represents the unfinished business of decolonization. It also insisted that the Tamils, who had not experienced any political freedom since the collapse of their independent Tamil kingdom in the sixteenth century, were as eager as the Sinhalese to be a free nation. The Federal Party also rejected the Sinhala Only legislation on grounds that the Tamil population had to acquire proficiency in a language that was totally different, both in the spoken and written forms, similar to what had been required of both Sinhalese and Tamil people during the British colonial period. The concept of a Tamil traditional homeland, however, did not exist in the minds of the Tamil people until S. J. V. Chelvanayakam advanced this concept as a legitimate demand of the Tamil people during the early 1950s (Wilson 1994: 125).

The Federal Party was determined to defend the rights of Tamils using nonviolent methods, but peaceful demonstrations were viewed by the Buddhist clergy and Sinhalese extremists as thinly disguised steps toward establishing a separate Tamil state. They were forcefully suppressed. Communal disturbances also erupted in the Gal Oya colony, a colonization scheme under which hundreds of Sinhalese peasants were settled in the Tamil-dominated eastern province. Many of the Tamil colonists were killed, maimed, or forced to abandon their homes and farms. Prime Minister Bandaranaike, concerned that the persistent demonstration by the Tamil community would create political instability, communal disturbances, and economic chaos, met with S. J. V. Chelvanayakam to explore ways to redress some of the Tamil grievances.

After lengthy negotiations, the Bandaranaike-Chelvanayakam Pact of 1957 was signed by both leaders. Among its provisions, this pact provided for the recognition of Tamil as a language of a national minority and as the language of administration of the two Tamil provinces, the establishment of one regional council for the northern province and one or more for the eastern province, direct elections to the regional council, and the right of Parliament to delegate wide-ranging powers to the regional councils over subjects ranging from agriculture, industries, land development, colonization, and water schemes to taxation and borrowing (Government of Ceylon 1957; A. J. Wilson 1988: 116–118).

Unfortunately, the government abrogated the pact because of the strong opposition from the Buddhist clergy and the United National Party, which had previously taken a pro-Tamil stand on most issues. Similarly, Prime Minister Dudley Senanayake, of the United National Party, failed to receive the support of the Sri Lanka Freedom Party and the Buddhist clergy required to enact the provisions of the 1965 Senanayake-Chelvanayakam Pact (Wilson 1988: 123–126). Sinhalese leaders not only rejected Tamil demands, but Tamil nationalists claimed continued discrimination against Tamils in matters dealing with employment, university admissions, and allocation of resources to develop Tamil areas, while at the same time proceeding with their policy of settling Sinhalese peasants in Tamil-dominated provinces.

Peasant Colonization Schemes

Peasant colonization schemes were sponsored by the government to settle peasants on public land, to increase food production, relieve population pressure in overcrowded regions, and raise the standard of living of the average peasant family. Major and minor irrigation projects, some of them involving the restoration of reservoirs and canals that had been abandoned in the past, were undertaken to settle peasant

families on parcels of land consisting of two to five acres of paddy land
and two to three acres of unirrigated highland, on which a house was
constructed (Farmer 1957). This policy of establishing colonization
schemes in the Dry Zone began in the 1930s, when the responsibility
of restoring old reservoirs and canals in the Dry Zone was transferred
from British officials to Sri Lankan officials in the colonial administration. Don Stephen Senanayake, the minister of Agriculture and Lands,
formed the Pan-Sinhalese Ministry by excluding Tamils from it in
order to implement an aggressive policy of settling Sinhalese peasants
in the Dry Zone. A major objective of colonization, according to Senanayake, who became the first prime minister of independent Sri Lanka,
was to aid the Sinhalese people to return to the land of their ancient
civilization in the Dry Zone (Moore 1985: 45).

Under the government-funded colonization schemes, all expenses
involved for construction of irrigation projects; moving peasants from
their original villages to the new locations; the preparation of the land
for cultivation; the construction of homes, schools, and hospitals; and
start-up money were completely financed by the government. It is estimated that almost a quarter of the island's population was moved from
the Wet Zone to the Dry Zone between 1946 and 1971, under peasant
colonization schemes (Oberai 1988; Indraratna et al. 1983: 79–136). Unfortunately, most of the areas targeted for colonization were predominantly in the Tamil-dominated northern and eastern provinces of the
Dry Zone. Although Sinhalese peasants moved in large numbers in the
direction of Tamil areas, no Tamil colonists were settled in the major
colonization projects established in the Sinhalese-dominated north
central, central, and southern provinces in the Dry Zone.

Sinhalese colonization of Tamil districts altered the ethnic composition of these districts beginning with the formation of the Pan-Sinhalese Ministry in the 1930s. The impact of the colonization on Tamil
areas can be demonstrated by comparing the ethnic composition of
Tamil districts for two separate census years. Because a census of population was not conducted from 1921 to 1946, the population data for
the year 1921 are compared with those of 1981 (Turner 1923; Department of Census and Statistics 1981; see Figure 9.1). The comparison
shows that the Sinhalese population in the Tamil-dominated Trico-
malee District, increased from 4.4 percent to 33.6 percent between 1921
and 1981, whereas the Sri Lankan Tamil population declined from 53.2
percent to 33.8 percent during the same period. Likewise, the Sinhalese
population increased from 8.6 percent to 37.6 percent, and the Tamil
population declined from 33.5 percent to 20.0 percent in the Tamil-
dominated Amparai District. The rapid increase in the Sinhalese population in the eastern province led to the creation of the Sinhalese elec-

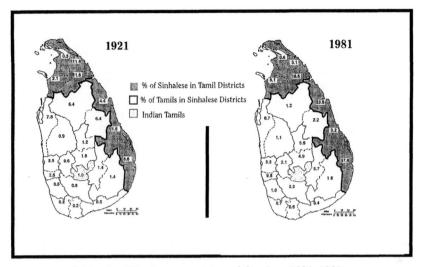

Figure 9.1   Sri Lanka: Ethnic composition of districts, 1921–1981

Source: L. B. J. Turner, *Report on the Census of Ceylon, 1921*, Government Printer, Colombo, 1923; Department of Census and Statistics, *Census of Population and Housing, Sri Lanka, Preliminary Report No. 1*, Colombo, 1981.

torates of Seruvila and Amparai in 1976. Sinhalese colonies were also established in the Mullaitivu District, which was inhabited exclusively by Tamils prior to the 1970s. Tamil colonists were driven out of Manal Aru in this district and were replaced by Sinhalese settlers (Manogaran 1994). The colony was renamed Weli Oya (in Sinhalese), and the colonists were armed and protected by security forces for fear they would be driven out by Tamil rebels. Tamil leaders believe that the location of this colony was intentionally planned to deny them both the rights to claim any area on the island as their traditional homeland and the merger of the northern and eastern provinces into a single Tamil province.

The Concept of Sri Lankan Tamil Nation

Sri Lankan Tamils justify their claim to a traditional homeland on grounds that they have inhabited the island as long as the Sinhalese, although they do not have any written history of their existence on the island from ancient times to legitimize their right to a traditional homeland. The Pali Chronicles refer to the presence of Tamils on the island from ancient times and to the war in which the Sinhalese prince,

Dutthagamani, defeated the south Indian Tamil prince, Elara, in 101 B.C. (Kearney 1978: 530).

Sinhalese nationalists regard the events leading to the defeat of Elara as the beginning of Sinhalese nationalism; the history of Sri Lankan Tamils was, thus, excluded from the history of Sri Lanka for almost 1,000 years (Rahula 1956: 76; Siriweera 1984: 160). To the Sinhalese, Sri Lankan history can only be the story of the Sinhalese people. Some Sinhalese historians, however, believe that the Tamils began settling on the island, both as peaceful immigrants and invaders, more than two thousand years ago (De Silva 1977: 37–38). Tamil scholars have cited examples of the existence of many ancient Hindu temples in predominantly Tamil areas to suggest that Tamil settlements persisted in northern and eastern Sri Lanka from ancient times (Arasaratnam 1964: 101; Tennent 1859: 483). The history of Tamils, as reconstructed by their scholars, also demonstrates that the Tamils inhabited the island as a distinct community beginning in the thirteenth century (Pathmanathan 1978). During the seven centuries of freedom from foreign domination and prosperity, Tamils of the northern and eastern parts of the island evolved a sense of collective identity based on language, culture, and territory, which are distinct from the Sinhalese and Tamils of Tamil Nadu. Howard Wriggins (1984) argues that Sri Lankan Tamils have "maintained their own separate and distinct continuum on the island for so many centuries that, in reality, the Tamil literary and cultural heritage of South India operates only as a source of historical inspiration."

Sri Lankan Tamil nationalists and politicians have used documentary evidence, especially letters and official documents left by British administrators and travelers, to suggest that the Tamils constituted a nation during the eighteenth and nineteenth centuries and that the Sinhalese people and Tamil people occupied two separate territories on the island from ancient times. In particular, Hugh Cleghorn, Colonial Secretary of Ceylon in 1798, even characterized the two nations in his famous minutes of 1799 as being of ancient origin and "differing entirely in their religion, language and manner" (Pieris 1953: 31). E. B. Denham, who reviewed the 1911 Census of Ceylon, also stated that "in spite of the closest political connection, the two races are as distinct today in Ceylon as the limits of their settlements are clearly defined" (Denham 1911: 196).

The differences between the two nations and the areas they occupied were distinct enough to persuade the British colonial government to designate the territory inhabited almost exclusively by Tamil-speaking people in the north and east of the island as the Tamil provinces in 1873. An examination of Arrowsmith's 1857 map of Ceylon indicates that the spatial distribution of Sinhalese and Tamil place-names, including those designated for natural and human-made features, was the criteria used by the British to define the boundaries of the Tamil provinces (Tennent 1859: frontispiece). Sinhalese place-names, such as Oya, Wewa, Gama, Gamwa, Wia, and so on, switched to Tamil names, such as Colom, Aar, Oor, Madoo, Tivoo, and so on, across the boundaries that separate Tamil provinces from Sinhalese provinces. An analysis of the census of population data for the year 1881 also indicates that the Tamil provinces were inhabited almost exclusively by Tamils in the late nineteenth century (Lee 1882). Sinhalese constituted only 1.8 percent (7,326 persons) of the total population of the Tamil provinces in 1881, most concentrated along the borders of both provinces.

Portuguese and Dutch records indicate that the Tamil provinces were governed as separate administrative units in the sixteenth and seventeenth centuries and that the colonial powers followed local customs and traditions in order to govern the Tamil-speaking people. Although the British government was fully aware that the island contained two distinct nations, it was determined to unite them under a unitary form of government (Farmer 1963). The unitary governmental structure, however, failed to unite the Tamil and Sinhalese communities into a single nation, because the members of each community adhered to their respective traditions and customs and made no serious effort to mingle freely with others. By the late 1970s, conflicting claims between the two communities over their respective space-related identities escalated the ethnic conflict, setting the stage for militant Tamil youth to use violent methods to confront the Sinhalese-dominated government over the Tamil question.

Tamil Reaction to Sinhalese Policies

Government policies and regulations dealing with colonization, university education, and employment affected the Tamil community adversely, especially its youth (Manogaran 1987). The origin of the Tamil youth militant movements can be traced to the year 1973, when emergency powers were introduced to arrest and hold in custody more than 100 young men, all of whom were suspected of being militants, for staging a black-flag demonstration during the visit of government ministers to Jaffna. Since then, harsh measures adopted by the government to deal with the youth movements led its members to organize underground militant movements.

Young Tamils became infuriated with the inability of the aging Tamil leaders to resolve the problem, and they demanded that the Tamil leaders form a single party to contest the general elections of 1977. This led to the formation of the Tamil United Liberation Front at a convention convened under the chairmanship of S. J. V. Chelvanayakam. Its members passed the Vaddukkoddai Resolution on May 14, 1976, which gave notice to Sinhalese politicians that Tamils would adopt new strategies to "establish an independent, sovereign, secular, socialistic state of Eelam that includes all geographically contiguous areas that have been the traditional homelands of the Tamil-speaking peoples in this country." The Tamil United Liberation Front, which contested the general elections of 1977 on a mandate for the establishment of a separate state, won overwhelming support from the Tamil people. A series of unfortunate events that followed the elections of 1977, including the anti-Tamil riots and the use of emergency powers to curb youth movements, contributed to the rise of Tamil militant movements. Elder statesmen and leaders of Tamil youth movements were united in their demand for the establishment of an independent Tamil nation, called Eelam, on the island of Sri Lanka.

Sinhalese leaders, for the most part, ignored Tamil threats, knowing that Sri Lankan Tamils had rarely displayed any tendency to resort to violence. Sinhalese politicians continued to justify their colonization of Tamil areas on grounds that Tamils had also been migrating to Sinhalese areas. Some Sinhalese were further enraged over the overwhelming support that the Tamil United Liberation Front received during the elections for establishing a separate Tamil state. Sinhalese-dominated security forces stationed in Tamil areas perpetrated violence against Tamil civilians and even set fire to the Jaffna Library, which was a repository of some of the most valuable documents and books on the history of Sri Lankan Tamils and their achievements. The government also enacted the Prevention of Terrorism Act of 1979 and dispatched its troops to Tamil areas in order to contain the militant movements. Tamil politicians who advocated separation for Tamil areas were subsequently debarred from participating in proceedings in Parliament.

Tamil militants, for their part, began targeting security forces, government establishments, and informants. These horrible incidents, and the reluctance of President Jayewardene's United National Party government to implement some of the concessions that it promised the Tamil people, contributed in the late 1970s to the formation of the most powerful and feared Tamil militant organization, the Liberation Tigers of Tamil Eelam Movement (LTTE), led by Veluppillai Prabhakaran (Narayan Swamy 1994). On July 23, 1983, the LTTE used a remote device that killed thirteen government soldiers in Jaffna. The incident, which is considered a watershed in the history of Sinhalese-Tamil relations, led to the most destructive anti-Tamil riots of 1983 (Obeyesekere 1984: 44–50).

A Political Solution: For Two Linguistic States within a Federal Union

The civil war between the LTTE and government forces continues, without any end in sight. Forty years have elapsed since the signing of the Bandaranaike-Chelvanayakam Pact, but no government has yet legislated any of the proposals granting substantial powers to the people of Tamil areas or implemented plans for the massive development of hitherto neglected war-torn Tamil areas. Proposals relating to the granting of regional autonomy to Tamil areas and to the government's policy of targeting Tamil areas for Sinhalese colonization have failed to materialize, because opposition parties and religious organizations have often refused to cooperate with the ruling party in order to reach a consensus on major issues. Even the thirteenth amendment to the constitution, establishing provincial councils, would not have received legislative approval, if it had not been linked to the Indo-Sri Lankan pact of 1987. The provincial councils, nevertheless, did not resolve the Tamil question, given the refusal of the LTTE to participate in the elections, the inability of the government to implement the provisions of the Tamil language legislation, and the reluctance of the government to funnel funds for the initiation of major reconstruction projects or to grant substantial powers to the North-East Provincial Council in order to limit Sinhalese colonization of Tamil areas. The creation of the northeast province, formed by the merger of the northern and eastern provinces, had the overwhelming support of Tamil politicians, but the permanent merger of the provinces was opposed by Sinhalese politicians. Tamil politicians insist that the permanent merger of the Tamil provinces is vital for the economic well-being of their people as well as for the preservation of the cultural and space-related identity of Sri Lankan Tamils (Manogaran 1988: 198–199).

Given the determination of the LTTE, as well as the grass roots support it has from the Tamil population, there is little prospect that the LTTE will be drawn into the political mainstream in the near future, unless a suitable alternative can be found for an independent sovereign Tamil Eelam. A viable alternative to Tamil Eelam would be the establishment of a federal system of government, which would fulfill LTTE demands concerning the preservation of both the distinct character of Tamil society and the territorial integrity of the Tamil traditional homeland. There are no signs that the army or the LTTE is willing to cease hostilities and to find a political settlement to the conflict. However, there are indications, given the statements made by the LTTE leader, Veluppillai Prabhakaran, in an interview to the British Broadcasting Corporation, that the militants may be willing to negotiate a political settlement, if the Sinhala-dominated government were willing to amend the constitution to grant regional autonomy to the Tamil-majority region under a full-fledged federal system (Tamil Times Ltd. 1993: 4–5).

Government forces captured the city of Jaffna, the capital of the northern province, in December 1995 and hoisted the Sinhalese Lion Flag. This act of raising the Sinhalese flag over the Tamil homeland kindled nationalistic sentiment among many Tamils who had not previously sympathized with the LTTE. Although armed forces have captured the city of Jaffna and a portion of the mainland, the government does not have complete control of either the northern or the eastern province. The president of Sri Lanka, Chandrika Kumarathunga, presented a set of devolution proposals, in January 1996, that would grant some measure of semiregional autonomy to Tamil areas (*Sunday Observer* 1996). Although the union of regions is designed to devolve the same degree of autonomy to both Tamil and Sinhalese areas, it does not recognize the territorial identity of the Tamil homeland. Moreover, provisions in the initial package of proposals have already been modified, or watered down, in order to accommodate the wishes of Sinhalese nationalists. There are indications that these proposals will meet the same fate as those previously proposed. Indeed, the government does not have the backing of Sinhalese parties and religious organizations to legislate its proposals. The Liberation Tigers of Tamil Eelam withdrew from the peace talks before the present phase of the hostilities was resumed on the grounds that the proposals did not even meet the prerequisites for a full-fledged federal system of government. The prospects for lasting peace and national reconciliation hinge on whether the Sinhalese politicians of all political persuasions and members of the Buddhist organizations are prepared to meet Tamil demands for the formation of a semiautonomous Tamil linguistic province formed by the merger of the northern and eastern provinces. The notion that the Tamil provinces have been "the historical habitation of Sri Lankan Tamil-speaking people," was recognized by the terms of the Indo-Sri Lankan Accord of July 29, 1987, the Bandaranaike-Chelvanayakam Pact of 1957, and the Senanayake-Chelvanayakam Pact of 1966 (Manogaran 1988: 196).

The degree of semiregional autonomy that the government has been willing to grant to the Tamil provinces, thus far, has been disappointing to Tamil nationalists. To meet their demands, a new proposal would have to focus on resolving the social, economic, and spatial-related identity problems that contributed to the ethnic conflict. The problems of the Tamil-speaking people are so unique and acute that, unless special powers are granted to Tamil areas under a full-fledged federal system of government and substantial funds are allocated for the rebuilding of Tamil area devastated by war and neglect, President Kumarathunga's devolution package will not resolve the Tamil question. Political developments in Belgium and Switzerland clearly suggest that, under a federal system of government, people belonging to different ethnic groups in a multiethnic society can remain united and committed to preserve, protect, and defend the constitution of a union of states.

References

Arasaratnam, Sinappah. *Ceylon*. Englewood Cliffs: N.J.: Prentice Hall, 1964.

De Silva, Kingsley M. *Sri Lanka: A Survey*. London: C. Hurst, 1977.

Denham, E. B. *Ceylon at the Census of 1911*. Colombo: Government Press, 1911.

Department of Census and Statistics. *Census of Population and Housing, Sri Lanka, Preliminary Report No. 1*. Colombo: Government Printing Press, 1981.

Farmer, Bertram H. *Pioneer Peasant Colonization in Ceylon*. New York: Oxford University Press, 1957.

———. *Ceylon: A Divided Nation*. London: London University Press, 1963.

Geiger, W. *The Mahavamsa or the Great Chronicle of Ceylon*. London: Oxford University Press, 1912.

Government of Ceylon, House of Representatives. *Parliamentary Debates (Hansard)* 30 (1957) cols. 1309–1311.

Hooson, David. *Geography and National Identity*. Cambridge: Blackwell, 1994.

Indraratna, A. D. V. de S., H. M. A. Codipilly, A. W. A. D. G. Abayasekera, and A. T. P. L. AbeyKoon. "Migration-Related Policies: A Study of the Sri Lanka Experience." In A. S. Oberai, ed., *State Policies and Internal Migration*. New York: St. Martin's Press, 1983, 79–139.

Jayawardena, Kumari. "Class Formation and Communalism." *Race and Class* 6 (11) (1984): 51–61.

Kearney, R. N. "Language and the Rise of Tamil Separatism in Sri Lanka." *Asian Survey* 18 (6) (1978): 521–534.

Lee, Lionel. *Census of Ceylon 1881*. Colombo: Government Printing Press, 1882.

Manogaran, Chelvadurai. *Ethnic Conflict and Reconciliation in Sri Lanka*. Honolulu: University of Hawaii Press, 1987.

———. "The Indo-Sri Lanka Accord of 29 July 1987." *The Round Table* 306 (1988): 195–200.

———. "Colonization as Politics: Political Use of Space in Sri Lanka's Ethnic Conflict." In Chelvadurai Manogaran and B. Pfaffenberger, eds., *The Sri Lankan Tamils: Ethnicity and Identity*. Boulder: Westview Press, 1994, 84–125.

Matthews, Bruce. The Situation in Jaffna—And How It Came About." *The Round Table* 290 (1984): 188–214.

Mikesell, Marvin W. "The Myth of the Nation State." *Journal of Geography* 82 (6) (1983): 1983, 257–260.

Moore, Mick. *The State and Peasant Politics in Sri Lanka.* London: Cambridge University Press, 1985.

Narayan Swamy, M. R. *Tigers of Lanka: From Boys to Guerrillas.* New Delhi: Konark, 1994.

Oberai, A. S. *Land Settlement Policies and Population Redistribution in Developing Countries.* New York: Praeger, 1988.

Obeyesekere, Gananath. "The Vicissitudes of Sinhala-Buddhist Identity through Time and Change." In Michael Roberts, ed., *Collective Identities, Nationalism, and Protest in Modern Sri Lanka.* Colombo: Marga Press, 1979, 279–312.

———. "Political Violence and the Future of Democracy in Sri Lanka." *Internationales Asienforum* 15 (1/2) (1984): 39–60.

Pathmanathan, S. *The Kingdom of Jaffna, Part 1 (circa A.D. 1250–1450).* Colombo: Arul M. Rajendran, 1978.

Pieris, Ralph. "Administration of Justice and Revenue on the Island of Ceylon under the Dutch government, (The Cleghorn Minutes)." *Journal of Royal Asiatic Society (Ceylon Branch)* 3(2) (1953): 131.

Poulsen, T. M. *Nations and States.* Englewood Cliffs, N.J.: Prentice Hall, 1995.

Rahula, Walpola. *History of Buddhism in Ceylon: The Anuradhapura Period, 3rd Century B.C.–10th Century A.D.* Colombo: M. D. Gunasena, 1956.

Siriweera, W. I. "Dutthagamani-Elara Episode: A Reassessment." *Ethnicity and Social Change in Sri Lanka.* Colombo: Social Scientists' Association of Sri Lanka, 1984.

Sunday Observer (January 21, 1996): 10–12.

Tamil Times Ltd. *Tamil Times* (London) 8(3) (March 15, 1993): 4–5.

Tennent, Emerson J. *Ceylon,* vol. 2. London: Longmans Press, 1859.

Turner, L. B. J. *Report on the Census of Ceylon, 1921.* Colombo: Government Printing Press, 1923.

Wilson, A. Jeyaratnam. *The Break-Up of Sri Lanka.* Honolulu: University of Hawaii Press, 1988.

———. *S. J. V. Chelvanayakam and the Crisis of Sri Lankan Tamil Nationalism, 1947–1977.* Honolulu: University of Hawaii Press, 1994.

Wriggins, W. Howard. *Ceylon: Dilemma of a Nation.* Princeton, N.J.: Princeton University Press, 1960.

———. "The Present Situation and Outlook for Sri Lanka." Oral Presentation before the Subcommittee on Asian and Pacific Affairs and the Subcommittee on Human Rights and International Organizations. Committee on Foreign Affairs, U. S. House of Representatives, August 2, 1984.

Part IV

Micro-Scale

Our last set of chapters concerns identities manifested at the micro-scale. Keeping with our previous categorizations, we have taken this to mean identities that exist below the level of the state. Very often, these micro-identities are substate nationalisms, which consider themselves nations and who desire autonomy. But micro-scale identities do not necessarily have to share in these goals. Moreover, it is important to note that "micro" is also relative; each micro-scale identity contains within it identities that exist at even smaller levels.

This subdivision of identities is particularly evident in Pauliina Raento's chapter. She shows how Basque identity, itself a substate nationalism, must coexist with compelling identities at both larger and smaller geographical scales. She argues that there are several Basque ideologies that must contend with one another, and that the most significant divisions are between provinces, within provinces, and between the rural and urban regions. These divisions frustrate attempts to construct a clear Basque identity and a unified nationalist front.

Oren Yiftachel discusses the marginal identity of the Palestinian-Arabs within Israel, caught between the larger Palestinian nationalism (which they do not fully share) and citizenship within a state that has long shunned their presence. Yiftachel argues that the Israeli Arabs have created a hybrid, ethnoregional identity that does not seek its own state but has come to ground its existence in the fractured Arab communities scattered throughout Israel.

George White's discussion of Transylvania gives an example of a borderland that, rather than occupying the edges of a larger national identity, lies at the very center of both Romania's and Hungary's geographical sense of self. These identities are manifested in specific places within the province that are spatially intermixed and that illuminate the tensions regarding Transylvania's political position. Yet,

Transylvania is more than a mix of two identities; as White argues, alongside there has also existed a distinctly Transylvanian identity.

Anne Knowles demonstrates that the voluntary character of Welsh emigration prevented a politicization of this experience as had been the case in Irish nationalism. This diaspora identity, based around the preservation of the Welsh language, initially prevented the establishment of a strong attachment to a Welsh homeland. Developments in the twentieth century altered this emphasis, with greater attention paid to the Welsh territory itself, especially in the Welsh redoubts of rural Wales.

10

The Geography of Spanish Basque Nationalism

Pauliina Raento

The century-long conflict between the Spanish central government and Basque nationalists is one of the most severe of its kind in contemporary Europe. The conflict has not faded away with the political transformation of the Spanish state after the death of dictator Franco in 1975. And European integration has not been of much help. Instead, today, the political debate over such issues as what is meant by "Basque national self-determination" and "Basque culture" and over how they should be promoted, is bitter and extremely polarized.

Although some valuable pieces of work (for example, Clark 1984, 1985, 1990) discuss this institutional and social fragmentation of Basque society in detail, they fail to root it in territorial issues. From a geographer's perspective, this leads to circularity that suggests that Basque people confront each other and the Spanish state because they do not agree with one another. Without recognizing the vital role of territorial elements in nationalist disputes, these studies also fail to explain the endurance and complexity of the current Basque conflict.

This chapter seeks answers to some of the previously untouched questions regarding the Basque conflict. These include questions such as "Why do Basque nationalists face difficulties in building national unity?" and "Why does their support vary considerably from one region to another?" A satisfactory analysis of any nationalist conflict should cover several geographical scales of inquiry. In the Basque case, European integration, the "New Spain," local, and provincial environments function as vital contexts for the current political actors. Each of these contexts interacts with one another in a complex manner that includes a variety of political, economic, cultural, and social elements that all evolve in both space and time.

Following this logic, the discussion proceeds from the national level of the conflict ("Spain" vs. "the Basques") toward the internal processes within the Basque territory. The study covers the four Basque provinces in Spain: Alava,[1] Guipúzcoa, Vizcaya (the Basque Autonomous Community), and Navarra, which has its own autonomy (Figure 10.1). The confrontation is more severe in this region than in the three Basque provinces in France. The focus will be on "radical" Basque nationalism, because it is arguably the most relevant actor at each examined scale.

Basque Political Ideologies

Basque nationalism first emerged as a middle-class reaction to the dramatic social and economic change of the Basque coast at the end of the nineteenth century (Corcuera Atienza 1979; Harrison 1983). Like many other self-declared "national" projects, it was place-specific in its ori-

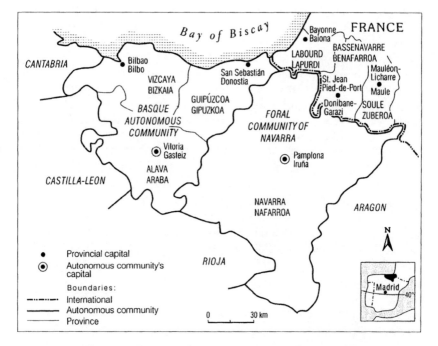

Figure 10.1   The seven historical Basque provinces in Spain and France

gin. Although the first nationalist party, Partido Nacionalista Vasco/
Eusko Alderdi Jeltzalea (PNV/EAJ), sought to protect the essence of
the Basque "race," its concerns focused mainly on the province of Vizcaya (Arana y Goiri 1978: 11–42).

The legacy of the bitter civil war in Spain (1936–1939) (Thomas 1961)
and the new industrial and demographic expansion on the Basque
coast after World War II led to the radicalization of Basque nationalism.
In the 1960s, a new organization named Euskadi Ta Askatasuna (ETA;
Basque Homeland and Liberty) launched an armed campaign against
the central government in Madrid. ETA also shifted Basque nationalism toward leftism and underscored the territorial unification of the
seven Basque provinces of Spain and France (Krutwig 1973; Jáuregui
1981; Clark 1984).

The political transition of Spain since 1975 broke the relative agreement of Basque nationalists. Previous internal tensions regarding the
goals and methods of the movement, already present in the 1920s, divided them bitterly. The actors currently present on the Basque political scene in Spain can be divided roughly into three groups, based on
their perception of the relationship between the state and the Basques
(see Corcuera Atienza 1991; Llera 1994):

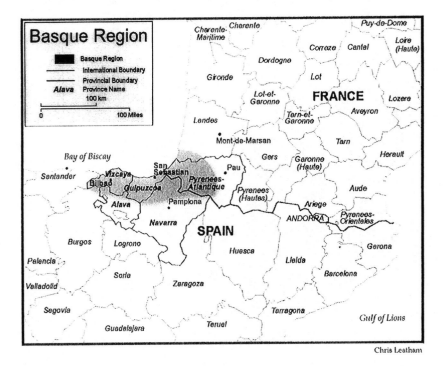

Chris Leatham

▶━━━◀

Area   Basque Autonomous Community 7,235 square km.
                              (provinces of Alava, Guipúzcoa, and Vizcaya)
                              Foral Community of Navarra 9,662 square km.
                              (province of Navarra)
                              Spanish Basque Country (four provinces) total
                              16,897 square km.
                              French Basque provinces 3,065 square km.
                              (provinces of Labourd, Basse-Navarre, and
                              Soule)
                              Basque Country (seven provinces) total 19,962
                              square km.

Population   Basque Autonomous Community 2.10 million
                              (provinces of Alava, Guipúzcoa, and Vizcaya)
                              Foral Community of Navarra 0.52 million (province
                              of Navarra)
                              Spanish Basque Country (four provinces) total 2.62
                              million
                              French Basque provinces 0.25 million (provinces of
                              Labourd, Basse-Navarre, and Soule)
                              Basque Country (seven provinces) total 2.87 million

Mono- and Bilingual   Basque Autonomous Community 24.1% (Alava 7.0,
Basque Speakers   Guipúzcoa 43.7, Vizcaya 16.5)
                              Foral Community of Navarra 9.6%
                              Spanish Basque Country (four provinces) total
                              21.3%
                              Basque Country (seven provinces) total 22.3%

NATIONALIST CONFLICT

- Provincial rights and privileges abolished: 1876
- First nationalist party (PNV) founded: 1895
- General Francisco Franco's dictatorship in Spain: 1939–1975
- ETA (Euskadi Ta Askatasuna) founded: 1959
- First killing by ETA: 1968
- Fatalities since 1968: some 800
- ETA-related prisoners in Spain and France: some 600

Sources: Euskal Herriko atlasa. Donostia: Erein, 1994. *Euskal urtekari estatistikoa/Anu-
ario estadístico vasco 1996.* Vitoria: Eustat, 1997. *La continuidad del euskera.* Vitoria:
Gobierno Vasco, 1995. Población de derecho en España 1.1.1995 por municipios. Insti-
tuto Nacional de Estadística.
<http://www.ine.es/~joseba/inre/inre51/muni00.htm>

The attempt to turn Spain into a unitary state in the nineteenth century led to the abolition of the medieval provincial rights and privileges of the Basque provinces in 1876. The subsequent liberalization of trade encouraged industrialization of the Basque coast and attracted thousands of workers from other parts of Spain. As a reaction to this profound social and economic change, nationalist ideas emerged among the Basque middle classes. The first Basque nationalist party, PNV/EAJ, was founded in 1895.

The harsh minority policy of General Franco's dictatorship in Spain (1939–1975) led to radicalization of Basque nationalism. In 1959, the separatist ETA was founded. It shifted Basque nationalist ideology toward leftism. In 1968, the organization committed its first political killing. Since then, some 800 deaths have been related to the conflict over the territorial composition and administrative status of the Basque territory and language.

After Franco's death, the new Spanish Constitution (1978) gave the Basques autonomy. The four historical Basque provinces, however, were divided into two autonomous communities (Basque Autonomous Community and Foral Community of Navarra) against the nationalists' will. Also, some transfers of power from the central to the regional governments remain to be completed. For the most radical nationalists, that is, ETA, the autonomy represents a betrayal of the original ideals. Currently, the Basques themselves disagree upon the acceptable goals and methods of the nationalist struggle. Both the ongoing conflict with the Spanish central government and the severe internal disagreements are further complicated by considerable regional differences within the four provinces.

▶━━━━━━━━━━━━━━━━━━━━━━━━━━━━━━━━━━━━◀

- The *nonnationalists* consider the Basque territory an essential part of the Spanish state and nation and see the Basque nationalist quest for "national self-determination" as satisfied by the autonomy.
- In turn, the *moderate Basque nationalist* parties, PNV/EAJ and Eusko Alkartasuna (EA), both oppose the Spanish state and its nonnationalist representatives in the Basque Country. In practice, they accept autonomy as a means of satisfying the quest for "Basque national self-determination" and condemn violence. These two form the Basque Autonomous Community's parliament together with the Spanish socialist PSOE.
- The *radical nationalist* Basque National Liberation Front (MNLV)

consists of the coalition party Herri Batasuna (HB) and various semiclandestine and clandestine activist groups (such as the ideological coordinator Socialist Patriotic Coordinator [KAS], and ETA). In its separatism, MNLV sees the Basque Country as "betrayed" and "occupied" by the Spanish (and the French) state. Accordingly, it seeks "liberation" by demanding political independence and monolingually Basque-speaking Basque territories by any means necessary. MNLV holds that by accepting autonomy and the territorial division into two autonomous communities and by cooperating with "the oppressor," the moderate nationalists, PNV/EAJ in particular, have betrayed the Basque people. In each election, HB garners some 15 percent of the vote in the Basque Autonomous Community.

In Basque politics, the territorial division—the acceptance of the Spanish state—overrides the traditional ideological division into right and left. This emphasizes the political nature of Basque identity especially in radical nationalism. Some moderate nationalists, as well as many nonnationalists, however, find it possible to identify with both the Spanish state and Basqueness simultaneously (Clark 1985; Linz 1985). Furthermore, all three main ideologies and related identities are *fundamentally territorial,* that is, they are primarily concerned with the vital composition and political structures of the Basque territory. This means that the state level and the regional context of the conflict are obviously interrelated.

Internal Territorial Pluralism

The political divisions are further enhanced by the internal pluralism of the historical Basque territory. Many of the internal problems of the Basques are directly related to the historically and politically distinct development of each province and to their subsequently unique personalities (Tuan 1975: 234–235). The Basque provinces differ from each other in terms of culture (language, lifestyle, and tradition), and there are considerable social and political contrasts between urban and rural, nationalist and nonnationalist, and Basque- and Spanish-speaking areas (see Douglass and Bilbao 1975: 13–16).

First, the contrast between rural and urban areas is remarkable. One-half of the Spanish Basque population of some 2.6 million is concentrated in the ten largest cities, which all have over 40,000 inhabitants. In contrast, more than three-quarters of the municipalities of the four provinces have population figures smaller than 5,000. The contrast is especially striking in Alava and Navarra, whereas on the coast industrialized "medium-size" centers are more numerous (EUE/AEV 1991; 49–51; *Censo de población 1991*). Second, 7 percent of the population in Alava is Basque-speaking, compared with 10 percent in Navarra, 17 percent in Vizcaya, and 44 percent in Guipúzcoa. Within the Basque-speaking zones, urban areas stand out as having relatively more Spanish-speakers. Many of the urban dwellers are non-Basque in their origin, and many of them do not know Basque at all (*La continuidad . . .* 1995). Third, as a consequence, these centers are distinguishable in voting patterns, with a higher percentage of the nonnationalist vote. Also, radical nationalism draws support from general urban radicalism present on the scene. It is in these centers where the nonnationalist, Spanish-speaking and the two nationalist, predominantly Basque-speaking worlds meet face-to-face and compete over political space in the fiercest manner.

The rural core area of "traditional" radical Basque nationalism lies in the small, predominantly Basque-speaking rural communities of the coast and of the mountain region in eastern Vizcaya, southern Guipúzcoa, and northern Navarra. In these areas, the strong nationalist sentiment has developed in a relatively protected environment without continuous contact with other realities and, thus, as very loyal to one dominant interpretation. Consequently, the explanation of these regional and local personalities can be sought in the relative geographical location and social composition of each "micro-world." Because of their historical development, many parts of the southern Basque borderland in Alava and Navarra are politically, culturally, and socially closer to Madrid than to the nationalist core areas on the Basque coast (Raento 1996: 47).

Along these lines, the Basque coast and the interior stand apart. In addition, the same distinctions take place within the provinces, particularly in Alava and Navarra. This heterogeneity has complicated the relationship between the two autonomous communities and their internal construction, posed difficulties to the Basque nationalist ideologies and tactics, and, in general, caused territorial disputes and rivalry. Both the national dispute and the provincial heterogeneity come down to the political development of the Foral Community of Navarra and the province of Alava within the Basque Autonomous Community.

Provincial Identities against Nationalism

Based on the Constitution of 1978, Spain was divided into seventeen autonomous communities in the early 1980s. In the Basque Country, the outcome was unacceptable especially for the radical nationalists. For them, the ancient Kingdom of Navarra represents the core of a medieval Basque state, which brought the Basque territories formally together during the Middle Ages (Tuñon de Lara et al. 1991: 86). Castile annexed the defeated kingdom to the new state of Spain in 1512. The MNLV insists that the current division into two autonomous communities represents "an imposition" of government and of false identity "by the victors upon the defeated" (*Egin,* December 2, 1994: 14), and that to "recover its own identity," Navarra should unite with the other Basque provinces in an independent state. The status of Navarra and the question of how, and by whom, it should be determined are among the most divisive issues of the Basque conflict.

The radical nationalist interpretation collides with a political identity called "Navarrism." It emphasizes Navarra's separate evolution from the other Spanish Basque provinces since 1512 and the province's role in creating modern Spain. Thus, Navarra is an essential part of the Spanish state, of its traditions and religion (see Payne 1985). This perspective is defended by two provincial parties, Unión del Pueblo Navarro (UPN) and Convergencia de Demócratas Navarros (CDN), which together garner almost one-half of the Navarrese vote (1995). They are supported especially in the Spanish-speaking central and southern Navarra, whereas the stronghold of Basque nationalism lies in the Basque-speaking north.

Within the Basque Autonomous Community, a similar movement has emerged in the province of Alava. Since 1990, Unidad Alavesa (UA) has attacked Basque nationalism and the dominance of the city of Bilbao in Basque economy and politics. Its core area of support is Vitoria, which experienced a dramatic process of industrialization and growth in the 1960s (López de Juan Abad et al. 1966: 21–22, 41–46) and which became the capital of the Basque Autonomous Community in 1980 (Rivera Blanco 1990: 37–38). The outcome is a strong local consciousness of the distinct character of the city and the province.

Many Alavese see that the ruling PNV/EAJ imposes Vizcayan interests on Alava—the provincial origin of the party and its doctrine are well-remembered. Although the Alavese consider themselves Basques (Hendry 1991: 170–195; de Pablo Contreras 1991), many see the strong presence of PNV/EAJ as an attempt to bring in "Basque" elements that are not genuine to the province and its southern borderland. In UA leader Pablo Mosquera's words, the party aims at recovering the "rights which make Alava capable of self-organizing and self-governing. Self-government in this context means the possibility to decide how to develop the territory and how to invest the money produced [in this territory]" (*Egin*, October 13, 1994: 16). In 1994, this message convinced 18 percent of the Alavese voters (EUE/AEV 1994: 550, 561).

For many nationalists, the antinationalism practiced by UA, UPN, and CDN is actually "anti-Basque" (*Egin*, October, 13, 1994: 17). Their rejection of the Basque language and some cultural issues is seen as an attempt to undermine the Basqueness of Alava and Navarra. In order to apply the term *anti-Basque*, however, there should be an agreement upon the definition of what is *Basque*, and this agreement does not exist. The term underscores the political nature of all identities present in the conflict. Also, it ignores the pluralist sociological reality of the southern borderland provinces and of the entire Basque territory.

Radical Nationalist Reaction

Talking about *anti-Basque-ism* reflects the difficulties both the moderate and the radical nationalists face in Alava and Navarra, where interpreting their message has been difficult. In particular, the term carries a hint of an attitude sometimes called "Vizcayan and Guipúzcoan mentality," which finds it difficult to understand, and accept, the antinationalist response in the Basque Country's culturally and ethnically multifaceted border zones (Payne 1985; Hendry 1991). Without paying attention to local circumstances, these regions have been treated with a certain paternalism and arrogance, leaving them in a position of relative weakness within the nationalist decision-making structures. The emergence and success of UA, UPN, and CDN within the historical Basque territory, however, have forced especially MNLV to review its tactics and long-term strategies (Raento 1996: 52–53). Consequently, the southern radical nationalists have acquired more power and real autonomy within MNLV's organization (see Mata López 1993: 122–125). Also, recent campaigns show greater sensitivity and skills of adaptation in relation to the specific characteristics of each *local* environment.

This adaptation is best exemplified by MNLV's street campaigns of public art (Chaffee 1988). Through graffiti, the national conflict is made visible at the local level and used as a means of grassroots mobilization in the street, the most important public space for Basque social activities. To gain the maximum impact, both the content and the frequency of the campaigns are modified according to their audience and its most intimate environment.

The most aggressive and homogeneous radical nationalist campaign of public art can be found in the densely populated urban neighborhoods of the coast. The details of each campaign and the reaction it creates reflect the social and political composition of each locale. For example, in San Sebastián, where MNLV is strong, the walls are simply wiped clean for new messages to appear. In the towns of southernmost Navarra, they are covered by fierce graffiti and countergraffiti. On the predominantly nationalist coast, few would replace such slogans as "Long live ETA" by "Long live Spain," or by "God, Fatherland, Old Laws, King," which expresses the core of the Navarrist identity (Payne 1985). In addition, the number of graffiti varies from one region to another. For example, the walls of Vitoria are covered by considerably fewer political messages than the ones in Pamplona, which MNLV considers the historical capital of the Basque territory (Raento 1996: 48–52). The differences show that "political mobilization . . . is place-specific, reflecting the history of integration into a national political system . . . local organizational capacity, and other facets of group formation" (Agnew 1987: 22).

The pattern is repeated in political demonstrations, which reveal the bitter internal divisions of Basque society. As well, they are organized most frequently in the provincial capitals, and in the industrial centers within MNLV's core area (Figure 10.2). These areas also produce the highest number of ETA militants (Llera et al. 1993: 125). In these towns, the demonstrations are also the most likely to lead to a physical confrontation, which happens especially between MNLV and PNV/EAJ. For example in 1994, the police registered 2,488 political demonstrations in the three provinces of the Basque Autonomous Community. Some 600 led to "incidents" in the form of roadblocks, stone-throwing, or fistfights (*Deia*, February 20, 1995: 6). A most severe episode took place in February 1997, when the Basque Autonomous Community's own police opened fire at radical nationalist demonstrators in Bilbao. Of the twenty-three wounded, two suffered injuries by bullets (*El País [Edición Europa]*, February 17, 1997: 1, 13, 14).

Challenged by Change

The changing overall context of Basque politics, especially European integration and Spain's increasing role as one of the EU members, adds up to the bitter atmosphere within the Basque territory. Consequently, both the radical and the moderate Basque nationalists are currently challenged in four geographical contexts.

First, locally, there is the dilemma of internal territorial diversity. This diversity complicates the nationalists' task of balancing the quest for internal unity with the quest for recognition of plurality. The crucial internal questions for each nationalist group are "On which basis

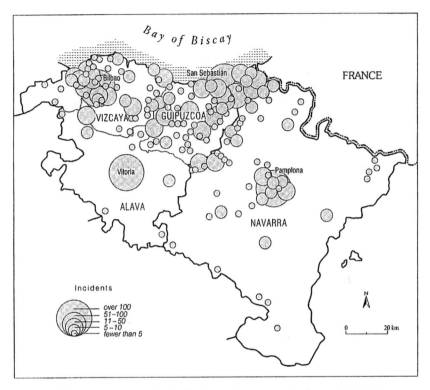

Figure 10.2   Cores of conflict in the Spanish Basque Country, 1988–1996

Note: Included are acts of repression by the police, attacks against freedom of expression, arrests related to opinion, arrests under the antiterrorist law, and sabotage.
Source: Anuario de Egin 1988, 1990, 1992, 1994, and 1996.

should the unity be built?" and "Who decides this, and how?" In an environment of multiple political options and competition, many nationalist ideologues now express the need to correct previously made mistakes. They call for patience and admit that giving up arrogance has become vital for attracting support.

The traditional focus of the nationalist ideologues has emphasized their most loyal core area in the coastal provinces. Despite the new adaptation to each local setting, this emphasis is not necessarily disappearing, which may complicate the maintenance of nationalist mobilization in the future. Therefore, even if the ideologues managed to answer the most fundamental questions concerning unity, they are still left with the practical problem of how to penetrate the distinct local realities of the entire claimed national territory and how to make them equally responsive to the cause. All these elements add up to the fragmentation of the nationalist world and its subgroups at the same time when the general framework of the nationalist movements in Europe is changing.

Second, in terms of the relationship between the Basque region and the Spanish state, it has become increasingly difficult to justify the use of violence as a political instrument for forwarding the radical nationalist cause. The justification, however, is still relatively strong in MNLV's core area in Guipúzcoa, northern Navarra, and eastern Vizcaya. In the new political environment, explanations that consider ETA's continuous success in recruiting new members and its violence to be a response to the poor relationship of the Spanish central government and the Basque Autonomous Community, or a reaction to continuous economic problems of the Basque industries, or to the alleged violation of human rights by the Spanish police have proved to be sufficient.

It appears instead that violence has created its own dynamics and logic of escalation and is self-sustaining (Clark 1984: 273–280; Raento 1994). ETA has used threats, intimidation, and violence within its own organization in order to maintain discipline (Douglass and Zulaika 1990: 251; Shabad and Llera Ramo 1995: 441–443). On each side of the conflict there are people who benefit from the violence. Also, some elements of Basque violence point to the importance of symbolic meaning of action and the prestige of those who carry out this action (Zulaika 1988). Therefore, it would be a mistake to see "Spain," "the Basque autonomous government," and "ETA" as single, homogeneous actors. Because of this complexity and despite numerous attempts to negotiate an end to the violence, there are many obstacles to a negotiated settlement. Each of the interested parties wants to end the violence on its own terms and for its own political benefit. There is considerable tension among different parties, they disagree upon the timing of a cease-fire, and they cannot agree upon the topics to be negotiated (Clark 1990: 226–230).

At its extremes, the contemporary conflict has become a question of *pride* and a matter of *principle* between very proud groups of people. Both views are understandable and explicable. For example, "Spain" is a former empire, and from any state's point of view, letting its regions go would mean losing its reason for being. Giving in to "terrorist blackmailing," as frequently stated by the former Spanish Prime Minister, Felipe González, would also be humiliating. "The Basque (radical nationalists)," in turn, have a centuries-long tradition of challenging the central government—why should they give up now, if there has been no reason to do so earlier? The difficulty of abandoning the armed struggle is understandable, when the ultimate goal of "full national self-determination" has not been reached. From ETA's perspective, abandoning the struggle would mean denying the sacrifices of the people it has fought for (Raento 1994: 41–43).

Third, in the continental context, there is a feeling of Basque distinctiveness being swallowed by European integration. Even if the Spanish Basques entered the European Union with the advantage of having their own autonomous government, the greatest weight in decision making still lies in Madrid. The Basque autonomous government's representatives lack special status in matters concerning their region, such as fishing. This may undermine the nonnationalist and the moderate nationalist belief that international boundaries and the ones within states are becoming increasingly alike and that, over the long run, this will peacefully enable the unity desired by the nationalists. The radical nationalists, and many moderate nationalists as well, challenge this belief as theoretically desirable but unrealistic in practice. They argue that contemporary states consolidate their power even further and point out the conflictive nature of Basque boundaries within Spain and France. Accordingly, these people see political independence as the only viable alternative in the contemporary continental (and global) context.

At the same time, however, the new openness of the international boundary between Spain and France has made it increasingly difficult to maintain the old (radical) nationalist argument concerning "Spanish and French colonialism" in the Basque territory. On the one hand, this contextual challenge may bring the nationalists closer to their dream of a territorially unified Basque Country. On the other hand, it may be argued that the strength of MNLV will diminish because of the erasure of the dividing line of "colonialism." Consequently, European integration has added a new context of division into local Basque politics over the desirable way of dealing with the central governments and with the European Union. The disputes have also complicated the implementation of some EU regional development projects in the Basque region.

Fourth, even if the nationalist groups were able to respond to these challenges, their quest for political power and their grassroots mobilization for the cause are still complicated by an intervening factor from a global level. Radical nationalists, especially, see that the continuity of their way of life is represented by the youth, who receive the ideology through social and interpersonal networks (Ramírez Goicoechea 1984; Arpal 1985). In the changing political environment, many radical nationalists consider this continuity endangered. Compared with the Franco years, Basque social networks have become relatively depoliticized, and the political content of cultural demonstrations and fiestas has diminished. The "traditional" scene of activities has been penetrated by a new, global alternative: modern mass media and, in particular, television. This intruder is *no longer place-specific* and, because of that, cannot be responded to with the same answers.

Conclusion

Many Basque nationalists claim that "It's all Madrid's fault." The discussed examples suggest, however, that the political conflict concerning the Basque Country takes place increasingly within the Basque Country itself and that the conflict is influenced by multiple factors that are all interconnected. For example, the bitter atmosphere and local disagreements within the Basque territory have a direct impact on the conflict between the central government and Basque nationalists and obviously complicate some continental processes. As long as the feelings of injustice and frustration are not resolved in a satisfying manner in *all* relevant contexts, the conflict is most likely to continue, in one form or another. Usually, one's satisfaction is another's disappointment.

The Basque example shows that a nationalist conflict is essentially about territory and political power. It is a conflict that *takes place* somewhere and, most importantly, affects regional configurations from the continental and state levels to the local and individual spheres of life within the disputed territory. To attend to the local context of politics in more detail is fundamental because it is the basis for all political mobilization: In order to be effective, any national(ist) propaganda must somehow touch the nerve at the local level. Therefore, political action cannot be studied in isolation from any of these geographical contexts. Their interconnectedness suggests that nationalism is an inherently territorial phenomenon that should be so studied. Likewise, the territorial and political nature of identities related to nationalism ought to be recognized in each and all of these scales.

The territorially multifaceted emphasis may offer a new insight into the fundamental dilemmas of nationalism, into what Benedict Anderson (1983: 14) has called *the three paradoxes of nationalism*. This refers to the dilemmas of combining a universal phenomenon with the variety of its real-life examples of very different settings; of matching nationalism's modernity with its ideological romanticism and historicist interpretation of the past; and of understanding why nationalism has an enormous power to mobilize despite its ideological vagueness in modern context. As the endurance and fierceness of the Basque conflict indicate, nationalism is most unlikely to just fade away. Instead, its inherently territorial logic underscores some universal elements within human nature, and suggests continuity. This is precisely what makes nationalism an important object of study.

Notes

1. For the sake of simplicity, I use Spanish toponyms (for their Basque counterparts, see Figure 10.1). Both the ethnohistorical Basqueness of Navarra and the jurisdictional pertinence of the four provinces to the Spanish state are treated as current facts. The geographical terms *region* and *territory* are used without any political connotation they may carry within the conflict over the territorial composition of the Basque Country. The terms *moderate* and *radical nationalist* are used in accordance with the Anglo-American literature on nationalism.

References

Agnew, John A. *Place and Politics: The Geographical Mediation of State and Society.* Boston: Allen and Unwin, 1987.

Anderson, Benedict. *Imagined Communities: Reflections on the Origin and Spread of Nationalism.* London: Verso, 1983.

Anuario de Egin: Euskadi 1988. Lizarra: Orain, 1988.

Anuario de Egin: Euskadi 1990. Lizarra: Orain, 1990.

Anuario de Egin: Euskadi 1992. Lizarra: Orain, 1992.

Anuario de Egin: Euskadi 1994. Lizarra: Orain, 1994.

Anuario de Egin: Euskadi 1996. Lizarra: Orain, 1996.

Arana y Goiri, Sabino de. *Obras escogidas. Antología política.* San Sebastián: L. Haranburu, 1978.

Arpal, Jésus. "Solidaridades elementales y organizaciones colectivas en el País Vasco (Cuadrillas, txokos, asociaciones)." In Pierre Bidart, ed., *Ibilbide zozialak, ideologiak eta ekintza kulturalak Euskal Herrian.* Pau: Université de Pau et des Pays de l'Abourd, 1985, 129–154.

Censo de población 1991. Resúmenes munipales. Pamplona: Gobierno de Navarra, 1993.

Chaffee, Lyman. "Social Conflict and Alternative Mass Communications: Public Art and Politics in the Service of Spanish-Basque Nationalism." *European Journal of Political Research* 16 (1988): 545–572.

Clark, Robert P. *The Basque Insurgents: ETA, 1952–1980.* Madison: University of Wisconsin Press, 1984.

———. "Dimensions of Basque Political Culture in Post-Franco Spain." In William A. Douglass, ed., *Basque Politics: A Case Study of Ethnic Nationalism.* Reno, Nev.: Associated Faculty Press, 1985, 217–263.

———. "Negotiating with ETA." *Obstacles to Peace in the Basque Country, 1975–1988*. Reno: University of Nevada Press, 1990.

La continuidad del Euskera. Vitoria: Gobierno Vacso, 1995.

Corcuera Atienza, Javier. *Origenes, ideología y organización del nacionalismo vasco (1876–1904)*. Madrid: Siglo XXI, 1979.

———. "Sistema de partidos en el País Vasco." In *Estudios sobre el estatuto de Autonomía del País Vasco III*. Oñati: HAEE/IVAP, 1991, 971–1063.

Douglass, William A., and Jon Bilbao. *Amerikanuak: Basques in the New World*. Reno: University of Nevada Press, 1975.

Douglass William A., and Joseba Zulaika. "On the Interpretation of Terrorist Violence: ETA and the Basque Political Process." *Comparative Studies in Society and History* 32(2) (1990): 238–257.

EUE/AEV 1991 = *Euskal Urtekari Estatistikoa/Anuario Estadístico Vasco 1991*. Vitoria: Eustat, 1992.

EUE/AEV 1994 = *Euskal Urtekari Estatistikoa/Anuario Estadístico Vasco 1994*. Vitoria: Eustat, 1995.

Harrison, Joseph. "Heavy Industry, the State and Economic Development in the Basque Region, 1876–1936." *Economic History Review* 36(4) (1983): 535–551.

Hendry, Barbara Ann. "Ethnicity and Identity in a Basque Borderland: Rioja Alavesa, Spain." Ph.D. Dissertation. University of Florida, 1991.

Jáuregui, Gurutz. *Ideología y estrategía política de ETA. Análisis de su evolución entre 1959 y 1968*. Madrid: Siglo XXI, 1981.

Krutwig, Frederico (Fernando Sarrailh de Ihartza). *Vasconia*. Buenos Aires: Norbait, 1973.

Linz, Juan. "From Primordialism to Nationalism." In Edward A. Tiryakin and Ronald Rogowski, eds., *New Nationalisms of the Developed West*. Boston: Allen and Unwin, 1985, 203–253.

López de Juan Abad, José Manuel, Angel María Campo, Ignacio Ibarrondo, and Juan Antonio de Zarate. *Dinámica socio-urbana de una capital: Vitoria 1950–1964*. Vitoria: n. p, 1966.

Llera, Francisco José. *Los vascos y la política. El proceso político vasco: elecciones, partidos, opinión pública y legitimación en el País Vasco, 1977–1992*. Bilbao: Universidad del País Vasco, 1994.

Llera, Francisco J., José M. Mata, and Cynthia L. Irwin. "ETA: From Secret Army to Social Movement—The Post-Franco Schism of the Basque National Movement." *Terrorism and Political Violence* 5(3) (1993): 106–134.

Mata López, José Manuel. *El nacionalismo vasco radical. Discurso, organización y expresiones*. Bilbao: Universidad del País Vasco, 1993.

de Pablo Conteras, Santiago. *Los problemas de la autonomía vasca en el siglo XX: La actitud alavesa (1917–1979)*. Oñati: HAEE/IVAP, 1991.

Payne, Stanley G. "Navarra and Basque Nationalism." In William A. Douglass, ed., *Basque Politics: A Case Study in Ethnic Nationalism*. Reno, Nev.: Associated Faculty Press, 1985.

Raento, Pauliina. "Baskimaan ETA—tarina poliittisesta väkivallasta." *Ulkopolitiikka* 31(4) (1994): 36–44.

————. "Baskimaan kansallinen konflikti ja alueellinen omaleimaisuus." *Kosmopolis* 26(4) (1996): 45–55.

Ramírez Goicoechea, Eugenia. "Cuadrillas en el País Vasco: Identidad local y revitalización étnica." *Revista Española de Investigaciones Sociológicas* 25 (1984): 213–220.

Rivera Blanco, Antonio. *La conciencia histórica de una ciudad: "El vitorianismo."* Vitoria: Diputación Foral de Alava, 1990.

Shabad, Goldie, and Francisco José Llera Ramo. "Political Violence in a Democratic State: Basque Terrorism in Spain." In Martha Crenshaw, ed., *Terrorism in Context.* University Park: The Pennsylvania State University Press, 1995, 410–469.

Thomas, Hugh. *The Spanish Civil War.* New York: Harper and Bros., 1961.

Tuan, Yi-Fu. "Space and Place: Humanistic Perspective." *Progress in Geography* 6 (1975): 211–252.

Tuñon de Lara, Manuel, Julio Valdeón Baruque, and Antonio Domínquez Ortiz. *Historia de España.* Barcelona: Labor, 1991.

Zulaika, Joseba. *Basque Violence: Metaphor and Sacrament.* Reno: University of Nevada Press, 1988.

Newspapers: *Egin, Deia, El País (Edición Europa)*

11

Regionalism among Palestinian-Arabs in Israel

Oren Yiftachel

The recent scholarly interest in nationalism has generated an impressive body of theories (for reviews see: Anderson 1996; Smith 1995). However, most theories of nationalism—despite their groundbreaking insights—have often ignored variations in ethnic spatial settings and citizen rights and have too easily conflated nation and state. Although nationalism is indeed a major engine of global transformation, it surfaces in a variety of dynamic forms and shapes, including ethnoregionalism among homeland minorities "trapped" within states controlled by other ethnic groups. These minorities are often caught in a position of *double marginality* vis-à-vis both their nations and their states. In such cases "ethnoregional" identities often emerge as a response, combining national and civic bases of identity with attachment to specific places or regions.

In this chapter I will attempt to focus on one such minority—the Palestinian-Arab citizens of Israel. I will attempt to present a political-geographical perspective, so often lacking in leading theoretical and empirical accounts, and will thus pay particular attention to the role of territory, geographical scale, and location as complementing other factors in the political mobilization and identity formation among the Arabs.

The analysis will lead me to argue that in response to their position of double marginality the Palestinian-Arabs in Israel are reshaping their group consciousness and collective identity by forging a (sub-state) ethnoregional community. Their emerging ethnoregionalism is being shaped by the "weight" of Jewish and Palestinian nationalisms and by their Israeli civil affiliation. Significantly, the process has also been influenced by the spatial existence of Palestinians in a "fractured region" within Israel, occupying a stable but divided "homeland territory" over the last fifty years. In that sense, the evolution of Arab ethnoregionalism in Israel provides a telling example of territorial ethnonationalism as expressed on a constrained substate level.

The chapter begins with a short discussion of the concept of ethnoregionalism, followed by analysis of four key processes shaping Arab political-geography within Israel. First, though, we need to provide some definition. The *Arabs in Israel* and the *Palestinian citizens of Israel* are interchangeable terms (with *Arabs* being often used in order to unequivocally include subgroups such as the Druze and the Bedouins). *Israel* denotes the country within its pre-1967 border, without the occupied territories or East Jerusalem. *Palestine* is the political-geographical unit that preceded Israel, stretching between the Jordan River and the Mediterranean Sea. *Ethnicity* is a collective cultural bond based on belief in a common past at a specific place, and *nation* denotes a cultural (usually ethnic) community, which controls or aspires to control a territorial state. *Region* connotes a sociospatial entity between the local and the state level, which provides a source of identity and mobilization for its community.

Nationalism, "Trapped" Minorities, and Ethnoregionalism

Among the collective identities shaping societies in the modern era, ethnonationalism has emerged as a hegemonic world order (Anderson 1991), and national identities have become "banal" (Billig 1995). This taken-for-granted political system confers enormous power on the nation-state to control its constituent communities, often concealing deep ethnic and social fragmentation (Chatterjee 1993). Yet, as the hegemonic nation-building discourse continues to penetrate the collective imagination of ethnic minorities, national identities often resurface in dynamic and flexible forms. This may destabilize multiethnic states challenged by peripheral demands for autonomy, regionalism, or sovereignty (Anderson 1996; Connor 1993; Hechter and Levi 1979; Smith 1995).

In the context of this hegemonic order, the case of marginal ethnic minorities is particularly telling. Because of border locations, such minorities usually find themselves "trapped" at the periphery of a state dominated by another ethnic group. Here national identity is often constrained by existing power structures, and minorities devise strategies that usually combine elements of nation-building citizenship in the reconstruction of their collective identities.

Israel

National Capital
Haifa • City
International Boundary
District Boundary

50 km

0   50 Miles

LEBANON

SYRIA

GOLAN HEIGHTS
(Israeli occupied, Unilaterally annexed by Israel in 1981)

• Nahariyya
• Akko

• Haifa   Tiberias •   Sea of Galilee
• Nazareth

Hadera
• Netanya
• Nablus

Herzliyya
• Tel-Aviv Yafo

Mediterranean Sea   WEST BANK *

Ramla •
• Ashdod
Jerusalem ✪
• Ashqelon   • Bethlehem

• Gaza
GAZA STRIP *
Rafah   • Hebron

• Beersheba   Dead Sea

• Dimona

Oron •

JORDAN

• Mizpe Ramon

EGYPT

Yotvata •

* Israeli occupied with current status subject to the Israeli-Palestinian Interim Agreement—permanent status to be determined through further negotiation.

Elat

Gulf of Aqaba

Chris Leatham

►───◄

DATA

In December 1995, the Palestinian-Arab citizens of Israel numbered 880,000 and constituted 16 percent of the country's population. This figure does not include the 170,000 Palestinians living in East Jerusalem (al-Quds), which was unilaterally annexed in 1967 without granting citizenship to its residents.

The Arab minority in Israel is distinct from the 2.3 million Palestinians residing in the territories occupied by Israel in 1967. The two groups share history, culture, and ethnicity but are separated by their different citizenship status. A fully fledged Palestinian national movement emerged in the territories but not inside Israel.

The Arab minority in Israel includes three main religious groups: Muslim (77 percent), Christian (13 percent), and Druze (10 percent). The community resides in three main regional concentrations, in the country's north, center, and south. It owns about 3.5 percent of Israel's land and controls about 2 percent of the country's local government area.

HISTORY AND CONFLICTS

During the 1947–1949 Palestinian-Jewish War, the Palestinians lost control over their homeland and became scattered in several states. Over 700,000 fled or were driven out of their towns and villages during that war. The Palestinian-Arabs remaining in Israel were placed under military rule until 1966, and about two-thirds of their land holdings were expropriated by the Jewish state.

During this period, the minority's position among Israel's lowest socio-economic and political strata was cemented by an Israeli regime that promoted Jewish interests, often at the expense of the state's Arab citizens. The marginalization of the Arabs was augmented by their geographical and social fragmentation and their isolation from the Arab world by Israel's sealed borders.

Following the 1967 war and the lifting of military rule, Arab political mobilization in Israel articulated two main goals: civil equality and Palestinian national independence in the occupied territories. This campaign became highly visible in Israeli politics and was highlighted by the events of Land Day (March 30, 1976), when six Arabs were killed during a mass protest against further land expropriation by the Israeli state. Peace Day (December 25, 1987) was another notable day of mass demonstration, protest, and general strike against Israel treatment of the Palestinian Intifada (uprising) in the occupied territories. Finally, the Oslo agreement of mutual recognition between Israel and the PLO (September 13, 1993) made clear that the Palestinian-Arabs in Israel are left outside the definition of the Palestinian political nation. The main conflict between them and the Israeli regime now revolves around the minority's continuing economic, territorial, cultural, and political marginalization in Israel.

▶━━━◀

Several studies have begun exploring the combination of national and civil elements in the identity construction of ethnic minorities. This brought some scholars to arrive at an "ethnoregional" interpretation of minority struggle and identity. The groundbreaking work of Hechter (1975) and Hechter and Levi (1979) and later contributions by Keating (1988, 1996), Mikesell and Murphy (1991), Shafir (1995), and Williams and Kofman (1989) have clearly demonstrated that under certain circumstances, the most likely result of minority organization and politicization is the emergence of an *ethnoregional* movement. The term has been used in a variety of ways, but here I wish to reintroduce it more rigorously to mean the mobilization of ethnic struggle *within* a nation-state, aiming to channel resources to specific ethnic territories, attain ethnic rights, preserve or rebuild a substate ethnic identity, and challenge the state's internal political structure.

Ethnoregionalism is thus one *dynamic* expression of the ongoing "weight" of a hegemonic ethnonational discourse superimposed over the existing grid of citizenship rights and geographical realities. It usually forms a reaction to the often exclusive, expansionist, or exploitive nature of majority ethnocentric nationalism that propels "trapped" minorities to campaign for goals such as territorial or cultural autonomy, devolution of government functions, power-sharing, or socioeconomic equality (Keating 1996; McCrone 1993; Mikesell and Murphy 1991). Ethnoregionalism characterizes homeland ethnic groups that do not wish to secede but still develop distinct and challenging identities within their polities.

Ethnoregionalism is different from both ethnonationalism and civic mobilization on a number of counts, making it a distinct, durable, and meaningful political movement. It is distinct from ethnonationalism by its lack of drive for ethnic sovereignty, by the self-perception of "its" territory as constrained, containing specific places or regions (and not a holistic national territory or state), and by its attempt to reconcile ethnic and civil bases of identity. It is distinct from civil group mobilization by its emphasis on specific homeland living spaces where the group's identity is grounded and by its steadfast demands to restructure the foundations of the polity and not merely redistribute its material resources.

I claim here that an ethnoregional campaign reflects a new "hybrid" group identity that emerges after a period of living in a state controlled by another ethnic group. This identity synthesizes ethnonational and civil motives, as illustrated by a growing number of such groups, including, for example, Catalonians in Spain, Tyroleans and Slovenians in Italy, Flemish in Belgium, Hungarians in Romania, Chinese in Malaysia, or Welsh and Scots in Britain. I further claim that this emerging "hybrid"entity is likely to proliferate under the current world order, increasing self-assertion of minorities in a gradually democratizing and globalizing world.

Ethnoregionalism is thus both a *territorial reality and a political process*, whereby a homeland ethnic minority reimagines its collective identity as forming a region (that is, a substate) and territorial and political community. The region forms the basis from which the minority challenges the privileged access to state power of other ethnic groups and the legitimacy of dominant power structures. Ethnoregionalism is also tied to economic disparities between region and state, which generate a mobilization of discontent (regardless, it seems, whether the region is economically advanced or retarded!), rooted in what Shafir (1995: 16) terms "the diminished value of the state for further economic development." It may evolve over time into fully blown separatist ethnonationalism or into gradual integration into the general political community, depending on the political circumstances. However, in most cases it is a distinct and lasting group identity that presents a notable challenge to the current nation-state order.

Ethnoregionalism is a movement that combines both *ethnonational and civil* causes and thus offers a promising avenue for synthesising the two approaches. The case of Palestinian-Arabs in Israel, to which we now turn, demonstrates the potential of this synthesis.

Palestinian-Arabs in the Israeli "Ethnocracy"

The Palestinian-Arabs in Israel are a telling case of a "trapped" minority, situated in double marginality, between the main body of Palestinians (chiefly in the occupied territories) and the Jewish majority in Israel (see al Haj, 1993b). The minority, which in late 1996 numbered 910,000, or 16 percent, of Israel's population, includes all Arabs with Israeli citizenship (as distinct from the 2.3 million disenfranchised Palestinians in the occupied territories of Gaza and the West Bank; see Figure 11.1). Arabs in Israel belong to three main religions (Moslems are 76 percent, Christians, 14 percent, and Druze, 10 percent) and re-

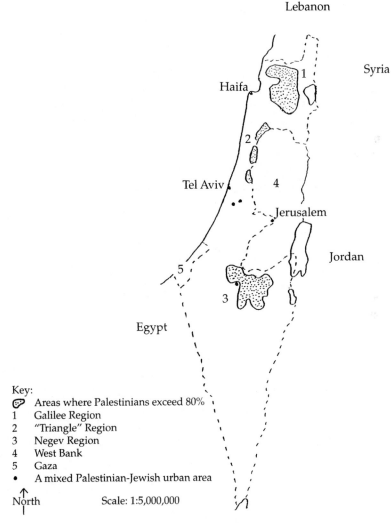

Lebanon

Syria

Haifa

Tel Aviv

Jerusalem

Jordan

Egypt

Key:
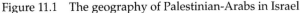 Areas where Palestinians exceed 80%
1   Galilee Region
2   "Triangle" Region
3   Negev Region
4   West Bank
5   Gaza
•   A mixed Palestinian-Jewish urban area

North   Scale: 1:5,000,000

Figure 11.1   The geography of Palestinian-Arabs in Israel

side in three principal regional concentrations—the Galilee, the "Triangle," and the Negev—as well as several scattered villages and six mixed cities (Figure 11.1).

The historical and political background to Arab-Jewish relations in Israel is covered extensively elsewhere (see: Smooha 1978; Yiftachel 1992b). As a necessary background, it should be briefly noted here that the evolution of these majority-minority relations has been strongly influenced by the construction of the Israeli Jewish-dominated "ethnocracy," by the Arab-Israeli conflict in general and the Jewish-Palestinian struggle in particular. Palestinian-Arabs who remained in Israel (on their own historical homeland) following the 1948 disastrous defeat to the Jews and the expulsion or escape of some 650,000–750,000 Palestinians, were considered by many Jews as enemy-affiliated and found themselves marginalized and disempowered in Israel.

Beyond the widespread association of the Arabs with Israel's enemies, their plight in the Jewish state was strongly affected by a rapid and relentless process of Zionist–Jewish nation- and state-building. The Zionist project was a reaction to centuries of Jewish persecutions in a hostile (mainly European) diaspora, where ethnonationalism was taking root alongside democratization and emancipation—all threatening the survival of a Jewish people. Thus a prevailing goal of Jewish survival in its historical homeland was a fundamental driving force behind the Zionist movement, endowing it with striking levels of resilience, vigor, and intransigence (Yiftachel 1995). Zionism was hence predicated on instilling an indigenous bond to the land to masses of Jewish refugees and migrants returning to a homeland they had never seen (Ram 1995). Arab-Jewish relations in Israel/Palestine must therefore be first and foremost understood as an ongoing conflict between two homeland ethnic communities vying to control a common territory (Yiftachel 1992a).

The goal of "indigenizing the Jews" necessitated the eradication of the Arab memory from the landscape, achieved by the destruction of most emptied Arab villages (Falah 1996b) and by a concerted effort to settle Jews in most regions historically populated by Arabs (Pappé 1995; Yiftachel 1992b). In the resulting Israeli-Jewish settlement, land and development policies have therefore continuously attempted to erode Arab territorial control and encourage Jews to settle in places promoted as "internal frontier" areas (Newman 1989; Yiftachel 1996). The upshot was a virtual ghettoization of the Arab minority associated with economic neglect and political disempowerment, as will be further discussed.

Israel has thus evolved quickly into a *Jewish ethnocracy*, where nearly all state resources, energy, and programs—with significant assistance from world Jewry—were aimed at furthering Jewish control. The process of rapid Jewish nation and state building can explain the legitimacy accorded by the Jewish public to these expansionist and ethnocentric policy measures as well as to the 1949–1966 imposition of military rule on the state's Arab citizens and to the widespread confiscation of minority land in a country self-proclaimed to democratic principles (Lustick 1980). The state capitalized on the scarring legacy of past Jewish traumas, on the enormous challenge of absorbing large numbers of Jewish refugees, on continuing security problems, and on genuine Jewish yearnings for forming a physically, culturally, and politically safe nation and proceeded to implement its ethnocentric nation-building policies, largely at the expense of Palestinian-Arabs.

As the name suggests, the focus of the Israeli ethnocracy was thus nearly totally *Jewish* and—in the eyes of the state's architects—had to remain exclusively Jewish in order to rally vital support from Jewish diasporas. Further, the state's Ashkenazi (European-oriented) elites feared a possible integration between Jewish immigrants from Arab countries and local Arabs that would leave the Ashkenazis as a cultural minority in Israel. Thus they proceeded to create a critical distance between Arab-Jews and the state's Arab minority by rapidly stripping Arab-Jews of their "Arabness" (Shohat 1988) and by virtually shutting out local Arabs from the process of creating the new state and society. The Israeli agenda thus became synonymous with (Ashkenazi) Jewish concerns, interests, and aspirations, despite always having a sizable Arab minority. Jewish education, public discourse, politics, and legislation were therefore entirely devoted to the ethnocentric project of constructing a Zionist-Jewish nation. Under the veil of formal democracy, the state in effect created a republican order, where only those contributing to a common (Jewish) good deserve full membership and the others are controlled (Peled 1992). This ideology quickly infiltrated into Israel's popular culture where Arabs were portrayed as primitive, dangerous, violent, and untrustworthy (Shohat 1996).

Later, Arab-Jewish relations have of course evolved. Tied with a gradual process of democratization, Israel has relaxed some of its control policies and practices over the Arabs, allowing their partial incorporation into Israeli society (Smooha 1992). However, despite this (slow) trend, the Arabs are still the least mobile and the most politically, economically, spatially, and culturally marginalized sector in Israeli society. The ethnocentric nation- and state-building efforts of successive Israeli governments and the continuing deprivation of Arabs are indeed two sides of the same coin. We can thus clearly see how the plight of the Arabs in Israel was shaped by the force and weight of Jewish-Zionist nationalism.

In parallel, however, other forces have been at work, most notably Palestinian nationalism and Arab awareness of their civil status as Israeli citizens. There is no need to elaborate here on the critical importance of contemporary Palestinian nationalism, which emerged in full force following Israel's conquest of the West Bank and Gaza. This nationalism never explicitly embraced the Palestinian-Arab citizens of Israel but still left a marked influence on their identity, struggle, and position vis-à-vis the Jews (Rekhes 1989). It legitimized the contacts between the Arabs in Israel and national Palestinian leaders, and has caused the minority to voice strong support and demonstrate in favor of the Palestinian national issues, as well as to nurture some of the most well-known Palestinian authors and poets, such as Emil Habibi, Mahmud Darwish, and Samih al-Khasem. As Rouhana and Ghanem (1993) convincingly show, the Arabs in Israel were and are Palestinians, and the construction of their own identity is framed within their Palestinian past and present.

Beyond national affiliation, the Arabs' Israeli citizenship has also been highly significant. It has gradually but steadily been used as a political, social, and cultural foundation of the rebuilding of their community. Nearly all Arabs are bilingual, and most educated Arabs attend Israeli universities. They consume the Israeli media and culture and see Israel as a central agent in a relatively rapid process of modernization. Repeated surveys have shown that even if an independent Palestinian state is established in the territories, the vast majority of the Arab minority (80–95 percent) would prefer to stay in Israel (al Haj 1993b). The Arabs' increasing awareness and use of political rights draws heavily on Israel's parliamentary democracy, and their awareness of an inferior class position is premised on their (uneven) integration into the Israeli economy. In similar fashion, their social and political perceptions have been influenced by the norms and practices of Israeli society at large (Smooha 1992). Although Rouhana (1997) argues strongly that the "Israeli" part of their identity has remained devoid of any emotional bond, even he concedes that it has had a significant impact on their collective identity and patterns of political mobilization.

Three main factors have thus shaped the identity and struggle of the Arabs in Israel: Jewish nationalism, Palestinian nationalism, and Israeli civic affiliation. However, most of the growing body of research on the subject has not attempted to carefully synthesize these factors as they are played out in the *specific political-geographic settings* of the Arabs in Israel (for a review: see Yiftachel 1995). In that research, two leading interpretations of Arab orientation have dominated: (a) *Politicization*, which claims that the growing assertion and militancy of the minority reflects, first and foremost, a struggle for Arab civil equality within Israel and an acceptance of life as an ethnic minority with a Jewish "ethnic democracy" (Smooha 1990, 1992; Ginat 1989; Lehman-Wilzig 1993); and (b) *Radicalization*, which argues that the strengthening Arab struggle for civil rights masks a deeper process of Palestinian nationalism, implicated with profound disloyalty to the Israeli state; this is likely to lead toward Arab separatism and irredentism (Landau 1993; Regev 1989; Soffer 1988, 1991).

Notably though, despite its groundbreaking importance and centrality to the understanding of Arab-Jewish relations in Israel, I have critiqued the politicization-radicalization debate as presenting a false dichotomy, because there is little theoretical or empirical evidence to suggest that the two are mutually exclusive (Yiftachel 1995). Further, the following analysis shows that *neither* politicization nor radicalization of the Arabs can adequately explain the political mobilization of the Arab minority.

In addition, the politicization and radicalization approaches have largely mirrored the theoretical approaches reviewed earlier and thus replicated their limitations and deficiencies. The politicization approach is rooted in a civic understanding of ethnic mobilization and accepts Gurr's (1993) classification of the Arabs in Israel as an "ethnoclass." As such, it regards the Palestinian component of Arab identity as one of many factors affecting their mobilization and ignores the central influence of global nationalism and the Arabs' homeland setting. On the other hand, the radicalization perspective is explicitly national, perceiving the Palestinian-Arabs to be marching on an almost inevitable path toward separation from the state. I claim that both these interpretations are too rigid and deterministic. Like their respective theoretical foundations, they have failed to treat seriously the nuances and intertwining of nationalism and civic concerns, have not examined in earnest the contradictions embedded in the construction of the Israeli nation-state, and have ignored the impact of Israel's ethnic geography.

Palestinian-Arab Mobilization and Identity in Israel

Clearly, any collective ethnic identity, and particularly that of the Arabs in the contradiction-riddled Israeli environment, is slippery, dynamic, and often difficult to pinpoint. However, my central claim is that the weight of both Zionist and Palestinian nationalisms and the civil affiliation of the Arabs with Israel have combined to cause a discernible redefinition of Arab collective identity in Israel. Whereas before 1948, they formed an integral part of a fledgling Palestinian nation and between 1948 and 1967 were isolated as "Israeli Arabs," since the 1970s, they have been in the process of collective reimagining, which sees their activities, struggle, and identity as a *distinct ethnoregional community.* That ethnic community is caught in a fixed geography, positioned in a double periphery in both Israeli and Palestinian societies (al Haj 1993b), thus forced to reformulate its identity using the main building blocks at its disposal: homeland localities and regions, Palestinian attachment, political and socioeconomic opportunities, and a recent—but meaningful—history of struggles, events, and places within Israel.

To be sure, the regionalization process is still embryonic, implicit, and only rarely discussed. It may take years before it becomes the explicit goal of any Arab organization. However, it is already in train, through the dynamics of local Arab governance, statewide Arab networks, the patterns of Arab economic activities, and daily Arab practices within Israel. Following from the definition of ethnic regionalism noted previously, the Arabs in Israel are indeed occupied with channeling resources into their localities and regions and are using these localities to defend and reshape their identity. In the process, they are beginning to forge a quiet, yet profound, challenge to the Israeli nation-state.

Why should this process be interpreted as ethnoregionalism and not simply a drive for "better terms of co-existence" (Smooha 1992: 3); or a movement whose "next step means an attempt to secede . . . from Israel and be annexed to the Palestinian entity across the border" (Soffer 1991: 198)? In the following sections, I will focus on four key dimensions of Arab political existence in Israel, which point to the emergence of an ethnoregional identity: their geographic setting, socioeconomic niche, antistate protest, and voting patterns. The scope of this chapter does not allow us to cover other central spheres of the Arab public domain, such as public discourse, print media, literature, and art. Nonetheless, the four dimensions to be covered provide ample evidence of the reshaping of the Palestinian-Arab collective identity in Israel.

Ethnic Geography

A most striking feature of the geography of the Arabs in Israel has been its (forced) stability over time. The Palestinian-Arab areas identified on Figure 11.1 have been virtually stable since 1948. We can therefore note that a stable Arab region has existed within Israel for the last five decades. This is particularly astonishing given Israel's dynamic history of settlement and rapid geographical change (Gonen 1995). Yet, since the upheavals of 1948, and apart from the establishment of several new towns for the concentration of seminomadic Bedouin-Arabs (Fenster 1993), the pattern of Arab localities has by and large remained unchanged (Figure 11.1). The original villages have of course grown, urbanized, and suburbanized, but there has been only scant Arab migration into non-Arab parts of Israeli cities (Ben Artzi 1996; Falah 1996a).

As shown in Figure 11.1, the Palestinian-Arab region is spatially fractured—a feature to which we shall return later. The political geography of the Arab region has also been shaped by its close spatial proximity to two significant entities: Jewish settlements and the Palestinian heartland in the West Bank and Gaza, with a significant set of interactions with each sector.

Because we have noted that ethnic regionalism denotes both a geography and a political process, we must elaborate on the way in which this exceptionally stable geography was created and maintained. Here we have to turn back to the Zionist project and to Jewish state-building practices, which have been consistently characterized by a single-minded mission to Judaize the country. Territory—above all else—has been the prime resource sought by the Zionist movement (Kimmerling 1983), engendering a relentless drive to control any piece of Arab land it could claim. The specific human geography of the Arabs in Israel was thus chiefly shaped by the most enduring feature of Israeli ethnocentric nationalism—the system of Jewish territorial control (see Yiftachel 1996).

As a result of this overriding quest, about 60 percent of Arab land in Israel was transferred to the state (Kimmerling 1983), and Arabs now control less than 2 percent of the country's local government areas—an eighth of their proportional share. Following the transfer of land to the state, over 400 Jewish settlements were constructed in all parts of the country. The Jewish Agency and Jewish National Fund—two bodies representing world Jewry and hence not accountable to Israeli democratic procedures—were granted rights to settle and develop the land on behalf of the state and the "Jewish People." The upshot was the penetration of Jews into most Arab areas, the encirclement of most Arab villages by exclusively Jewish settlements (where Arabs are not permitted to purchase housing), and the near total ghettoization of the entire Arab minority in Israel. In the process, Arabs have not only lost individual property but have also been dispossessed of much of their collective territorial assets and interests, because nearly all land transferred to the state (ostensibly for "public purposes") was earmarked for Jewish use (Yiftachel 1991).

Arabs have of course attempted at times to rupture their spatial containment. They have staged an intense wave of protest against further land expropriation (as will be further discussed) and have attempted to enlarge their local government boundaries, both with some success (Yiftachel 1991). They have attempted to initiate the creation of Arab regional planning committees, which even in heavily populated Arab areas are usually controlled by Jews, and have lobbied for ending discrimination in the provision of public housing (Khameissi 1992). In addition, individual Arabs, especially in recent years, have moved to Jewish towns and Jewish neighborhoods, at times demonstrating the ability to overcome intense Jewish opposition but usually being contained within Israel's urban areas by a combination of uneven public policies, social practices, and prejudice and by their limited capital resources (Ben Artzi 1996; Rabinowitz 1997).

We must of course remember that some of this residential segregation and stability has been voluntary, relating to a general concentration tendency among distinct ethnic groups (Peach 1996) and to a specific bond of Palestinians to their ancestors' land, embodied in the age-long custom of *summud* ("steadfastly clinging to the land"), and by generations of Palestinian peasant lifestyle and traditions (Doumani 1995). Yet, the creation of a constrained and ghettoized "Arab region" was, as shown, equally the result of Arab territorial containment and expansionist policies and activities by the Israeli state on behalf of Jews in Israel and abroad.

In terms of the reconstruction of collective identity, the spatial confinement of the Arabs has had some important effects. Although being obviously restrictive and painful, it has provided a unifying experience distinctive to that community and has spawned what Rabinowitz (1994: 117) terms a "collective memory of loss." This new geographic reality has erected visible and almost impregnable boundaries between "us" and "them," "in" and "out." This reality is largely shared by all Arab localities in Israel (in clear distinction to all other types of localities).

The translation of this stark reality into attitudes and patterns of interactions and movements is well documented by Schnell (1994) in his fascinating study of Arab territorial perceptions. Schnell, using interviews, surveys, and the drawing of mental maps, finds similar Arab sentiments of solidarity and comfort toward other Arab spaces, localities, and regions within Israel. Conversely, Arabs are usually indifferent, uncomfortable, or even hostile toward Jewish localities and spaces. Most striking is the high level of Arab alienation from nearby Jewish settlements built most recently around Arab villages.

The result is the creation of a "fractured Arab region," connecting segregated spaces and localities across the country in a set of common perceptions, experiences, affinities, and agendas. Therefore, a fractured Arab ethnic-region already exists in Israel, functioning to a large extent as one political, cultural, and social unit rooted in its own (constrained) homeland spaces.

Socioeconomic Status

Despite Israel's self-declared socialist ideology during the twenty-nine-year reign of the Labor movement (1948–1977), it constructed a hierarchical and exploitive dual system of separate Arab and Jewish labor, termed by Grinberg (1991) "split corporatism." This system derived its logic from the Jewish colonialist strategy of separating Jewish and Arab workers, dating back to the beginning of the twentieth century (see Shafir 1989; Shalev 1992). Following independence, the system's first and foremost objective became the provision of employment to Jewish immigrants in order to avoid social upheaval among potentially unemployed Jews (particularly among Jews of Arab origins in Israel's peripheral regions). Arabs were thus kept under military rule for eighteen years, during which their daily movement was controlled and restricted, effectively locking them out of the Israeli labor market. Further, their membership in the Histadrut—then Israel's all-powerful labor organization—was only granted (to "loyal non-Jews") in 1959. As Shalev (1992: 49) observes, "until the late 1950's, then, when the labour market experienced a transition from substantial unemployment to excess demand, the Histadrut's local institutions actively took steps to limit Arab employment." Even in the 1990s, Arabs remained underrepresented in most rungs of Israel's labor organizations, despite their concentrations among the country's working classes and the poor.

As documented by Zureik (1979), who used Hechter's (1975) analytical framework, the Palestinian-Arabs in Israel were subject to a regime of "internal colonization," whereby the majority uses minority resources (such as land and labor), and the ethnocentric state apparatus to further its own economic position. Zureik convincingly shows how the widespread state expropriation of Arab land and the construction of an industrial economy in Israel has caused a transformation of the class situation of the Arabs from peasantry to a commuting "proletariat." Part and parcel of that internal colonization process was a widespread—often institutional—ethnic division of labor and a constant sharpening of ethnic occupational hierarchies—all in the name of majority interests, legitimized through the "national" discourse of Jewish cultural, technological, and economic superiority (see also Haidar 1991).

The late incorporation of the Arabs into the Israeli labor force and the practices of "internal colonialism" meant of course that their occupational opportunities were severely limited, not only by their stigma as Arabs in a Jewish state but also by the fact that they had to enter the labor market from its lowest strata. This disadvantage was amplified by their low levels of professional qualification, paucity of capital resources, peripheral location, and exclusion from many of Israel's security-related industries. As a result, Arabs have been incorporated into the Israeli economy mainly as low-skill and menial laborers, especially in agriculture, manufacturing, transport, and local public bureaucracies, prompting Semyonov and Lewin-Epstein (1987) to label their niche as "hewers of wood and drawers of water."

During the 1970s and 1980s the incorporation of mass disenfranchised labor from the occupied territories "pushed" Israel's Arab citizens up the occupational ladder, placing them in better-paid and more managerial positions, albeit mostly in their "traditional" branches of the economy. This has continued to some extent during the 1990s with the importation of some 300,000 foreign temporary workers into Israel's expanding economy, who partially replaced the (potentially rebellious) Palestinian labor. However, despite the pervasive incorporation of noncitizens into the Israeli economy, and despite the Arabs' rapidly rising levels of education and skills, their occupational mobility remained highly constrained in an economy still stratified according to ethnic and national affiliations (Lewin-Epstein and Semyonov 1993; Smooha 1993).

Accordingly, Khalidi (1988) concludes that the Arabs are gradually forming a "region" within the Israeli economy, drawing their resources, directing their energies and economic aspirations, and performing most transactions within the Arab enclave of the Israeli economy. This was largely supported by a comprehensive industrial study during the mid–1990s (Schnell et al. 1995), which revealed that although most Arab firms attempt, and would prefer, to expand their trade into the Jewish industrial sector, they remained constrained to specific menial niches and still perform some three-quarters of their transactions with Israel's Arab localities.

Needless to say, this economic stratification and "enclavement" has been translated into social polarization, with Arabs and Jews generally occupying different class positions within Israeli society. Data on poverty, for example, has shown that in 1989, 39.8 percent of Arab households and 48.7 percent of Arab children lived under the poverty line, as opposed to 12.8 percent of households and 18.6 percent of children among Jews (Social Security Institute 1996). This polarization has worsened in the subsequent years, and in 1995, 44 percent of Arab households and 56 percent of Arab children were under the poverty line, as opposed to roughly half these proportions among Jews. Income data, too, shows, for the last fifteen years, Arab household income has consistently been around 60–70 percent of that earned by Jews (Sikkuy 1996; Social Security Institute 1996).

A recent study has shown that Arab deprivation in Israel has a clear geographical dimension, being expressed by the socioeconomic status of Arab localities. When Israeli localities were ranked by their socioeconomic status and grouped into deciles, a marked distinction became apparent between Jews and Arabs. Accordingly, Arab localities (which make up 23 percent of the number of Israeli local authorities) constituted 54 percent of the localities ranked in the lowest 20 percent. Even more strikingly, there was not even one Arab locality ranked in the top 60 percent of Israeli localities (CBS 1996). It is clear that the rapid development and economic growth experienced by Israel during the last four decades has largely bypassed most Arab (as well as some Jewish) localities. This demonstrates again that the material reality of Arab deprivation is not abstract but grounded in "their" spaces, which form a central part of the "identity infrastructure" of most peripheral minorities in industrial societies (Hechter and Levi 1979: 266).

Returning to the earlier themes of nationalism, state policies, and collective identity, we can draw a direct link between the all-embracing commitment of the Zionist project to bring Jews into the country and keep them (employed) in Israel and the systematic economic exclusion and marginalization of the Arabs. Israel's "split corporatism" (Grinberg 1991) is thus rooted in the political economy of Judaization and the exploitive use of Palestinian-Arab resources. As we have learned from Hechter and Levi (1979: 268), the emergence of a "reactive ethnic regional movement" is tied to inferior socioeconomic prospects within the state and to the existence of an ethnic occupational niche. Here too, then, Arab collective identity in Israel is beginning to bear the hallmarks of ethnic regionalism.

Protest and Mass Mobilization

Ethnic protest generally reflects the changing nature and emphases of ethnic demands vis-à-vis the central state. As such, it is an especially useful prism through which to study the mobilization of ethnic groups and other minorities. However, beyond a mere reflection of other demands and problems, ethnic protest also acts as a symbol and a generator of collective identity. As noted by Lofland (1985), the process of planning, preparation, and the act of protest itself have often fueled and accelerated the emergence of ethnic and other social movements.

Key protest events, and particularly those occurring in highly conflictual circumstances, often find their way into the group's collective memory, thereby forming a key role in the shaping of its communal identity (Jenkins and Klandremans 1995).

Since the mid-1970s, the Arabs have become increasingly organized politically and have staged an antigovernment protest campaigns. The most clear event that marks their arrival as an organized force in Israeli policies was Land Day, a 1976 mass demonstration against land expropriation in the Galilee, where six Arab protesters were killed. Figure 11.2 displays the intensity and key issues of that protest. Several broad observations can be made on both the fluctuation and content of Arab protest. First, its intensity has steadily increased from the mid-1970s until about 1990, reflecting the growing political awareness and self-assertion of the Arabs and their more proficient use of extraparliamentary politics in the highly politicized Israeli environment (Lehman-Wilzig 1993; Smooha 1990).

The relative decline in protest level since 1990 (except for 1994) may be linked to the Arab-Israeli peace process and to the policies of the 1992-1996 Labor government, which increased state financial support to most Arab localities (Sikkuy 1995). Alternative accounts have been offered for the decline. For example, Ghanem (1995: 14) observes that "the Arabs have scaled down their protest as a result of a deepening condition of 'communal distress' born by continuing discrimination, Arab political ineptness and subsequent inability to achieve meaningful integration into Israeli society." Rouhana (1997) sees this process

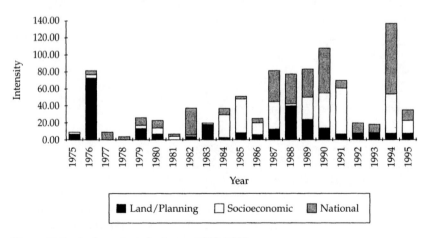

Figure 11.2 Arab protests by issue, 1975–1995

as part of a "delusion" gripping most Arabs, who believe their full integration into Israeli society is likely once Arab-Jewish hostilities subside.

However, if we return to our main argument of "ethnic regionalism," we should also note that antistate protest is generally fueled by expectation for some efficacy. A politically savvy reaction to persisting irresponsiveness by the state is likely to be the transformation of the Arab struggle into different modes of action. There is a prevailing feeling among Arabs (see Bishara 1993) that under its current structure, the Israeli state is constrained in its ability to make substantial policy changes, except for financial matters (which indeed formed an important focus of a 1994 wave of protest). Hence, mass antistate protest may be losing its appeal, while other modes of operation gain favor, including formal state-level politics and the strategic use of the Arabs' growing electoral clout (Lustick 1989), or the channeling of Arab energies into a quiet construction of a political, social, economic, and cultural enclave within Israel.

The unpacking of political protest reveals that three key issues have consistently dominated Arab protest: land control and planning, socioeconomic condition, and Palestinian nationalism (Figure 11.2). What is striking is the continuing prevalence of all three issues, in almost equal intensity: In the 1975–1996 period, 33 percent of the total number of protest events were about land control and urban planning issues (such as boundaries, house demolitions, and zoning), 42 percent were on socioeconomic issues (such as budgets of Arab local governments, services, and infrastructure), and 25 percent addressed Palestinian national issues (mainly responding to events in the occupied territories and Lebanon). If we measure protest by intensity, however, land and planning issues were the basis for 33 percent of Arab protest, socioeconomic grievances, 28 percent, and Palestinian national issues, 38 percent.

Clearly, then, we can see that these three issues have jointly dominated the mobilization of Arab mass politics, with Palestinian national issues relatively low on numbers but high on intensity, socioeconomic protest, the reverse, and land and planning issues, in the middle category on both counts. Despite obvious peaks and troughs in Figure 11.2, among the collective identities constructed by and within states, ethnonationalism should be seen as a hegemonic order from which most other identities emanate in the modern era. This taken-for-granted political objective confers enormous power on the nation-state to control its constituent communities, homogenize subnational cultures, and conceal internal deprivation, class conflicts, and human rights issues, in the name of the all-encompassing nation-building project (Chatterjee 1993). However, we should recognize not only that national identities are "banal" (Billig 1995) but also that because of this very banality, they are dynamic in scope and modes of expression. This is because the hegemonic nation-building discourse continuously penetrates the self-identity and collective imagination of ever-smaller ethnic groups and regions. This may destabilize existing political structures with campaigns for autonomy, regionalism, or sovereignty (Anderson 1996; Connor 1993; Hechter and Levi 1979; Smith 1995). The persistence and roughly equal strength of all three issues over time is most significant. This lends support to the ethnic regionalism thesis, which places Arab struggle between nation(s) and state. If Arabs were "radicalizing" and moving toward secession, the national cause would gradually prevail. Conversely, if they were striving for full integration into the state as an ethnoclass, as many observers claim, the socioeconomic strand would dominate. The continued concern of the Arabs for all three issues, and especially their persisting rallying to protect and expand their rights and power over *land,* indicate a campaign grounded in Arab spaces and localities. In short—a campaign of a budding ethnoregional movement.

A final aspect of Arab protest regards its leadership. The Arab campaign has been orchestrated and led by a range of bodies, most notably the National Committee of the Heads of Arab Councils (the "National Committee"), the "Following Committee" (composed of the National Committee, Arab parliamentarians, and other prominent leaders), and —most recently—the Moslem Movement. These are all voluntary bodies, receiving their support from a growing Arab focus on grassroot and village-based politics, illustrating a process of "Arab political localization" (al Haj 1993a: 84). The role of the National Committee has been particularly instrumental, prompting its labeling as "the parliament of the Arabs in Israel" (al-Haj and Rosenfeld 1990: 164).

Here lies another important clue to the political process experienced by the Arabs: The minority has rallied behind these voluntary organizations, often in open defiance to state attempts to ignore or even disallow their activities (al Haj and Rosenfeld 1990; Lustick 1989). In some respects, Arab political organization and institution building is thus bypassing the formal procedures and institutions of state and local governance. Given the explicit goal of the National Committee to work for Arab collective rights, total ethnic equality, and the restructuring of the Zionist nature of the state, the very impact and endurance of this voluntary body points to the emergence of a distinct oppositional ethnopolitical community, "within but not inside" Israel's main political arena.

Electoral Behavior

The analysis of minority voting can complement the examination of extraparliamentarian protest by further illuminating its evolving grievances and agendas. The Israeli proportional representation system encourages the representation of minorities, thus according added salience to electoral patterns. The main trend to emerge from the analysis of Arab vote to Israel's parliament—the Knesset—shows gradual polarization between Arabs and Jews, particularly since the Arab protest campaign for minority rights and equality began in the mid-1970s. Arab electoral behavior reveals a steadily growing level of support for "non-Zionist" parties, which have always been predominantly Arab, and have continuously posed a challenge to the existing Zionist nature of the state. Although the level of the non-Zionist vote hovered around 20 percent until the 1970s, it rose to twice that rate during the 1980s and early 1990s, and reached 68 percent in the 1996 elections. Conversely, Zionist parties, which were totally dominant in the Arab sector until the 1970s (often polling around 80 percent), have since steadily declined, reaching an all-time low of 32 percent in the 1996 elections.

To be sure, many other factors affect the vote of the large and diverse Arab population. Yet a genuine chasm is developing between the near total majority of Jews who support Zionist or Jewish parties (some 98 percent in the 1996 elections) and over two-thirds of the Arabs who prefer to vote for Knesset members who challenge—implicitly or explicitly—the Israeli ethnocentric regime. The gradual shift to the extreme left is more striking when we consider that for decades the political organization of Arabs in Israel was under strict surveillance, that Arabs were not allowed to run in all-Arab parties until 1988, and that the dominance of Zionist parties has been so pronounced, that many of the most prominent Arab political leaders actually still represent Zionist parties. Despite these mitigating factors, the Arabs are now increasingly supporting predominantly Arab parties whose platforms reflect a desire to restructure Israeli society.

Results of the 1996 election lend further support to the "regionalization" argument, chiefly by illustrating both the Arabs' growing distance from the dominant (Zionist) Israeli regime and also their drive to actively change that regime. We must note here that a new electoral system introduced in 1996 assisted small parties by allowing voters to split their prime ministerial and party votes. Yet, other indicators show that the shift here is more than tactical. First, the electoral turnout reached 79 percent for the first time in 20 years during which turnout was lower, indicating a growing will to participate and influence change. Second, the platforms of three predominantly Arab parties—

for the first time—explicitly voiced their desire for a "new state order" in Israel. The Arab Democratic List and the Progressive Union (which received over 14,000 votes but did not qualify for the Knesset) used variations of the call to "transform Israel into a state of all its citizens," which of course challenges Israel's self-definition as "the state of the Jewish People" and the associated policies that favor resident (as well as incoming nonresident) Jews over the country's Arab citizens.

Further, all three main non-Zionist parties called for the first time for a recognition of the Arabs as a "national" minority, opposing their current classification as "religious minorities." Part of the Hadash-led Front (the Democratic National Union) went even further by making a groundbreaking demand for "Arab cultural autonomy" in its platform. Although this demand was not binding for the other partners in this leftist bloc, it remained associated with some of its candidates, who continued to promote the idea even after the election (Ozacky-Lazar and Ghanem 1996: appendix 1).

An equally significant aspect of the 1996 elections is the participation—again, for the first time—of two previously rejectionist organizations: the Moslem Movement and the Sons of the Village group. The Moslem Movement, after much deliberation, soul searching, and a damaging split, joined with the Arab Democratic List under the new banner of the United Arab List and assisted the doubling of its representation from two to four Knesset seats. The Sons of the Village group, for a long time one of the most nationalistic organizations among the Arabs, was the leading element in the newly formed Democratic National Union that created a political bloc with Hadash. The new bloc received a sizable 37 percent support among the Arabs (as compared with 23 percent support for Hadash in 1992), resulting in five Knesset seats.

The decision of these two organizations to participate in the Israeli elections is highly significant, mainly because: first, from their own previous rejectionist perspective, this step and its associated rhetoric amount for the first time to a recognition and acceptance of an Israeli state; and second, their decision to run was accompanied by a widely expressed agenda of *restructuring* the state from within. This agenda, and its links to both Israeli and Palestinian concerns, was articulated by Dr. A. Bishara, leader of the Democratic National Union, in a May 1996 preelection rally: "by running in this election we are of course accepting the existence of Israel, thus toeing the line with the Palestinian people who did the same by endorsing the Oslo agreement and by electing Arafat as President . . . our project addresses the next urgent goal: restructuring the Israeli political system which is totally based on the definition of the state as belonging to the Jewish people more than to its Arab citizens . . . only by working to change the system can we achieve our status as a national minority, our need for cultural autonomy, and our fundamental right for genuine collective equality."

Beyond the unifying trend evident in the building of two major political blocs (after decades of debilitating internal divisions), another event signaled a political change: the last-minute withdrawal of the well-known personality Dr. Ahmad Tibbi (Arafat's chief adviser for Israeli affairs). Tibbi, whose party (the Arab Alliance for Progress and Renewal) was lagging in the polls, quit in an unprecedented move, citing fears of splitting the Arab vote. Tibbi's withdrawal and the nature of the Arab vote highlight a further point: a growing distance between the Arabs in Israel and the main Palestinian national leadership (now in the territories). This was reflected by the low popularity of Tibbi's party (which was strongly associated with Arafat) and by the general low profile kept by the Palestinian leadership during the campaign, contrary to previous campaigns. Thus, the Arabs are distancing themselves at the same time both from the Zionist parties and from the Palestinian leadership, thereby carving themselves a separate political niche between nation and state.

In addition, the 1996 results show a growing convergence among Arab localities, ethnic groups, and socioeconomic strata. One of the most noteworthy shifts occurred among the Druze, for long the most "Israelized" Arab group and at times openly hostile to the Palestinian national cause. In the 1996 elections, however, Hadash and the Arab Democratic List more than doubled their vote among the Druze, reaching 19 percent, whereas the vote for other left-wing parties, such as Labor and Meretz, rose by 30–35 percent. Conversely, the vote for Likud and Jewish religious parties plummeted from 41 percent in 1992 to only 22 percent in 1996. Returns among Arab subgroups display a similar trend toward the left. This has been most prominent in two sectors in which Zionist parties had a solid majority for forty-five years: small villages and Negev Bedouins. This time the non-Zionist vote doubled in both sectors, reaching 49 percent in the former and 76 percent (!) among the latter (Ozacky-Lazar and Ghanem 1996: appendix 1).

In sum, electoral trends among the Arabs point to parallel processes of Arab-Jewish political polarization, growing Arab aspiration of working to reform and restructure the Israeli political system from within, and increasing levels of Arab cohesion and unity. These trends are consistent with the formation of ethnoregionalism, which generally struggles for rights and resources within a multiethnic state, and for the restructuring of such states to reflect fairly their interethnic geography and demography (see Hechter and Levi 1979; Keating 1996; Mike-sell and Murphy 1991).

Geographical Scale, Division, and Cohesion

To complete the picture of political mobilization and identity forma-tion among the Arabs, we should return to three key and related fac-tors discussed earlier: the geographical scale of identity, the impact of nationalism on their cohesion and fragmentation, and the construction and "imagination" of a regional collective identity in a "fractured" territory.

First, it may be illuminating to note that the geographical scale of the Arab identity in Israel has changed dramatically a few times dur-ing the twentieth century. Prior to the disastrous 1948 defeat, they were an integral part of the agrarian Palestinian society that was gradually building its national consciousness. During the third and fourth de-cades of the century, Palestinian nationalism was emerging under Brit-ish rule in a similar fashion to other anticolonial Arab national move-ments (as in Egypt or Syria). The conflict with Zionism, although highly influential in determining the specific characteristics of the Pal-estinian movement, did not impinge on the pre-1948 perception of the community as a countrywide ethnic and political community.

However, following the defeat and the expulsion or dispersal of most Palestinians and the strict control imposed by Israel, the core of Arab identity shifted back to the village and the clan. Israeli policies encouraged, co-opted, and coerced the dominance of traditional prena-tional leadership and prevented most forms of intervillage and interre-gional political cooperation. It was only in the 1970s that political mo-bilization started to broaden the geographical scale of Arab identity, aided greatly by the well-publicized events of Land Day 1976. During the last two decades a further integration of the Arabs into a statewide political community has been evident, as heralded by the statement of Hanna Moyas—the first chair of the Arab National Committee—in a Land Day commemoration rally in 1978. "We, the Arabs in Israel, are like one body; our limbs are Arab lands from north to south. When parts of our body are confiscated in the Negev, we all hurt; when parts are taken in the Galilee, we all hurt again. . . . Only if we act together, as one, we can perhaps overcome the pain of further land losses and rebuild ourselves in the lands, villages and towns that have always been ours" (Land Day leaflet, Archives of National Committee, Sh-fa'amar)

Regarding the forces of nationalism, our analysis points to a dual impact of Jewish nationalism on the Arabs. It did, as noted, exclude and marginalize them from effective participation in the Israeli nation-building project (Peled 1992). Still, it also diffused a prevailing ethno-national order, citizenship rights, and democratic norms into their practices, mobilization, and political activities. Because the domain of the Arabs in Israel is confined to their fractured region, and because the ethnonational order could not be expressed as open nationalism—given the perceived immense cost to the Arabs—Arab identity is developing as an ethnonational minority, residing in its homeland territories. In other words—an ethnoregional community.

Here also lies a main difference between Palestinian regionalism within Israel and the full expression of Palestinian nationalism in the occupied territories. Palestinian nationalism in the West Bank and Gaza aims to achieve full sovereignty over the totality of its territories and replace Israeli with Palestinian sovereignty. In contrast, the Palestinian minority in Israel has now developed an identity that accepts its existence within the Israeli state, combining national (Palestinian) and civil (Israeli) building blocks in building its collective identity and political campaign. Palestinian-Arab regionalism in Israel aims to ground its civil, cultural, and ethnic rights in the fragmented Arab places, aiming to increase the share of resources and autonomy of the Arab region vis-à-vis the Israeli state (see also Rouhana 1997).

The content of the emerging collective identity and the process of its reimagination have relied on the unbroken attachment of Arabs to their villages and localities, on their continuing—albeit changing—ties with the mainstream of Palestinian nationalism but also on the events, institutions, opportunities, norms, and practices embodied in their civil affiliation as Israeli citizens. Chief among these has been, as noted, the collective memory of loss, dispossession, and deprivation (Rabinowitz 1997) and their common struggle for recognition, acceptance, and equality in Israel. Thus events such as Land Day (an annual day of commemorating a 1976 mass demonstration against land expropriation in the Galilee where six Arab protesters were killed), institutions such as the National Committee, or a campaign to establish an Arab university in Nazareth, all work to create, reinforce, and strengthen an "Israeli variety" of a Palestinian-Arab collective identity.

To be sure, cleavages and fragmentations among the Arabs are also pronounced and will continue to abate the crystallization of a unified Arab identity within Israel. The Israeli state has traditionally attempted to widen and exploit the divisions with Arab society (Lustick 1980), particularly those separating Druze, Christians, and Moslems, as well as nomads and peasants. The state, through policies of patronage and co-optation, has also attempted to promote the interests of loyal Arabs and present political and economic obstacles to those challenging Jewish domination (Haidar 1990). This has been particularly effective through the traditional clan-based "notables" still dominant in many Arab villages (Rouhana and Ghanem 1993).

Although the forces of class and religious and subregional fragmentation are still vividly apparent in Arab society, the mobilization of the minority during the last two decades has worked to gradually diminish these divisions. There are now hundreds of voluntary associations in the Arab sector working across traditional boundaries (al Haj 1993a), and Arabs have been forging a range of intervillage regional organizations in the fields of urban and regional, industrial and environmental development (Yiftachel 1995). The examination of Arab protest, too, reveals that the major issues draw participation from all parts of the country and that in each of the main Arab areas—the Galilee, Triangle, and Negev as well as the main urban centers–the three protest topics of land, development, and nation have played a reasonably even role (see Meir 1997; Yiftachel 1997). Last, as analyzed previously, the recent 1996 Knesset elections demonstrated a convergence of electoral trends among all sectors of the Arab minority.

The understanding of Arab political mobilization in ethnoregional terms also allows us to anticipate the likely shape of future Arab-Jewish politics. Given the regional homeland orientation, Arabs are likely to heighten the push for gaining recognition as a national minority, with associated cultural and (later) territorial autonomy, press for land rights, and campaign for the closing of Arab-Jewish social and economic gaps (see also al Haj 1993a: 85). This will be combined with a drive to devolve the functions of the highly centralized Israeli state, which may receive significant assistance from a similar agenda of other sectors in Israeli society, especially the ultra-orthodox Jews. However, the Arabs will not accept the ethnocentric Zionist character of the state or confine their struggle merely to "better terms of coexistence" (Smooha 1992). Using the ethnoregional framework, we can also anticipate that the Arab struggle in Israel will intensify following Arab-Jewish reconciliation in the Middle East and not subside as many assume. Arab regionalism is thus likely to pose a serious challenge to the Israeli "ethnocracy," by intensifying the drive against its exclusive ethnic (Jewish) character. As such, it may form an increasingly coherent force in the struggle to decentralize and democratize the Israeli state.

References

al Haj, M. "The Changing Strategies of Mobilization among the Arabs in Israel: Parliamentary Politics, Local Politics, and National Organization." In E. Ben

Zadok, ed., *Local Communities and the Israeli Polity*. New York: State University of New York Press, 1993a, 67–88.

——. "The Impact of the Intifada on Arabs in Israel: The Case of a Double Periphery." In A. Cohen and G. Wolsfeld, eds., *Framing the Intifada: People and Media*. Norwood: Ablex, 1993b, 64–75.

al Haj, M., and H. Rosenfeld. *Arab Local Government in Israel*. Boulder: Westview Press, 1990.

Anderson, B. *Imagined Communities: Reflections on the Origin and Spread of Nationalism*. 2d ed. London: Verso, 1991.

——. "Introduction." In G. Balakrishnan, ed., *Mapping the Nation*. New York: Verso, 1996, 1–16.

Ben Artzi, Y. "Normalization under Conflict? Spatial and Demographic Changes of Arabs in Haifa, 1948–92." *Middle Eastern Studies* 32(4) (1996): 281–295.

Billig, M. *Banal Nationalism*. London: Sage, 1995.

Bishara, A. "On the Question of the Palestinian Minority in Israel." *Teorya Uvikkoret (Theory and Critique)* 3 (1993): 7–20 (Hebrew).

CBS (Central Bureau of Statistics). *Statistical Yearbook for Israel*. Jerusalem: Government Publishers, 1996.

Chatterjee, P. *The Nation and Its Fragments*. Princeton, N.J: Princeton University Press, 1993.

Connor, W. "Beyond Reason: The Nature of the Ethnonational Bond." *Ethnic and Racial Studies* 16(2) (1993): 373–388.

Doumani, B. *Rediscovering Palestine: Merchants and Peasants in Jabal Nablus, 1700–1900*. Berkeley: University of California Press, 1995.

Falah, G. "The 1948 Israeli-Palestinian War and Its Aftermath: The Transformation and De-Signification of Palestine's Cultural Landscape." *Annals of the American Association of Geographers* 86(2) (1996a): 256–285.

——. "Living Together Apart: Residential Segregation in Mixed Arab-Jewish Cities in Israel." *Urban Studies* 33(6) (1996b): 823–857.

Fenster, T. "Settlement Planning and Participation under Principles of Pluralism." *Progress in Planning* 39(3) (1993): 169–242.

Ghanem, A. "Political Mobilisation among the Arabs in Israel." In *The Arab Minority in Israel*. Tel Aviv: Dayan Centre (proceedings), 1995.

Ginat, Y. "Voting Patterns and Political Behaviour in the Arab Sector." In J. M. Landau, ed., *The Arab Vote in Israel's Parliamentary Elections, 1988*. Jerusalem: The Jerusalem Institute for Israel Studies, 1989, 3–21.

Gonen, A. *Between City and Suburb: Urban Residential Patterns and Processes in Israel*. Aldershot: Avebury, 1995.

Grinberg, L. *Split Corporatism in Israel*. Albany: State University of New York Press, 1991.

Gurr, T. *Minorities at Risk: The Global View of Ethnopolitical Conflict*. Arlington: Institute of Peace Press, 1993.

Haidar, A. *Arabs in the Israeli Economy*. Tel Aviv: International Centre for Peace in the Middle East, 1990.

——. *Social Welfare Services for Israel's Arab Population*. Boulder, San Francisco, and Oxford: Westview Press, 1991.

Hechter, M. *Internal Colonialism—The Celtic Fringe in British National Development, 1536–1966.* Berkeley: University of California Press, 1975.

Hechter, M., and M. Levi. "The Comparative Analysis of Ethnoregional Movements." *Ethnic and Racial Studies* 2 (1979): 260–274.

Jenkins, J. C., and B. Klandremans. "The Politics of Social Protest." In J. C. Jenkins and B. Klandremans, eds., *The Politics of Social Protest: Comparative Perspectives on States and Social Movements.* London: UCL Press, 1995, 3–14.

Keating, M. *State and Regional Nationalism.* New York: Harvester and Wheatsheaf, 1988.

———. *Nations against the State: The New Politics of Nationalism in Quebec, Catalonia, and Scotland.* Basingstoke: Macmillan, 1996.

Khalidi, R. *The Arabs Economy in Israel.* London: Croom Helm, 1988.

Khameissi, R. *Planning, Housing, and the Arab Minority in Israel.* Boulder: Westview Press, 1992.

Kimmerling, B. *Zionism and Territory.* Berkeley: Institute of International Studies, University of California, 1983.

Landau, Y. *The Arab Minority in Israel: Political Aspects, 1967–1991.* Jerusalem: Am Oved, 1993.

Lehman-Wilzig, S. "Copying the Master? Patterns of Israeli Protest, 1950–1990." *Asian and African Studies* 27 (1 and 2) (1993): 129–147.

Lewin-Epstein, N., and M. Semyonov. *The Arab Minority in Israel's Economy: Patterns of Ethnic Inequality.* Boulder: Westview Press, 1993.

Lofland, J. *Protest: Studies of Collective Behavior and Social Movements.* New Brunswick: Transaction Books, 1985.

Lustick, I. *Arabs in the Jewish State: Israel's Control over a National Minority.* Austin: University of Texas Press, 1980.

———. "The Political Road to Binationalism: Arabs in Jewish Politics." In I. Peleg and O. Seliktar, eds., *The Emergence of a Binational Israel.* Boulder: Westview Press, 1989, 97–124.

McCrone, D. "Regionalism and Constitutional Change in Scotland." *Regional Studies* 27 (1993): 507–512.

Meir, A. *When Nomadism Ends: The Transformation of Negev Bedouins in Israel.* Boulder: Westview Press, 1997.

Mikesell, M., and A. Murphy. "A Framework for Comparative Study of Minority Aspirations." *Annals of the Association of American Geographers* 81 (1991): 581–604.

Newman, D. "Civilian Presence as Strategies of Territorial Control: The Arab-Israeli Conflict." *Political Geography Quarterly* 8 (1989): 215–227.

Ozacky-Lazar, S., and A. Ghanem. *The Arab Vote for the 14th Knesset.* Givat Haviva: Center for Peace Studies (Hebrew), 1996.

Pappé, I. "The Uneasy Coexistence: Arabs and Jews in the First Decade of Statehood." In S. I. Troen and N. Lucas, eds., *Israel—The First Decade of Independence.* Albany: State University of New York Press, 1995, 617–658.

Peach, C. "The Meaning of Segregation." *Planning Practice and Research* 11(2) (1996): 137–150.

Peled, U. "Ethnic Democracy and the Legal Construction of Citizenship: Arab

Citizens of the Jewish State." *The American Political Science Review* 86(2) (1992): 432–443.

Rabinowitz, D. "The Common Memory of Loss: Political Mobilisation among Palestinian Citizens of Israel." *Journal of Anthropological Research* 50 (1994): 27–49.

———. *Overlooking Nazareth: The Ethnography of Exclusion in Galilee.* Cambridge: Cambridge University Press, 1997.

Ram, U. "Zionist Historiography and the Invention of Modern Jewish Nationhood: The Case of Ben Zion Dinur." *History and Memory* 7(1) (1995): 91–124.

Regev, A. *The Arabs in Israel: Political Issues.* Jerusalem: Jerusalem Institute for Israel's Studies, 1989.

Rekhes, E. "Israeli Arabs and the Arabs of the West Bank and Gaza Strip: Political Ties and National Identification." *Hamizrach Hachadash* 32 (1989): 165–191.

Rouhana, N. "Accentuated Identities in Protracted Conflicts: The Collective Identity of the Palestinian Citizens in Israel." *Asian and African Studies* 27 (1 and 2) (1993): 97–128.

———. *Palestinian Citizens in an Ethnic Jewish State: Identities and Conflict.* New Haven, Conn.: Yale University Press, 1997.

Rouhana, N., and A. Ghanem. "The Democratisation of a Traditional Minority in an Ethnic Democracy: The Palestinians in Israel." In E. Kaufman and A. El Abed, eds., *Democracy and Peace in the Middle East.* Boulder: Westview Press, 1993, 67–87.

Schnell, Y. *Perceptions of Israeli Arabs: Territoriality and Identity.* Aldershot: Avebury, 1994.

Schnell, Y., M. Sofer, and I. Drori. *Arab Industrialisation in Israel.* Westport, Conn.: Praeger, 1995.

Semyonov, M., and N. Lewin–Epstein. *Hewers of Wood and Drawers of Water.* Ithaca, N.Y.: CLR Press, 1987.

Shafir, G. *Land, Labor and the Origins of the Israeli-Palestinian Conflict 1882–1914.* Cambridge: Cambridge University Press, 1989.

———. *Immigrants and Nationalists: Ethnic Conflict and Accommodation in Catalonia, the Basque Country, Latvia, and Estonia.* Albany: SUNY Press, 1995.

Shalev, M. *Labour and the Political Economy of Israel.* Oxford: Oxford University Press, 1992.

Shohat, E. "Sepharadim in Israel: Zionism from the Standpoint of Its Jewish Victims." *Social Text* 19–20 (1988): 1–35.

———. "Columbus, Palestine, and Arab-Jews: Toward a Relational Approach to Community Identity." In K. Ansell-Pearson, B. Parry, and J. Squires, eds., *Cultural Identity and the Gravity of History: On the Work of Edward Said.* New York: Lawrence and Wishart, 1996, 101–132.

Sikkuy. *Report on the Achievement of the Government in Promoting Jewish-Arab Equality in Israel, 1992–5.* Jerusalem: Sikkuy, 1995.

———. *Arabs and Jews in Israel: Comparative Data Over Time.* Jerusalem: Sikkuy (Hebrew), 1996.

Smith, A. D. *Nations and Nationalism in a Global Era.* Cambridge: Polity, 1995.

Smooha, S. *Israel: Pluralism and Conflict*. Berkeley: University of California Press, 1978.

———. "Minority Status in an Ethnic Democracy: The Status of the Arab Minority in Israel." *Ethnic and Racial Studies* 13(3) (1990): 389–412.

———. *Arabs and Jews in Israel: Change and Continuity in Mutual Intolerance.* Boulder, San Francisco, and Oxford: Westview Press, 1992.

———. "Class, Ethnic, and National Cleavages and Israel's Democracy." In U. Ram, ed., *Israeli Society: Critical Perspectives*. Tel Aviv: Brerot, 1993, 134–155.

Social Security Institute. *Annual Report on Poverty in Israel*. Jerusalem: Social Security Institute, 1996.

Soffer, A. *The Demographic and Geographic Situation in the Land of Israel: Is It the End of the Zionist Vision?* Haifa: Author's Printing, 1988.

———. "Israel's Arabs Towards Autonomy: The Case of the Galilee Sub-System." *Mechkarim Begeografia Shel Eretz Yisrael (Studies in the Geography of the Land of Israel)* 12 (1991): 198–209 (Hebrew).

Williams, C., and E. Kofman, eds. *Community, Conflict, and Nationalism*. London: Routledge, 1989.

Yiftachel, O. "State Policies, Land Control and an Ethnic Minority: The Arabs in the Galilee, Israel." *Society and Space* 9 (1991): 329–362.

———. "The Ethnic Democracy Model and Its Applicability to the Case of Israel." *Ethnic and Racial Studies* 15(1) (1992a): 125–136.

———. *Planning a Mixed Region in Israel: The Political Geography of Arab-Jewish Relations in the Galilee*. Aldershot: Avebury, 1992b.

———. "Arab-Jewish Relations in Israel: Policy, Disparities, and Political-Geographical Implications." *Medina, Mimshal Veyachasim Benleumiyim (State, Government and International Relations)* 40 (1995): 185–224 (Hebrew).

———. "The Internal Frontier: The Territorial Control of Ethnic Minorities." *Regional Studies* 30(5) (1996): 493–508.

———. "The Political Geography of Ethnic Protest: Nationalism, Deprivation, and Regionalism among Arabs in Israel." *Transactions: Inst. of British Geographers* 22(1) (1997): 91–110.

Zureik, E. T. *Palestinians in Israel: A Study of Internal Colonialism*. London: Routledge and Kegan Paul, 1979.

12

Transylvania: Hungarian, Romanian, or Neither?

George W. White

As the geopolitical order of the Cold War era has unraveled with the disintegration of the Soviet Union, political instability has increased in many areas of the world. Southeastern Europe is one of the places where violence has been a notable feature of the post–Cold War era. Although Bosnia-Hercegovina has captured the world's attention, relationships have been strained between ethnic groups in Kosova and Macedonia as well. Moreover, conflict has not been limited to the former Yugoslavia. The overthrow of Ceauşescu in Romania was explosive, albeit short in duration, and tensions between ethnic Romanians and Hungarians have resulted in incidents of violence.

As much of the world has looked upon events of the post–Cold War era, popular perception often has led to the general conclusion that the violence essentially has been chaotic. While ethnic hatred clearly is fueling the violent acts, the acts themselves are viewed as little more than the desire by those involved to obtain and control more territory. This perception stems from a general geographical ignorance in society, an ignorance that simply views territory as nothing more than a resource to be fought over. This popular but ignorant perception of territory explains the lack of insight regarding the nature of territorial conflicts as well as the nature of ethnic and national conflicts. Territory is not merely a resource to control but something much more. Territory is a component of ethnic and national identities, and because of that, ethnic groups and nations become very protective of the territories that they use to define their identities. The control and maintenance of territories is as crucial as the control and maintenance of a national language, religion, or a particular way of life. Indeed, a language, religion, or way of life is difficult to maintain without control over territory. Consequently, ethnic groups and nations will act with the same intensity and determination in defense of their territories, as they will in defense of their language, religion, or way of life.

By recognizing the meaning and significance of territory, clearer explanations arise concerning the nature of ethnic and national conflict. A closer examination of the territory known as Transylvania will illustrate the significance of territory and hence shed light on the nature of the Romanian-Hungarian conflict that has arisen over Transylvania. In short, Transylvania is significant because it represents fundamental components of both Romanian and Hungarian national identities. Transylvania is important for both the Romanian and Hungarian nations in two regards. At the macro-scale, Transylvania is seen as an integral component of a broader national territory that is viewed as an organic and inviolable unit; within these broader organic units Transylvania is the cradle for both Romanian and Hungarian civilizations. At the micro-scale, Transylvania contains within it a number of places of great cultural and historical significance.

Transylvania between Romania and Hungary

Beginning at the macro-scale, the significance of Transylvania only becomes apparent when Romania and Hungary are considered in their entireties. For the Romanians, Romania is seen as a natural physiographic unit that has political legitimacy. The center of Romania is dominated by the eastern extension of the Carpathian Mountains, which are seen as a fortress that protects the Romanian people in times of crisis. Encircling the mountains are a series of rivers that serve as the moat for the natural fortress. These rivers—the Danube River (Dunerea), Tisa River (Tisza), and Nistra (Dniester)—along with the Black Sea, are viewed as Romania's "natural" boundaries (see Figure 12.1). Together they complete an almost circular boundary for Romania (Ceauşescu 1983: between 18 and 19; Stoicescu 1986: 9–13).

Taken as a whole, the many regions of a Romania bounded by these rivers are seen to be the basis of a strong and self-sufficient nation. At the same time, Hungarian control of Transylvania—the very "heart" of Romania—for much of the last thousand years is seen as the cause of the arrested development of the Romanian nation. Romanian nationalists believe that Walachia and Moldavia were slow in developing and then were weak political states because they lacked the contributions of the Romanian territory of Transylvania (Stoicescu 1986: 9–10).

Despite the supposed "natural" unity of Romania, political unity

Chris Leatham

of Romania's territories was only achieved in the twentieth century, following World War I. In the last 2,000 years, little precedent for political unity can be found. The eight-month reign of Michael the Brave in the year 1600 inadequately provides the historical precedent for establishing legitimacy for the conceptions of the modern Romanian state. To find some sort of historical precedent, history has to be traced back to Roman times and the pre-Roman times of the Dacians. Romanian nationalists have combined the Roman period with the earlier Dacian period to create the Daco-Roman theory. In short, the legitimacy of modern Romanian identity and the territorial extent of Romania are founded on the belief that modern Romanians are the descendants of a Daco-Roman blend. Assuming that this theory is correct, the Romanians place themselves in the hall of great nations by being the descendants of one of the greatest empire builders in human history. The Romanians also are able to legitimize their control over their described territory because no other nation in southeastern Europe can claim that their ancestors inhabited Romanian land before the Romanians. The crucial aspect of the Daco-Roman theory is the fact that the Dacian state and the Roman province of Dacia were politically and economically centered in Transylvania.

Hungary, as seen by the Hungarians, is the Carpathian basin; the Carpathian basin is a territory that consists of the Tisza and middle

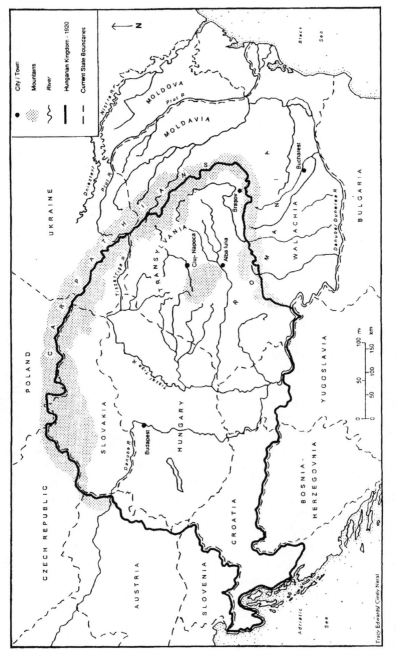

Figure 12.1   Romanian and Hungarian conceptions of national territory

CURRENT REGIONAL DATA

Transylvania is approximately 39,000 sq. miles (101,000 sq. km.). The total population is approximately 7.5 million. The following is a list of the ethnic groups who inhabit Transylvania: Romanians, Hungarians, Szeklers, Saxons, Germans, Gypsies, Jews, Slovaks, Ruthenians, and Armenians. Romanians are found throughout Transylvania but historically have lived in rural areas. Hungarians are predominantly in the urban areas but are also found in the rural areas as well. Szeklers dominate in an extensive mass in eastern Transylvania. The Saxons and Germans historically resided in the urban areas along with the Hungarians but are found in large concentrations in southern Transylvania. Small pockets of Slovaks and Ruthenians are found in the north and northwest.

The classification of ethnic groups is controversial, and for a few reasons. First, simplistic nationalistic conceptions have resulted in the lumping together of differing groups. For example, Szeklers are often classified as Hungarians. Saxons, as well as Swabians if the Banat is included in Transylvania, are put together with Germans. Slovaks and Ruthenians are routinely classified as Slavs. Second, many disputes have arisen concerning the population numbers of each of the ethnic groups. The number of individuals classified as Hungarians (including Szeklers) ranges from 1.5 million to 3.5 million. Hungarian nationalists tend to argue for the higher number, and Romanian nationalists use the lower number. Most figures depend on the method of classification. When language is used as an identifier, the count of minorities tends to be lower. Language policies of the Romanian government over the last seventy-five years have encouraged many minorities to adopt Romanian as their language. Other governmental policies have encouraged many minorities to emigrate. In 1914, when Transylvania was part of Hungary, Romanians accounted for approximately 54 percent of the population, whereas Hungarians made up 31 percent and the Germanic group made up 10 percent. Currently, Romanians are more than 68 percent, and Hungarians are less than 25 percent. The Germanic group has dropped enormously, especially over the last decade. Czechs, Serbs, and Croatians were also present but are now virtually gone.

HISTORY OF TRANSYLVANIA
(INCLUDING PERTINENT CONFLICTS)

Information about Transylvania's history extends back more than 2,000 years. From about the sixth century B.C.E., Transylvania was geographically and politically the very center of a series of Geto-Dacian states that stretched from the Carpathians to the Balkan Mountains. In 106 A.D., Roman emperor Trajan conquered the Dacians and incorporated their territories into the Roman Empire. The Dacian Empire became the Roman province of Dacia, with Transylvania as its administrative center. Transylvania remained within the Roman Empire until the year 271 when Emperor Aurelian ordered all Roman forces out of the province on the grounds that the territory was too vulnerable to invasion. Transylvania failed to stay together as a single political unit but, instead, was ruled by petty lords who acted independently of one another. Little is known about this period of Transylvania's history, which lasted several hundred years. Beginning in the tenth century, the recently established Hungarian Kingdom began expanding eastward into Transylvania. By the eleventh century, Transylvania was integrated into the Hungarian Kingdom (see Figure 12.3). Following the destruction of the Hungarian Kingdom at the Battle of Mohács in 1526, Transylvania became a vassal state of the Ottoman Empire. It was during the Ottoman period that Transylvania exercised its greatest autonomy. It even experienced a "golden age" in the seventeenth century and was even recorded as a sovereign state in the Treaty of Westphalia (1648). In 1688, five years after the crushing defeat of Ottoman forces outside of Vienna, the Transylvanian Diet renounced Ottoman suzerainty and accepted Austrian protection. Transylvania remained as a distinct administrative unit within the Austrian Empire until the Compromise of 1867, which created the Austro-Hungarian Dual Monarchy. In the agreement, Transylvania was reunited with the Hungarian Kingdom. Following the defeat of the Central Powers at the end of World War I, the Austro-Hungarian Empire was dismantled and Transylvania was awarded to Romania. Sections of Maramureş, Crişana, and the Banat were also awarded to Romania and subsequently have often been collectively included under the name "Transylvania." In the 1940s, Hitler manipulated Hungarian irredentist feelings toward Transylvania, as well as those feelings toward other lost territories, to bring the Hungarian state into the Axis alliance. For the Hungarians' participation in the war effort, Hitler awarded northern Transylvania to Hungary in 1940. Following the Axis defeat in 1945, northern Transylvania was returned to Romania. Transylvania has remained an integral part of Romania since then.

▶━━━━━━━━━━━━━━━━━━━━━━━━━━━━━━━━◀

Danube watersheds (see Figure 12.1). These watersheds are created and bounded to a large extent by the Carpathian Mountains. Physiographically, the Carpathians are seen as the "natural" political boundary of the Hungarian state as well. The naturalness of the political boundary has been reinforced by the fact that the Carpathians have indeed served as the political boundary for the Hungarian state for much of the last thousand years, albeit with periods of interruptions.

The significance of Transylvania (*Erdély*) is illustrated by the phrase *két haza*, which means two homelands (Czigány 1984: 537). Many Hungarians view Transylvania as their other homeland because the territory played a very important role in Hungarian history. Transylvania preserved the highest degree of independence of any of the territories of the Hungarian Kingdom when the Ottomans occupied Hungary. Moreover, Transylvania even experienced a "golden age" of its own in the seventeenth century. As a result, Transylvania is seen as a refuge of Hungarian culture, largely untarnished by the Ottomans, or even the Austrians who ruled over Hungary following the Ottomans.

The political power of Transylvania in the seventeenth century contributes greatly to ideas about the historical continuity of the Hungarian nation. Hungarian civilization initially is seen as having emerged in the central part of the Carpathian Basin; during Ottoman occupation it transferred itself to Transylvania; afterward, Hungarian political power reestablished itself in the central part of the basin. This view also underscores the belief that the various territories of the Hungarian Kingdom work in harmony with one another and are even mutually dependent. If we emphasize all the political and cultural accomplishments made in Transylvania, particularly in the seventeenth century, Hungarian culture can be described as having continuous vitality throughout history.

Romanian Place Identity in Transylvania

An examination of Transylvania at the micro-scale brings to light a number of specific places that act as fundamental components of both Romanian and Hungarian national identities. Romanian national identity is intimately tied to a number of places within Transylvania (see Figure 12.2). Some of these places are the oldest of Romanian places. They are tied to two cultures that are seen by the Romanians as their progenitors—the ancient Dacians and the Romans. The ancient Dacian state was centered in Transylvania, and the Roman Empire, although obviously centered elsewhere in Europe, set up important administrative centers in Transylvania to govern the territory that is now Roma-

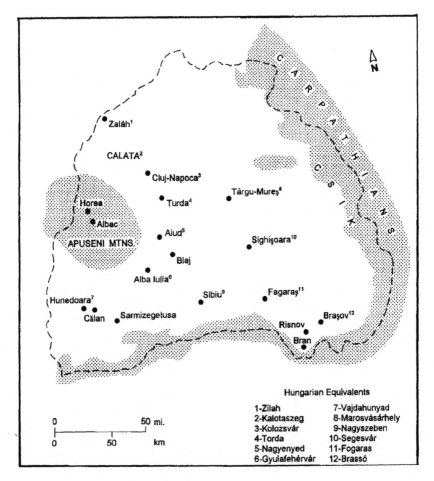

Figure 12.2   Transylvania: significant places

nia. These places testify to the grandness of what it is to be Romanian by illustrating both the ancient Dacian culture and the Roman roots of modern Romanian national identity. Numerous statues of Dacian leaders and the "She-Wolf" suckling Romulus and Remus (the original of which is found in Rome) are found all around Transylvania.

As the center of ancient Dacia and the Roman province of Dacia, Transylvania holds within it many of the great cities of these periods of early "Romanian" history. The capital of the Dacian state was Sarmizegetusa. Sarmizegetusa remained important during Roman times as one of the provinces' eight *colonia*. In addition to Sarmizegetusa, four other *colonia* were also found in Transylvania: Apulum (now Alba Iulia), Aquae (now Călan), Napoco (now Cluj-Napoca), and Potaissa (now Turda) (Giurescu 1981: 64). All of these places provided tangible evidence for the Daco-Roman theory.

In the 1970s, the Roman name *Napoca* was added to the name of the Romanian city of *Cluj*, thus making the city's name Cluj-Napoca. This recently created toponym serves as an ever-present reminder in the landscape of the connection that modern Romanians have with their Daco-Roman past. The subtle implication is that the longer name existed throughout history and thereby legitimizes Romanian control of Transylvania. It also is noteworthy to point out that Romania's leaders decided to Romanize the name of a city that has not only been historically Hungarian in character but is Transylvania's largest and most important city. Much of the ethnic conflict that has occurred in Transylvania has taken place in Cluj-Napoca.

The conflict, however, does not simply stem from the mere fact that both Romanians and Hungarians live in the city together. Rather conflict revolves around the meaning of place and how each national group has found and expressed its national identity in places. For example, the Romanian nationalist mayor has had a "Memorandum" monument constructed on the corner of the main square of the town that primarily consists of Hungarian elements. The fact that a Romanian monument stands among Hungarian ones is not the problem per se. Rather the Romanian monument commemorates a petition written in 1848 that protested Hungarian rule over Transylvania. Similarly, a few blocks away in front of the main Romanian Orthodox church the Romanian nationalist mayor of Cluj had a monument built to Avram Iancu, a figure who led the revolutionary struggle against the Hungarians in 1848. The statue to such a figure may not necessarily be offensive to the Hungarians, however, it stands opposite the Hungarian state theater, towers above it, and the individual that the statue represents looks down upon it. Further conflict has resulted concerning the statue of the Hungarian king Matthias, which stands on the central square of the city. The plaque on the statue originally read "Matthias Corvinus," however, the plaque was recently changed to read "Matthias Rex," a Latin name. Finally, Roman ruins have been found under the main square where the statue to the Hungarian king stands in front of the Hungarian Roman Catholic church. Excavations have begun and likewise have threatened to damage the Hungarian monument and church. Even if the excavations do no damage, the Hungarians will have another Romanian monument next to theirs, "invading their space."

Not all places are in Transylvania are associated with the Romans or

Dacians. From medieval times, Fagaraş stands out as one of the earliest places of importance. It is the supposed origin of Negu-Vodă who migrated south in the thirteenth century and founded the Walachian state (Seton-Watson 1934: 24–25). Sighişoara is the birthplace of Vlad Ţepeş (the Impaler; popularly known as Dracula), prince of Walachia (McNally and Florescu 1994: 15–16); he and members of his family resided in or traveled to a number of places in southern Transylvania. Besides Fagaraş, Vlad Ţepeş and his family also stayed at the castles of Bran and Risnov. Histories of Negu-Vodă and Vlad Ţepeş, and many of the others like them, establish a close connection between Transylvania and the other Romanian territories of Walachia and Moldavia.

The town of Hunedoara is known for one of the largest castles in all of Romania (see Figure 12.2) (Giurescu 1981: 272). The castle was built by a figure that the Romanians call Iancu Hunedoara. Although this individual is closely tied to the Hungarian ruling families, and the Hungarians even view him as one of their great leaders (János Hunyadi), Romanian historians have depicted Hunedoara as one of Romania's great national heroes. Because Hunedoara was from Transylvania, Romanian historians are forced to depict him as a Romanian. This fact aside, claiming this figure as a national hero can be and is, in fact, a great source of national pride. Hunedoara led many victories against the Ottomans.

Considering that Transylvania was under Hungarian control for a number of centuries, it is important for Romanian historians to illustrate the centuries-long desire of the Romanians of Transylvania to free themselves and their territory from the Hungarian Kingdom. This has been done through the depiction of the Horea-Cloşca uprising in 1784 as a national uprising. This peasant uprising began in the Apuseni Mountains near the small town of Brad. The uprising spread in all directions and even into the large towns of Alba Iulia and Hunedoara. Subsequently, these towns, along with the Apuseni Mountains where the rebels also found final refuge, have become very important to Romanian territorial identity. A number of monuments in the area underscore the importance of many of these towns. For example, a bust of Horea was erected in his hometown of Albac (Edroiu 1978: 74, 77); a small town in the area was subsequently named Horea; and an obelisk stands in Alba Iulia, dedicated to all three leaders of the uprising: Horea, Cloşca, and Crişan. In fact, statues of Horea, Cloşca, and Crişan are in a number of towns throughout Transylvania, particularly in Hungarian towns such as Deva.

Alba Iulia, Braşov, and Sibiu are large towns in Transylvania that represent significant historical events in Romanian history. For example, it was in Alba Iulia that Michael the Brave—the Walachian

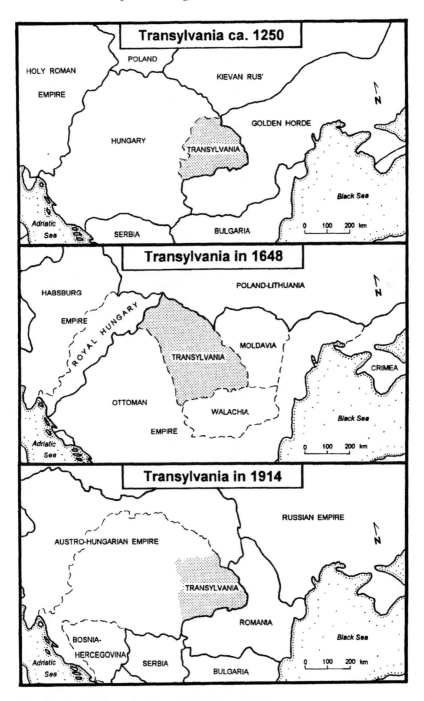

Figure 12.3 Transylvania in 1250, 1648, and 1914

leader—had himself crowned as ruler of a united Walachia, Moldavia, and Transylvania in the year 1600. Michael the Brave had a coronation church built for the occasion, and a recently constructed replica of that church now stands in the town. Later, in 1918, the National Assembly of the Romanian Nation gathered in Alba Iulia and proclaimed the unification of all the Romanian territories (Giurescu 1981: 396–397). King Ferdinand, the first king of modern Romania, was crowned in the same city in 1922. In many ways, the modern Romanian state and king legitimized themselves by declaring their authority in the same place where the medieval act was performed. Alba Iulia has by no means diminished in significance. During the spring of 1996, the Romanian government actively discussed the idea of moving the national capital to Alba Iulia. Such an act would not do more to solidify Romanian control of Transylvania, but it would do much to dilute the presence of Hungarians in Transylvania by bringing thousands, even tens of thousands, of Romanians from Bucharest to Transylvania.

Alba Iulia, Braşov, and Sibiu are also significant places because they were among the first places for Romanians to have active printing presses. Hence, these places were important centers for the dissemination of information relating to Romanian culture. Braşov had the first printing press (1535) in Transylvania. Sibiu had the first printing press that printed the Romanian language in the Latin script. Alba Iulia was the place where the new testament was translated from Greek into Romanian (Giurescu 1981: 312–314).

Transylvania is also significant because the modern Romanian national movement began in a number of Transylvania's religious and educational centers. Blaj is the most significant. Beginning as the headquarters for the Romanian Uniate Church in 1738, this small town developed into the nucleus of the modern Romanian national movement (Seton-Watson 1934: 178). In fact, the Daco-Roman theory developed in large part in Blaj.

Hungarian Place Identity within Transylvania

Hungarian national identity also is intimately tied to a number of political-cultural centers within Transylvania (see Figure 12.2). Kolozsvár (Cluj-Napoca) is one of the most important. Kolozsvár is the birthplace of one of Hungary's great kings, Mátyás (or Matthias Corvinus), and the statue of him in front of the great Hungarian Gothic church symbolizes the city. The Hungarian university, before being converted to a largely Romanian university, was one of the most prestigious in the Kingdom of Hungary. Also in the city is the Hungarian state theater as

well as many museums and other institutions that are or were regarded among the greatest cultural institutions created by the Hungarian nation in modern times (Erdei 1968: 212, 556, 560, 569, 590, 618,
677, 679, 732, 792, 804, 809–810, 919).

Kolozsvár is not the only administrative center and home of great
Hungarian families and institutions. At times, Gyulafehérvár (Alba
Iulia) served as the administrative center as well as the home of one of
Hungary's ruling families, the Bethlens. Found in the town is the Bethlen Palace and the university that Gábor Bethlen founded. As much as
the Bethlens are Hungarian, Gyulafehérvár is Hungarian. Nagyenyed
(Aiud) is an important place now because Gábor Bethlen moved his
college there. The college still exists and has within it a library containing an old collection of Hungarian books.

Hungarian national identity also is closely tied to another great cultural center of Transylvania, Marosvásárhely (Târgu-Mureş). The university there represents many great accomplishments in Hungarian
science. Many great Hungarian leaders either came from or resided in
Marosvásárhely; the Telekis, General Bem, and Lajos Kossuth are some
of the more noteworthy (Légrády Brothers 1930: 99). The Telekis
founded a library that became one of the finest libraries in the Kingdom of Hungary (Erdei 1968: 590). Following World War II, Marosvásárhely became important in another context to the Hungarians because
it served as the administrative center of the Magyar Autonomous Region that the Romanian government created. The autonomous region
was eventually abolished, but Marosvásárhely has remained an important cultural and political center for Hungarians in Transylvania.

Hungarian national identity is also tied to Vajdahunyad (Hunedoara). The castle was built by one of Hungary's greatest leaders—János
Hunyadi. As part of the celebrations of the thousand-year anniversary
of the Hungarian Kingdom, the Hungarians built a replica of Vajdahunyad castle in middle of Budapest in 1986 (Légrády Brothers 1930: 62–
63). That replica still stands in Budapest and reminds modern Hungarians of the importance of Vajdahunyad and of Transylvania in general
to the Hungarian nation.

A battle that was fought against the Russians in 1849 makes Segesvár
(Sighişoara) an important part of Hungarian national consciousness.
Although many battles were fought in the war, the one outside of Segesvár is significant because Hungary's greatest poet, Sándor Petöfi,
died during the struggle here. A monument was erected to Petöfi, and
it symbolized the heroic devotion and self-sacrifice that he made for
the Hungarian nation (Légrády Brothers 1930: 93).

Transylvania is significant to Hungarian national identity culturally
as well as politically. Many of the folk songs and folk customs collected

by Hungarian Romantics were collected in Transylvania. Hungarian Romantics saw Transylvania as a source of folk customs because Transylvania, being isolated from much of the rest of Europe, had remained unchanged for centuries. Therefore, many Hungarian Romantics viewed Transylvania as a preserve of true Hungarian culture and went to places like Torda (Turda), Zilah (Zalâu), and Kalotaszeg (Calata) to collect information on Hungarian folk tradition (Erdei 1968: 985).

Although many Hungarians may see Transylvania as a preserve of Hungarian culture, many of the inhabitants of Transylvania who accept a Hungarian identity really think of themselves as Szeklers (Székely). The Szeklers are a tribe who traveled to the Carpathian Basin with the Magyar tribes or possibly migrated there soon after the Magyars. In either case, the Szeklers were politically integrated into the Hungarian Kingdom from an early period (Palmer 1970: 11–12) and adopted a Hungarian identity. Despite assimilation, the Szeklers are culturally distinct from other Hungarians. The cultural distinctiveness of the Szeklers notwithstanding, Hungarian Romantics heralded Szekler culture as true Hungarian culture. Bartók and Kodály, for example, collected folk songs in the Szekler areas of Csik county (Suchoff 1981: 95).

Divided Claims and the Creation of a Transylvanian Identity

Transylvania often is considered to be an isolated and peripheral area of Europe. For the Hungarians and Romanians, Transylvania is by no means a peripheral territory. Both at the macro- and micro-scales, Transylvania represents fundamental aspects of each nation's identity. At the macro-scale, Transylvania has served as a refuge, a cultural center, and heart of political independence. An examination of Transylvania at the micro-scale has revealed myriad places that underscore the importance of the territory at the macro-scale for each group. A closer examination of Transylvania also illustrates that the significant places for each nation are spatially intertwined. It would be difficult from a practical point of view to draw a political boundary that would separate the important Romanian places from the Hungarian ones. In fact, it would be impossible to accomplish such a task because a number of places in Transylvania are important to both groups. Alba Iulia/Gyulafehérvár, Cluj-Napoca/Kolozsvár, Hunedoara/Vajdahunyad, Sighişoara/Segesvár, and Turda/Torda are only the places mentioned in this chapter. Moreover, one historical figure from Transylvania in particular is seen as both a great Romanian and a great Hungarian by both groups: Iancu Hunedoara/János Hunyadi.

When tensions arise between ethnic groups, political leaders and diplomats either assume that the best solution is to separate the groups with a political boundary or they decide to award the territory to one of the sides that claim it. The fact that members of each group may be spatially intertwined unfortunately has not deterred diplomats from drawing lines on maps that divide the groups. Bosnia-Hercegovina is just as complex if not more so than Transylvania; yet Vance and Owen produced plans for its division. Unfortunately, such failures have not caused diplomats to question their assumptions about the need to divide; undeterred they head back to the drawing board to create new disasters. They fail to recognize that division will just as likely exacerbate conflict as solve it. Fortunately, few diplomats and political leaders historically have argued for the division of Transylvania. Instead, many have been caught up in the argument as to whether Transylvania is really Romanian or Hungarian. This "either-or" limitation in thinking is just as tragic because it fails to recognize that other identities may exist, namely in this case, a Transylvania one.

When examining nations around the world, it is important to keep in mind that national identities have formed in more than one manner (Smith 1986: 134–138). In one form, national identities can emerge among people who share a single territory, regardless of language and religion. This type of national identity is by no means unique. Not only have a number of nations developed in this manner, but this form of nationalism is considered to be the earliest form of nationalism. Nations from North America and Western Europe, such as the Swiss, French, Dutch, English, Americans, and so on, all developed within state territories that existed prior to the rise of modern nationalism (Kohn 1994: 163–164). The form of nationalism that places emphasis on language, religion, and historical continuity regardless of existing state territories emerged later and never came to represent all forms of nationalism (Kohn 1994: 163–164). Ironically, many diplomats, although of the former form of nationalism, fall victim to the rhetoric of nationalists of the later form as they focus on language, religion, and historical continuity. The diplomats most likely would use language and religion to divide Transylvania as they have tried to do with Bosnia-Hercegovina; however, Romanian and Hungarian nationalists do not wish to divide Transylvania. Instead, each side is trying to claim all of Transylvania on historical grounds. Consequently, diplomats have become caught up in the historical arguments of these nationalists. Unfortunately, they have allowed themselves to be forced into deciding whether Transylvania is historically Romanian or historically Hungarian without realizing that it may be neither.

In their attempt to legitimize their claims to Transylvania, ethnic nationalists (whether Romanian or Hungarian) have interpreted and written about Transylvania's history to illustrate their respective nationalist perspectives. Many facts in Transylvania's history, however, fail to support nationalist arguments and, in fact, refute both Hungarian and Romanian nationalist claims. Transylvania's history is punctuated by struggles of the people of Transylvania (whether Hungarian, Romanian, or otherwise) from being incorporated into either the Romanian or Hungarian national states.

The Romanian nationalist perspective would have us believe that the Romanians of Transylvania, supposedly being imbued with a strong sense of Romanian national identity, have spent their history fighting against their Hungarian oppressors to unite Transylvania with the other Romanian states of Walachia and Moldavia. The historical facts, however, do not completely support this nationalist argument. Although the Romanians of Transylvania recognized their close cultural affinity with Romanians of Walachia and Moldavia, their historical struggle has been one in which they primarily sought to gain recognition within a Transylvanian state. The *Supplex libellus Valachorum*, for example (touted as the most important political act of the Romanian national movement in the eighteenth century), simply asked that Romanians receive equal political status with the Magyars, Szeklers, and Saxons, and that Romanians should have representation within Transylvania's governing structures (Hitchins 1969: 119–120). No desire was even expressed to unite Transylvania with either Walachia or Moldavia.

Even as national revolutions swept across Europe in 1848, Romanian revolutionaries did not call for union with Walachia and Moldavia but instead demanded that the Romanians of Transylvania be placed on an equal footing with the other peoples of Transylvania (Hitchins 1969: 213–217). Even after it was clear that the Hungarians were not willing to extend equal status to the Romanians, Romanians turned not to Moldavia and Walachia but to the Austrian emperor to create a Romanian autonomous principality within the Hapsburg Empire (Hitchins 1969: 221, 260–261). Despite hostile fighting between the Romanians and Hungarians of Transylvania in 1848–1849, it should be noted that Romanian revolutionary leaders continued to address the Hungarians as "brothers" (Hitchins 1969: 273). Romanian nationalists only gave up their goal of self-determination for Romanians within Transylvania after the Austro-Hungarian Compromise of 1867 was reached. The compromise not only created the Dual Monarchy of Austria-Hungary, but it allowed Transylvania to be incorporated into the Hungarian part of the empire. Consequently, the Romanians of Transylvania were subjected to intense Magyarization policies in the latter part of the nineteenth century. It was this setback that forced the Romanian nationalists of Transylvania to abandon their goal of self-determination within the empire and begin formulating a national goal of union with Walachia and Moldavia (Hitchins 1969: 280–281).

The Hungarian nationalist perspective likewise would have us believe that the Hungarians were in a perpetual struggle to liberate and reunite the Hungarian Kingdom after it was destroyed and torn apart by the Ottomans at the Battle of Mohács in 1526. Transylvania's Hungarian leaders, however, showed little interest in uniting Transylvania with the other Hungarian territories beyond any opportunity to expand the territory of Transylvania and Transylvania's power (Sugar, Hanák, and Frank 1990: 129). The Hungarians of Transylvania historically fought for Transylvania's independence and secured it in the Treaty of Westphalia in the seventeenth century. They attempted to regain it in the early eighteenth century after it was lost.

By the end of the eighteenth century, many Hungarians of Transylvania did, in fact, try to unite Transylvania with Hungary proper. However, such attempts were made at a time when Transylvania and Hungary proper were both part of the Hapsburg Empire and subject to the same imperial policies; these imperial policies had the intent of transferring political power from the local and regional levels to the imperial government in Vienna (Kann and David 1984: 224–226). The commonality that the Hungarians of Transylvania found with Hungarians from other territories was more likely a commonality derived from a shared predicament rather than the expression of some long-held historical desire of national unity. Unification in the face of a greater enemy (i.e., the Austrians) increased the likelihood for successful resistance.

The fact that Germanization was part of the imperial government's centralization policies can be overemphasized from a nationalistic perspective. Germanization was less of an affront to Hungarian national consciousness than it was part of the erosion of the local and regional nobilities' power. Language policy, however, was (and still is) an effective political tool. Local and regional leaders were able to combat the centralization policies of the imperial government in Vienna by rallying around the language issue. The fact that Hungarian leaders saw the language issue as a political tool rather than an affront to Hungarian national identity is exemplified in two ways. First, the campaign to make Hungarian the official language within Hungary came from the Slovak areas, not the Hungarian areas of central Hungary (Kann and David 1984: 226). Second, even though Hungarian leaders saw the political value of using the language issue, many were at times reluctant to push this issue too heavily because many Hungarian leaders spoke

Hungarian poorly (Kann and David 1984: 231), at least until the middle of the nineteenth century.

Language policy, along with the other centralizing policies of the Austrian government, did, in fact, serve as a catalyst for bringing the Hungarians of Transylvania together with Hungarians in other territories. However, this process was not inevitable as nationalists might argue. The "Hungarians" only saw themselves as one nation as long as they suffered from the same predicament. Once the catalyst was removed, the desire for unification ended and the "Hungarians" of Transylvania sought their independence again. This counterargument is supported by the fact that the Hungarian leaders of Transylvania began speaking of an independent Transylvanian state following the destruction of the Austro-Hungarian Empire at the end of World War I (Dreisziger 1975). Furthermore, in the 1920s and 1930s, Hungarian and Saxon intellectuals formed a movement to foster a Transylvanian national identity (Illyés 1982: 75).

A close examination of Transylvania reveals that the history of conflict within the territory is better described as class conflict rather than ethnic conflict. Although many more Hungarians and Saxons enjoyed ruling class status than did Romanians, ethnic and class differences were hardly the same. Michael the Brave, heralded as a great Romanian by the Romanians, virtually ignored the Romanian peasants in Transylvania as he courted the ruling class (Seton-Watson 1934: 67–68). At the same time, it is also inaccurate to depict the Horea-Cloşca Uprising of 1784—a peasant uprising—as purely a Romanian national movement, when Hungarian peasants joined in the cause (Welsch 1992).

Conclusion

The difficulty in recognizing Transylvania as something other than Romanian or Hungarian stems from the unfortunate fact that Transylvania has been controlled by either the Romanian or Hungarian national governments throughout much of its history. As a result, Transylvanians have spent much of their lives being "Romanianized" or "Magyarized." A Transylvanian identity has not had the ability to develop and mature as have other territorial national identities such as Swiss and American identities. The independent political states of Switzerland and the United States have been instrumental in the development of Swiss and American national identities.

Despite the absence of a Transylvanian state, many ingredients for a Transylvanian identity are still present, particularly in regard to the meaning of place and territory. At the macro-scale, Transylvania is a territory that distinguishes itself from both Hungary and Romania in its ethnic and religious diversity. In terms of ethnicity, not only do Hungary and the non-Transylvanian territories of Romania not have Transylvania's ethnic blend, neither even has Szeklers, who are completely unique to Transylvania. In terms of religion, although Hungary and the non-Transylvanian territories of Romania have Roman Catholicism and Eastern Orthodoxy, neither has both existing together. Moreover, in contrast to Hungary and the non-Transylvanian territories of Romania, Transylvania has Protestantism and the Uniate Church. Significantly, these religious sects have greatly shaped Transylvania's history. Of course, Protestantism exists in eastern Hungary, but it has never enjoyed the autonomy or exerted its influence in Hungary to the degree that it has in Transylvania. The political climate in Transylvania, especially during times of greatest autonomy, provided Transylvania's Protestant sects (e.g., Calvinists and Lutherans) and its Uniate Church the freedom to engage in intellectual pursuits and activities. It was the Protestant sects, for example, which set up the previously mentioned printing presses and distributed Bibles and other documents. It was the Uniate Church, for example, that wrote the history of the "Romanian" people. At the micro-scale then, it was the activities of Transylvania's various religious sects that created so many places of significance within the territory.

Ironically, the less-restrictive political climate of Transylvania allowed the religious sect to develop ideas and engage in activities that also became crucial components of both Romanian and Hungarian national identities. No wonder then that the Hungarian and Romanian nations have been so determined to incorporate and assimilate Transylvania into their respective national states. In recent decades, Ceauşescu's repressive nationalist policies in regard to ethnic minorities cultivated both a disdain for minorities among Romanians and a distrust of Romanians among the minorities. In the years that followed Ceauşescu's execution, the well-nurtured disdain and distrust led to tension and violent incidents between Transylvania's ethnic groups. In the 1990s, however, the Romanian national government has progressively granted more rights to ethnic minorities, even invited them into the government, despite the rhetoric of narrow-minded nationalists and even the ascendancy to power of nationalists in some localities. In 1996, the Romanian government even signed a basic treaty with the Hungarian government. With the Hungarian government's willingness to recognize Romania's boundaries, the Hungarians of Transylvania became less of a threat to the Romanian nation. Thus, the Romanian government was willing to grant even more rights to the Hungarians of Transylvania in the treaty.

The conciliatory efforts made by the Romanian government in recent years have done much to avert the violence that occurred in Bosnia-Hercegovina. Moreover, the Romanian government may be unwittingly fostering a Transylvanian identity now that it is allowing the non-Romanians of Transylvania to express themselves and thus shape Transylvania into a territory that is different from other Romanian territories. Transylvania will not simply become a territory where Romanians, Hungarians, Szeklers, Saxons, Gypsies, and so on coincidentally live. Transylvania will be a territory where these peoples interact and create something unique, for lack of a better word, something *Transylvanian*. Indeed, a Transylvanian identity can be built on the fact that all of the places thus far mentioned, despite being significant to Romanian and Hungarian national identities, exist within Transylvania and are historically significant for Transylvanians regardless of their individual ethnic backgrounds. In fact, all of these places, taken as a complete collection, can serve as the basis of a Transylvanian national identity. Despite decades and even centuries of domination by outside forces, ethnic Romanians and Hungarians of Transylvania still stand apart from their ethnic brethren who live outside the region. Although it seems unlikely that Transylvanians will establish a political state that is necessary to cultivate a distinct Transylvanian national identity, the uniqueness of Transylvania as a place will continue to make Transylvanians stand out from the peoples around them.

References

Ceauşescu, Ilie. *Transylvania—An Ancient Romanian Land*. Bucharest: Military Publishing House, 1983.

Czigány, Lóránt. *The Oxford History of Hungarian Literature: From the Earliest Times to the Present*. Oxford: Clarendon Press, 1984.

Dreisziger, N. F. "Count Istvan Bethlen's Secret Plan for the Restoration of the Empire of Transylvania." *East European Quarterly* 18 (January 1975): 413–423.

Edroiu, Nicholae. *Horea's Uprising: The 1784 Romanian Peasants' Uprising*. Translated by Alexandru Bolintineau. Bucharest: Editura Stiintific Si Enciclopedic, 1978.

Erdei, Ferenc, ed. *Information Hungary*. New York: Pergamon Press, 1968.

Giurescu, Dino C. *Illustrated History of the Romanian People*. Bucharest: Editura Sport-Turism, 1981.

Hitchins, Keith. *The Romanian National Movement in Transylvania, 1780–1849*. Cambridge, Mass.: Harvard University Press, 1969.

Illyés, Elemer. *National Minorities in Romania: Change in Transylvania*. Boulder, Colo.: East European Monographs, 1982.

Kann, Robert A., and Zedněk V. David. *The Peoples of the Eastern Habsburg Lands,*

1526–1918. Vol. 6 of *A History of East Central Europe,* edited by Peter F. Sugar and Donald W. Treadgold. Seattle: University of Washington Press, 1984.

Kohn, Hans. "Western and Eastern Nationalisms." In John Hutchinson and Anthony D. Smith, eds., *Nationalism.* New York: Oxford University Press, 1994, chap. 24.

Légrády Brothers. *Justice for Hungary: The Cruel Errors of Trianon.* Budapest: privately published, 1930.

McNally, Raymond T., and Radu Florescu. *In Search of Dracula: The History of Dracula and Vampires.* New York: Houghton Mifflin Company, 1994.

Palmer, Alan. *The Lands Between: A History of East-Central Europe since the Congress of Vienna.* New York: The Macmillan Company, 1970.

Seton-Watson, R. W. *A History of the Roumanians: From Roman Times to the Completion of Unity.* Cambridge: Cambridge University Press, 1934.

Smith, Anthony D. *The Ethnic Origins of Nations.* New York: Basil Blackwell, 1986.

Stoicescu, Nicolae. *Age-Old Factors of Romanian Unity.* Bucharest: Editura Academiei Republicii Socialiste România, 1986.

Suchoff, Benjamin, ed. *The Hungarian Folk Song by Béla Bartók.* Translated by M. D. Calvocoressi. Albany: State University of New York Press, 1981.

Sugar, Peter F., Péter Hanák, and Tibor Frank, eds. *A History of Hungary.* Bloomington and Indianapolis: Indiana University Press, 1990.

Welsch, Darron Ray. "The Horea-Cloşca Uprising of 1784 and Nationalist History." Eugene, Oregon: Honors College Paper University of Oregon, 1992.

13

Migration, Nationalism, and the Construction of Welsh Identity

Anne K. Knowles

One of the defining moments in the history of Welsh nationalism was a speech broadcast on BBC radio in 1962. Titled *"Tynged yr Iaith"* (The Fate of the Language), this speech crystallized years of thinking by Saunders Lewis, the leading intellectual of the Welsh nationalist party. It was an urgent cry to save the Welsh language from extinction and to make it the sole focus of the political struggle to free Wales from English domination. "The language is more important than self-government," Lewis declared, "and no government is worth having that does not safeguard and revive the language." Much of the speech was a catalogue of crimes against the language, emphasizing not those committed by an oppressive English government but those committed by the Welsh themselves, whom Lewis accused of failing to value and defend their own culture. Searching for a historical precedent for his position, Lewis harkened back to an obscure and largely failed attempt to plant a Welsh colony on the dry prairies of Patagonia in the middle of the nineteenth century. He praised the Patagonia settlement as "that heroic experiment to create a Welsh homeland" and singled out its leader, Michael D. Jones, for daring to envision a society governed by Welsh institutions. "[A] chapel and school and senate-house, with the old language as the medium of worship and trade, learning and government. It would be a strong nation, a Welsh-speaking home. Revolutionary words, a revolutionary program. Even today, our lack of national consciousness prevents us from grasping the significance and heroism of the venture in Patagonia" (Lewis 1962).[1]

Lewis's speech galvanized a new generation of Welsh nationalists and made the language a powerful focus for political action. His rever-

ential reference to the Patagonia colony also created one of the founding myths of linguistic nationalism in Wales. The myths that political
movements adopt can be revealing, both for their symbolic truths and
the ways they distort the history they claim to portray. This chapter
will explore the actual and the mythologized roles that migration has
played in the formation of Welsh cultural and political identity, beginning with the Patagonia colony and other overseas ventures and concluding with internal migration. I will argue that Saunders Lewis's
portrayal of emigration to Patagonia as a political act echoed the view
of earlier Welsh leaders who had tried to cast emigration as an effort
to preserve Welsh cultural identity. Their vision, however, did not reflect the opinions or motivations of most Welsh people, who saw emigration as one choice among many for improving their economic
status. Thus, Welsh efforts to politicize emigration repeatedly failed,
and Welsh emigration neither became a source of inspiration for Welsh
nationalism nor fostered a strong attachment to the Welsh homeland.
This stands in marked contrast to the success of Irish nationalist leaders in promulgating a highly political and national interpretation of
Irish emigration, encapsulated by the metaphor of emigration as exile.
Emigration from Wales also failed to become an important political
issue because internal migration had a far more profound impact upon
Welsh identity, creating a cultural and political divide within the country that Welsh nationalists have yet to bridge.

The Patagonia Settlement in Myth and Reality

The Welsh settlement in Patagonia was the brainchild of a Welsh Con-
gregational minister named Michael D. Jones (1822–1898). As a young
man, Jones became distressed by the assimilation of Welsh people into
English culture. In letters published in Welsh and Welsh-American
newspapers during the 1840s and 1850s, Jones berated the Welsh for
ignoring the peril of their situation and for refusing to acknowledge
the value of their own language and cultural institutions (*Drych* 1857,
1863; *Cenhadwr* 1848–1854). The solution he proposed was to establish
a new Welsh homeland beyond the reach of English influence. Initially
he hoped to locate this homeland (*gwladfa*) on the American frontier,
but visits to Welsh-American settlements convinced him that assimilation was erasing Welsh culture just as quickly in America as it was in
Britain. Only a large settlement in a remote location, like the Mormons'
state of Deseret in Utah, could avoid the inexorable decay of language
and the corruption of morals by Anglo-American society ("Michael
Daniel Jones" 1895; 211–212; Rhys 1902; M. D. Jones 1857).

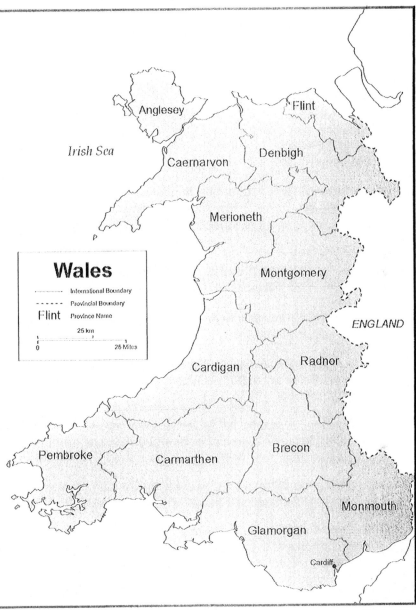

Wales

International Boundary
Provincial Boundary
Flint   Province Name

25 km

0   25 Miles

Irish Sea

Anglesey

Flint

Caernarvon

Denbigh

Merioneth

Montgomery

ENGLAND

Cardigan

Radnor

Pembroke

Carmarthen

Brecon

Monmouth

Glamorgan

Cardiff

Chris Leatham

▶────────────────────────────────────◀

CURRENT COUNTRY/REGION DATA

Population   2,835,073 (1991 census)

Area   7,469 sq. miles/19,419 sq. km.

Welsh-speaking   18.6 percent
  population
  (according to the
  1991 census)

Geography of Welsh   Strongest in rural areas and small towns of
  language use   NW Wales; growing numbers in cities and
                        among school-age children in SE Wales

**CONFLICTS AND PROTESTS RELATED
TO LINGUISTIC NATIONALISM**

1847 Publication of "The Blue Books" incites defense of Welsh lan-
      guage and traditions.

1936 Leaders of Plaid Cymru (Welsh Nationalist Party) set fire to the
      RAF Bombing School at Penyberth on the Lleyn Peninsula,
      North Wales.

1957 Parliament passes bill to drown the Tryweryn valley in North
      Wales to create reservoir for Liverpool; years of sporadic protest
      follow.

1963 First protests by Cymdeithas yr Iaith Gymraeg (Welsh Language
      Society) demanding equal legal status for Welsh and English.

1969 Plaid Cymru boycotts the investiture of the Prince of Wales; vio-
      lent protests by a splinter group, Mudiad Amddiffyn Cymru
      (Movement for the Defense of Wales).

1980 Proposed "fast unto death" by Gwynfor Evans, president of
      Plaid Cymru, compels Parliament to establish a Welsh-language
      television channel.

1996 The queen's visit to Aberystwyth is called short because of dis-
      ruptions by Welsh protestors; Cymdeithas yr Iaith claims sym-
      bolic victory.

HISTORICAL BACKGROUND

Welsh was the majority language in many parts of Wales until the middle of the nineteenth century, when internal migration and improved communications between England and Wales accelerated the adoption of English as the language of commerce and education. English had long been considered the key to success by ambitious Welsh people, many of whom migrated to London and other English cities to pursue economic opportunities unavailable in the impoverished Welsh countryside.

A turning point in national regard for the language came in 1847 with the publication of Reports of the Commissioners of Inquiry into the State of Education in Wales, infamously known as "The Blue Books." The Blue Books' portrayal of the Welsh as an ignorant, morally degenerate people outraged religious and political leaders, giving rise to the first sustained defense of the Welsh language (particularly as a medium for religion) and Welsh traditions. At the same time, a new Welsh political identity was being forged in the industrial valleys of southeast Wales, where conflicts over wages and working conditions eclipsed concerns about language. Neither Lloyd George's Liberal Party nor the Labour Party in Wales argued for Welsh independence. Their concern for social welfare and the rights of working people reflected the main issues of everyday life in a country whose economy was dominated by heavy industry and subsistence agriculture well into the twentieth century.

But the class-based identity born in industrial areas made language and religion lesser issues, if not outright irrelevancies. Nationalist claims that language defined Welshness angered many Anglo Welsh, who felt that their distinctive working-class heritage constituted a cultural identity as uniquely Welsh as the rural heritage emphasized by nationalists. Hostility against the linguistic definition of Welshness was an important contributing reason for the resounding defeat of the 1979 referendum on devolution and an elected assembly for Wales, which won support from only 20 percent of voters (Davies 1993: 675–677). A second referendum was narrowly approved in September 1997 by a margin of just 0.6 percent. Support for a Welsh assembly remained very weak in the northeast districts bordering England and in the urban belt along the south coast. The most intriguing change reflected in the geography of the 1997 vote was the strong support for devolution in inland industrial towns such as Merthyr Tydfil and former coal-mining valleys such as the Rhondda, places where outside funding from the European Union has softened the hardship of chronic unemployment and persuaded many people of the benefits of a Welsh presence on the European stage.

The crux of Plaid Cymru's continuing dilemma lies in the small proportion of the electorate who identify themselves with the Welsh language and the party's inability to appeal to significant numbers outside
its traditional heartland.

▶━━━◀

Jones's definition of Welshness focused on the cultural traits he saw
disappearing from Welsh-American communities, particularly use of
the Welsh language and adherence to the tenets of Welsh Nonconformist religion, characterized by an emphasis upon the Bible and following
strict moral guidelines. He referred to cultural melding or fusing (*yr
elfen doddawl*) "as the basic obstacle to the maintenance of a discrete
immigrant community" (G. A. Davies 1995: 45). The evidence of cultural decay in Welsh-American settlements proved that geographical
isolation was essential to achieve the aim of preserving Welsh culture.
Having abandoned hope of finding a suitable location in the United
States, Jones looked to South America. In 1857 he announced to readers
of the leading Welsh-American newspaper, *Y Drych* (*The Mirror*), that
he had entered negotiations with the government of Argentina to establish a Welsh colony in the Chubut Valley in central Patagonia (M.
D. Jones 1857).

Jones was disappointed by the generally lukewarm reception his
plan received in the United States. Established immigrant farmers were
unwilling to abandon their comfortable standard of living in flourishing Welsh-American communities in order to help pioneer the Patagonia settlement, and their monetary contributions were negligible. By
the late 1850s Jones's missives in the Welsh-American press had a bitter, scolding tone. He accused immigrants of having forgotten their
homeland and the suffering that the poor in Wales continued to endure
at the hands of oppressive landlords. Some readers were incensed by
Jones's criticism of their accommodation to American culture. They
lambasted his plan as being ill-conceived and pointless, given the
ready availability of excellent, cheap land in the United States. Others
took umbrage at Jones's description of Welsh Americans as servile,
spineless creatures, little better than slaves to their "English" (i.e.,
American) masters. Successful immigrant farmers found the comparison of their situation to slavery offensive and absurd (*Drych* 1857,
1863).

Industrial Welsh-American communities responded more positively
to Jones's appeal, at least to the extent of providing financial support.
Most of the known American contributors to the Patagonia venture
were working men in industrial towns such as Youngstown and Iron-

dale, Ohio; Wilkesbarre and Pittston, Pennsylvania; and the slate-quarrying district of Vermont (List of subscribers . . . undated). A spokesman for the Welsh Colonization Society in Pittston wrote in 1857, "One hopes that soon we shall have, in just this sort of settlement, . . . a justification, as Welsh people, of the right to be respected by the world as we are not at present." David James of Minersville, Pennsylvania, wrote to *Y Drych* in 1863 that the Welsh in the old country had no rights, no voice; they labored "throughout the year to enrich the English." Another supporter from Castleton, Vermont, urged Welsh immigrants in 1863 to remember that their first loyalty was to Wales, echoing Jones's declaration that the Civil War was "the American's war . . . to them belongs the main glory of losing or winning, and the Welsh [in the United States] will be extinguished as a nation by the North as much as by the South, whichever of them gains the victory."[2] The rhetoric of freedom from slavery made sense to Welsh industrial workers in the United States and Wales, for they were long familiar with the militant view of industrial work as "wage slavery." Workers' sympathy for the cause, along with the enduring desire among many Welsh industrial workers to become landowners, helps explain the successful recruitment of colonists from the south Wales coalfield and from slate-mining communities in North Wales. These two regions accounted for half of the first group of 163 emigrants who finally sailed for Patagonia in May 1865. Most of the rest came from Liverpool, the port of departure and home of the venture's promotional publication, *Y Ddraig Goch* (*The Red Dragon*) (G. Williams 1975: 35–38; G. A. Davis 1995: 48–49).

The colonists were woefully unprepared for what lay ahead of them. Hopeful scouting reports had led them to expect Patagonia to be a fertile country, ideally suited to agricultural settlement. Upon arriving they were stunned to learn that the land acquired for them was scrub desert and that it was virtually impossible to grow any crops without irrigation, a technology unfamiliar to the few farmers among them. Too poor to book return passage, the settlers were marooned in a harsh landscape that their nominal leader, Michael D. Jones, had never visited and would in fact never see. Several colonists died during the first winter, and it took years for the survivors to master irrigation and flood control so that the colony could become self-sufficient (G. Williams 1975: 39–53, 59–65; R. B. Williams 1942). No Welsh settlement suffered greater hardship or such extreme physical isolation during its pioneer years. Genuine heroism and group effort enabled them to survive and to establish a string of farming settlements that attracted several hundred more immigrants from Wales over the next fifty years.

The drama of the Patagonia colonists' struggle for survival clearly appealed to Saunders Lewis, as it has to Welsh audiences ever since his speech. Despite its distance from Wales and its small immigrant population, the Patagonia colony has become the best known overseas Welsh settlement, especially among Welsh speakers (G. Williams 1991: ix), thanks largely to Lewis's speech and to broadcast documentaries such as the four-part television series called *Plant y Paith* (*Children of the Prairie*). The colony's history was not always interpreted in heroic terms, however. At the turn of the twentieth century, for example, when a number of Welsh Patagonians appealed to the British government for financial assistance in order to relocate to more fertile farms in western Canada, the Welsh press portrayed the colony as a miserable failure. Stories about the early settlers' trials carried headlines such as "The Welsh Settlement in Patagonia: Pathetic Story of a Brave but Futile Attempt at Founding an Independent Colony" and "Welsh Colonists Who Sought Independence and Found Ruin" (Press cuttings . . . undated). These stories highlighted the continuing hardship of trying to farm in the desert and the poverty of the Patagonia Welsh.

Saunders Lewis's reinterpretation of the Patagonia venture transformed it from a sorry tale of near tragedy into a brave attempt by protonationalists to found an independent Welsh state. The difficulties the colonists encountered only added poignancy to their effort. In his appropriation of the story, Lewis emphasized Michael D. Jones's original plan rather than the way events actually unfolded. He particularly stressed the settlers' courage in planning to establish Welsh-language institutions, even though not all the institutions envisioned by Jones came to fruition. Negotiations with the Argentine government failed to secure political independence for the colony. The Welsh language did persist for an exceptionally long time as the language of many Welsh homes, schools, and chapels, but its survival was mainly owing to the remoteness of the colony (particularly the western-most settlement located in the Andean foothills, where the language hung on longest) and to the fact that other residents of the region were predominantly either native Indians or Spanish-speaking Catholic immigrants, whom the Protestant Welsh were slow to accept as marriage partners (G. Williams 1975: 149–150, 185–186).

To Lewis, however, what mattered was the colonists' *intention* to create "a strong nation, a Welsh-speaking home." His emphasis upon Welsh-language institutions acknowledged the particular difficulty Welsh nationalists faced because of the historical lack of indigenous Welsh political institutions. Many scholars point to this as the fundamental difference between Wales and Scotland in their relations with England; Scottish law, its courts, and the Scottish educational system survived that nation's union with its imperial neighbor, whereas in Wales, no distinctly Welsh institutions survived the Acts of Union with

England in 1536 and 1542 except those in the cultural realm.[3] Had Jones's original plan been fully realized, the Patagonia colony would have provided a working model for a Welsh nation along the lines that Lewis wished for Wales itself: a communal society, anchored to the land by subsistence agriculture and religious devotion, a society whose sole language was Welsh. Lewis's view has strongly influenced subsequent presentations of the Patagonia story, including Glyn Williams's geographical studies. Like Lewis, Williams attributes nationalist motives to the first Welsh colonists in Patagonia and to those who established a new settlement in the Patagonian Andes between 1885 and 1900. "[F]or those who were Welsh among the settlers" in the Andes, he writes, ". . . one cannot help feeling a sense of tragedy mingled with the success, the tragedy that is to be found in a group of people who are obliged, because of what they saw as an oppressive government, to forsake their homeland in search of a new land where their cultural and economic ideals could be realized. This was the price to be paid for wanting to be Welsh." (G. Williams 1978: 83). In *The Desert and the Dream*, his authoritative historical geography of the colony, Williams writes that "[t]he organization of the emigration was undertaken by a group of nationalists whose interests lay in establishing an isolated unit of Welsh culture whose values would hinge upon religion and language. These values would be promoted through the religious institutions aimed at making their religious writings the basis of all social interaction. This point cannot be over-emphasized in considering the strong internal cohesion of the Welsh as a culture group in Patagonia" (G. Williams 1975: 38).

The largest rural Welsh settlements in the United States during the nineteenth century were also characterized by strong internal cohesion based upon religious values and institutions, but they were not planned by individuals who espoused the kind of extreme separatism that Michael D. Jones sought for his colony. Welsh culture persisted in places such as Jackson and Gallia Counties, Ohio, because the immigrants who settled there came mainly from one part of Wales, bought land in close proximity to one another, and achieved sufficient economic success to retain a large proportion of the second and third generations in the community, thus maintaining its ethnic character. Nationalistic ideals were not necessary for the maintenance of Welsh language and religion in immigrant communities. The Jackson/Gallia community and other relatively large rural settlements show that the more important factors were a degree of physical isolation, a diverse economic base that provided local employment over a long period, and sufficient numbers (at least 1,000 Welsh) to provide a pool of marriage partners over an extended period (Knowles 1989, 1997). It may be significant that Michael D. Jones spent much of his time in the United States in Cincinnati and Paddy's Run, Ohio, two of the least-insular Welsh settlements in the United States. Had he stayed in Jackson County, Ohio, his choice of location for a Welsh colony might have been different.

One might question whether the organizers of the Patagonia colony were in fact nationalists. Michael D. Jones's chief concern throughout his life was the preservation and elevation of Welsh culture. During his later years he argued for self-governance for Wales (R. T. Jones 1986: 116), but during his advocacy of the Patagonia venture his goals were more modest, focusing mainly on building up Welsh self-respect and fostering conservative religious morals. Jones and those who supported his colonial scheme found outright rebellion unthinkable, as one would expect of ministers and members of Welsh denominations whose values were dominated by a severe, authoritarian strain of Calvinism. They took pains to distinguish their methods from the overtly political, sometimes violent actions of Irish nationalists. The Rev. W. Roberts, president of the Welsh Colonizing and General Trading Company (which assumed organizational and commercial control of the Patagonia venture in 1866), declared that he was glad to see the Welsh making a peaceful attempt to establish a state under a watchful government of Welsh courts and officials in Patagonia, "in contrast to trying to achieve this through rebellion . . . as the Fenians were doing" (Welsh Colonizing and General Trading Company 1866: 8).

The concept of a Welsh homeland thousands of miles from Wales reveals a fundamental distrust of the Welsh people's ability to maintain their unique identity, a distrust that in Michael D. Jones and Saunders Lewis sometimes bordered on contempt. In his arguments for the Patagonia venture, Jones suggested that Welsh identity would only become strong if the Welsh were physically removed from the corrupting influences of English and American society. Lewis's speech on the fate of the language expressed a righteous anger at the Welsh for being their own worst enemies. "There will be no Wales without the Welsh language," Lewis declared (S. Lewis 1962). The nation of Wales meant little if it were not peopled by Welsh speakers. The corollary of this fixation upon the language was that a Welsh nation could exist anywhere that the Welsh language thrived.[4] For Lewis as for Jones, the idea of the *gwladfa* was not tied to a particular territory; in theory, at least, a Welsh homeland might succeed anywhere so long as it was far away from England. The problem Lewis faced as a self-proclaimed nationalist was the immutable proximity of Wales to England. Forced by this geographical fact to try to change the Welsh themselves, Lewis pointed to the Patagonia colony as a model of self-sacrifice for the cause of Welsh national identity. If the Welsh were willing to suffer for their language as the colonists had, they could save it.

Emigrants and Exiles

Personal suffering is a common thread running through the founding myths enshrined by many nationalist movements. It is also a theme common to popular accounts of nineteenth-century emigration from European countries to the United States. How could emigrants bear to leave their homeland unless they were downtrodden, impoverished, driven by hunger and oppression to seek a better life in a strange land? In Ireland, real hardship was manipulated by nationalist politicians to create an enduring image of emigration as the suffering of a whole nation at the hands of its oppressors. According to historian Kerby Miller, the Irish conception of emigration as exile developed gradually over centuries of English occupation and rule. Its first incarnation portrayed the Irish as internal exiles who suffered injustice and deprivation as the dispossessed poor of their own country. By the time of the Famine in the 1840s, a growing number of emigrants saw themselves as being forced into permanent exile overseas. Both readings of exile were inherently political, based upon the imbalance of power between Irish Catholics and their British and Anglo-Irish masters. What Miller calls the "bitter nourishment" of "forced banishment" became an important source of inspiration for Irish nationalism in Ireland and among immigrants in the United States. The notion of emigration as exile also fixed the emigrant's regard for "Mother Ireland" as the true home of the Irish people and fostered an ideological and emotional attachment that moved many immigrants to send remittances back home, to return whenever they could, and to raise funds for the nationalist cause (Miller 1985: 103).

To every Irish emigrant who perceived his or her decision to leave Ireland in this light, emigration was a political act. In Wales, men whom Saunders Lewis and others have claimed as early nationalists tried to convince their contemporaries that emigration should be a political act and that leaving Wales could be a way to preserve Welsh culture. The individuals to whom I will now turn were not as determined or as radical in their thinking as Michael D. Jones, but as his intellectual precursors they were important figures in the history of Welsh emigration overseas. Their view of emigration's relation to national identity directly influenced Jones, and their misunderstanding of the way emigrants themselves regarded their decision and their identity foreshadowed the Patagonia venture's failure to generate widespread support.

Perhaps the first Welshman to advocate emigration as a means of preserving Welsh culture was William Jones (1726–1795), a country philosopher from the mid-Wales county of Montgomeryshire. Jones was an ardent admirer of Voltaire and the French Revolution. He argued in pamphlets and correspondence that Welsh patriots' main goal should be the rejuvenation of Welsh culture in Wales, but he also urged " 'All Indigenous Cambro-Britons' to summon up the courage to abandon their oppressed native land and make for the Land of Liberty in America." Jones advocated the organized emigration of Welsh folk to the American frontier in order to "establish a separate state whose affairs would be administered through the medium of the Welsh language" (Jenkins 1995: 365, 384). His vision was partly inspired by the Welsh Quakers and Baptists who had tried a century before to create an independent Welsh colony in Pennsylvania (H. M. Davies 1995). Another of the Welsh "transatlantic brethren" who set his eyes on America was the Baptist preacher Morgan John Rhys (1760–1804). Like Williams Jones, Rhys made explicit political connections between emigration and independence. He tried to realize his vision of a Welsh society freed from oppression by organizing a colony called Beulah in central Pennsylvania, near the location of the later settlement of Ebensburgh (G. A. Williams 1980). Beulah failed to attract significant numbers of settlers and served mainly as a stopping point for later Welsh immigrants traveling westward to more fertile regions.

Jones and Rhys set a precedent by suggesting that Welsh identity could be preserved—indeed, that it might be saved—through colonization. Theirs was an aspatial conception of national identity that decoupled Welsh identity from its native soil and stressed the goal of individual liberty rather than national liberation. They identified the Welsh language and Nonconformist Welsh religion as the two most important elements of Welsh culture, as did Michael D. Jones fifty years after. In this regard, these leaders' view accurately reflected contemporary trends in Welsh culture, which during the early nineteenth century increasingly "emphasized the new puritanical Sunday as 'The Welsh Sunday,' the new 'Welsh way of life' being that of the chapel, the singing school (for hymns not ballads), the temperance assemblies, the *Cymanfa Ganu* [a hymn-singing assembly] . . . and much else which is familiar to the twentieth century as the typical Wales" (P. Morgan 1984: 95). These institutions could be, and were, readily transplanted to virtually all overseas Welsh settlements in the nineteenth century, from rural communities in upstate New York and the coal towns of eastern Pennsylvania to the colonies established by Welsh immigrants in Australia (Lloyd 1988). But the very strength of Welsh Nonconformity and the dominance of the Welsh language in religious life in Wales itself made calls for their preservation seem superfluous.

The desire for greater personal liberty clearly motivated many emigrants to set sail for America, but for most of them the liberty to secure a better livelihood was more important than abstract principles of political freedom. One example will serve to represent this general point. The emigrant in whom William Jones placed his highest hopes was a young man named Ezekiel Hughes. In 1795, Hughes led a small party of emigrants from his home parish of Llanbryn-mair, Montgomeryshire, with the intention of joining Morgan John Rhys's settlement in Pennsylvania. Before the year was out, however, Hughes and his cousin Edward Bebb had left the party and headed west for the Ohio frontier, where they patiently waited to claim sections of prime agricultural land for their own farms and to sell as land speculators. Hughes's inheritance as the second son of fairly wealthy tenant farmers gave him more money to buy land and to travel than many of his fellow emigrants possessed. He was nevertheless typical of the emigrants who founded Welsh agricultural settlements in the United States. For Hughes as for many Welsh people, emigration was not a flight from poverty or oppression but rather a way to earn a better return on his investment of capital and labor (Knowles 1995b).

Another minister and journalist who advocated emigration as a solution to the endemic poverty in Wales was Samuel Roberts (1800–1885). Roberts was an early and vehement opponent of landlordism in Wales. He published a number of tracts attacking absentee landlords and their avaricious, unprincipled agents. At the same time he harangued Welsh folk for being subservient and unenlightened. His ideal citizen was the yeoman farmer, represented in a piece of rhetorical fiction entitled "*Ffarmwr Careful.*" The eponymous hero is the tenant of a large farm who works hard to improve the land and to introduce modern methods of agriculture. His family's efforts are for naught, however, as the improvements they make merely enrich their landlord and inspire the spiteful envy of their neighbors. Roberts argued that Farmer Careful was just the sort of industrious Welshman who should emigrate to the United States. Only there could he and his family reap the rewards of their labor.

Roberts's interest in the United States dated from his days as a student, when he began a lively correspondence with relatives who had emigrated to Ohio (Taylor 1974). As a middle-aged man he decided to establish his own Welsh colony on the American frontier. He and one of his American-born relatives, William Bebb, tried to organize a Welsh colony on 100,000 acres of woodland in northeastern Tennessee just before the Civil War. Neither Roberts's enthusiasm for the project nor Bebb's experience as a lawyer, land speculator, and former governor of Ohio proved sufficient to make the plan succeed. Only a few dozen Welsh families, most of them from Roberts's home district, expressed interest in joining the settlement, and of the few who emigrated with him in 1857; none remained more than a few months in Tennessee (Taylor 1974; Shepperson 1961; Tennessee Colonization Papers). In addition to the land's dubious title, the site was far away from any established Welsh community. By the late 1850s, when Roberts and Bebb were trying to attract settlers to Tennessee, there were over twenty substantial rural Welsh settlements in the United States where new immigrants could settle among friends and relatives, including promising new communities on the fertile prairies of Minnesota and Iowa. The location of the Tennessee colony south of the Mason-Dixon line was also a serious impediment to Welsh emigrants, who almost universally opposed slavery and identified themselves with the free North. For financial, social, and political reasons, the Tennessee colony simply did not appeal to Welsh emigrants (Taylor 1974; Knowles 1997: 25–28; M. A. Jones 1985: 122–127; Conway 1961: 96, 283–284, 112–117).

In the summer of 1858 it was clear to Bebb that the colony would never get off the ground if it were limited to Welsh settlers. He wrote Roberts that the Welsh were too naïve, too inexperienced, and too blinded by their prejudice against slavery to recognize the opportunity awaiting them in the South. Rather than continue trying to persuade them he recommended opening the settlement to *"all the world."* "Organised emigration is suited to the genius of the Yankees," he concluded, "but I fear the Welsh are not suited for it."[5] He had recognized one of the characteristics that distinguished the Welsh from other European immigrant groups throughout the nineteenth century; namely, that they did not respond to religious or political leaders' efforts to organize emigration projects. In Wales, lay leaders generally held more power in Nonconformist congregations than did ministers or unlicensed preachers, and the emigration parties they organized tended to involve relatively small numbers of close friends and relatives—as indeed the typical membership of a Welsh chapel was small in comparison to Catholic church memberships in many European countries (Knowles 1989: 26–28). I have emphasized examples of rural Welsh emigration up to this point, but the same pattern of small-scale, family-led chain migration characterized emigration from industrial districts in Wales throughout the nineteenth century, including the highly skilled workers who responded to recruitment campaigns by agents for American industrial concerns (W. D. Jones 1993).

What William Bebb called the unsuitability of the Welsh for organized emigration also reflected the fact that individualism had transformed many aspects of traditional Welsh culture by the early nineteenth century. Nonconformist religion, which became the first true national religion of Wales between 1750 and 1850, brought with it a new mentality that stressed personal responsibility and the belief that one should respond positively to God's commandments. By the early nineteenth century, Welsh society was much further along the road to modernization than was Catholic Ireland, whose worldview was dominated by communalism, fatalism, passivity, and dependence (Miller 1985: 428). Welsh people's worldview was also revolutionized by dramatic economic changes during the early nineteenth century, changes that created a new kind of Welsh identity that directly competed with the rural, religious, linguistically defined identity so important to Saunders Lewis and the nineteenth-century advocates of overseas emigration.

Internal Migration and the Geography of Welsh Identity

Until the end of the eighteenth century, Wales was a country of farms, hamlets, and market villages, with only scattered pockets of small-scale industry such as coal and lead mining and the cottage manufacture of textiles. One sign of the lack of urban and industrial development was that London functioned as the expatriate capital of Wales. There were long-standing traditions of Welsh professionals and craftspeople setting up businesses in the capital, and of Welsh agricultural laborers migrating to central and southeastern England for seasonal employment. A new kind of migration began to eclipse these traditional movements during the first decades of the nineteenth century, as the rapid development of first the iron industry and then coal mining turned parts of southeast and northeast Wales into leading centers of heavy industry in Britain. By 1830, the iron furnaces and rolling mills of southeast Wales were producing up to 40 percent of all British iron. The capital of Welsh iron was the town of Merthyr Tydfil, which in 1851 boasted forty-one blast furnaces that employed approximately 30,000 people. Merthyr's total population of over 60,000 in 1851 made it the largest urban center in Wales and the center of the principality's largest industrial conurbation (Riden 1986: 128–129; Carter and Wheatley 1982: 8, 18; J. Davies 1993: 328–330).[6]

The remarkable transformation of rural hinterlands into centers of economic development prompted an unprecedented and massive shift in population from rural to industrial areas (see Figure 13.1). Between 1801 and 1851, the combined population of the two leading industrial

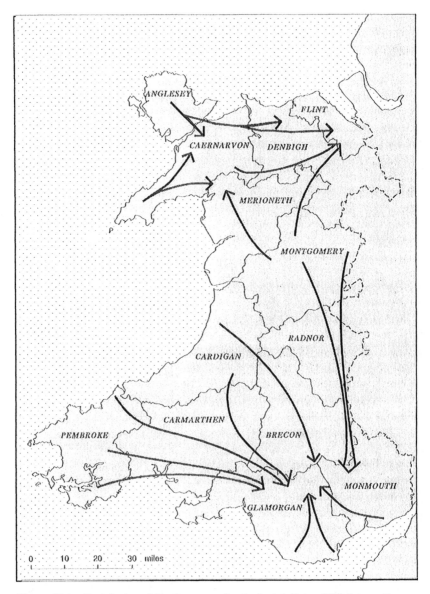

Figure 13.1   Population shifts from rural to industrializing Welsh counties,
1830–1880

Sources: P. E. Jones (1989); P. N. Jones (1987); Knowles (1997: 56–71); Pryce (1975).

counties, Glamorgan and Monmouthshire, leaped from 56,061 to 203,097, an increase of 362 percent, almost ten times the average growth for Wales as a whole (Census 1852: 3). During the same period, iron and coal mining operations in Denbigh and Flintshire attracted significant numbers of migrants, as did the rapid growth of Liverpool as the leading port for the cotton and textile trades (Pryce 1975; Pooley 1983). Most of the population increase in northern and southern industrial areas up to mid-century was due to migration from other Welsh counties. Rural populations also increased during this period, but at a slowing rate as more and more agricultural workers exchanged the miserly wages on Welsh farms for the promise of better-paying jobs in industry. Migration peaked during the last quarter of the century, when the expansion of deep-pit anthracite coal mining in south Wales created jobs for tens of thousands of workers and spurred the development of port towns such as Cardiff and Swansea. By 1901, internal migration had radically restructured the distribution of the Welsh population, with 58 percent residing in Glamorgan and Monmouthshire and 81 percent in the six most industrial counties, leaving just 19 percent in the seven predominantly rural counties (see Table 13.1) (Census 1903).

TABLE 13.1   Welsh Population in 1901, by Administrative County

North Wales	
Anglesey	50,606
Carnarvon	125,649
Denbigh	131,582
Flint	81,485
Merioneth	48,852
Montgomery	54,901

South Wales	
Brecknock	54,213
Cardigan	61,078
Carmarthen	135,328
Glamorgan	859,931
Monmouth	298,076
Pembroke	87,894
Radnor	23,281
TOTAL	2,012,876

Source: Census of England and Wales (1903), passim.

According to the economic historical Brinley Thomas, the migration of rural Welsh folk to industrial south Wales saved the Welsh language by preventing tens of thousands of Welsh speakers from leaving the country who otherwise would have sought employment in England or fled poverty by emigrating overseas as did millions of Irish (Thomas 1987). Many immigrants to the iron works and coal fields did continue to speak Welsh and to practice the religion they had learned in the countryside, but the experience of industry in cramped urban conditions fundamentally changed Welsh workers' sense of identity. A new kind of Welsh society emerged, particularly in the densely populated valleys of the southeast: a self-confident, militant working class who were inspired by the radical politics of English socialism and the early trade union movement. These Welsh men and women identified more strongly with fellow workers around the world than with the pious agricultural communities they had left behind. A permanent rift developed between the working-class, increasingly Anglicized southeast, and the predominantly Welsh-speaking, agricultural northwest, a divide encapsulated by historian Gwyn A. Williams as the archetypal identities of the *gwerin* and the working class (G. A. Williams 1985: 234–240). Even though the absolute number of Welsh speakers in the urban and industrial southeast and northeast remained fairly high, their proportion dwindled to a small fraction of the population. This is still true today. The 34,671 Welsh-speakers in Cardiff and Swansea in 1991 accounted for just 6 percent and 10 percent, respectively, of those cities' populations, whereas the 36,026 Welsh speakers in Ceredigion (formerly Cardiganshire) were 59 percent of that rural county's population (Aitchison and Carter 1995: 92–93).

Although one may debate whether internal migration saved the Welsh language, there is no question that the availability of employment within Wales significantly dampened the outflow of Welsh emigrants overseas. Estimates of emigration from Wales as from the rest of Great Britain are very approximate because of the lack of comprehensive sources that correctly identified nation of origin. Official government statistics counted just 42,076 Welsh immigrants entering the United States in 1820–1900, but the actual number was probably about 150,000. This compares with between 1.1 and 1.8 million emigrants from England, about 400,000 from Scotland, and nearly 4 million from Ireland[7] (Thernstrom 1980: 1047–1948; Berthoff 1980: 1013; Erickson 1980: 324–325, 335; Donaldson 1980: 910; Blessing 1980: 528). Emigration never became a national tragedy for Wales as it did for Ireland. More to the point, emigration from Wales did not become a political act. Nationalist political leaders in Ireland promoted the notion of emigration as exile because it embittered ordinary Irish folk against their

British rulers and helped foster enduring loyalty toward the mother country, as well as ensuring strong political and financial support for the nationalist cause by those who settled overseas. Welsh leaders were hampered in their efforts to politicize emigration both by their own reluctance to openly oppose the British government and by the lack of crises comparable to the demographic catastrophe that afflicted Ireland. Just when many Irish families were compelled to leave their homes because of evictions or imminent starvation, the rise of industry gave poor Welsh families new reasons to stay in Wales.

From the founding of Plaid Cymru in 1925, the Welsh nationalist movement has struggled to come to terms with the consequences of nineteenth-century industrialization and the population shift it brought about. In the early years, the party's policies and philosophy reflected Saunders Lewis's conviction that the main goal of the nationalist movement should be not political independence but resisting cultural assimilation, which Lewis believed could be achieved by promoting traditional rural values (D. H. Davies 1983). In the same spirit that gave rise to movements to preserve folk cultures in continental European countries, Lewis idealized rural Wales as the rootstock of national character and argued that industrialization had undermined the nation's moral foundations. Yet, this new focus on traditional Welsh territory did not mark a complete departure from the earlier aspatial notion of Welsh identity, for language was still the key element.

In his analysis of Lewis's "back to the land" ideology, Pyrs Gruffudd notes that, "during its first twenty years Plaid Cymru was not a political party at all but a cultural and educational movement seeking to elicit a sense of common ethnic identity" (Gruffudd 1994: 69–70). That identity was based in language. "As we saw it," wrote novelist and founding Plaid member Kate Roberts, "whoever controls the language controls the soul of a nation" (Humphreys 1988: 25). But the class-based identity born in industrial areas made language and religion lesser issues, if not outright irrelevancies. Nationalist claims that language defined Welshness angered many Anglo Welsh, who felt that their distinctive working-class heritage constituted a cultural identity as uniquely Welsh as the rural heritage emphasized by nationalists. Hostility against the linguistic definition of Welshness was an important contributing reason for the resounding defeat of the 1979 referendum on devolution and an elected assembly for Wales, which won support from only 20 percent of voters (Davies 1993: 675–677).

The crux of Plaid Cymru's continuing dilemma lies in the small proportion of the electorate who identify themselves with the Welsh language and the party's inability to appeal to significant numbers outside its traditional heartland. As John Aitchison and Harold Carter have written, "To associate itself too closely with language issues means association with less than 20 percent of the voters; to distance itself from the language alienates its basic core of support in Welsh-speaking Wales" (Aitchison and Carter 1995: 7). The cultural and political divide created by nineteenth-century industrialization still marks today's political landscape (see Figure 13.2). In the landslide election of May 1, 1997, the Labour Party won every seat in most urban and industrial counties of south and north Wales, whereas Plaid Cymru won just four seats in the most rural counties of the northwest, despite putting forward candidates in every Welsh constituency.

The percentage of Welsh speakers declined steadily in all counties through most of the twentieth century, from a national average of 50 percent in 1901 to just under 19 percent in 1981, a level that has remained fairly stable because of the rising proportion of children learning Welsh in school. What was once a continuous Welsh-speaking territory called "Welsh Wales" (*y Fro Gymraeg*) has shrunk and become fragmented into islands (Aitchison and Carter 1995). The largest remaining contiguous areas are in the physically most remote regions, giving credence to earlier notions that isolation was necessary to the preservation of Welsh culture. Thus, the changing statistics and geography of the language that lent urgency to Saunders Lewis's message in 1962 continue to fuel the linguistic arguments of Welsh nationalists. The same patterns also explain why linguistic nationalists remain unable to persuade anything like a majority of Welsh people to listen.

Conclusion

Overseas and internal migration have influenced the formation of Welsh identity symbolically and in very concrete ways. Emigration to the United States and to Patagonia became a part of the rhetoric of nineteenth-century arguments for preventing the assimilation of Wales into English culture, a rhetoric that Saunders Lewis later appropriated to be a guiding metaphor for a Welsh nationalism based in language and Welsh institutions. Lewis was correct in pointing out the singular nature of the Patagonia colony. Few of the founders and even fewer of the residents of other Welsh settlements overseas held anything like the Patagonia organizers' ambition to create an embryonic Welsh state. Like the far greater number of Welsh men and women who migrated to developing industrial districts within Wales, most emigrants to the United States, Australia, and other destinations sought better economic conditions first and foremost. Both internal and overseas Welsh migrants initially maintained many aspects of their native culture in their

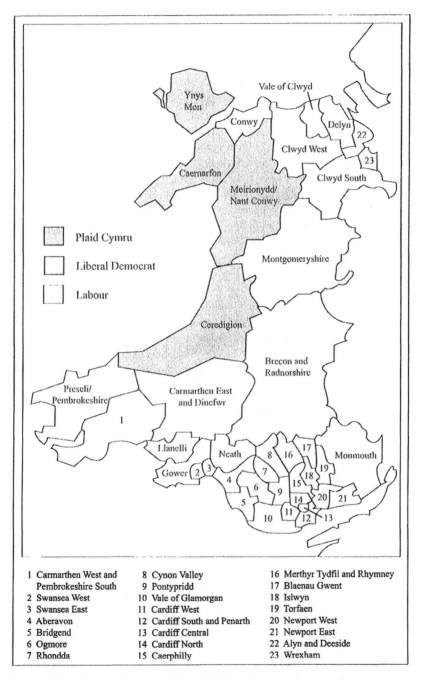

1	Carmarthen West and	8	Cynon Valley	16	Merthyr Tydfil and Rhymney
	Pembrokeshire South	9	Pontypridd	17	Blaenau Gwent
2	Swansea West	10	Vale of Glamorgan	18	Islwyn
3	Swansea East	11	Cardiff West	19	Torfaen
4	Aberavon	12	Cardiff South and Penarth	20	Newport West
5	Bridgend	13	Cardiff Central	21	Newport East
6	Ogmore	14	Cardiff North	22	Alyn and Deeside
7	Rhondda	15	Caerphilly	23	Wrexham

Figure 13.2 Electoral results of the 1997 British parliamentary elections in Wales

Source: *The Guardian*, election supplement, May 3, 1997, p. 12.

new communities, thus for a time extending the territory of Welsh-speaking, Nonconformist Welsh identity. But experiences of different living conditions, new modes of work, exposure to people from other cultures, and the formation of new axes of political allegiance forged new Welsh identities, including both the militant working-class identity prevalent in southeast Wales and in industrial Welsh communities in the United States and the politically conservative identity rooted in religiosity and respectability that developed in many Welsh and Welsh-American farming communities. The range of Welsh identities generated over the past 150 years reminds us that national and ethnic identities are always prone to change and reinterpretation. Appreciating the variety of Welsh identities helps one understand just how wide the gulf stands between the idealized, Welsh-speaking rural identity upon which Saunders Lewis based his nationalist vision and the gritty reality of working-class life in urban-industrial Wales.

In comparing the role of nationalism in Welsh and Irish emigration, two key differences emerge. The first was the real and perceived force behind Irish emigration and the voluntary nature of emigration from Wales. This difference, which deeply affected emigrants' regard for their homeland and their identity, was neatly summarized by a Welsh minister named David Price in his farewell address to a group of emigrants about to set sail from North Wales to America in 1848. Price acknowledged that leave-taking always causes grief and sorrow, but told his congregation to take comfort from the fact that

> This departure is not a necessity. It is a source of comfort to you who are leaving your country to think that you are [freely] *going* and not being driven away. You voluntarily came to the decision to leave. It is a better country that you seek. . . . Some were exiled across the mighty ocean. A departure such as that is worse than death itself, Jer. 22:10 [Weep not for him who is dead, nor bemoan him; but weep bitterly for him who goes away, for he shall return no more to see his native land.]. But that is not the manner in which you go. You who remain behind may suck comfort from this. Your sons are taking their leave amidst the most tender feelings of their neighbors, yea, in the midst of the love and prayers of God's Church. (Price 1848: 198)

The second difference was that Irish nationalism made Ireland itself the central character in the tragedy of emigration, focusing emigrants' grief on the place they called home, whereas early Welsh emigrant leaders tried to argue the aspatial notion that culture constituted homeland even if divorced from its native soil. The latter idea by no means typifies all Welsh nationalist rhetoric or actions; quite the contrary. Saunders Lewis and two other nationalists set fire to an RAF training base on the Lleyn Peninsula, Carnarvonshire, in 1936, declaring after they turned themselves in to the police that they aimed to prevent the despoliation of one of the hearths of indigenous Welsh culture by the English military. In 1957, protests against the drowning of the Tryweryn valley in Merionethshire by a reservoir built to supply water to Liverpool demonstrated that territory could matter very much to Welsh nationalists, as have occasional arson attacks on English-owned holiday cottages in North Wales since then. The difference is that for Welsh nationalists, the territory that matters has always been the land inhabited by native Welsh speakers, not Wales as a whole, or Wales as an independent political entity.

Choosing to leave one's homeland is rarely easy, but it is undoubtedly a less-wrenching experience than being forced to leave. This emotional aspect of forced emigration played an important part in making the metaphor of exile a potent weapon in the arsenal of Irish nationalism. To early Welsh nationalists such as Saunders Lewis and perhaps even Michael D. Jones, the metaphor of emigration as exile may have made sense on two levels. First, they could more readily imagine a free and independent Wales on a remote frontier than in Wales itself, given the enormous difficulty of reversing the course of Welsh history and what seemed the inexorable trends of cultural assimilation. Second, the extreme views of Lewis and Jones made them in some respects exiles in their own country; or, to use a metaphor closer to their religious beliefs, prophets crying in the wilderness, unable to convince the majority of Welsh people to heed their warnings and join the struggle to stave off the gradual destruction of Welsh Wales. It is ironic that their sense of Welsh identity, so deeply rooted in the values and experience of rural Wales, achieved its symbolic fulfillment in an imagined territory impossibly far away from its only enduring *habitus.*

Notes

1. This and all other translations from the Welsh are by the author.

2. Correspondence in *Y Drych,* 1857–1863; quotations from letters to the editor from Shadrach Griffiths, Ava, New York, May 16, 1857, p. 158; David James, Minersville, Pennsylvania, April 25, 1863, p. 122; John P. Jones, Castleton, Vermont, February 7, 1863, p. 33; Michael D. Jones, February 21, 1863, p. 49.

3. The existence and power of Welsh political institutions before the Acts of Union is a matter of debate. The general view, articulated by J. Davies (1993), is that medieval Welsh law, its courts, and the rule of powerful princes were indigenous institutions that, if not actually constituting a Welsh state, were well on their way to forming a distinct Welsh polity and political culture whose full development was presented by the Acts of Union. The spatial extent and

effectiveness of political power and thus the actual function of political institutions during the medieval period, however, is extremely difficult to ascertain, which makes the argument difficult to prove. A recent attempt to do so is R. Jones (1996).

4. I have frequently encountered a personal version of this attitude among native Welsh speakers who regard me as being Welsh, in spite of my being a recent immigrant from the United States who has learned the Welsh language, imperfectly, as an adult.

5. Letter from William Bebb to Samuel Roberts dated August 13, 1858, transcribed in Taylor, *Samuel Roberts*, emphasis in the original.

6. The 1851 census gives a total population of 63,080 for the town without specifying the parishes this figures includes; Census of Great Britain (1852): 892.

7. Richard A. Easterlin gives a much higher aggregate figure for Great Britain of 3,026,000 for the period 1821–1900 (Easterlin 1980: 480). Dudley Baines estimates much higher figures for the second half of the nineteenth century, with total emigration (not accounting for return migration) of 4,946,000 from England and Wales in 1825–1900 and 1,070,000 from Scotland in the same period (Baines 1985: 299–305). On the difficulties of calculating the number of British emigrants, see Erickson 1994: 87–125 and Knowles 1995a.

References

Aitchison, John W. "The Welsh Language in 1981." Plate 3.4 in Harold Carter, ed., *National Atlas of Wales*. Cardiff: University of Wales Press, 1988.

Aitchison, John W., and Harold Carter. *A Geography of the Welsh Language*. Cardiff: University of Wales Press, 1995.

Baines, Dudley. *Migration in a Mature Economy: Emigration and Internal Migration in England and Wales, 1861–1900*. Cambridge: Cambridge University Press, 1985.

Berthoff, Rowland. "Welsh." In Stephan Thernstrom, ed., *Harvard Encyclopedia of American Ethnic Groups*. Cambridge, Mass.: Harvard University Press, 1980, 1011–1017.

Blessing, Patrick J. "Irish." In Stephan Thernstrom, ed., *Harvard Encyclopedia of American Ethnic Groups*. Cambridge, Mass.: Harvard University Press, 1980, 524–545.

Y Bywgraffiadur Cymreig hyd 1940 (The Welsh Biographical Dictionary to 1940). London: Honourable Society of the Cymmrodorion, 1953.

Carter, Harold. "The Welsh Language in 1971." Plate 3.2 in Harold Carter, ed., *National Atlas of Wales*. Cardiff: University of Wales Press, 1988.

Carter, Harold, and Sandra Wheatley. *Merthyr Tydfil in 1851: A Study in the Spatial Structure of a Welsh Industrial Town*. University of Wales Board of Celtic Studies, Social Science Monograph no. 7. Cardiff: University of Wales Press, 1982.

Y Cenhadwr Americanaidd (The American Missionary). (1848–1854).

Census of England and Wales, 1901, Enumerators' Returns (1903). London: His Majesty's Printing Office.

Census of Great Britain, 1851 (1852). Population Tables I, Numbers of the Inhabitants . . . in England and Wales, vol. 2, Welsh Division. London.

Conway, Alan, ed. *The Welsh in America: Letters from the Immigrants.* Minneapolis: University of Minnesota Press, 1961.

Davies, D. Hywel. *The Welsh Nationalist Party 1925–1945: A Call to Nationhood.* Cardiff: University of Wales Press, 1983.

Davies, Gareth Alban. "Wales, Patagonia, and the Printed Word: The Missionary Role of the Press." *Llafur: Journal of Welsh Labour History* 6(4): (1995): 44–59.

Davies, Hywel M. *Translatlantic Brethren: Rev. Samuel Jones (1735–1814) and His Friends, Baptists in Wales, Pennsylvania, and Beyond.* Cranbury, N.J.: Lehigh University Press, 1995.

Davies, John. *A History of Wales.* London: Allen Lane/Penguin, 1993.

Donaldson, Gordon. "Welsh." In Stephan Thernstrom, ed., *Harvard Encyclopedia of American Ethnic Groups.* Cambridge, Mass.: Harvard University Press, 1980, 908–916.

Y Drych (The Mirror). 1857, 1863 (issues from intervening years have not survived).

Easterlin, Richard A. "Immigration: Economic and Social Characteristics." In Stephan Thernstrom, ed., *Harvard Encyclopedia of American Ethnic Groups.* Cambridge, Mass.: Harvard University Press, 1980, 476–486.

Erickson, Charlotte J. "English." In Stephan Thernstrom, ed., *Harvard Encyclopedia of American Ethnic Groups.* Cambridge, Mass.: Harvard University Press, 1980, 319–336.

———. "Who Were the English and Scots Emigrants to the United States in the Late Nineteenth Century?" In *Leaving England: Essays on British Emigration in the Nineteenth Century.* Ithaca, N.Y.: Cornell University Press, 1994, 87–125.

Gruffudd, Pyrs. "Back to the Land: Historiography, Rurality, and the Nation in Interwar Wales." *Transactions of the Institute of British Geographers,* new series 19 (1994): 61–77.

Humphreys, Emry. *The Triple Net: A Portrait of the Writer Kate Roberts, 1891–1985.* London: Channel 4 Television, 1988.

Jenkins, Geraint H. " 'A Rank Republican [and] a Leveller:' William Jones, Llangadfan." *Welsh History Review* 17 (1995): 365–386.

Jones, Maldwyn A. "Welsh-Americans and the Anti-Slavery Movement in the United States." *Transactions of the Honourable Society of Cymmrodorion* 1985, 105–129.

Jones, Michael D. "Y Wladychfa Gymreig" (*The Welsh Colony*). *Y Drych,* May 16, 1857: 153.

Jones, Peter Ellis. "Migration and the Slate Belt of Caernarfonshire in the Nineteenth Century." *Welsh History Review* 14 (1989): 610–629.

Jones, Philip N. *Mines, Migrants, and Residence in the South Wales Steamcoal Valleys: The Ogmore and Garw Valleys in 1881.* Occasional Paper in Geography, no. 25. Hull: Hull University Press, 1987.

Jones, R. Tudor. "Michael D. Jones a Thynged y Genedl (Michael D. Jones and the Fate of the Nation)." *Cof Cenedl: Ysgrifau ar Hanes Cymru* (*Memory of the Nation: Writings on the History of Wales*), vol. 1. Llandysul: Gwasg Gomer 1986, 95–123.

Jones, Rhys. "Daearyddiaeth Wleidyddol a Sefydliadol Cymru yn yr Oesau Canol (The Political and Institutional Geography of Medieval Wales)." Ph.D. dissertation, Department of Geography, University of Wales, 1996.

Jones, William D. *Wales in America: Scranton and the Welsh, 1860–1920.* Cardiff: University of Wales Press, 1993.

Knowles, Anne Kelly. "Welsh Settlement in Waukesha County, Wisconsin 1840–1873." Unpublished master's thesis, Department of Geography, University of Wisconsin–Madison, 1989.

———. "Immigrant Trajectories through the Rural-Industrial Transition in Wales and the United States, 1795–1850." *Annals of the Association of American Geographers* 85 (1995a): 246–266.

———. "Llanbryn-mair a'r Amerig: Cofio'r Ymfudo Cyntaf/Llanbryn-mair and America: Remembering the First Emigration." Unpublished address delivered at Hen Gapel, Llanbryn-mair, Montgomeryshire, July 9, 1995b.

———. *Calvinists Incorporated: Welsh Immigrants on Ohio's Industrial Frontier.* Chicago: University of Chicago Press, 1997.

Lewis, Saunders. "*Tynged yr iaith*" ("The Fate of the Language"). Radio broadcast, BBC Radio, February 13, 1962.

List of subscribers for shares in the Welsh Colonizing and General Trading Company, Limited. David Stephen Davies Papers, NLW Ms. 4616B, undated.

Lloyd, Lewis. *Australians from Wales.* Caernarfon: Gwynedd Archives, 1988.

"Michael Daniel Jones, Y Cenelwr (Michael Daniel Jones, the Nationalist)." *Y Ceninen* 13 (1895): 211–213.

Miller, Kerby. *Emigrants and Exiles: Ireland and the Irish Exodus to North America.* Oxford: Oxford University Press, 1985.

Morgan, Prys. "From a Death to a View: The Hunt for the Welsh Past in the Romantic Period." In Eric Hobsbawm and Terence Ranger, eds., *The Invention of Tradition.* Cambridge: Cambridge University Press, 1984.

"Plant y Paith: Hynt a Helynt Cymry Patagonia" ("Children of the Prairie: The Trials and Travails of the Welsh in Patagonia"). BBC broadcast in eight parts, second broadcast in December 1981. Written and presented by Owen Edwards.

Pooley, Colin G. "Welsh Migration to England in the Mid-Nineteenth Century." *Journal of Historical Geography* 9 (1983): 287–306.

Press cuttings on the Welsh in Patagonia (undated). NLW Ms. 10816E.

Price, David. Address to his congregation, Denbigh, reprinted in *Y Cenhadwr Americanaidd.* 1848, 197–199.

Pryce, W. T. R. "Migration and the Evolution of Culture Areas: Cultural and Linguistic Frontiers in Northeast Wales." *Transactions of the Institute of British Geographers* 65 (1975): 79–107.

———. "The Welsh Language 1750–1961." Plate 3.1 in Harold C. Carter, ed., *National Atlas of Wales.* Cardiff: University of Wales Press, 1988.

Rhys, W. Casnodyn. "Fifteen Years in Patagonia." Lecture delivered April 22, 1902, NLW Ms. 16653B.

Riden, Philip. "Iron and Steel." In John Langton and R. J. Morris, eds., *Atlas of Industrializing Britain, 1780–1914*. London: Methuen, 1986.

Roberts, Samuel. "Ffarmwr Careful, Cilhaul-Uchaf." In *Gweithiau Samuel Roberts* (*The Works of Samuel Roberts*). Dolgellau: Evan Jones, 1856, 73–106.

Shepperson, Wilbur S. *Samuel Roberts: A Welsh Colonizer in Civil War Tennessee*. Knoxville: University of Tennessee Press, 1961.

Taylor, Clare. "Samuel Roberts and His Circle: Migration from Llanbrynmair, Montgomeryshire, to America, 1790–1890." Typescript volume, privately issued, Aberystwyth, Wales, 1974.

Tennessee Colonization Company Papers, Duke University Archives.

Thernstrom, Stephan. "Immigration by Country." In Stephan Thernstrom, ed., *Harvard Encyclopedia of American Ethnic Groups*. Cambridge, Mass.: Harvard University Press, 1980, 1047–1048.

Thomas, Brinley. "A Cauldron of Rebirth: Population and the Welsh Language in the Nineteenth Century." *Welsh History Review* 13 (1987): 418–437.

Welsh Colonizing and General Trading Company, Limited. "*Llythyrau a ddaethant o'r Sefydlwyr yn y Wladfa Gymreig* (Letters which have come from the Settlers in the Welsh Colony)." R. Bryn Williams Papers 32, NLW Ms. 18206C, 1866.

Williams, Glyn. *The Desert and the Dream: A Study of Welsh Colonization in Chabut 1865–1915*. Cardiff: University of Wales Press, 1975.

———. "Cwm Hyfryd—A Welsh Settlement in the Patagonian Andes." *Welsh History Review* 9 (1978): 57–83.

———. *The Welsh in Patagonia: The State and the Ethnic Community*. Cardiff: University of Wales Press, 1991.

Williams, Gwyn A. *The Search for Beulah Land: The Welsh and the Atlantic Revolution*. London: Croom Helm, 1980.

———. *When Was Wales? A History of the Welsh*. London: Penguin, 1985.

Williams, R. Bryn. *Cymry Patagonia* (*The Welsh in Patagonia*). Aberystwyth: Gwasg Aberystwyth, 1942.

Afterword: Nested Identities—Nationalism, Territory, and Scale

David B. Knight

The term *nested identities* nicely captures an essential attribute or "identity," inasmuch as each person gains an understanding of who she/he is by considering "self" in relation to "others" in a variety of different ways that can and generally do include differing scales or levels of abstraction. Group identities rather than personal identity are the concern of the authors within this volume though ultimately, of course, the individual "self" is at the core. At least from a Western perspective, the simple question "who am I?" may lead to one to consider oneself in relation to changing geographical scales. For example, the following may pertain: residence, neighborhood, local organizations (such as school, service club, church), village/town/city, an identifiable (even if only vaguely understood) group sense of attachment to a region within the state, and what it means to be a citizen of the state and to relate (or not) to a sense of national identity associated with it.[1] In addition, some people may genuinely reflect on their "place" within at least subcontinental if not also global "societies." Other elements of identity exist, of course, including, perhaps especially, ethnicity, but the notion of "nesting" is important and, consistent with the concern in this book, it undergirds what is included in this chapter.

The word *self* was used above rather than *person*. Why? Although the reader can reflect on its application in a quite personal way, it is important to reflect also the notion of *group* "self," a notion, admittedly, that can cause definitional problems (see, e.g., Bloom 1990; Isaacs 1975; Neuberger 1986; Shafer 1980). Consider the following pairings: Muslim versus Christian and Republican versus Democrat. They encompass values and expectations that may find reflection in behaviors, but they do not necessarily have a readily observable territorial component. They also have the notion of "we/they" implied: "believers" and "nonbelievers." A different type of pairing is explicitly territorial: Californian versus Vermonter, German versus Canadian. Implied here too is the notion of "we/they" but, in addition, these pairings refer to regions defined by political bounding to which values may be attributed. Generalizations have been made about being a Vermonter, for example, honest, hardworking, frugal, reserved, being given to understatement, caring for neighbors yet wary of strangers, being active in democratic government, having a deep love for the land, and so on. Whether these attributes are based on reality is another thing: They are said by some to exist, or are held to be ideals, and that is enough. These personal attributes are tied to where the people are from, in the territorial sense. Being a Vermonter—as with being from Saskatchewan within Canada (Morse 1980)—can have a positive impact on the way identification is made with the nation, for local and regional attachments can reinforce and do not necessarily compete with a national identity that is derived from an attachment to the nation and the associated nationalism.

Guntram Herb, in Chapter 1, has identified something of the confusion related to the meaning of and bases for nation, nationalism, and national identity. As he notes, there is a huge literature on these fundamentals of societal structuring and interaction. Herb usefully concludes that there are three commonalities: The sense of nation "evokes a stronger loyalty from its members than other communities"; that, as a collective identity, it "shares an idyllic and often primordial past" with the history being written (and rewritten) to give it "genetic legitimacy"; and each nation has "a goal or destiny" whereby it seeks "to reinforce and preserve the unique character of its community." Part of the problem is one of definition: Who is to decide if a nation exists or not, and if it has any claim to territory? A. Cobban has an easy but "loaded" answer: "Any territorial community, the members of which are conscious of themselves as members of a community, and wish to maintain the identity of their community, is a nation" (Cobban 1945: 48). Cobban's suggestion could cause havoc if all groups could so self-identify and proceed to claim "nationhood" in a sovereign territory!

There is considerable discussion in the literature on the expressions of and links among ethnicity, nation, and other collective identities that, in varying ways, are linked in plural societies within many states (e.g., Kliot 1989). Herb (Chapter 1) suggests that a key difference between a nation and ethnicity is that "only a nation is considered worthy of the ultimate sacrifice—to give one's life for its continued existence." I cannot agree for, sadly, there is plenty of evidence to suggest otherwise. However, I do agree with his point that people have long been willing to die for their nation. Though at different times and for different reasons our priority of belonging may change (as needed and appropriate for a particular moment), ultimately most people, when called upon to refer and even act upon the priority of belonging to the "nation," will respond. David Kaplan (Chapter 2) notes that although "national identities are situated among a cascade of geographically based identities," there is "nothing 'natural' about its preeminent position." Even so, as a nationalist historian put it, there is "a *belief* that an individual should be loyal to his nation, its land, its values, and its state," even to the point of laying down one's life (Shafer 1972: 17; stress added). This touching and ofttimes disturbing fact has been demonstrated in many wars, not least the two tragic World and subsequent wars of the twentieth century. I thus fully agree with Herb, and also the other contributors to this book, that "identities of state and nation are tied to territory" (Chapter 1).

Territory—a human construct—is fundamental (Gottmann 1973; Knight 1982). In his "toward a definition of nationalism," Boyd Shafer (1955) identifies ten "conditions," the first of which is "a certain defined (often vaguely) unit of territory (whether possessed or coveted)." Although seldom thereafter explicitly considering the geographical implications of this listing, Shafer nevertheless implicitly identified the identity (nation/nationalism) link with territory. As his former student, I have since explored the links from a distinctive geographical perspective while drawing upon writings in history, the social sciences, indigenous thought, and international law. Clearly the authors of the chapters in this book also have found it necessary to range wide, judging from their cited literatures. In so doing, however, they and I have remained geographers, committed to revealing the geographical dimensions of the identity-territory linkages.

What are the key terms? *Identity, territory, state* and *statehood, nation, nationalism, nation building, power, territorial control* and, relatedly, *territoriality, regions, landscapes,* and *scale.* Each of these terms can be defined in isolation, yet each should also be seen in an interactive sense, as demonstrated in varying ways by the authors in this book. The dynamics of interaction (institutionally, behaviorally, spatially, and in terms of human-landscape)—especially in relation to the fundamental geographical concepts of space, place, spatial distribution, and spatial interaction—all undergird the geographical approach. Also central to a geographical perspective is the realization that group identities can be at once asymmetrical (spatially within a territory and in power relationships) and also unevenly nested within the hierarchy of possible identities, from personal to "humankind," and divided areally in many ways, not least by the bounding of the international system of states.

The identity-territory link is complicated, in a sense, by the existence of states, and the priority attributed to the states as *the* structure for politico-territorial organization of the earth's surface. This is not to deny the importance and power of the world economy and the removal of so many economic decisions from governments; it is simply to highlight states' external boundings as the basis frame for world spatial organization and the interaction of peoples within and divided by states. Indeed, the chapters in this volume clearly reveal that the state remains of great importance (see also Jackson and James 1993, and Demko and Wood 1994). The state itself is a geographical factor (Knight 1993).

Attachments to place cannot be reduced only to the territorially defined state, for, as suggested in the opening paragraph of this chapter, other scales also apply. For any geographically bounded community, it is necessary to take account of its rootedness in its individual culture, history, and place, for in so doing the "moral particularity" of the community may help us identify the significance of its distinctiveness (Wallace and Knight 1996). An element of the relationship between communities and the territory they claim as theirs includes meanings that are attributed to and also gained from the territory and its landscape (e.g., Tuan 1977; Knight 1982; Williams and Smith 1983; Rumley and Minghi 1991; Lowenthal 1994; Johnson 1997). National anthems and other patriotic songs and music, flags, monuments, literature, art, propaganda, parades, and so on may all reflect this attachment, that is, the attachment to the nation and the national territory, and may aid the development of a national identity (see, e.g., Zelinsky 1984, 1988; Lowenthal 1994; Johnson 1997; Kong and Yeoh 1997; Unwin in Chapter 7).

The chapters in this book reinforce the existence of the "problem" that not all who live within existing international boundaries identify with the states within which they live. Accordingly, there may be conflict, although there are a variety of ways states can seek to accommodate societal plurality (e.g., Murphy 1988a). Although some substate people—as group politico-territorial identities—have accommodated themselves to being reasonably satisfied regional groups within a state, as with the Catalans in Spain, others find the incongruence between their largely culturally based "national identity" and the so-called state identity imposed on them to be such that they challenge the bounding of the present state as they call for separation and the gaining of independence, as with some Basques in Spain (Chapter 10), some Walloons and Flemish in Belgium (Murphy 1988a, 1988b), and Québecois in Canada (Knight 1997).

The bases for a secessionist process under international law is at first glance wide open because various UN documents declare that "all people have the right to self-determination," but there are limitations that result from the primacy given to an existing state if effective control of the state's territory has integrity and can be maintained (Knight 1985; Alfredsson and Macalister-Smith 1996). Secession can thus only occur if the existing state permits the politico-territorial separation of a region from the state so the secessionist group can gain sovereign status for the people in that split-off territory. This interpretation—and limitation—of international law is inconsequential to leaders of groups desirous of separation from an existing state and the attainment of a new statehood, which, among other attributes, would include sovereignty and international recognition (Knight 1992). As a counter, governments of existing states, understandably, generally react negatively to any threat of separation, sometimes with resulting violence, as, for instance, in the United States in the nineteenth century and Nigeria (Biafra), Ethiopia (Eritrea), and Sri Lanka (Tamil northeast) in the twentieth century. The desire and push for partition and secession, linked with nationalistic sentiments, cause both instability within states and destabilization of the international system of states (Waterman 1996).

The ultimate tussle is over the control of territory, with each "side" exhibiting contrasting expressions of territoriality. Territoriality has been defined as "the attempt to affect, influence, or control actions and interactions (of people, things, and relationships, etc.) by asserting and attempting to enforce control over a specific geographic area" (Sack 1981: 55). We can take Sack's interesting definition further by making explicit the link between territory and identity: "territory is . . . space to which identity is attached by a distinctive group who hold or covet that territory and who desire to have full control over it for the group's benefit" (Knight 1982: 526). The essential elements underlying the nature of the identity-territory link need to be isolated, including the relative role of "nested" identities.

The notion of "nesting" has been evident in political-geographical thinking for some time, in ways other than previously identified. "Nesting" has served as a useful classification tool. For instance, Burnett and Taylor (1981) identify three scales of generalization and interaction—local, national, and international—as the three principal scales of consideration in the literature. Their triple division demonstrates that the older bifocal attention to intrastate political geography versus international political geography was limited. Peter Taylor ([1985], 1993) takes the criticism further in his world-systems approach to political geography, wherein he explores three interrelated scales, "world-economy, nation-state, and locality."

Many problems arise from the fact that international political boundaries do not conform nicely to the distribution of peoples who claim senses of community, perhaps as nations. For example, although some substate regional identities are focused within one state (e.g., the Scots in northern U.K.), others are divided by an international boundary (as with the Basques in northern Spain/southwestern France). In the first instance, relationships are with one state (the U.K.) and may be managed with relative ease, including, as is now being explored, by means of a quasi-federal structure within what has been a unitary state; in the other the divided people may relate to different states. An example of the latter would be the Kurds who are split between five states. The degree of acceptance and involvement in states' polities by substate group politico-territorial identities may vary, and the people's aspirations may differ (see Mikesell and Murphy 1991).

Jean Gottmann (1973) identifies that territory offers contrasting and competing perspectives: inward-looking (with a stress on security) versus outward-looking (with a stress on opportunity). These perspectives can be viewed as being two ends of a spectrum, though, in reality, a state will either seek to achieve a balance between the extremes or will emphasize this or that end of the spectrum at varying times, in terms of its foreign relations. With respect to nationalism, I have suggested that a similar continuum exists, with tensions existing between the contrasting pull of an inward-looking (security) perspective versus an outward-looking (opportunity) one.

With the notion of continua in mind for both territory and identity (the latter, here, as a regionalism or a nationalism), consider the following questions. Are the Basques, split as they are between Spain and France, thus two separate regional identities? Yes, if one confines oneself to the existing state boundaries. Perhaps not, if the people of the two substate regions accept themselves as one broader culture region within Europe. Being simplistic, do each of the groups have separate inward-looking orientations as they seek to set themselves apart from the respective states within which they are located—Spain versus France? Or, if they accept the existence of a cultural cross-political community boundedness, do they share outward-oriented opportunities for cross-border cooperation and broader identity development? What are the roles of the French and the Spanish states in encouraging outward-looking perspectives for their respective substate group politico-territorial identities? Who is to say that Basques in Spain, for instance, should hold ultimate allegiance to the Spanish state, in contrast to holding only to a "lower-order" allegiance to being Basques in Euskadi? The issues are complex (see Raento, Chapter 10). George White, with respect to Transylvania (Chapter 12), explores difficulties when deciding who belongs to which state.

There are also extrastate identities, that is, those that are at the macro-scale, to use Herb's and Kaplan's organization schema. To what extent do people of any state also have an attachment to or, at least, a vague appreciation for, a level of identity that transcends the state, an identity that is not tied to ethnic/national identification? By this I mean some form of internationalism, but not necessarily at a world scale. The role of religion may be cited, as with believers of a particular inter- pretation of a religious ideology that links people from a variety of states. Geographical dimensions to such beliefs and the distribution of the believers exist, and religion may represent a key element in either a nationalism or an internationalism. There is also the form of interna- tionalism that is believed to exist among people who have developed a sense of group self that lies beyond the national, which links accept- ers from various countries. Taken together, the believers may form an (interstate) regionalism. This new type of identity deserves critical at- tention, as with the instance of people in western Europe who identify themselves as being "European" and not just from this or that state within Europe (see Murphy, Chapter 3; Gamberale 1977), or with peo- ples from the many island communities in the Caribbean (see Elbow, Chapter 4). Another form of international attachment is found in the postcolonial sense of "belonging." People in many states have to either belong to the Commonwealth of Nations (Yeung 1966) or, for others, *La Francophonie* (Old 1984); these remain to be explored from a geo- graphical perspective.

As implied previously, there is great importance given to words (see also Murphy 1990) regarding how people identify themselves in rela- tion to their territory. Germans live in Germany, but Bavarians, as Ger- mans, are especially attached to Bavaria. In turn, BaKwena and BaK- gatka, although accepting that they are also Botswana, are especially attached to two different regions in Botswana. The identification is both self- and territory-centered. The link is also nicely illustrated by the Inuit in the Northwest Territories in Canada, who are to gain politi- cal control in 1999 of part of the NWT (within the Canadian state). They are the numerically dominant people in the region. The name for themselves is Inuit—"The People" or "Real People"—who live in Nunavut—"our land."[2] The link between the identity and the territory is clear.

People may have names for themselves, as with the Inuit, but schol- ars also have devised analytical terms for groups that have regional distinctiveness within states. These include *substate regionalisms, ethnic-*

nationalisms, subnations, mini-nationalisms, plus others, all of which
evoke thoughts that may not always have been intended. Likewise,
broad, extrastate regional groupings are also said to exist, as with
"Central Americans" and "Europeans." The diverse language led me
to suggest (Knight 1982, 1994) that we needed neutral terms, hence,
group territorial identities and, if politicized, *group politico-territorial identities* were proposed and have since been used by others.

In this volume, Herb and Kaplan, aware of using terms that may be
defined differently by different authors, escaped the issue by letting
each author define their terms for themselves; however, fully aware of
the role of scale, they grouped the chapters into three scales: macro (or
suprastate), meso (or, more or less, state), and micro (or substate) and
thus follow the example of Burnett and Taylor identified previously.
Given that political geographers of today are sensitive to the pervasive-
ness of the world economy in relation to politico-territorial organization, Herb and Kaplan's warning in the introduction to this volume is
vitally important, that is, that the three scales used for organizing this
volume—macro, meso, and micro—"are not only fluid, but also interconnected or nested." To give one person's experience: A former student of mine, from eastern Zimbabwe, grew up knowing of his tribal
identity; only when he left the country to study overseas did he fully
appreciate that he was Zimbabwean; while overseas he also discovered
he was African.

Permit me to add a personal note. The identity-territory issue is
problematic for me because I am a citizen, with passports for each, of
three states—the U.K., New Zealand, and Canada—and have lived for
a decade in a fourth (the United States). The question, "where do you
come from?" thus poses a problem for me, as it does for all migrants,
whether forced to move or to have done so voluntarily. All migrants to
a greater or lesser degree consider their identity and the ties and pulls
of different ethnic and national identities related to specific territories.
Where is "home" for such people? In my case, I feel powerful senses
of belonging to four "nations" or, more particularly, to their territories,
to which (or to parts of which) I have profound attachments. Each contributes to my sense of self, to my identity. Each has elements of
"home" for me. Though I cannot claim to have a strong personal sense
of nation or of nationalism that overrides all other levels of identity,
"nation" and "nationalism" have been a focus of my academic study
for more than thirty years! I am intrigued—but also too often deeply
troubled—by the power of nationalism, notably when it is linked with
excessive patriotism, or is tied to blinkered isolationist thinking that
can lead to persecution, conflict, and even war.

My personal circumstance, of course, is atypical because most people in the world do not have the freedom—or luxury or privilege—of being a part of several group territorial identities. Most people are born into a territory and thus are "told" that they belong to the group. Indeed, being born within a state's territory generally conveys the rights of citizenship, which serves as a "badge" of belonging. Under certain circumstances citizenship can be bestowed by a state, but a state cannot bestow its nationalism. The latter must be learned and accepted by immigrants, if they can or wish, even as they may develop a sense of belonging to the nation. Delineating one's personal attachment to a nationalism is not always easy. To which national identity can a migrant, for instance, give priority of belonging—the "old" or the "new"? Or is it possible to give priority to neither, to claim instead to be part of each—that which was left behind and also the new one in the host territory? For some, notably those forced out of a homeland, the choice may be hard, even impossible, to make.

Let me conclude with some questions for the reader: Where is "home" and how does the perspective from that place influence your geographical view of the world? What are your identity-territory linkages? To what level in the possible hierarchy of attachments do you place ultimate priority? If the latter level of priority is not to the state, what does this mean for your attachment to the "nation" and the "state" within which you live? To what degree is your priority of attachment influenced by factors other than nationalism? What are they? How do they relate to your sense of nationalism? If your responses mirror those of a large regionally focused minority of people within your state, what are the politico-geographical implications and potential consequences of your answers? Does it matter what you and like-minded individuals feel, if you believe (correctly?) that the state dominates ultimate decisions regarding identity-territory priorities and actions, whether at intrastate or international levels of interaction? What is the importance of culture to your (personal and group's) sense of nation? How do state policies and actions feed the development of a nationalism? How does the nationalism find expression in education, in the role of the military, in foreign relations? What is the role of historical understanding? Of language? Of relationships with the landscape? What if your society is a pluralistic one, with two or more significant cultures—and perhaps nations—within the state? How do the dominant nationalism and also any minority nationalism(s) find expression in state policies? Are your state's policies ameliorated in any way by pressures from other states, perhaps with reference to international human rights expectations? How does your state deal with powerful regionalisms within the state, especially if they have reached the point of demanding special recognition? If your state faces secessionist demands you cannot agree to, how do you react? How does your state react?

Answers to these and similar questions may take time to enunciate and fully appreciate, but in pondering the answers it may then be possible for the reader to better reflect on how these questions may be responded to by others, not only within one's own state but elsewhere, notably in states where discord and conflict is the order of the day because of a clash between competing identities located within contested territories. In such explorations, a deeper, perhaps fuller appreciation may develop of the importance of ideas, of the links between identities and territory, and, notably, of the importance of territorial ideologies (see, e.g., Murphy 1991a), the most notable of which is nationalism. Murphy's observation deserves our attention. "What lies behind the framework of political territories or formal ethnic regions are spatial constructs with deep ideological significance that may or may not correspond to political or formal constructs. These ideologies are forged in the territorial struggles that produce particular regional arrangements and understandings, and these in turn shape ideas, practices, activities and routines" (Murphy 1991b, p. 29). The authors in this volume have tackled aspects of his summary declaration, have revealed new insights, and have pointed the way to further research needs. More thus awaits to be done if we are to more fully appreciate the social construction of the myriad links between nested identities and territories and their politico-geographical consequences.

Notes

1. In a paper subsequently identified as a seminal integrative geographic work on nationalism and regionalism, it was stated that "whatever our reference levels, we have the astonishing ability to 'flick a switch' in our minds and change levels of abstraction" as we reflect on our identity-territory links (Knight 1982: 515). Without assuming responsibility for what followed in the years since the publication of that paper—for other geographers too were exploring identity-territory issues, including Fisher (1968), Smith (1979), Burghardt (1980), Sack (1981), Williams (1981), and Orridge and Williams (1982)—it is nevertheless rewarding and encouraging to note that the ties have since been explored in a wide ranging literature by many geographers, such as those in this volume (and see R. J. Johnston et al., 1988, including the essays by Anderson, Murphy, Portugali, van der Wusten, and Williams).

2. The outside world anglicized the contemptuous Cree word for their neighbors to the far north, i.e., *Eskimantsies*, or "eaters of raw flesh." Understandably, the people detested being called Eskimos because of its origins, hence, Inuit are today called by their own name for themselves.

References

Agnew, John. "Political Regionalism and Scottish Nationalism in Gaelic Scotland." *Canadian Review of Studies in Nationalism* 8 (1981): 115–129.

Alfredsson, Gudmunder, and Peter Macalister-Smith. *The Living Law of Nations.* Kehl: N. P. Engel, 1996.

Bloom, William. *Personal Identity, National Identity, and International Relations.* Cambridge: Cambridge University Press, 1990.

Burghardt, Andrew. "Nation, State, and Territorial Unity." *Cahiers de géographie du Québec* 24 (1980): 123–134.

Burnett, A. D., and P. J. Taylor. *Political Studies from Spatial Perspectives.* Chichester and New York: Wiley, 1981.

Cobban, A. *National Self-Determination.* Oxford: Oxford University Pres, 1945.

Demko, George, and William B. Wood, eds. *Reordering the World: Geopolitical Perspectives on the 21st Century.* Boulder: Westview Press, 1994.

Fisher, Charles A., ed. *Essays in Political Geography.* London: Methuen, 1968.

Gamberale, Carlo. "European Citizenship and Political Identity." *Space and Polity* 1 (1997): 37–59.

Gottmann, Jean. *The Significance of Territory.* Charlottesville: The University Press of Virginia, 1973.

Isaacs, Harold R. "Basic Group Identity: The Idols of the Tribe." In N. Glazer and D. P. Moynihan, eds., *Ethnicity: Theory and Practice.* Cambridge, Mass.: Harvard University Press, 1975, 29–52.

Jackson, R. H., and A. James, eds. *States in a Changing World.* Oxford: Oxford University Press, 1993.

Johnson, Nuela. "Cast in Stone: Monuments, Geography, and Nationalism." In J. Agnew, ed., *Political Geography: A Reader.* New York: Wiley, 1997, 347–364.

Johnston, R. J., David B. Knight, and Eleanore Kofman, eds. *Nationaism, Self-Determination and Political Geography.* London: Croom Helm, 1988.

Kliot, Nurit. "Mediterranean Potential for Ethnic Conflict: Some Generalizations." *Tijdschritf voor Economische en Sociale Geografie* 80 (1989): 147–163.

Knight, David B. "Identity and Territory: Geographical Perspectives on Nationalism and Regionalism." *Annals of the Association of American Geographers* 72 (1982): 514–531.

———. "Territory and People or People and Territory?: Thoughts on Postcolonial Self-Determination." *International Political Science Review* 6 (1985): 248–272.

———. "Statehood: A Politico-Geographic and Legal Perspective." *GeoJournal* 28 (1992): 311–318.

———. "Geographical Considerations in a World of States." In R. H. Jackson and A. James, eds., *States in a Changing World.* Oxford: Oxford University Press, 1993, 26–45.

———. "People Together, Yet Apart: Rethinking Territory, Sovereignty, and Identities." In G. J. Demko and W. B. Wood, eds., *Reordering the World: Geopolitical Perspectives on the 21st Century.* Boulder: Westview Press, 1994, 71–86.

———. "Canada's Political Fault-lines: Regionalisms, Nationalisms, and the

Threat of Secession." In Gordon Bennett, ed., *Tension Areas of the World*. Dubuque, Iowa: Kendall-Hunt, 1997, 207–228.

Kong, Lily, and Brenda S. A. Yeoh. "The Construction of National Identity through the Production of Ritual and Spectacle: An Analysis of National Day Parades in Singapore." *Political Geography* 16 (1997): 213–240.

Lowenthal, David. "European and English Landscapes as National Symbols." In D. Hooson, ed., *Geography and National Identity*. Oxford: Blackwell, 1994, 15–38.

Mikesell, Marvin W., and Alexander B. Murphy. "A Framework for Comparative Study of Minority-Group Aspirations." *Annals of the Association of American Geographers* 81 (1991): 581–604.

Morse, S. J. "National Identity from a Social Psychological Perspective: A Study of University Students in Saskatchewan." *Canadian Review of Studies in Nationalism* 7 (1980): 299–312.

Murphy, Alexander B. *The Regional Dynamics of Language Differentiation in Belgium*. Chicago: University of Chicago Research Series in Geography, No. 227, 1988a.

———. "Evolving Regionalism in Linguistically Divided Belgium. In R. J. Johnston, David B. Knight, and Eleanore Kofman, eds., *Nationalism, Self-Determination, and Political Geography*. London: Croom Helm, 1988b.

———. "Historical Justifications for Territorial Claims." *Annals of the Association of American Geographers* 80 (1990): 531–548.

———. "Territorial Ideology and International Conflict: The Legacy of Prior Political Formations." In Stanley Waterman and Nurit Kliot, eds., *War, Peace, and Geography*. London: Belhaven, 1991a, 126–141.

———. "Regions as Social Constructs." *Progress in Human Geography* 15 (1991b): 23–35.

Neuberger, Benyamin. *National Self-Determination in Post-Colonial Africa*. Boulder: Lynne Reinner, 1986.

Old, Colin. *Quebec's Relations with Francophonie: A Political Geographic Perspective*. Ottawa: Carleton University, Geography Discussion Paper no. 1, 1984.

Orridge, A. W., and C. H. Williams. "Autonomist Nationalism." *Political Geography Quarterly* 1 (1982): 19–39.

Rumley, Dennis, and Julian V. Minghi, eds. *The Geography of Border Landscapes*. London: Routledge, 1991.

Sack, Robert D. "Territorial Bases of Power." In A. D. Burnett and P. J. Taylor, eds., *Political Studies from Spatial Perspectives*. Chichester and New York: Wiley, 1981, 53–71.

Shafer, Boyd C. *Nationalism: Myth and Reality*. New York: Harcourt, Brace, and World, 1955.

———. *Faces of Nationalism: New Realities and Old Myths*. New York: Harcourt Brace Jovanovich, 1972.

———. "If Only We Knew More about Nationalism." *Canadian Review of Studies in Nationalism* 7 (1980): 197–218.

Smith, Graham E. "Political Geography and the Theoretical Study of the East European Nation." *Indian Journal of Political Science* 40 (1979): 59–83.

Taylor, Peter J. *Political Geography: World-Economy, Nation-State, and Locality.* 3d ed. London: Longman, 1993 [1985].

Tuan, Yi-Fu. *Space and Place: The Perspective of Experience.* Minneapolis: University of Minnesota Press, 1997.

Wallace, Iain, and David B. Knight. "Societies in Space and Place." In F. O. Hampson and J. Reppy, eds., *Earthly Goods: Environmental Change and Social Justice.* Ithaca, N.Y.: Cornell University Press, 1996, 75–95.

Waterman, Stanley. "Partition, Secession, and Peace in Our Time." *GeoJournal* 39 (1996): 345–352.

Williams, Colin H. "Identity through Autonomy: Ethnic Separatism in Quebec." In A. D. Burnett and P. J. Taylor, eds., *Political Studies from Spatial Perspectives.* Chichester: John Wiley, 1981, 389–418.

Williams, Colin H., and Anthony D. Smith. "The National Construction of Social Space." *Progress in Human Geography* 7 (1983): 502–518.

Yeung, Yue-man. "Geography and the Commonwealth in a Changing World: A Silver Jubilee Overview." In Yue-man Yeung, ed., *Global Change and the Commonwealth.* Hong Kong: The Chinese University of Hong Kong, Institute of Asia-Pacific Studies, 1996, 3–24.

Zelinsky, Wilbur. "Oh Say, Can You See? Nationalistic Emblems in the Landscape." *Winterthur Portfoliio,* 19 (1984): 277–286.

————. *Nation into State: The Shifting Symbolic Foundations of American Nationalism.* Chapel Hill: University of North Carolina Press, 1988.

Index

Abiola, Mashood, 191
Abrahams, R., 161
African-Caribbean-Pacific Group
  (Lomé Agreements), 78, 82(fig.),
  92, 93(table)
Agnew, John, 22, 58
agriculture, 153, 155, 159, 162
Aitchison, John, 307–8
Åland Island, 133(map), 140
Amazon Cooperation Treaty,
  93(table), 94
Andean Group, 78, 82(fig.), 93(table),
  94
Anderson, Benedict, 13, 14, 232
Anderson, Thomas, 90
Antilles, 76, 86, 89
Arab Democratic List (Palestinian-
  Arab), 258, 259
Arab National Committee (Palestin-
  ian-Arab), 260
Arabs, 40. See also Palestinian-Arabs
Assembly of European Regions
  (AER), 63
assimilation, 141, 143, 290, 307
Association of Caribbean States
  (ACS), 82, 88, 94–96, 97
Atlanticism, 113
Austro-Hungarian Empire, 272
Awolowo, Obafemi, 185, 186, 188
Azikewe, Nnamdi, 185, 186, 188

Bandaranaike, S. W. R. D., 206, 207
Bandaranaike-Chelvanayakam Pact
  (1957), 207, 214

Barber, Benjamin, 42, 43
Basque National Liberation Front
  (MNLV), 223–24, 226, 227, 230, 231
Basque Region (Spanish), 16, 219–20,
  221(map), 222–23, 322–23; and au-
  tonomy, 223, 224, 226, 231; and Eu-
  ropean integration, 231; language
  in, 222, 225; nationalist/antina-
  tionalist sentiment in, 221, 223,
  225–32; political ideologies of,
  220–21, 223–25, 227, 229–30
Bebb, Edward, 301, 302
Benítez Rojo, Antonio, 88
Berlin Conference (1884, 1885), 182
Biafra, 12, 179
Bishara, A., 258
Blue Books (Wales), 292, 293
borderlands, 37–38, 45
boundaries. See nation, and bound-
  aries
Breuilly, John, 13, 15
Brubaker, Rogers, 106
Buddhists, in Sri Lanka, 200, 205
Burghardt, Andrew, 87

capitalism, 14, 183
Caribbean, 75–76, 77(map), 79–82; colonial heritage of, 75, 78, 79, 81, 83,
  84–86, 87, 90–91, 92, 96; culture in,
  88–89, 91, 97n2; identity of, 83, 85–
  87, 88, 90, 96; integration of, 78, 81–
  82, 87–88, 89, 90–92, 93(table),

Contributors

Valentin Bogorov is a Ph.D. student in geography at the University of Wisconsin–Madison. He received his Master of Science degree from Moscow University in 1986 and has presented several papers on Russian nationalism at professional conferences.

Gary S. Elbow is professor of geography and director of the Latin American Area Studies Program at Texas Tech University. He received his Ph.D. in geography from the University of Pittsburgh in 1972. His publications include "Territorial Loss and National Image: The Case of Ecuador," *Yearbook, Conference of Latin Americanist Geographers* 1996, vol. 22.

Jouni Häkli is senior lecturer at the Department of Geography at the University of Joensuu, Finland. He received his doctoral degree in 1994 from the University of Tampere, Finland. His publications include the monograph "Territoriality and the Rise of Modern State," *Fennia* 172:1, 1994.

Guntram H. Herb teaches geography at Middlebury College. He received his Ph.D. in geography from the University of Wisconsin in 1993. His publications include *Under the Map of Germany: Nationalism and Propaganda 1918–1945* (London: Routledge, 1997).

Rex D. Honey is associate professor of geography at the University of Iowa. He received his Ph.D. in geography from the University of Minnesota in 1972. In addition to coauthoring a textbook, *Human Geography* (St. Paul: West Publishers, 1987), and articles in professional journals, he just completed two books with Nigerian scholars on the political geography of Nigeria.

341

David H. Kaplan teaches geography at Kent State University. He received his Ph.D. in 1991 from the University of Wisconsin. He has published widely in the topics of nationalism and ethnic segregation, including articles in the *Annals of the Association of American Geographers, Political Geography, The Professional Geographer,* and *The American Review of Canadian Studies.*

David B. Knight is professor of geography at the University of Guelph, where he served as Dean of the College of Social Science from 1993 to 1998. He was educated in New Zealand, Scotland, and the United States, receiving his Ph.D. from the University of Chicago. He was the first Chair/President of the International Geographical Union commission on the World Political Map and has been a visiting professor at institutions in England, Israel, and Russia. His books include A Capital for Canada; Choosing Canada's Capital: Conflict Resolution in a Parliamentary System; Our Geographic Mosaic (editor); Self-Determination (coauthor); Nationalism, Self-Determination and Political Geography (coauthor); and Making Sense in Geography and Environmental Studies (coauthor).

Anne K. Knowles is lecturer at the Institute of Earth Studies, University of Wales–Aberystwyth, UK. She received her Ph.D. in geography from the University of Wisconsin–Madison in 1993. Her publications include *Calvinists Incorporated: Welsh Immigrants on Ohio's Industrial Frontier* (Chicago: University of Chicago Press, 1997).

Nicholas J. Lynn is a lecturer in the Department of Geography at the University of Edinburgh, Scotland, UK. He finished his Ph.D. in 1996 at the University of Birmingham, UK, and has published articles on nation building and state formation in the republics of the Russian Federation and is currently embarked on a research project (funded by the Royal Geographical Society) examining the idea of "federal democracy" in Russia's Far East region.

Chelvadurai Manogaran is professor of geography at the University of Wisconsin–Parkside. Born in Kuala Lumpur, Malaysia, he received his Ph.D. from Southern Illinois University at Carbondale in 1972. His publications include *Ethnic Conflict and Reconciliation in Sri Lanka* (Honolulu: University of Hawaii Press, 1978) and *Sri Lankan Tamils: Ethnicity and Identity* (Boulder, Colo.: Westview Press, 1994).

Alexander B. Murphy is professor of geography at the University of Oregon. He received his J.D. from Columbia University in 1981 and his

Ph.D. from the University of Chicago in 1987. His publications include *The Regional Dynamics of Language Differentiation in Belgium: A Study in Cultural-Political Geography* (Chicago: University of Chicago Press, 1988).

Pauliina Raento is assistant professor of geography at the University of Helsinki, Finland. She received her Ph.D. in Basque studies (geography) from the University of Nevada–Reno in 1996. In addition to her recent dissertation on Basque nationalism, she has presented numerous papers at professional conferences and published articles in Finnish professional journals.

Tim Unwin is reader in geography at Royal Holloway, University of London, and honorary secretary of the RGS-IBG (Royal Geographical Society–Institute of British Geographers). His books include *The Place of Geography* (Longman, 1992), *Wine and the Vine* (London: Routledge, revised paperback edition 1996), and his edited *Atlas of World Development* (New York: John Wiley and Sons, 1994).

George W. White is assistant professor of geography at Frostburg State University. He received his Ph.D. in geography from the University of Oregon in 1994. His publications include "Place and Its Role in Serbian Identity," in *Reconstructing the Balkans: A Geography of the New South-East Europe*, edited by Darrick Danta and Derek Hall (New York: John Wiley and Sons, 1996).

Oren Yiftachel teaches at the Department of Geography, Ben Gurion University, Be'er Sheva, Israel. He studied urban studies, urban and regional planning, and political geography in Australian and Israeli universities. Among his recent books are *Guarding the Grove: Policy and Resistance in a Palestinian Village*, Center for the Study of Arab Society, Bet Berl (Hebrew) (1996); and *Ethnic Frontiers and Peripheries: The Politics of Development and Inequality in Israel/Palestine* (with A. Meir, eds.); Boulder: Westview Press, 1997.